REALISM AND NATIONALISM

1852-1871

harper torchbooks

A reference-list of Harper Torchbooks, classified by subjects, is printed at the end of this volume.

THE RISE OF MODERN EUROPE

Edited by WILLIAM L. LANGER
Harvard University

Edward P. Cheyney	THE DAWN OF A NEW ERA, 1250-1453. TB/3002
Myron P. Gilmore	THE WORLD OF HUMANISM, 1453-1517. TB/3003
E. Harris Harbison	THE PROTESTANT REVOLT, 1516-1560.*
Philip Hughes	THE CATHOLIC REFORMATION, 1560-1610.*
Carl J. Friedrich	THE AGE OF THE BAROQUE, 1610-1660. TB/3004
Frederick L. Nussbaum	THE TRIUMPH OF SCIENCE AND REASON, 1660-1685. TB/3009
John B. Wolf	THE EMERGENCE OF THE GREAT POWERS, 1685-1715. TB/3010
Penfield Roberts	THE QUEST FOR SECURITY, 1715-1740. TB/3016
Walter L. Dorn	COMPETITION FOR EMPIRE, 1740-1763. TB/3032
Leo Gershoy	FROM DESPOTISM TO REVOLUTION, 1763-1789. TB/3017
Crane Brinton	A DECADE OF REVOLUTION, 1789-1799. TB/3018
Geoffrey Bruun	EUROPE AND THE FRENCH IMPERIUM, 1799-1814. TB/3033
Frederick B. Artz	REACTION AND REVOLUTION, 1814-1832. TB/3034
William L. Langer	LIBERALISM, NATIONALISM AND SOCIALISM, 1832-1852.*
Robert C. Binkley	REALISM AND NATIONALISM, 1852-1871. TB/3038
Carlton J. H. Hayes	A GENERATION OF MATERIALISM, 1871-1900. TB/3039
Oron J. Hale	THE GREAT ILLUSION, 1900-1914.*
Bernadotte Schmitt	THE WORLD IN THE CRUCIBLE, 1914-1919.*
Raymond Sontag	REVOLT AGAINST THE OLD ORDER, 1919-1939.*
Gordon Wright	THE SECOND WORLD WAR, 1939-*

*** In preparation**

David Oakley

REALISM AND NATIONALISM

1852-1871

BY ROBERT C. BINKLEY

HARPER TORCHBOOKS THE UNIVERSITY LIBRARY

HARPER & ROW, PUBLISHERS, NEW YORK

To

The Memory of

William Forbes Adams

Scholar and Comrade

REALISM AND NATIONALISM

Printed in the United States of America

This book was originally published in 1935 by Harper & Brothers in The Rise of Modern Europe series, edited by William L. Langer.

First HARPER TORCHBOOK edition published 1963 by Harper & Row, Publishers, Incorporated, New York, Evanston, and London.

TABLE OF CONTENTS

MAPS

LIST OF ILLUSTRATIONS

The illustrations, grouped in a separate section, will be found following page 168

Acknowledgments

This page can be only a token payment on the heavy debts to which this book has given rise. Professor John Hildt will recognize his influence in the paragraphs on *civis Romanus sum*, Major T. H. Thomas will judge how well or ill I have used the reflections born of our pleasant conversations, Professor Mervyn Crobaugh has so far shared his thought with mine that the book is in a measure his. Richard Breithut has saved me from some pitfalls. And without the loyal and painstaking assistance of Miss Adeline Barry the book would have had to wait another year for completion. The generosity of the librarians of Widener Library, Cleveland Public Library, Western Reserve University and the New York Public Library has given me every material aid that time permitted me to use. My son, with the wisdom and kindness of his six years, has tolerated my remaining late at the office and benevolently excused me again and again from the evening story that is his right. My wife has been a constant aid in drawing together thoughts woven into the book. Whoever has worked with Professor W. L. Langer will bear witness to the value of his inspiring leadership.

INTRODUCTION

Our age of specialization produces an almost incredible amount of monographic research in all fields of human knowledge. So great is the mass of this material that even the professional scholar cannot keep abreast of the contributions in anything but a restricted part of his general subject. In all branches of learning the need for intelligent synthesis is now more urgent than ever before, and this need is felt by the layman even more acutely than by the scholar. He cannot hope to read the products of microscopic research or to keep up with the changing interpretations of experts, unless new knowledge and new viewpoints are made accessible to him by those who make it their business to be informed and who are competent to speak with authority.

These volumes, published under the general title of *The Rise of Modern Europe*, are designed primarily to give the general reader and student a reliable survey of European history written by experts in various branches of that vast subject. In consonance with the current broad conceptions of the scope of history, they attempt to go beyond a merely political-military narrative, and to lay stress upon social, economic, religious, scientific and artistic developments. The minutely detailed, chronological approach is to some extent sacrificed in the effort to emphasize the dominant factors and to set forth their interrelationships. At the same time the division of European history into national histories has been abandoned and wherever possible attention has been focussed upon larger forces common to the whole of European civilization. These are the broad lines on which this history as a whole has been laid out. The individual volumes are integral parts of the larger scheme, but they are intended also to stand as independent units, each the work of a scholar well qualified to treat the period covered by his book. Each volume contains about fifty illustrations selected from the mass of contemporary pictorial material. All non-contemporary illustrations have been excluded on principle. The bibliographical note appended to each volume is designed to facilitate further study of special aspects touched upon in the text. In general every effort has been made to give the reader a clear idea of the main movements in European history, to embody the monographic contributions of research workers, and to present the material in a forceful and vivid manner.

. . .

The period of Cavour and Bismarck has supplied the theme for a vast literature, most of it glorifying the victory of nationalism and exalting the accomplishments of the realists in politics. Professor Binkley has preferred to strike out on a fresh line and to evaluate the achievements of these years in a thoroughly critical spirit. His introductory chapters have little to do with politics, and are devoted to a study of the growth of the scientific mentality and of the related spread of the ideas of realism in literature, art and religion. Considerable attention is given to the evolution of business and the appearance of new social problems after the first impact of the industrial revolution. Many of these aspects of the period have been very generally neglected in historical surveys of these stormy decades. But Professor Binkley has not allowed his treatment of them to interfere with an adequate presentation of the more colorful political and military events. Without attempting to follow the diplomacy of Cavour, Bismarck or Napoleon III in all its intricate details, he gives the essentials of the great national problems and views them as yet another manifestation of the spirit of realism. The reader will find here a most stimulating contrast of the ideas of federalism and European comity so characteristic of the preceding period with the ideas of aggressive and exclusive nationalism. Like other volumes in the series, the treatment here is of Europe as a whole, and not of a dozen separate national compartments.

William L. Langer

PROLOGUE

THE THIRD QUARTER of the nineteenth century was an epoch recognized in the history of many countries as having decisive political significance. In Italy it was the age of the *Risorgimento*; in Germany, of the *Reichsgründung*; in Russia of the Great Reforms; in the Hapsburg Empire it was the last great period of constitutional experiment before the political system was fatefully immobilized by the Compromise of 1867; in America it was the time of Civil War and Reconstruction; in Japan, the moment of Awakening, the beginning of the Meiji Era. The international system of the European states took on during these decades those characteristics that came to be called "The Armed Peace," which paralleled the development and spread of the centralized national state as a standard political form. The evolution of that complex of technological processes, economic institutions and juridical norms to which the generation gave the name of capitalism took place in a cultural environment that was in well-defined contrast both to the age that preceded and to the one that followed. For France it was the period of the Second Empire, for England the middle of the Victorian Age, and for Europe generally the era in which "science" won, at the expense of other intellectual interests, the dominion it was to exercise for the next two generations over the European mind.

When the quarter-century opened, the dominant European attitudes of mind were those of reaction against the excesses of the preceding era—reaction against democracy in politics, against romanticism in literature, against all sentiment and idealism and philosophy. By 1871 the universe had been redesigned in partial conformity with these attitudes. With increasing certainty through these twenty years, it was established that the whole realm of "matter," of tangible things, was understood by science and was far more stable and important than the realm of ideas which the philosophers had once vainly explored. It seemed that the course of politics was determined by material forces and interests rather than by ideal principles or ethical truth, and that material forces and interests themselves were measurable in terms of commodities, of things produced and exchanged rather than by any other scale. The generation that made the new national states made a new universe to environ them; it was left for another generation to discover how they would fare therein.

The universe that was coming into existence may be analyzed from three angles: the intellectual, the economic, and the political. In its intellectual aspect, it was a very hard and tangible universe, mapped by science (not philosophy) and described by such catchwords as "positivism" or "materialism." In its economic aspect, it was predominantly a world of moving commodities; it owed its existence to the development of transportation with the corresponding industrial and financial innovations. In its political aspect the new world had by 1871 become at once highly organized and highly anarchic. Behind sharply drawn frontiers the authoritarian territorial states (none of them any longer feudal states, and most of them already national states), operated with perfected administrative machinery; across these frontiers they dealt jealously with each other, the continental states on terms of *Realpolitik*, England on the basis of isolation, both principles being a denial of obligations to international society.

The account of European development that follows will of necessity be fragmentary. It may differ somewhat in emphasis and design from many current accounts of the same era. The difference will be the result of a systematic effort—only partially successful—to find the basis of a European history that will not be a sum obtained by adding up the histories of the various states, together with a history of diplomacy. The political contours of contemporary Europe, with its large number of national states, render such an approach more necessary than ever, for what has endured as a problem of interstate relations in central and eastern Europe was then formulated as a series of intrastate problems of the Russian, Austrian, and Ottoman Empires.

Two devices have suggested themselves as means of bringing more clearly to the fore those elements of European history that are common to the whole continent and culture. One of them is to begin the story with an account of the non-political side of Europe's development, with the analysis of culture as it was manifested in science, letters, art, religion and business life, where the national units do not press themselves so insistently upon the historian. Then, in the analysis of political history, recourse is made to a concept which has not received the benefit of theoretical exposition in the hands of political theorists, but which seems none the less useful to the historian. This is the concept of "federative polity," applied herein to problems of federalism within a state, confederation among states, and quasi-confederal relations of states generally. *Federative polity,* as the term is used in this narrative, is the polity that emphasizes the political relations of adjustment among equals rather than the political relationships of inferiority and superiority, and of methods of law rather than methods of force. The term will be applied to federalism in the Danube monarchy as it was proposed in 1860, to federalism or confederation in *Mitteleuropa* as it was promoted by the *Grossdeutsch* reformers of the 1860's, to the confederal program for the reorganization of Italy, to the use of the European congress as a legislative body for Europe, and even to arbitration as a means of adjusting disputes between states. For Europe as a whole, federative polity declined almost to the point of extinction in this era, but survived among Anglo-Saxon peoples, in the United States of America, the British Empire, and in the relation of Britain to the United States.

There is an element of enforced fiction in any periodization of history. All historic sequences have unbroken continuity. But since periodization is necessary as a device for study and exposition, the historian has the task of finding the rhythm and meaning that makes a unity of the particular period to which he addresses his attention. A period of twenty years, wherever in the long course of history it may lie, has one characteristic that will never escape it. It is always a period sufficiently long to set its seal upon the minds of its generation. The ranks of the men who are at the height of their powers when such a period begins are thinning when it ends. If there take place within it events that mark themselves with emphasis upon the minds of the young, the consequences of such events will not be fully realized until youth has grown to age and had its day of power.

Under the cultural conditions obtaining in Europe in the nineteenth century, the members of the middle and upper classes saw all the facets of civilization. They followed diplomatic events, they read about scientific achievements, they knew something of letters and art and had opinions about religion. If they were not actually drawn into the nexus of the business world as investors or participants, at least they watched its marvelous achievements. That which, in a history, is separated into chapters was in these lives brought together as a sum of experience. Georges Clemenceau as a doctor knew about Lister; as a young Paris intellectual he followed the art controversy over Courbet; as a political leader he bore his part in the tragedy of the Commune and the Bordeaux Assembly. Paul von Hindenburg, a cadet during the war of 1866, a young officer in the war of 1871, saw Europe with the eyes of the Prussian officer corps, as Clemenceau saw it with the eyes of Parisian radicalism. These are two individuals out of millions. In their lives, as in the lives of millions, there was perpetuated the grandeur, the conflict, the tragedy of the years of their youth.

Chapter One

THE AGE OF SCIENCE: SYNTHESIS, POPULARIZATION AND UTILITY

1. SCIENCE VERSUS PHILOSOPHY

THE FIRST HALF of the nineteenth century was an age of philosophy; the second half of the century was an age of science. The science of the second half of the century crowded philosophy into the background in three ways and for three reasons. Science became comprehensive, where previously it had been fragmentary and disconnected; it made itself understandable to the multitude where later it passed in many of its branches beyond the power of the layman to grasp; it established a claim to utility, for it contracted in the presence of the public its marriage with technology.

The displacement of philosophy by science was evident in the practical affairs of the world. Down to the fiasco of the revolutions of 1848, philosophies and theories of all kinds had seemed to have tremendous practical importance. They were regarded as a kind of dynamite likely to destroy the social order, or as a sovereign remedy for social ills. Hegelian philosophy in its original German form, or as reformulated by the Neo-Guelphs in Italy or the Slavophils of Russia, had seemed potent and important; so also had the constructions of the Utopian socialists, or the romantic nationalism of the Young Europe cult, or the theoretical creations of the authoritarian school. The revolutions of 1848 had seemed to prove, not only that certain theorists were wrong, but that all theories were unimportant. This was precisely the time chosen by science to begin to reverse its relations with technology. For in the first half of the nineteenth century natural science was more like an array of parlor tricks than a force contributing to practical life.

The shift in interest on the part of the intellectual classes was evidenced by the desertion of philosophy courses in the German universities, the home of philosophy. The public at the same time evinced a desire to learn of the world of science. Humboldt's *Cosmos* achieved a wide circulation in the early 1850's as the forerunner of a host of popular-science books. When the rise of Napoleon III fixed the expression *"coup d'état"* in Europe's language, reviewers wrote of the "*coup d'état* of science." A diarist in Paris, Anthony B. North Peat, was struck by the popular interest in scientific lectures and jotted down in 1865:

> But a few years have elapsed since the custom brought over from England of lecturing in public has been introduced into Paris, and this custom has spread with tremendous rapidity over every part of the Empire. The multitude of *salles de conférence* which have been opened in France for the purpose of disseminating useful knowledge and ennobling ideas is to the philanthropist one of the most encouraging features of the present state of society. In all the principal towns, and even in the smaller villages, men distinguished either by great scientific or literary attainments have come forward to lend an earnest aid to the cause of social progress by the diffusion of knowledge.[1]

Some of the classics of western European scientific writing are the product of this rapprochement between the scientists and the public.

To this shift in interest there corresponded a very important accomplishment of the natural scientists themselves. Theirs was the outstanding intellectual achievement of the age—the synthesis of natural science by the integration of its various branches. The historical significance of the development of the science of the mid-nineteenth century is not wholly confined to the formula of the historians of science that the discoveries of this period contributed to later discoveries and pressed forward a continuously advancing frontier of knowledge. The science of the mid-nineteenth century differed from the science of the early part of the century in its internal style. Scientists became bolder in making generalizations; they sought more widely for relationships; they drew from a vast accumulation of separate items of experimental data certain great synthetic conclusions which they contrived to make meaningful to the public.

[1] Anthony B. North Peat, *Gossip from Paris during the Second Empire.* (New York, 1903), 147.

In the first half of the century, while the philosophers had the spotlight of public attention, the natural scientists were the enemies of nature philosophy. They took pride in abstaining from generalizations. They tinkered and mixed and measured and reported their experiments to each other. They had a neat system of rules relating to priority of discovery, and competed with each other as if in a game.

"In that race which Sig. Nobili and Antinori ran against me, they obtained the spark from the common magnet before me," wrote Faraday in 1832.

Then, after 1850, the spirit changed. It became permissible for experimental scientists to generalize. They then came forward with their great synthetic concepts: thermodynamics and evolution. They defined with a gesture of finality the three ultimate constituents of the universe: matter, energy, and æther. They contrived in all of this not to lose touch with the public.

The mid-nineteenth century was an age of science, indeed, but how much scientific work was done therein? How can intellectual achievement be given quantitative expression? Some statistical tables of so-called "scientific discoveries" in physics have been drawn up by T. J. Rainoff from Auerbach's *Geschichtstafeln der Physik* and from other sources. Rainoff has plotted a curve of scientific productivity based, of course, on the number of reported experiments that have since been thought worthy of inclusion in histories of science. This curve falls off sharply in the 1850's and does not recover to the pre-1850 level until after 1871.[2]

Judged by the number of reported experiments, this great age of science was not highly productive. Its productivity was in synthesis of theory and practical application to technology. This was the age in which there was built up that whole system of scientific materialism which differed from the materialisms of all previous times in the amplitude of its experimental bases.

The scientists organized their accumulation of separate observa-

[2] T. J. Rainoff, "Wave-like Fluctuations of Creative Productivity in the Development of West-European Physics in the Eighteenth and Nineteenth Centuries," *Isis*, XII (1929). 298.

tions under a few great general concepts (matter, energy, æther, organism, environment, evolution) and wove the connective tissue between the sciences. Thus they developed a system of thought that exceeded in scope the world of Newton, as it exceeded in experimental certainty the world of Goethe. While the age looked on and marveled, the different parts of the structure of science were falling into position. The study of atomic weights, thermodynamics, and the kinetic theory of gases brought together Newtonian physics and chemistry; investigations of the spectrum, of light pressure and heat radiation revealed the relation of light to matter and energy. Then electro-magnetic phenomena took their place in the picture, using the same æther with light, and taking part in the same energy transformations with matter. Organic chemistry was reaching out to relate this world with the world of biology. In the biological sciences the Darwinian synthesis showed its capacity to draw in and use the evidence submitted by geology and the testimony taken with the microscope, while it lent its great thought-pattern to the study of mankind. And in the study of human nature the experimental psychologists, Fechner, Helmholtz, Wundt, were exploring the physical basis of psychic phenomena. It was no wonder that science won prestige and popularity at the expense of idealistic and romantic philosophies, for it rivaled them in completeness and surpassed them in its appeal to a sense of fact.

II. THE CONCEPT OF MATTER

The process by which significant generalizations were deduced from the abundant experimental data accumulated by 1850 can be illustrated in the development of the concept of matter. Matter was the ultimate reality of nineteenth-century science. From it all certainties proceeded, to it all investigation returned. The essential laboratory quality of matter was its weight, because the principal laboratory tool was the balance which measured weight. When the twentieth century developed new tools, such as the ionization chamber, it quickly evolved a very different conception of matter.

In the nineteenth century the chemists rather than the physicists took the lead in the study of matter. Their work rested upon two fundamental observations in each of which the balance played a leading part. The first was of the late eighteenth century: Lavoisier's demonstration that the products of combustion weigh neither more nor less than the materials combined in the burning. This seemed to prove that matter was indestructible—or to use the more provocative word of the German popularizers, immortal. This quality of matter prevailed during the entire century from Lavoisier and Dalton to Madame Curie.

The second fundamental observation dated from the first years of the nineteenth century: Dalton noted that for every five ounces of carbon, ethylene gas contains one ounce of hydrogen, and methane gas two ounces. Why should these elements, carbon and hydrogen, combine with each other such simple numerical proportions by weight? Dalton explained the fact by assuming that the primal form of carbon was a small particle or atom weighing just five times as much as the corresponding particle of hydrogen, and that this atom of carbon would sometimes combine with one atom of hydrogen to make ethylene, sometimes with two atoms of hydrogen to make methane. The idea of the atomic structure of the universe, as old as Greek philosophy, received its experimental demonstration from Dalton.

In the half-century following Dalton the chemists determined a multitude of combining weights (also called atomic weights), and they were overloaded with data which they found difficult to interpret. The relations of atom to molecule were in the 1850's, like the electron and nucleus in the 1930's, a central problem to those who studied "matter."

The confusion over the interpretation of weight data became so great in the 1850's that the system of chemical notation was breaking down. For instance: should the formula for water stand as HO, or should it be written H_2O as Gerhardt began to write it about 1856? Some chemists talked of abandoning the atomic theory. The great problem—and the great achievement—of the chemistry of the 1850's and 1860's was to clarify the relationship of atomic weight to other chemical qualities of substances.

To clear up the question of chemical notation, an international convention of chemists met at Karlsruhe in 1860. The whole atomic weight concept was really at stake. At the close of the meeting

Stanislao Cannizzaro, who was then a professor in the Royal University of Genoa, distributed a pamphlet he had written two years before, describing his plan of a course in "chemical philosophy." The pamphlet made a great impression. Lothar Meyer, who later shared with Mendeléyev the honor for the discovery of the periodic table, describes the effect of Cannizzaro's pamphlet upon his mind. He read it on the train returning to Breslau from the convention.

> The scales seemed to fall from my eyes. Doubts disappeared and a quiet feeling of certainty took their place. . . . Like me it must have affected many others who attended the convention. The big waves of controversy began to subside, and more and more the old atomic weights of Berzelius came into their own.[3]

It is highly significant in the history of thought that science should have been in such a state that the outline of a general university course in chemistry should clear up a controversy raging among the leading chemists of Europe. The incident illustrates the fact that the forefront of scientific knowledge was not at that time so remote from the comprehension of the average man as it became in the twentieth century.

What Cannizzaro did was to harmonize the data on combination weights with the data derived from the almost forgotten observations of Avogadro on gas volumes. Avogadro had noted that while the weight relations of oxygen and hydrogen in water stand at eight to one, the volume relations are one to two. Cannizzaro did no new experimenting; he merely suggested that atomic proportions could be taken as those established by weight, molecular proportions those established by gas volume. His suggestion standardized the atomic weight system on a firm basis, gave water the formula H_2O and oxygen the atomic weight sixteen. Like so many other achievements of the time, it was a drawing together of previously disparate elements of a science. And it prepared the way for the work of the 'sixties, toward the understanding of molecular structure as Kekule saw it in the benzene ring, and of atomic weights as Mendeléyev interpreted them in the periodic table.

Both Cannizzaro and Kekule used in their thinking a simple and

[3] Forris J. Moore, *History of Chemistry* (New York, 1918), 176

easily comprehended imagery. Cannizzaro presented a table of combining weights and then went on to explain:

> To fix this well in the minds of my pupils, I have recourse to a very simple artifice: I say to them, namely, "Suppose it to be shown that the half molecule of hydrogen weighs a millionth of a milligram, then all the numbers of the preceding table become concrete numbers, expressing in millionths of a milligram the weights of the molecules and of their components."[4]

So also Kekule in 1854, with an imagery as simple as Cannizzaro's, had dreamed of the dance of the atoms. While riding in a London omnibus, he saw in his mind's eye how,

> frequently two smaller atoms united to form a pair; how a larger one embraced the two smaller ones; how still larger ones kept hold of three or even four of the smaller whilst the whole kept whirling in a giddy dance. I saw how the larger ones formed a chain dragging the smaller ones after them, but only at the ends of the chain.

Eleven years later, in 1865, he was again dreaming. Again the atoms danced before his eyes in long, snakelike lines, among them the benzene molecule, which now, because of Cannizzaro's contribution to the science, linked twelve rather than six atoms in its chain. "But look—what was that? One of the snakes has seized hold of its own tail."[5] Thus, in the words of Kekule, did the benzene molecule first appear as the benzene ring.

Kekule's vision of the structure of the molecule was only one of many new insights into the nature of matter made possible by the standardization of the atomic weights. Of even greater importance was the periodic table, the most comprehensive systematic achievement of mid-nineteenth-century chemistry. Independently of each other, in 1869, Lothar Meyer and Dimitri Mendeléyev announced that various chemical qualities of the elements, such as those that were observed as "electropositive" and "electronegative" in the early nineteenth century, or those that had begun to be called "valencies of combinations" in the 1850's, together with the obvious physical

[4] S. Cannizzaro, "Sketch of a Course in Chemical Philosophy," *Alembic Club Reprints*, No. 18 (Edinburgh, 1910).

[5] Quoted in John Hohnyard, *The Great Chemists* (London, 1928), 107.

qualities, such as solid or gaseous state at normal temperatures, were all related to atomic weight. The elements, arranged in order of atomic weights, divided themselves into groups; the properties of an element in one group resembled those of an element in a corresponding position in another group. By 1871, Mendeléyev had perfected the statement of the periodic law, and ventured to predict the discovery of three elements to fill vacant places in his table—predictions that came true during his lifetime. When science accepted his dictum that "the magnitude of the atomic weight determines the character of the element," the varied properties of matter were subordinated, to a degree not reached before nor long retained thereafter, to the common denominator of weight.

III. POPULARIZATION

While the chemists were perfecting their conception of matter, the popularizers were preaching it with missionary zeal. In 1855 Ludwig Büchner wrote *Kraft und Stoff*, a book that was to run through nine editions, and to serve as a bible for that whole generation of German and Russian youth that was then deserting Hegel. Büchner was still able to find a few men who doubted or denied the universal application of the principle of the conservation of matter. He noted one writer who asserted that water originated in clouds, another who held that animals produce nitrogen, a third who questioned whether organisms create or transform the materials they contain. He turned upon these intellectual laggards the full force of his powers of exhortation:

> How can anyone deny the axiom, that out of nothing, nothing can arise. . . . An atom of oxygen, of nitrogen, or of iron, is everywhere and under all circumstances the same thing, endowed with the same immanent qualities, and can never in all eternity become anything else. Be it wheresoever it will, it must remain the same; from every combination, however heterogeneous, must it emerge the selfsame atom. But never can an atom arise anew or disappear; it can only change its combinations. For these reasons matter is immortal: and for this reason it is, as already shown, impossible that the world can have been created.[6]

[6] L. Büchner, *Kraft und Stoff* (Frankfurt, 1855), chap. ii.

Great scientists like Clerk-Maxwell stated the principle more cautiously, in language that did not so closely as Büchner's suggest the thought-world of Lucretius, but with whatever reservations it was stated it remained the working hypothesis in the laboratory as well as an article of popular scientific belief.

The popularization of this scientific dogma illustrates the fact that the science of the mid-century was not only comprehensive, but comprehensible. It was constructed on patterns with which people were familiar. Its time and space and matter and force were nearer to common experience than the Hegelian Absolute that had preceded it or the Einstein space-time continuum that was to follow. Scientists could use the same language to the public that they used to their colleagues. The *Origin of Species* was not a vulgarization, and yet it was a popular book. The ninth edition of the *Encyclopædia Britannica* was perhaps the last monument to this great age of truly popular science.

IV. THE STEAM ENGINE AND THERMODYNAMICS: THE ENERGY CONCEPT

Another important characteristic of mid-century science was its rapidly changing relationship to invention. Increasingly the findings of the scientists found industrial application. This feature of the history of the period can be illustrated in the field of thermodynamics and electro-magnetic studies, for in thermodynamics the scientists borrowed from the artisans, in electro-magnetic developments they repaid the debt. The steam-engine did not arise in the laboratory, it came up from the millwright's workshop; the dynamo, on the contrary, was evolved directly as a result of laboratory findings.

The steam-engine was the greatest gift of the artisans to the scientists, for it presented very clearly the problem of finding the relationship of heat to motion. The idea that heat might be a mode of motion was old, but the problem of measuring the amount of heat that would give rise to a given amount of motion was as new as the steam-engine. Even the basic concepts of "work" and "power," in terms of which the mechanical equivalent of heat was to be stated when found, were not defined except by implication in the old Newtonian mechanics. James Watt defined these units in the late eighteenth century—foot-pounds as a measure of work, foot-pounds-per-second as a measure of power—because he needed some way of explaining to his customers the value of the engines he was manufacturing at Soho.

Almost half a century passed before scientists saw that the steam-engine illustrated some specific relationship of heat to work. In 1824 Carnot published a pamphlet on the motive power of fire, posing for the first time the question of the mechanical equivalent of heat, but no one paid any attention to his ideas at the time.

The energy concept, as it was developed in the body of doctrine which in the 1850's began to be called thermodynamics, was the most comprehensive synthesizing concept in nineteenth century physics. It furnished a common denominator for the phenomena of mechanics, heat, electro-magnetism and chemical affinity. It permeated the physics of the 1860's as relativity and quantum mechanics do the physics of the 1930's, compelling the restatement of old laws and the rewriting of textbooks.

It took the characteristic mid-century form of a series of broad generalizations of which the first was the most important and the most widely understood. This first law of thermodynamics, the law of conservation of energy, was stated by Helmholtz in this way:

> Nature as a whole possesses a store of force which cannot in any way be either increased or diminished . . . therefore the quantity of force in Nature is just as eternal and unalterable as the quantity of matter.[7]

The demonstrations of this principle traced energy from heat to motive power, from motive power to electrical and thence to chemical energy, and back again to heat. Herbert Spencer, who was just then starting to run his prodigious race with all the branches of science at once, wove this great generalization into the whole pattern of his thought. For him the "persistence of force" was the fundamental truth underlying all science.

There was coördinated with this first law of thermodynamics a second law, even more rich in philosophical implications—the law of the degradation of energy, with its warning that the sun would

[7] Ludwig Helmholtz, "The Conservation of Energy," *Classics of Modern Science* (New York, 1927), 286.

ultimately cool down, the tides halt the revolutions of the earth, and the universe die as its store of energy reached equilibrium. The eschatological thought of Europe had been committed for centuries to the prospect of a final combustion of the earth; henceforth it would dwell more upon the prospect of an ultimate refrigeration. This second law of thermodynamics offered good grounds for cosmic despair. The twentieth century was able to feed no inconsiderable pessimism upon it. But the mid-nineteenth century gave scant heed to this second law and its eschatological implications. It drew its pessimism from Schopenhauer, finding none in Spencer.

The emergence of the laws of thermodynamics in the mid-century illustrates not only the debt of the scientists to the inventors, but also the characteristic shift of scientific interest from small experiments to large conclusions. Before 1850 the physicists had been given many opportunities to accept the principle of conservation of energy, but had resisted them all. They not only paid no attention to Carnot's pamphlet in 1824, but neglected the suggestions of two or three scientists in the 'thirties, and almost a dozen in the 'forties, who approached in one way or another a statement of the new law of nature. Poggendorf's *Annalen der Physik*, the leading German journal of experimental physics, rejected three papers in which the doctrine or some part of it was set forth: Mohl's in 1837, Mayer's in 1843, and Helmholtz's in 1847. The editors were trying to keep their field clear of the taint of armchair philosophy, and suspected such titles as "The Nature of Heat," "The Forces of Inorganic Nature," or "The Conservation of Energy" as too suggestive of speculation rather than experiment. The basic experimental data were gathered about 1843 by Joule in England and Colding in Denmark. James Prescott Joule, a one-time pupil of Dalton's, found that water was warmed by being churned with a paddle. He measured the rise in the temperature of the water and the amount of work spent on the paddle. The resulting ratio, the mechanical equivalent of heat, had implications comparable in range with those of Galileo's law of falling bodies, but the significance of the discovery was not then appreciated. It was only in the sessions of the learned societies of London, Edinburgh and Berlin in the years 1850 to 1852 that the whole doctrine was matured and given a nomenclature and a mathematical demonstration.

Ten years later the popularizers fell into line. Büchner was still unaware of the new idea when he published *Kraft und Stoff* in 1855, but in the fifth edition he included an appropriate chapter on *The Immortality of Force.* John Tyndall's *Heat a Mode of Motion* spread the gospel with more adequate proofs in 1863. Thomsen and Tait's *Treatise on Natural Philosophy* in 1867 was the conclusive and systematic summary of the new physics. These works ran all through Europe in translation.

Meanwhile the drive toward synthesis went on. Physics and chemistry drew closer together. Clerk-Maxwell took up the gas molecules where Cannizzaro had left them in 1860, and formulated the kinetic theory of gases. He developed the mathematical consequences of the assumption that molecules of gas were like little balls that bounded against each other and against the walls of a containing vessel. An increase in their speed of motion was exactly the same thing as an increase in temperature, and it had the effect of increasing gas pressure because it increased the number and momentum of their collisions. The tattoo of speeding molecules on the surface of a piston was the motive power of steam. Then, in the hands of Julius Thomsen (1869) and Berthelot, the measurement of heat transformations in chemical reactions led to an explanation of chemical affinity. Their doctrine in chemical science was for a time called "the third law of thermodynamics": namely, that such chemical transformations take place as are accompanied by the greatest amount of energy liberated as heat.

V. THE ELECTRO-MAGNETIC TELEGRAPH AND THE ÆTHER CONCEPT

Electro-magnetic studies in the mid-century were productive in two ways: they developed practical applications and extended the great scientific synthesis by defining the concept of æther.

When the nineteenth century opened, there were three kinds of electro-magnetic phenomena under investigation, each with some tinge of practical interest. The study of magnetism was applied in navigation, of static electric charges in lightning rods, and of battery currents in chemical electrolysis. Both electricity and magnetism lent themselves to interesting class room and laboratory tricks, but they opened no vast insight into the nature of the physical universe. They seemed to be the by-products of nature. Magnetism had no definite relation to electricity.

In 1819 Oersted had happened accidentally upon the discovery that an electric current would deflect a magnetic needle. Thereupon Ampère found he could produce magnetism from electricity and Faraday electricity from magnetism. The two fields of scientific investigation, electricity and magnetism, became one.

Industrial applications followed this stride toward synthesis in the science. The magnet, activated by a battery current of electricity, became the electric telegraph in the 'thirties and 'forties; the forerunner of the modern dynamo, generating electricity by forcing wires to move through an electric field, appeared at the same time. Efforts were made to find industrial application for these early dynamos. One American inventor thought he had solved the problem of perpetual motion with such a device. He would decompose water with an electric current, burn the hydrogen as fuel for the steam-engine, use the steam power to run a generator, and the generator current to decompose the water. In 1850 Nollet, professor of physics in Brussels, invented a generator which he thought could be used commercially to supply illuminating gas by decomposing water. The company promoted for this purpose failed, but ten years later steam-generated electricity was used commercially for lighting purposes. In 1862 the British government accepted an arc-light installation for Dungeness Lighthouse. Iron and steam, bone and breath of the new age, had grown without the ministrations of science, but electricity was nursed by it at every stage.

When the first Atlantic cable ceased functioning soon after it was laid in 1858, Sir William Thomson (later Lord Kelvin) brought all contemporary physical science to bear upon the problem of making a workable cable. The success of the second cable in 1866 was due to his researches. Meanwhile in Germany Ernst Wilhelm von Siemens had left his army career after the Danish War of 1848 to combine business and science in one enterprise, the great electrical firm of Siemens and Halske.

In the meantime the intellectual enterprise of explaining the place of electro-magnetic phenomena in the physical universe was being carried forward. The starting-point of nineteenth-century speculation on this point was the suggestion that the presence of certain mysterious fluids, such as austral and boreal magnetic fluid, a positive and a negative electric fluid, accounted for electro-magnetic behavior. These were not the only weightless fluids of that scientific era. Caloric, the weightless fluid of the heat present in hot substances like water in a sponge, had hung on despite the protests of certain physicists, till the laws of thermodynamics disposed of it. As late as 1850 John Ericsson was promoting a "caloric engine" that was supposed to use the same caloric over and over again. But these weightless fluids did not sit well with a materialistic science, and their diversity was troublesome to a unified and comprehensive scientific synthesis. Faraday had preferred another imagery in explaining electro-magnetic action. He chose to think of the space surrounding a magnet or an electric wire as an area run through and through with "lines of force," such lines in fact as are exhibited in the arrangement of iron filings in the presence of a magnet. It was here that the concept of æther began to be helpful about 1851.

The æther was an extraordinary space-filling substance. It had been called into existence in the first half of the century as a means of explaining the transmission of light. Its reality was denied by the proponents of the corpuscular theory of light, whose doctrine that light is a stream of particles was not finally scotched until Foucault proved in 1850 that light travels faster in air than in water. It was doubted by Comte and John Stuart Mill as an unduly speculative entity, too remote from direct observation to have good status in the world of science. Its properties became increasingly curious as the century advanced. At first it was only a rarefied interstellar atmosphere, carrying light as air carries sound, but in the 1840's it became a jelly, sufficiently rigid to carry a shudder through infinite space, and yet so soft and yielding that the planets could plow through it without friction. It then seemed too subtle, as in the twentieth century it began to seem too gross, to serve as a wholly satisfactory scientific entity. And yet it was more satisfactory than a lot of miscellaneous weightless fluids, and it became an indispensable construction in the great scientific synthesis, for it brought together the phenomena of light and electro-magnetism. Only a few months after Foucault had ended the controversy over the wave theory of light, Faraday was talking of æther as a medium for magnetism. "If there be an æther," he told the Royal Society, "it should have some other uses than simply the conveyance of radiation."[8] These "other uses" the scientists were quick to provide.

Faraday's suggestion of 1851 that the medium in which lines of force are present might be precisely the same as the light-bearing æther was supported in 1862 when Clerk-Maxwell showed that the mathematical qualities of an æther that would serve as a medium for electro-magnetic forces were precisely those of an æther transmitting light waves.

From this point the physical science of the mid-Victorian era moved to its most adventurous speculation—the vortex theory of matter. Perhaps this strange æther might be the primal world-stuff, and the atoms and molecules merely knots and whirlpools in it! Notions of this kind, reminiscent of the Cartesian philosophy of the seventeenth century, were propounded in the 'fifties by the engineer scientist Macquorn Rankine, and taken up in the 'sixties by Sir William Thomson and Clerk Maxwell. This line of thought was worked out in terms of mathematics, and remained a little beyond the level of popularization. It had no currency outside of England. Even Germany, once the favored land of speculative thought, gave it no reception.

German science was none the less pushing forward the great synthesis. Between 1859 and 1862 Bunsen and Kirkhoff developed spectrum analysis, thus making the study of light contribute to chemistry. They began with the "Bunsen burner," which gave them a hot but colorless gas flame. They noted that each of a number of substances when heated in this burner gave rise to a flame of characteristic color. By passing the light of the flame through a prism they determined accurately the exact color character—the spectrum, that is to say—of each element. Then they observed that when a stronger light is passed through the flame, the flame will

[8] Faraday, "Experimental Researches in Electricity" (London, 1852), *Philosophical Transactions—Royal Society of London.*

kill those very colors which it is itself giving forth, and the spectrum will have black lines where bright lines would otherwise be found. With this double check on the relation of flame color to chemical character, the two investigators examined the spectrum of the sun's light, and found evidence of the existence of a number of common metals in the sun. In 1868 Lockyer identified in the solar spectrum the element *helium*, not then known on earth. Spectrum analysis was a new tool, the effect of which was only beginning to be felt in physics and astronomy by 1871.

VI. THE UTILITY OF SCIENCE

Even as the extreme forefront of scientific speculation was moving by 1871 to regions the public could not so easily enter with its understanding, to doctrines like the vortex theory of matter or experimental tools like the spectroscope, the public confidence in science was fortified by a growing conviction that science was useful. This conviction was the result of an exaggeration of the past rôle of science in industry, and a well-founded expectation of its future contribution.

What was the relation of the great technological achievements of the era to the development of pure science? The state of technology was one to which Lewis Mumford has applied the term "paleotechnic." The coal-iron complex had replaced or was replacing the wood-wind-water complex in technics, but the electricity-alloy complex had not yet appeared.

The achievements of industry and engineering that were at the time most conspicuous and which absorbed the largest proportion of capital, had to do with the development of transportation equipment and the extension of steam-power manufacturing plants in textiles and fabricated products. This involved the construction and improvement of ports and navigation facilities, in which concrete as a relatively new building material was developed. The Suez Canal, built between 1856 and 1869, was the most striking product of this kind of constructive energy. It involved also the building of cities, or their enlargement to wholly new dimensions. Traditional brick, stone and wood remained the dominant building materials for houses and factories, although structural iron began to make its way, especially with the wrought-iron I-bar in the 'fifties. The Crystal Palace, built for the great London Exhibition of 1851 of cast-iron frame and glass, was regarded as a triumph of the builders' art. In ocean transportation, the age began with the supremacy of the American clipper ship and ended with the challenge of steam to sail. The steamship had increased its ocean-going capacity by means of the screw propeller in the 'fifties and the compound engine, which meant less coal and more cargo, in the 'sixties. Of all the apparatus of industry and commerce, the most important by far was the railroad. The great and enduring monument left by the nineteenth century to the twentieth was the railway network. As the thirteenth century built cathedrals, so the nineteenth built railways. The world's mileage stood at 38,000 in 1850, at 204,000 in 1870. Railway-building revolutionized the iron industry on the Continent, forcing the substitution of coke for wood charcoal in the blast furnaces. The turning-point came in the 1860's. Though this mileage was destined to be trebled before the building boom slackened and died in the twentieth century, the technics and business management of railways were matured by 1871. Later locomotives might be more powerful, but not much faster. The 4-foot-8½-inch gauge was standardized, and the steel rail was already beginning to replace iron. The problem the railroad presented to the world after 1871 was no longer technical nor even financial, but a problem of social control.

What did science contribute to these achievements? The process of popularization which gave intelligent artisans knowledge of contemporary development in science obscured somewhat the distinction between pure and applied science. The man at the workbench was able to understand what the man in the laboratory was doing, even if he made no direct use of the information. If by science is meant the tradition of inquiry and experiment that runs from Galileo and Newton through such men as Lavoisier and Dalton to men like Einstein and Morgan, the answer must be that the contributions were small and indecisive. Out of this tradition had come such things as the miner's safety lamp, or Leblanc soda-ash, not large-scale production, nor concrete. Neither the Crystal

Palace nor the railway system nor the use of coal in metallurgy nor the cotton-mills nor the Suez Canal were in debt to nineteenth-century science. The first workings at Suez in 1856 were carried on with forced labor and equipment not much different from what Ptolemy must have used, and when the withdrawal of forced labor led to the greater use of machinery after 1863, the dredges and diggers that were built made use of no new scientific principles. And yet there was an increasing application of science to industry in the mid-century. The change can be illustrated in metallurgy. Henry Bessemer was a man of the inventor type, half promoter, half mechanic; he was not a scientist. He dabbled in many bright ideas. Among them was one which made him a fortune—the idea of blowing air through molten iron to burn the carbon and cinder from it. His process, which worked very well with certain ores, was the last great rule-of-thumb innovation in iron and steel. After him came the chemists who found out how to deal with phosphorus in the ore. Soldy in England (1868), Tchernoff in Russia, founded the science of metallography (the microscopic examination of the structure of iron and steel), which prepared the way for the age of alloys.

One of the turning-points in the relations of pure science to technology was undoubtedly the great London Exhibition of 1851, which brought together under one roof samples of the products of all lands. The exhibition established clearly that England led the world in the mechanical arts, despite the fact that technical education was in England less developed than on the Continent. At the same time it brought together the contributions that the scientists were making to industry, and publicized their possibilities. When the Austrians exhibited "some models of Lucifer matches made with amorphous phosphorus" the *Edinburgh Review* commented:

> The uninformed reader would hardly guess that this simple statement involves the solution of one of the most curious problems of Vulcanic chemistry. . . . We have reason to think that the distinguished scholar to whom we owe this important discovery, Professor Schroetter, the Secretary of the Academy of Sciences at Vienna, is not without

strong hopes of speedily resolving some other elementary crystallized substances into a similarly amorphous state.[9]

Comment on the Great Exhibition usually linked mechanical arts and science, but not in the sense that science was the leader and art the follower. Whewell, the historian of science, in his summing up of the "General Bearing of the Great Exhibition of the Progress of Art and Science" took it for granted that the natural and "proper sequence" was for creative activity in the arts to go first, and science to follow after with its speculations—exactly the process that was taking place in the development of the doctrine of thermodynamics from the steam-engine.[10] In 1867, when Paris held its second World Exhibition, the place of science in its relations to industry was noticeably changing. By that time the aniline dyes had arrived as the products of organic chemistry, and a number of electric dynamos were on exhibit. When Michel Chevalier, the free-trade economist, wrote his introduction to the jury reports of the Exhibition, he attributed increase in productive power to the advance of science. Making due allowance for the difference between France, where technical education was long established, and England, where it was not, and for the ambiguity in the meaning of the word "science," the difference between Whewell's attitude in 1851 and Chevalier's in 1867 can be taken as marking the point at which science established before the public a claim to the leadership in the industrial arts which in the ensuing fifty years was to be made good, especially in chemical, electric and metallurgical fields.

Thus science had the double merit that it not only explained the universe, but fructified it.

VII. CONCLUSION

An intellectual atmosphere is not a simple consensus of all people upon all things, but a very complex structure. It exhibits different levels of enlightenment; great minds are creating at one level, while the understanding of the masses is keyed to a lower

[9] *Edinburgh Review,* October, 1851, p. 305.
[10] Whewell, "Inaugural Lecture on the Great Exhibition of 1851," *American Journal of Science* (New Haven, 1852), XIII, 352.

level. There is a time lag between creative thought or publication and the response of a public to new ideas. While it was a remarkable characteristic of the mid-nineteenth century that the creative thinkers and the public kept close together, and the time lag was short, still the time lag and the popularization differential were present.

Moreover, intellectual life is defined as much by polarity as by consensus. It is most clearly manifested when Stoic is opposed to Epicurean, Christian to pagan, nominalist to realist. Science did not succeed in mowing down all opposed views of the world, but it made itself the rallying-ground for at least one party in every battle in the world of thought. Sometimes both parties claimed the support of science and accepted its postulates. This was particularly true of the doctrinal controversies relating to economic life.

The postulates of physical science, carried to their logical conclusion, reduced the whole universe to a material and mechanical system, operated automatically by an iron determination of cause and effect. This was not the first time that such a view of the world had found expression in European culture. The issues it raised were familiar to the mind of the west; they had often been explored to their uttermost speculative limits. More than any other issues in the world of thought the questions raised by the opposition of matter to spirit, realism to idealism, were basic in the tradition of the Western mind. With other cultures, other issues have prevailed. When Gandhi formulated for his people a political principle that would hold in their culture, he set the formula in terms of soul-force and the antithesis of action to non-action. The metaphysics of this problem runs in a true line all the way from the Bhagavad-Gita. When Sun Yat-sen undertook to give a philosophical basis to his political program, he took one side of the great antithesis between knowledge and action. "To know is difficult, to act is easy," he said. This is a problem deep-rooted in the history of Chinese thought. Karl Marx went for his metaphysical foundation to materialism. As a university student, he had written a thesis on Epicurus, and resisted the idealism of Hegel. The antithesis between materialism and idealism goes back just as far in the tradition of Western thought as the antithesis of action and non-action in Hindu culture, of knowledge and action in Chinese. These observations are important because they suggest that in the rhythm of the movement of Western civilization, the swing of the pendulum between materialism and idealism is not an incidental event, but something that may be charged with profound meaning. On the chart of Western culture, it is an important line to follow.

There are two great secular dogmas that have been brought down into the twentieth century in a form they assumed in the nineteenth. These are the dogmas of socialism and nationalism. Both of these dogmas received in the middle of the century the stamp of the age of science. They crystallized in a time when the intellectual pendulum was swinging to realism and materialism. Socialism became associated most closely with the materialist teachings of physical science, nationalism with the struggle-for-existence ideas that crowned the synthesis of the biological sciences. The scientists of the twentieth century may dissolve the matter of the nineteenth, yield the principle of determinism in favor of a principle of indeterminacy, remold the universe in a new design, and even leave some place in it for the human personality;[11] but the science of the nineteenth century is not thereby expelled from the body of thought that was nourished in its atmosphere.

[11] R. C. Binkley, "The Twentieth Century Looks at Human Nature," *Virginia Quarterly Review*, July, 1934.

Chapter Two

SCIENCE AND LIFE

I. ORGANIC CHEMISTRY

IT WAS INEVITABLE that an explanation of the universe in purely physical terms should reach out to include living things in its synthesis. How would science interpret life, and how would its interpretation receive practical application? The mid-century followed three lines of thought in establishing a scientific view of life: the first stemmed from Liebig and organic chemistry; the second came to a point with Pasteur and Lister; and the third with Darwin. The principal direct applications of these scientific achievements came in medicine, the indirect applications in social thought.

Organic chemistry, even before it synthesized dyestuffs, had come to the aid of agriculture with chemical manures and suggestions for food preservation, two practical applications of a chemical study of the life process. It also provided a point of view from which life as a whole could be explained. Moleschott offered this chemical explanation of life in his *Kreislauf des Lebens* (1852), a book that shared popularity with Büchner's *Kraft und Stoff*. For Moleschott life was a cycle of chemical change in which matter moved from inorganic to organic and back again to inorganic form. Since brain tissue on chemical analysis showed a high phosphorus content, he concluded that thought itself was merely a form of phosphorus. Feuerbach, who had revolted against Hegel and become the philosopher of materialism, carried this type of thinking to a characteristic conclusion when he declared that the Revolutions of 1848 had failed because the poorer classes had been made sluggish by a potato diet.

Shall we then despair? Is there no other foodstuff which can replace potatoes among the poorer classes and at the same time nurture them to manly vigor and disposition? Yes, there is such a foodstuff, a foodstuff which is the pledge of a better future, which contains the seed of a more thorough, even if more gradual, revolution. It is *beans*.[1]

Neither the experimental technique nor the conceptual system of science could at that time sustain anything as recondite as a vitamin or a hormone. For an applied science of dietetics the world had to wait fifty years, until the consequences of the principles of conservation of energy had been fully thought out and given physiological application. It was natural, therefore, that the chemical interpretation of life involved only simple deductions from the quantitative analysis of animal tissue, which revealed the presence of phosphorus in the brain (and in fish), and of nitrogen in muscle tissue (and in beans).

II. BACTERIOLOGY AND MEDICINE

Bacteriology contributed more than organic chemistry in this era to an understanding of life, and to the useful arts. Every improvement of the microscope since the seventeenth century had made the scientists more familiar with "germs," and yet the germs were not found engaged in any important occupation until the time of Pasteur and Lister. Like early electricity, they were a scientific curiosity merely. Then Louis Pasteur, whose training was in pure chemistry, began in 1854 to study fermentation. He identified microscopically the yeasts of good and bad beer and the ferments of good and bad wine, then solved a silkworm disease by bacteriological methods. Thence he worked toward the application of his findings to animal, and ultimately to human, diseases. He worked up through chicken cholera and anthrax to rabies. Though he was not himself a medical man by training or profession, his great contribution was made to medicine. For this reason he can be taken as a symbol of the growing utility of experimental science.

Lister received his medical degree in 1852, and began soon afterwards to study the suppuration of wounds. He interpreted suppuration as a kind of fermentation, and in the 'sixties he applied to this kind of fermentation the principles Pasteur had worked

[1] Feuerbach, Sämtliche Werke, Bolin and Jodl, X, 23, quoted in S. Hook: *Towards an Understanding of Marx* (New York, 1933), 127.

out for beer and wine. For Pasteur had proved that fermentation could not take place except in the presence of micro-organisms, that these were not spontaneously generated, and that they could be introduced only from some external contact. Lister used pure carbolic acid to destroy germs on the surface of a wound, and carbolic acid spray to clear the air of them. By 1871 his "germ theory" and his system of aseptic and antiseptic surgery had won general acceptance.

Pasteur was in mid-course in 1871. His germs, and his technique of immunization, had to wait for the 1880's and 1890's for their greatest triumphs. Meanwhile public sanitation, which later became deeply indebted to him, had been well launched without his specific explanation of the relation of filth and germs to disease. The great sanitarians before Pasteur, Pettenkofer in Munich, Chadwick and Sir John Simon in England, learned from rule-of-thumb observations that filth was associated with disease, and made use of the indisputable æsthetic fact that open sewers stink. Simon, who became central medical officer of the British General Board of Health in 1855, saw the root of the public sanitation problem in the average Englishman's indifference to dirt.

> Against accumulated obvious masses of filth, against extreme atrocities of stench, local protests, no doubt, are pretty commonly to be heard, and, at moments when there is panic about disease, may often rise to a considerable warmth of indignation, but in regard to the less riotous forms of uncleanliness, far too much insensibility is widely shown.[2]

As the steam-engine developed before its explanatory physics, so nineteenth-century sanitation got under way before bacteriology.

Another important practical innovation in mid-century medicine was anæsthesia, imported from America in 1847. It came as the result of the happy idea of two New England dentists, and was no more closely related to the development of science as Pasteur practiced it than was McCormick's reaper, which was making a great stir at the London Exhibition of 1851, to the development of physical science.

Darwinism itself had an important indirect effect upon medical

[2] C. A. Winslow, *The Evolution and Significance of a Modern Public Health Campaign* (New Haven, 1923), 24.

science. The *Origin of Species* stimulated among medical men a dissatisfaction with the traditional classifications of diseases, and brought about an era of scepticism in the course of which the superficial interpretation of symptoms was outmoded. "Fever," for instance, ceased to be regarded as an adequate diagnosis, and the "humours" of venerable standing in medical lore were dropped from the medical vocabulary.

III. THE ORIGIN OF SPECIES

The Darwinian theory of the origin of species was of all the products of the scientific imagination of the mid-century the most typical and the most provocative. It drew together not only varied evidences from natural science, but concepts that had matured in political economy, and levied also upon the workaday world. The collection of fossils that gave Darwin his geological background came from excavations in canal, railroad, and port building; the data on selective breeding came from practical agriculture.[3]

All the elements of the Darwinian theory were lying about, waiting to be put together. The idea of evolution was the starting-point of all philosophical and political thinking of the early nineteenth century, and Lamarck in 1800 had applied it to the differentiation of species. Comte, Karl Marx, and Herbert Spencer were already, before Darwin, transforming the romantic and idealistic varieties of evolution that had flourished in the early century into hard, scientific kinds of evolution. The disposition to see all living things as fundamentally related to each other—the principle of the unity of life—had flourished in the mind of Goethe as a kind of nature-philosophy, had been defended by Geoffrey St. Hilaire as a convenience in classification, and had been confirmed in the 'thirties by the improved microscope, which showed the similarities of cell structure in all living tissue. The idea of environment, the totality of surrounding conditions as something determining life had been defined in speculation about human society, and was being used in the 'fifties by such men as Taine and Buckle, whose *History of Civilization in England* antedated the *Origin of Species* by two

[3] O. S. Crawford, "The Dialectical Process in the History of Science," *Sociological Review*, XXIV, April-July, 1932, 165-73.

years. The Malthusian principle of the geometric rate of natural increase and its resulting misery had long done service in the Dismal Science, and was at this very moment ceasing to be interesting to the practical world because of better food supplies, higher living standards, and increasing consciousness of the value of a large population for war purposes. The notion that competition is a vitalizing principle in economic life had become a platitude of political economy. Lyell's geology had clinched the idea that natural changes occur by the slow operation of uniform causes over long periods of time. The elements that Darwin drew together came from all the corners of European thought.

Darwin was restrained from stating his theory when he first formulated it in 1842 by precisely the same considerations that had led to the neglect of the first formulations of the principles of thermodynamics, namely the resistance of the inductive science of the 1840's to any general ideas. His letter to Hooker in 1844 shows how tough that resistance was:

> I have read heaps of agricultural and horticultural books and have never ceased collecting facts. At last gleams of light have come, and I am almost convinced (quite contrary to the opinion I started with) that species are not (it is like confessing a murder) immutable. Heaven forfend me from Lamarck's nonsense of a "tendency to progression," "adaptation from the slow willing of animals," etc. But the conclusions I am led to are not widely different from his, though the means of change are wholly so. I think I have found out (here's presumption) the simple means by which species become exquisitely adapted to various ends.[4]

In 1856, by which time the air had become more inviting to general theories, Lyell, the great geologist and friend of Darwin, advised him to write out his theory. When Wallace's essay came to his attention in 1856, Darwin was spurred to hasten the publication of his own views. The *Origin of Species* appeared in November, 1859, at a moment when the Italian national state was in the making and business was recovering from the first really international depression following a boom in railway building operations and the expansion caused by California gold.

[4] *Life and Letters of Charles Darwin* (New York and London, 1919), I, 384.

IV. DARWINISM, MORALITY, AND NATIONALISM

The effect of Darwinism upon European culture was felt in two waves, the first of which broke immediately after the publication of the *Origins,* while the second was not fully realized till the end of the century.

The first controversy had to do with the relations of evolution to religion and personal morality. The first popularizers, Haeckel and Huxley, had to encounter the objections of people who did not like to see mankind incorporated so completely in the animal kingdom, nor to have the biblical account of the origins of species set aside in favor of the testimony of science. This was the problem that occupied Tennyson in the poem "To an Evolutionist"; it is the question to which various writers in all countries addressed themselves. In Germany, for instance, Paul Ree argued that the moral impulses were useful to a society in which they were found and helped it to survive; Dr. Georg von Gizycki was worried because Darwinism proved that men were too near the animals, while Dr. G. Jaeger was comforted by the vision that the trend of evolution is to develop in man non-brutish qualities. These are the problems of Darwinism in the first decade. The later nineteenth century had no practical difficulty in connection with them. No collapse of personal morality accompanied the spread of the theory of evolution. But it was otherwise when the imagination of Europe came to see the nations, organized as centralized states, engaged with each other in a struggle for existence.[5]

For ultimately Darwinism, which summarized the science of the nineteenth century, came to be synthesized with nationalism, which included all its politics. In the decades of the reign of philosophy, in the time of Young Europe and the Hegelian inspiration, nationalism had been associated with the idea of harmony among nations, not conflict, except perhaps on the level of ideas. The rivalry of nationalities in the days of Mazzini and Gioberti centered on the

[5] Statements of the theory, mostly from the late nineteenth century in George Nasmyth, *Social Progress and the Darwinian Theory* (New York, 1916); also Edward Krehbiel, *Nationalism, War and Society* (New York, 1916); Raymond G. Gettell, *History of Political Thought* (New York, 1924), 428 ff.

various "contributions" each would make to civilization, not on struggle with each other for survival.

The marriage of the offspring of the doctrines of nationalism with the theory of survival of the fittest, which came to be known as "Social Darwinism," exhibits the interplay of sequences that seem to stand independently in the world of thought with sequences that seem to explain themselves completely in the world of action. All the elements of social Darwinism had been assembled by 1871, ready to be put together.

Nationalism as a practical political movement had set itself, ever since 1815, against the European treaty structure, but it did not propose to substitute anarchy for legality. It had its own jurisprudence, the principle of nationality, which was dramatized by the Italian War in 1859, the very year of the *Origin of Species.*

At the same time, within the sphere of cabinet policy among the European states, the principle of *Realpolitik* found expression. Schwarzenberg, Napoleon III, Cavour and Bismarck each contributed something toward its development. Political literature gave it a defense and exposition, beginning in 1853 with Rochau's *Grundsätze der Realpolitik, angewendet auf die Staatlichen Zustände Deutschlands.*[6] Comte in 1854, in his *Cours de Politique Positive,* asserted that force was the basis of political relations. The principles of *Realpolitik* demanded recognition of the preëminence of force in political relations, but these men did not set forth a theory of international relations in terms of a Darwinian struggle for existence.

This stage in the development of nationalist theory towards fusion with Darwinism is illustrated in that bible of the Pan-Slavs, *Russia and Europe,* written by the scientist Danilevsky between 1865 and 1867. The Pan-Slavs of the last half of the nineteenth century differed from the Slavophils of the first half in that the latter had a soft, cultural program associated with philosophy, while the former had a hard, political program associated with science and war. Danilevsky's program for the Pan-Slavs demanded that Russia break away from the European system of balance of power and the tradi-

[6] Friedrich Meinecke, *Die Idee der Staatsräson in der Neueren Geschichte* (Munich and Berlin, 1929), 493 ff.

tional respect for the treaty system, and face the certainty of war with Europe. For Russia, he argued, was not a European state, but the predestined leader of a Slavic confederation which would be separate from Europe. Some elements of Danilevsky's thought are analogous to the separatist principles of the Monroe Doctrine. In forging ahead with her policy, Russia should turn

> indifferently to Reds and to Whites, to demagogy and despotism, to legitimacy and revolution, to the French, the English, the Italians, to Napoleon, Bismarck, Gladstone, Garibaldi; we must be true friends and allies of those who will and can further our single and unchanging aim.[7]

This is simple *Realpolitik*; there is no Darwinism in it. Although Danilevsky was writing a two-volume work on Darwin when he died, he did not make the synthesis of Darwinism and nationalism.

The first political application of Darwinism, according to an American historian, came in the slavery controversy in the United States, where the new theory arrived just in time to help to prove the inferiority of the Negro race, before the Civil War shifted the forum of decision.[8] The next political application was made by Walter Bagehot, who was writing and publishing for five years, from 1867 to 1872, his *Physics and Politics, or Thoughts on the Application of "Natural Selection" and "Inheritance" to Political Society*. Bagehot quickly found his way to the "First Law" that "Those nations which are strongest tend to prevail, and in certain marked peculiarities the strongest are the best," though he encountered a troublesome doubt as to how far "the strongest nations really are the best nations."[9] As a good English liberal, faithful to all the orthodoxies of his day, he could not do otherwise than conclude that industrial society is better than military society, and parliamentary agencies of discussion superior to military agencies of force. He was able to protect his theory from embarrassing contact with the wars that were going on across the Channel by considering the warlike phase of nation-making only in connection with primitive peoples, and allowing advanced peoples to exhibit

[7] Nicholas Danilevsky, *Russland und Europa* (Stuttgart and Berlin, 1920), 244.
[8] Arthur H. Cole, *The Irrepressible Conflict* (New York, 1933), 54.
[9] *Fortnightly Review*, IX, April, 1868, 453, 470.

their survival value by industry and discussion. His chapters on the "Use of Conflict" and "Nation Making," written between 1869 and 1872, while the most bitter national conflict in Europe was setting up the strongest national state, still went for political illustration of the Darwinian principle, not to the war-torn valleys of the Rhine and Moselle, but to distant Australia, where English settlers were exhibiting their fitness to survive at the expense of the native black-fellow.

On the Continent there was a readier disposition to think of the relation of a general theory of conflict to contemporary affairs. Oncken has noted a French pamphlet by Charles Muller, published in 1868, *Nos Frontières sur le Rhin,* in which war is praised as the supreme motive power in human progress. When the Franco-Prussian War came, it was accompanied by a controversy over its cultural significance, a controversy which Friedrich Nietzsche watched with sour disapproval. In his *Thoughts out of Season* (1873) Nietzsche denounced the "world-wide, general error, the error of public opinion and of those who make public opinion, that German culture won the war." He argued that victory in the war proved nothing but an unimportant superiority in certain material things. Thus he combated the very doctrines that came later to be associated with his name.[10]

It was undoubtedly the violent crash of war in 1870-71 that made Social Darwinism the natural theology of nationalism. This was the first war since the publication of the *Origin of Species* that could be interpreted as a war between rival cultures and peoples—the rest had been civil wars. Moreover, this war completed the alignment of interests that came to find the Darwinian idea useful as a scientific rationalization of the place of the army in society.

For the wars culminating in 1871 changed the place of the army in Europe's public life. In 1850 the army was still the defender of order against revolution; by 1871 it had become the protector of one national state against another. In 1850 the army was still fundamentally allied with the agrarian economic interest; by 1871 railroads and industrialization had established the alliance with heavy

[10] Friedrich Nietzsche, *Gesammelte Werke* (Leipzig, 1899), I, 179-80.

industry. In 1850 the army was still professional. Though Austria and the German states had the *cadre* and reserve system, the training was not actually universal, and France and Russia were both using long-term conscript enlistment armies. By 1871 the conception of the "nation in arms" had triumphed and all military institutions were either adapted or in process of adaptation to it. These changes will be followed in more detail in the chapters on political history; for the present it is sufficient to note that the army of the late nineteenth century came to assume a position analogous to that occupied by the Church in the early part of the century. The officer corps, like the clergy of the era of throne and altar, enjoyed a special position in the state because it was regarded as the indispensable protector of the state's most vital interests. The general staff, like the hierarchy in the time of reaction, worked closely with the civil government, and yet retained its own special character and tradition. The army as a whole, like an established Church, touched the lives of all citizens, not only because it was supported by general taxation, but also because it drew all males into its membership. Any institution so vast as the late nineteenth-century army might be expected to have some broad doctrine corresponding to its sphere of action.

The older officer corps had not felt the need of going to science for a doctrine, for it drew its respect for the military virtues from a romantic-aristocratic tradition, its faith that war was a part of the divine order from religious conviction, and the generalization that war is the "father of all things" from its classical education. But when the later army had to make terms in parliament and journalism with minds not bred in the military families, and adapt itself to an atmosphere in which scientific materialism was dominant, it welcomed the synthesis of Darwinism and nationalism as its most persuasive philosophy. This Social Darwinian theory did not arise as the product of any great mind, nor was it laid before Europe originally and decisively in any great book; it grew to maturity almost impersonally from the scientific ideas that offered a pattern, the social forces that furnished a pressure, and the harsh political events that supplied it a convincing illustration in the era of national wars.

V. THE IMPACT OF SCIENCE ON SOCIAL AND ECONOMIC THOUGHT

Social thought, like nationalism, received the stamp of the age of science.

The relations with science were easily established. In fact, all the political economists, as well as that precursor of all sociologists, Auguste Comte, had been almost belligerently scientific, even in the age of philosophy. The English utilitarians were consistently hostile to any taint of metaphysics. John Stuart Mill had been much influenced by Comte, and had given Comte's positivism an introduction to England in his *Inductive Logic* (1844) which furnished an organon for science as Hegel's logic had offered one for philosophy. Although the political economists were actually deductive rather than inductive in method, still they felt themselves to be in very close touch with the hard and dismal facts. On the Continent, where their doctrines were still a gospel and not yet an orthodoxy, the alliance with science was an effective means of propaganda. In Italy the average liberal believed in science as a beneficent agency that would bring tax and tariff reduction in one hand, railroads and efficient manures in the other. The various doctrines that had been promulgated before 1848 as socialism or communism were on another footing. They were regarded as non-scientific, for indeed they were not in agreement with the true science of political economy. They were soft, romantic, idealistic, Utopian—hopelessly identified with the qualities of the defeated revolutionists of 1848. It was therefore appropriate that socialism should be born again into a scientific environment, and come forth as "scientific socialism."

The most typical mid-century science of society was not, however, socialistic. It was the social science of Herbert Spencer, that last and least of the encyclopædists, who made his synthetic philosophy a catch-all for every popularized scientific concept. He was sufficiently ambitious, and at the same time sufficiently myopic, to put the thought of his generation into a form that would seem to his contemporaries to be the summit of enlightenment, and would become after his death a caricature of the Victorian mind. Into his lengthening shelf of books went everything that was commonplace in the attitudes and popular in the science of the day: the prevailing distrust of metaphysics, the concepts of evolution and organism that served to make sociology a pseudo-biology, the principles of conservation of energy taken directly from physics, the pleasure-pain calculus of utilitarian psychology, and the political ideal of laissez-faire carried to the ultimate limit which would leave the poor to starve. His magnificent powers of intellectual digestion enabled him to believe that society is an organism, and yet to repudiate organized social responsibility, to apply the principle of struggle and survival of the fittest to societies and yet deny that war may be indicated as the means of struggle, to give over the ultimate problems of philosophy to the realm of the "unknowable" and yet leave the Victorian mind unshaken by doubt. The event proved that it would not be Spencer who would keep alive in the twentieth century the materialistic presuppositions of the nineteenth. That function was reserved for Karl Marx on the one hand, and the epigones of the classical economists on the other.

VI. THE "COMMODITY" AND THE "INDIVIDUAL" IN ECONOMIC THOUGHT

Just as the modern historian in analyzing the doctrinal disputes of Lutherans and Catholics of the sixteenth century will often so fix his attention upon the differences as to ignore the vastly greater similarities of the creeds, so the writer on economic doctrines, in contrasting Marxian socialism with classical economics, is prone to neglect the important respects in which they resembled each other.

Both the classical economics, which had arisen as a negation of the mercantilist doctrine, and the Marxian socialist theory that defined itself as a refutation of the classical scheme, shared the same fundamental concept of human nature. Both were preoccupied with the kind of causes that flow from the past to the present, the one conceiving of "supply" and "demand" as preëxisting quantities, the other thinking of value as labor already congealed in the form of a labor-product. Thus classical economics, which was the creed of business, did not deal with intangibles and expectancies; and socialist economics, which was set forth as a creed for labor, did not include the concept of "planned economy." Both systems reached doctrinal maturity without receiving the impact of those three makers of the modern economic world, the corporation, accountancy, and statistical measurement of business activity.

The corporation form of ownership was known at the time, but regarded by the classical economists as an exception, by Marx as a mere vehicle for concentration of ownership. The standard assumption made by socialist and classical theorists was that in a capitalist society each individual enterprise is managed by an individual owner who has accumulated his capital in the past. The one party averred that it was accumulated by his abstinence, the other asserted that it was accumulated by withholding from labor its just due. The potential influence of the corporation on the relations of ownership to management, and of the accumulation of capital to the credit mechanism and the general securities market, could hardly have been appreciated. For at that time European legislation was just clearing the way for the widespread use of the limited liability company. French laws of 1863 and 1867, English statutes of 1855 and 1862, the common commercial code adopted by the German Confederation in 1861, and the law of the North German Confederation in 1870 are the milestones along this legislative path. The Crédit Mobilier was just beginning to teach its lessons on investment finance in 1852.

The accountant, when Marx and Mill wrote in 1848, was still a bookkeeper on a high stool. Such basic accountancy concepts as overhead costs, depreciation and good will had not been developed, except perhaps as the phenomenon of overhead costs was to some extent implied in the "law of increasing returns" in industry, and depreciation taken for granted as a painless way in which capital could be withdrawn from one enterprise to be invested in another. The beginnings of professional accountancy were indicated by the incorporation of the Society of Accountants of Edinburgh in 1854, of Glasgow and Aberdeen in 1855, and of London in 1870. The crisis of 1866 taught English business the importance of professional financial accounting, and the conversion of family enterprises into limited-liability corporations was instrumental in developing the early techniques and standards of accountancy. The illustrations of cost behavior that appear in most of the economic writings are quite innocent of contact with the concrete instances encountered in business operations.

Moreover, the business man, economist and social reformer were compelled to move in a world uncharted by statistical guides. Statistics of various kinds were cited in parliamentary debates over policies, but the application of statistical method to business problems was in its infancy. In 1851, at the London Exhibition, the Belgian scientist, Quetelet, was just starting his movement for the international standardization of statistics; Tooke completed his *History of Prices* in 1857, but without diagrams or any general pictures of price trends; Stanley Jevons in 1862 told the British Association that commercial trends had not been investigated "according to the same scientific methods with which we are familiar in other complicated sciences";[11] he then began to work up the forerunners of the modern chart of business activity, and in 1869 the London *Economist* was beginning to publish its famous index number of wholesale prices. In the absence of these implements for giving mathematical analysis to economic phenomena, the economists tended to ascribe the scientific character of their conclusions to the rigor of their deductive method; they had escaped the rigorous discipline of induction from which the natural sciences were emerging. And the premises from which their deductions were made were derived, inevitably, from the experiences of the fifty years that lay behind them, not from a vision of new things springing into life.

Marx and the classical economists like Mill agreed that the phenomena they studied resembled those of any other science in that they were subject to general natural laws, superior to the vagaries of human control. For Mill, the law was manifested in the operations of supply and demand; for Marx, in "dialectical materialism," the inevitable movement from a capitalist to a proletarian economic system. Both believed in competition and struggle; for Mill the contenders were individuals, for Marx, embattled classes. Both accepted for the purposes of their doctrines a simplified interpretation of human nature. The economic man of the classical school and the proletarian and bourgeois type of the Marxian system were alike in

[11] J. H. Clapham, "Work and Wages," *Early Victorian England* (London, 1934), I, 64.

their subjection to the rule of acquisitive instincts. When Ruskin proclaimed in *Unto this Last* (1862) that man was Soul, he was stating a principle that to the classical economists was irrelevant, to the Marxians an impudent distraction. The motivation of a human being, as it was analyzed in economic science, exhibited no more complexity than the structure of the human body as analyzed by organic chemistry. And finally both schools accepted the tangible commodity as the prime datum of their science. They drew their illustrations from the consumer goods industries, especially textiles, and from intensive farming. Economic value was something that inhered in commodities, its ultimate source being in labor. Money was a commodity, its value being determined like that of any other commodity by relations of supply to demand. Commodities, like the matter of the physical universe, were completely divisible; they could be added to or consumed in any small increment. And since the main business of Europe's economic system in that day was to enjoy the consequences of increased facilities of transportation by developing long-distance interchange of raw materials and manufactured goods, this was an appropriate point of view from which to examine economic life. But in its way it was, like the mercantilist identification of wealth with gold which it superseded, a limited and partial view.

From this array of postulates, it followed that the antithesis of socialism vs. capitalism would not be stated as a contrast between a planned and unplanned economy, but only as a contrast between various wealth-sharing systems, each of which, when once in operation, would be self-regulating.

The character of this teaching is brought out clearly if one puts to Marx and Mill the same question, namely, "How are we to decide upon the proportion of this year's product that should go into building of factories and railroads and other capital goods, and the proportion that should go into shoes and cotton garments and other consumption goods?" This question became a more important one with each advance in technology. How did the economic doctrinaires, socialist and classical, meet it?

Marx would have had a ready reply in favor of giving the workers the full product of their toil, and this presumably in a form in which they could consume it, but he would have been very vague about providing resources for new factory building. When the Russian Communists in the twentieth century tried to apply Marxian doctrine in a situation where they had to divert consumption goods from workers in order to build factories—to export wheat taken from hungry peasants in order to buy machines—their use of the Marxian doctrine was something of a *tour de force*. Marx did not envisage the problems of a planned economy.

Mill appreciated the fact that an economic society must in some way divide its efforts between making capital goods and consumption goods, but thought that the division was effected automatically by an interest rate. Capital, he believed, came from savings, from thrift, from the innumerable decisions of the countless individuals who preferred not to use their purchasing power to the limit in satisfying their immediate wants, but to lay something by for the future. A high interest rate, he thought, would cause more people to be more thrifty because thrift would pay them better. Then, to balance his theory of saving as a process encouraged by a high interest rate, he envisaged investment as something encouraged by a low interest rate. A falling interest rate would continuously uncover opportunities for more factory and railroad building. Thus without taking thought society would always apportion its labor automatically between the production of capital and consumption goods, and without any purposive intervention the interest rate would always set itself at the point which would exactly reward the savers for saving the exact amount that the entrepreneurs wished to invest.

The conditions that might have led Mill to doubt the adequacy of his theory were just then appearing in the development of investment banking and the manipulation of the discount rate by the Bank of England. The analysis of these conditions can be deferred to the chapter on the world of business. It is sufficient to note here that twentieth-century capitalist society found the theory of Mill as inadequate as the communists found Marx's theory on the same point—the point, namely, where economics shifts from the appraisal of the results of past action, which is summarized in the idea of accumulation, to the impact of the foreseen future upon the present, which is summarized in the idea of purpose and plan. The thought-world of economics was as crudely materialistic as the thought-world of physics.

Yet the advance signals of another thought-world were present in the science of society. Just as Clerk-Maxwell with his vortex theory of the universe went beyond the crude materialism of physical science and anticipated the conceptual system of twentieth-century physics, just as Nietzsche's ideas of "culture" as something existing in a dimension other than that of matter and force was a precursor of Spengler and Fascist and Nazi myth-makers of the twentieth century, so Jevons in England and a group of scholars in Austria prepared a shift of base for economic doctrines.

They undertook to divert economic thought from its preoccupation with commodities as the embodiments of value and lead it toward the realm of psychology. Jevons' *Political Economy* (1871) for the first time set forth with appropriate appraisal the predicament of the consumer who has a very great desire for one loaf of bread, a somewhat less insistent longing for a second loaf, and an attitude amounting to indifference to the tenth loaf. The so-called "marginal" theories of economic value that entered European thought at this time were an indication—slight indeed—that if the hard material universe of the mid-nineteenth century, with its tangible economic commodities and simple dynamics of conflict were ever to dissolve, it would be through some more ample understanding of the complexity of human motives and behavior.

VII. PROPERTY AND CONTRACT IN PRIVATE LAW

The concepts of economic thought had their counterparts in the system of private law, whether English or continental. The legal concept of property was the counterpart of the economic concept of commodity; like a commodity, it was essentially a tangible and useful object in the possession of an owner. The free individual was the legal equivalent of the acquisitive economic man. The competitive market mechanism had its legal existence in the free right of contract. Just as the classical economists believed that their economic laws were natural laws, so the jurists entertained the presumption that legal systems which permitted free individuals to contract with out restraint concerning the disposal of property were especially cherished of nature. Marxian socialism, on the contrary, diagnosed the whole system of private law as a device by which capitalists protected interests.

These juristic principles were derived in direct descent from the eighteenth century. By the middle of the nineteenth they were already beginning to show the effects of criticism. In Germany Ihering, in his analysis of the spirit of Roman law, developed the thought that law is indeed a device for protecting interests rather than a cold rational deduction from natural principles. In England, Sir Henry Maine brought the force of great historical erudition to support the dictum that the movement of a progressive society is from status to contract, but even as he wrote, (*Ancient Law,* 1861), English legislation was departing from the principles of absolutely free contract. Duguit, in his analysis of the evolution of continental law; Dicey, in his account of the development of English legislation agree in setting the period following 1850 as the era in which judges and legislators began to take down the great juristic edifice that had been reared on the principle of absolute property right and freedom of contract. When the Court of Colmar in 1855 ordered an owner to take down a blind wall he had erected on his land, it started the trend away from the strict interpretation of the Code Napoleon with the doctrine that, even though an owner's right in property might be "in a sense absolute," yet its exercise must be "limited to the satisfaction of a serious and lawful interest."[12] So also in England, laws limiting the free use of property and the free right of contract multiplied at an increasing rate, principally in connection with factory legislation.

VIII. CONCLUSION

There is no evidence that the triumph of physical science in offering a proved and ample explanation of the physical universe was an effective and adequate cause of the development of social thought. Darwin did not wait upon Helmholtz, the commodity concept of economic thought was not dependent upon a prior proof of the

[12] Léon Duguit, "Les Transformations générales du droit privé depuis le Code Napoléon," tr. in *Progress of Continental Law in the 19th Century* (Boston, 1918), 141.

validity of atomic concepts of physics. And yet there was between these varied achievements of the human mind a relationship of harmony or pattern. It was easy to believe in both of them at once—in a science of society and a science of nature, a dynamics of energy and a dynamics of conflict and competition.

Chapter Three

REALISM AND MATERIALISM

I. REALISM IN LITERATURE

IT WAS NOT alone in the scientific and pseudo-scientific writings of politics and economics that the great social problems of the day received their statement. Literature took an increasing part in the analysis of society. This was the social function of the realistic novel which tended to replace printed sermons and devotional books as the intellectual food of an earnest and humanitarian public. Turgenev's *Sportsman's Sketches* (1852) forced discussion of the problem of serfdom in Russia; Harriet Beecher Stowe's *Uncle Tom's Cabin* (1852) had in the same year the same influence on the slavery controversy in America. Disraeli's *Sybil*, Mrs. Gaskell's *North and South*, Kingsley's *Alton Locke*, Frederika Bremer's *Hertha*, Dickens' *Bleak House*, Henri Dunant's *Souvenirs de Solferino*, and Chernyshevsky's *What Is To Be Done* (1864) set before the public the evils of the factories and the law courts, the problem of the emancipation of women, the inhumanity of war, and the vision of a future society. It was Marx who persuaded Heine to stop worrying about the sufferings of passionate lovers and devote himself to the sufferings of the oppressed. The *Westminster Review*, in its notice of Mrs. Stowe's book in 1852, remarked that "since Miss Martineau published her gamelaw tales, specific social evils have successively adopted this method of laying their grievances before the world."

If literature was able after 1850 to assume this function of social criticism to an increasing degree, this fact is to be attributed to a change in the literary fashion and to the development of a reading public. The change of fashion is the one known in the literary history of all European countries as the shift from romanticism to realism. The word "realism" first appeared in France as applied to Courbet's painting in 1850, and was soon thereafter applied to literature. It appeared in the *Westminster Review* in 1856 in connection with the work of Frederika Bremer, and in 1857 it was used to describe George Eliot's *Scenes of Clerical Life*. Its German variant, *Realismus*, was applied to Freytag's *Soll und Haben* (1855), and when Flaubert's *Madame Bovary* appeared (1856) it was evident that the literature of the whole continent had been captured by the new spirit.[1] Writers who had previously devoted themselves to other styles wrote in the new fashion, taking their subject matter from close at hand and portraying the ugly with the beautiful. Hugo, a leader of the romantics in 1830, published *Les Misérables* in 1862; Bulwer-Lytton turned away from tales of high adventure to write *The Caxtons* (1852). Tolstoi, in 1853 a soldier in the Caucasus, read Turgenev's *Sportsman's Sketches* and noted in his diary that "Pushkin's prose is already old-fashioned, not in its language, but in the manner of its exposition."[2] The change of fashion struck Germany at the same time. An English reviewer noted (1852) that

> in Germany . . . the modern school of novel writing differs widely from the old. Instead of metaphysical subtleties, fantastic theories of character and action, equivocal morals, wild unearthly fancy and grotesque humor, we have scenes and characters of everyday life and real history, average men and women.[3]

One can pick illustrations almost at random from any national literature, any vehicle of literary art, and find the same movement of fashion recorded. There was, for instance, the obscure Joseph Autran, who had been publishing poetry since 1835, and who now in 1852 suddenly found himself famous with his *Poems of the Sea*, in the preface of which he declared that there are only three great subjects of poetry: agriculture, war and the sea. Love is conspicuous by its absence. Realism appeared on the French stage with Augier, and the phenomenal popularity of Dumas' *La Dame aux Camélias* in 1852. Stage scenery became realistic. A so-called "natural style" of rendering lines competed with a declamatory style. It is needless to catalogue all the great names. In England they were

[1] E. E. Hale, "The Earlier 'Realism'," in *Faculty Papers of Union College*, XXV, No. 2, 1932.
[2] *Private Diary of Leo Tolstoi*, 1853-1857, edited by Aylmer Maude (New York, 1927), 18, 34.
[3] *Westminster Review*, 1852, LVIII, 305-306.

the children of Dickens, in France the children of Balzac, in Russia the followers of Belinsky. They grouped themselves in circles in London, Paris, Petersburg, rubbed elbows with scientists and political figures, knew and influenced each other. It was from Proudhon that Tolstoi got the inspiration to write his great *War and Peace*; Turgenev's life touched that of Bakunin, Flaubert, Herzen, and Henry James. When the young medical student, Georges Clemenceau, at a table in the Brasserie Andler in 1860, drew up his first political document—the manifesto of the "Do as you Think Association," there were among those who signed it the artist Courbet and the young Emile Zola, who was destined to carry realism in the novel to its extreme conclusion. If it stood as one of the great achievements of mid-nineteenth century civilization that man's immediate surroundings were made to appear intelligible, the credit for this goes no less to the novelists than to the scientists and political economists.

II. THE READING PUBLIC

The great age of the novel was also the great age of the reading public. Just as popular science was not far removed from authentic science, so best-seller literature was in general of the type that has since been regarded as great literature. It was this reading public that made the realistic novel effective in politics.

In journalism this was the time of the leading article, upon which the telegraphic news distributed by a news agency was only beginning to encroach. The European press agencies were young. Havas had started in 1835, Wolff in 1849, and Reuter in 1850. The great London newspapers scorned Julius Reuter's offer of news until he made a deal with the *Morning Advertiser* and scooped the London *Times* in reporting Napoleon's warlike words to the Austrian ambassador on New-Year's Day, 1859. The circulation of newspapers was growing with the increase of wealth and literacy, and with falling prices. The prices were helped to lower levels by the abolition of tax and paper duty in England (1855-61), by the economies of the rotary press, and by the popularizing editorial policies of such men as Émile de Gérardin of the *Presse* in Paris, who lowered the annual subscription price from eighty to forty francs and concentrated on news and continued stories—the *feuilleton*. August Zang took the new journalism to Vienna in the *Neue Freie Presse*. The stereotype of syndicated collateral printed matter appeared in Germany in 1858, in England in 1870.

The relations of the authors to their public were given increasing security by the development of copyright law. *La Dame aux Camélias* was protected in England by the new Anglo-French copyright convention of 1851; it was one of the books that led to the passage of the Obscenity Bill of 1857. The copyright law was buttressed by a series of international treaties of which France made eighteen between 1850 and 1865, and England seven. A satisfactory German copyright law did not come until 1871.

The wide market for solid reading matter was proved by the success of the publishing enterprises of Ernest Bohn, whose Standard, Scientific, Classical and Antiquarian Library series, starting in 1847, ultimately included six hundred volumes. Emerson said of him that he did for literature what the railroads did for commerce. In 1867 Reclam in Leipzig launched his *Universal Bibliothek*, a comparable series which ran into thousands of titles.

Literature met journalism on the one hand, science on the other, in a remarkable new genre of writing that achieved popularity in the mid-century—namely, the detective story. It began with Poe in 1840, and in the ensuing decades built up a popularity that compelled authors to contribute to it. The feuilleton was its vehicle. Eugène Sue took up the style in *Mystères de Paris*; Dumas in *Les Mohicans de Paris*; Balzac was forced by Sue's popularity to imitate; Gaboriau, after trying to succeed in various kinds of writing, hit his stride with *L'Affaire Lerouge* (1866); Dickens entered the field in 1853 with *Bleak House*; and Wilkie Collins with *The Moonstone* in 1867. Though the greatest heroes of this genre, Sherlock Holmes and Nick Carter, did not appear until 1887, the mid-century had established a definite canon and an assured popularity. The peculiar quality of the detective story is the strict use of the method of induction. Love and adventure are incidentals. If the realistic novel conformed to the preferences of an age of science in objectivity and in the rejection of fantasy, the detective story conformed to the scientific spirit in its use of a method of evidence.[4]

By what bonds was literary realism related to scientific materialism? The critics of the day saw the connection. Montégut wrote in 1861:

What dominates in our literature of imagination, as in modern criticism, as in science and history, is the love of facts, of reality, of experience.[5]

Taine expressed the same idea in 1865 when he wrote of the novel and criticism that both had become "a great inquest on man." Realism could have come without the scientific synthesis as a sheer reaction against romantic excess; the scientific synthesis ran true to the internal history of the experimental tradition, and did not require the aid of novelists. Yet it is unquestionable that the two reinforced each other, and lent each other the prestige-value of their respective achievements.

III. PICTORIAL ART

Pictorial art, like literature, made terms with the scientific temper of the times in a style of painting that was known for a time as "realism," and which then merged in another style that took the name of "impressionism."

The leader of the realistic school was Gustave Courbet, the son of a peasant, who retained through life a peasant's hearty love of earthy things. When Courbet found that Paris interpreted his pictures of common people in common situations as socialistic, he accepted political radicalism to parallel his artistic radicalism. His political radicalism made him a marked man. As an artist he was greater than his doctrine which, as he stated it, made art the servant of facts. "To render the customs, the ideas, the aspects of my time according to my understanding of them, not alone as a painter, but also as a man—in a word, to make living art—that is my aim."[6]

The critics and satirists opened war on Courbet. When he ex-

[4] Régis Messac, *Le "Detective Novel" et l'influence de la pensée scientifique* (Paris, 1929).

[5] Quoted in Bédier and Hazard, *Histoire de la littérature française illustrée* (Paris, 1923), II, 268.

[6] R. H. Wilenski, *French Painting* (Boston, 1931), 222.

hibited "The Wrestlers" (1853), the *Journal pour Rire* parodied it with a pair of misshapen figures and the explanatory note:

These two men are fighting to see which is the dirtiest. The victor will receive a four-cent bath ticket. None of the muscles of these wrestlers will be found in its usual place. The disorder is easily explained by the strain of the struggle. Often a beautiful disorder gives an artistic effect.[7]

"The Bathers" (1853), which for the first time in the memory of Paris art viewers put nude women into water without making them look like nymphs, shocked the art-lovers. But a group of younger artists flocked to Courbet; in 1861 he opened an *atelier* which drew a group of students. He had become the founder of a school.

The jokes about the ugliness of Courbet's pictures were still going the rounds in 1869. His "Fieste pendant la Saison des Foins" was greeted with the warning that even the most docile cows would soon refuse to enter his landscapes.[8]

The controversy between classicism and romanticism in art had ended by 1850; the new controversy that arose to take its place was between realism and idealism. Daumier, himself a great realist and satirist, caricatured the conflict in 1855. He portrayed a nude and scrawny "idealism" with spectacles and a Greek helmet brandishing a brush against a shabby hooligan "realism" in wooden shoes.[9] But the realists had no foothold in the Salon, except Courbet, who could not be excluded because he had won a prize which entitled him to exhibit regardless of the opinions of the jury. There is a cartoon that satirizes the panic of the members of the jury at the thought that Courbet might send some new horror to be hung in the Salon.[10]

The salon, as it was kept pure of radical influences, remained dull; the pictures hung by the jury conformed to official canons of taste, but remained without influence on art history. In 1863 Paul Mantz, reviewing the Salon of the year for the *Gazette des Beaux Arts*, commented:

There is serenely installed a somewhat banal array of bourgeois tal-

[7] *Journal pour Rire* (Paris, 1863). See illustration No. 17.
[8] See illustration No. 16.
[9] See illustration No. 15.
[10] See illustration No. 18.

ents, who please themselves in lukewarm temperatures, and who are above all afraid of isolating themselves on mountain tops or wandering too far in distant valleys . . . the Salon abounds in mythologies. All sorts of divinities have made rendezvous here. . . . Jupiter has aged, Mars is on half-pay, but Venus is eternally beautiful.[11]

It was from this dull Salon of 1863 that the jury had excluded Eduard Manet's "Déjeuner sur l'Herbe." The protest from the radical artists against their exclusion was so loud that Napoleon authorized a special *Salon des Refusés.* Manet's painting, exhibited although rejected, became the storm center of controversy.[12] Some attacked its morals, others its art. The subject was simple—a group of men and women resting in the shade near a stream. But the critics were horrified because the men were in strictly modern dress, while the women had removed their clothes. The cartoonists portrayed Courbet welcoming Manet into the realist school. And Manet's own statement of his principle of art was not unlike Courbet's: "There is only one thing true: to paint from the first what one sees. When that is done, it is done."[13]

The group of conscious rebels against the authority and standards of the Academy included Claude Monet, who did more than any other artist to put light on canvas, to give fully the feel of the open air into which Courbet and Manet invited art. In 1866 he painted his own "Déjeuner sur l'Herbe," imitating Manet in some respects, but giving his canvas more light. Monet's technique of rendering light and color and outline by the juxtaposition of small dabs of pigment of contrasting colors conformed to the principles of physics and optics that the scientists were expounding. Monet taught artists that shadows are not black. Edgar Dégas in 1866 became a recruit to Manet's school; from that year dates his interest in the themes of the racetrack and the stage. Wilhelm Hausenstein writes of Dégas:

He has an eye for everything that is mechanical in the human world. In this art there lives, as in the art of Manet, a cold, centrifugal atheism.[14]

[11] *Gazette des Beaux Arts* (Paris, 1863), 482-483.
[12] See illustration No. 20.
[13] W. George, "The Impressionism of Manet," *Apollo,* XVI (London, 1932), 1-6.
[14] Wilhelm Hausenstein, "Der Geist des Edgar Dégas," *Pantheon,* VII (1931), 161.

Auguste Rodin exhibited in 1864 his "Man with a Broken Nose," harsh and Roman in its realism.[15]

The word "impressionist" came into use after 1867 to describe the vital, combative, and permanently influential French painting of the 'sixties. Was there really an impressionist school? Did it really possess a creed and a technique? The painters who felt themselves united by their common antipathy to the vested interests of the Academy made much of their duty to truth; their horses were of the stable, not the battlefields; their women were laundresses and ballet-dancers and courtesans, not nymphs and goddesses. They convinced themselves at least that they were doing no more than to paint what they saw. They went out-of-doors, saw the beauty of light, and learned how to catch it and fix it upon canvas; they saw the tragedy and comedy of the human scenes about them, and their paintings became sometimes moving social documents.

Daumier, the Balzac of art, outdistanced his contemporaries in quantity of output and in the effectiveness of the criticism of society his work conveyed. For Daumier made the press rather than the Salon the vehicle by which he reached his public.

While realism and impressionism were the new schools of art in France, the Pre-Raphaelites were the artistic radicals of England. This group of devoted workers in art and letters were rebels against industrialism, as Courbet was a rebel against imperialism. Like Courbet, like Manet, they looked to nature for their model, and made a creed of accuracy in transcription. But while Courbet attacked the Church, they worshiped it.

The leading cartoonist of England was John Tenniel, who joined the staff of *Punch* in 1850, and began in 1862 to contribute weekly cartoons.

Among the great contributors to pictorial art must be included Jules Chéret, the pioneer poster artist who began in 1866 to combine art and color printing in dimensions previously unknown. All Paris was colorful with his theatrical posters and his advertisements of lozenges and kerosene (*pétrole de sureté*). Lithography had been serviceable in the preceding decades to the romantics in popularizing their iconography of the distant and remote; it had developed

[15] See illustrations Nos. 21-22 for Monet's *L'Argenteuil,* and Rodin's "Man with a Broken Nose."

an industry of obscene pictures, and lent itself to political caricature. Chéret made it serviceable to business.

The great artists of the time, like the great novelists, were in harmony with the prevailing realistic emphasis that had its primary manifestation in the achievements of science. But they were farther ahead of their public. The public took quickly to the realistic novel, and came more slowly to the appreciation of realism in art.

In architecture the cultural lag was even greater. There was no creative architecture in the mid-nineteenth century. The triumphs of building were triumphs of engineering rather than of architecture. And in the humble arts of furniture-making and fabricated iron, or working in wood and metals, the great problem of the day was not presented as a problem of art, but rather as one of factory technology. Tradition in the crafts was not attacked by artists, but by machines.

IV. MUSIC

The opera is the form of musical art most completely established in European culture as a social institution. It has been subsidized by the public in most cities, and has drawn a clientele from all classes. The gallery and the boxes had their traditions of dress and behavior. The highly formalized character of the opera as a combination of music and drama made it more resistant than other artistic media to the general change from romanticism to realism. The opera felt two impacts in the mid-nineteenth century: first, the continued encroachment of nationalism in a medium which was to some degree independent of the nationalistic implications of the great musical revolutionist, Richard Wagner.

Central and eastern Europe have leadership in music, as France has leadership in art, and England in technology. Verdi made his operas a covert vehicle of nationalist agitation. When he wrote in the libretto of "Rigoletto" "Io ho la lingua, egli ha il pugnalo," the Austrian censors let it stand, but the audience in Milan gave the phrase a contemporary political meaning. The very name of Verdi was used as a nationalist acrostic for Vittorio Emmanuele Re d'Italia.

Rimski-Korsakov was a typical musical nationalist; he found his themes in Russian folk music. Richard Wagner went to Germanic folklore for the subject-matter of his operas.

Wagner, according to Cecil Gray, was a Napoleon of music, in that he aimed to put all the arts under the empire of music. "In order to attain his ambition he was willing to sacrifice the lives of his French subjects."[16] The controversy aroused by Wagner has ended with the general recognition of his greatness as a creative genius, but not with a general acceptance of his whole program of merging the arts in a *Gesamtkunstwerk*.

For Wagner, like Goethe before him, was a great synthesizer, one who could overcome the contradictions of romanticism and realism in his own age as Goethe had overcome the contradictions of classicism and romanticism a half-century before. What he tried to do for art was what the scientists had done in their field—to bring everything together in a common scheme. He had his critics, as Darwin had his critics, and met them with satire in the *Meistersinger von Nürnberg*. His theory of *Gesamtkunst* survived no longer than Spencer's synthetic philosophy.

Realism in literature and pictorial art, synthesis of art with technology by the Pre-Raphaelites in the English scene, and of all the arts by Wagner in the German setting—these are the qualities which give distinctiveness to the æsthetic side of the culture of the third quarter of the century.

V. HISTORY AND BIBLICAL CRITICISM

The literature of history had been established in public taste in the first part of the century; it responded now to the demand for facts, the evidence of documents. This lesson was taught in Germany by the school of Ranke, exemplified in France by Fustel de Coulanges, in England by Bishop Stubbs.

The publication of collections of historical documents had been going on so long that by 1850 the historians had at hand great resources of printed "source material." The standard of research technique that developed accompanied the professionalization of research in history. The professional historian, salaried by an institution of learning, encroached relentlessly upon the amateur. The style of

[16] Cecil Gray, *The History of Music* (London, 1928), 207.

the monograph with its apparatus of footnote references to source material became standardized as a formal canon of historical research. As the realistic novel and the detective story brought some of the outlook and method of natural science into literature, so the reorganization of historical labor, the subdivision and professionalization of the work brought the methods of industry and of science into the study of history.

The change in public taste showed itself also in a shift of interest from the Middle Ages to the Renaissance.

Sismondi had written early in the century of the Italian Communes, glorifying an age that Gioberti tried to recall with his Neo-Guelph movement of the 'forties. Burckhardt in 1860 published *Die Kultur der Renaissance in Italien*, describing a statecraft which was at that very moment exemplified in the politics of Cavour. J. A. Symonds was inspired by Burckhardt, as Burckhardt had been inspired by Michelet. Froude revived the glamour of the sixteenth century in his *History of England*. Ranke settled down to the sixteenth and seventeenth centuries. Macaulay's *History of England*, appearing from 1849 to 1855, gave political liberalism on the continent ammunition no less valuable than what it received from the writings of the economists. The spirit of historical writing on the Renaissance was at least amoral, and at most anti-clerical. If a return to the Middle Ages was a natural orientation for a generation that supported a legitimistic political structure, an interest in the Renaissance (interpreted as a release from the restraints of an outworn system) was an appropriate concomitant for a faith in the principle of nationalities and an antipathy to the treaty settlement of 1815.

The material of religious history, which had been ornamented with sentiment by historians in the time of Chateaubriand, was now made subject to the common law of criticism and brought down to the level of the earth, Renan's *Life of Jesus* (1863) portrayed the founder of Christianity as a rather naïve person who had "no knowledge of the general state of the world. . . . The charming impossibilities with which his parables abound, when he brings kings and the mighty ones upon the stage, prove that he never conceived of aristocratic society except as a young villager who sees the world through the prism of his simplicity." J. R. Seeley in *Ecce Homo* (1866) wrote of Him as a "young man of promise, popular with those who knew him." This point of view outraged religious sensibilities, but it was fortified, by the rising school of biblical scholarship. Bishop Colenso of Natal was led in 1862 by the problem of explaining the Bible to Zulus into a criticism of the Pentateuch that looked in England like heresy. In 1860 there appeared in England the *Essays and Reviews* of a group of so-called Broad Church writers. When two of them were condemned in an ecclesiastical court, the Lord Chancellor reversed the decision, giving rise to the jest that he had "dismissed Hell with costs and taken away from the Orthodox members of the Church of England their last hope of eternal damnation." Reuss at Strassburg tried in 1850 to give France a school of biblical criticism which it lacked. Historical objectivity in the study of religion was especially troublesome because (unlike the criticism of the eighteenth century) it came at a time when the abdication of philosophy seemed to leave religion as the sole bulwark of morality.

VI. FREE WILL AND MECHANISM

The culture of a period, in its infinite complexity, revealed itself not only in the form of a consensus; it betrayed its nature also in the issues concerning which men disagreed, and in the inconsistencies into which they were forced by the imperious demands of existence. While the scientific synthesis, coördinated with the orthodoxy of political economy, had set up a universe completely dominated by natural causes and effects, and while the great novelists had coöperated to the extent of focusing their attention upon the world of their actual experience, it was self-evident that the world of science could not serve adequately as a world for man. The novelists saw this. Dickens in *Hard Times* satirized Coketown where there was "fact, fact, fact everywhere in the material aspect of the town; fact, fact, fact everywhere in the immaterial." Turgenev, with greater art and subtlety, created the character, Bazarov, the Nihilist of *Fathers and Sons*, who repudiated everything save what was confirmed by science. Matthew Arnold at Dover Beach (1867) saw the sea of faith recede, and railed against the consequences. There was at least one great artist who felt that realism was not enough. Cézanne, boyhood friend of Emile Zola, consorted with the impressionist artists in Paris, but protested inwardly that their view of the world lacked depth. Friedrich Lange, as instructor at the University of Bonn, accepted the situation with resignation and set out in 1857 to write *The History of Materialism*, which appeared in 1867 with the sad testimony that the spread of materialism was producing a "general enfeeblement of philosophic effort," "the perishable material to which our forefathers gave the stamp of the divine and the sublime . . . is devoured by the flames of criticism, like the organic body, which, when the vital spark dies out, becomes subject to the more general action of chemical forces and has its earlier form destroyed."[17] It was Lange's unconscious testimony to the power of the materialism he attacked that he should take his final metaphor from the natural sciences. In a comparable way, Fechner, having begun his academic life as a physicist, rebelled at the rise of what he called the *Nachtaussicht*—the view of nature that left consciousness out of account. He set forth to put the study of the mind on a scientific basis, and emerged from long years of study in 1860 with a mathematical theory of sensation—that sensation varies with the square of the stimulus.[18] Despite his good intention, he merely helped to put psychology on the barren road it followed into the twentieth century.[19]

The best students of the mind, the real rebels against the *Nachtaussicht* of science, were not of the school of Fechner; they were the novelists like Dostoyevsky and the poets like Browning, who analyzed profoundly and wrote convincingly of the human soul in action.

The effective challenge to the supremacy of materialism did not come from half-inhibited professorial critics like Lange and Fechner, nor from disgruntled æsthetes like Ruskin and the Pre-Raphaelites in England or the Parnassian poets in France, nor yet from the passive resistance of respectable people, but from the cult of the Hero and the philosophy of the Will.

17 Friedrich Lange, *History of Materialism* (London, 1892), III, 359.
18 E. Boring, *History of Experimental Psychology* (New York, 1930).
19 Wundt had been working along this line since 1851.

When a man who has lived and written in obscurity for a long period is suddenly made a celebrity, when books that have remained unsold and unread for decades are suddenly in demand, it argues not that the man has changed, nor that the books have altered their content, but that the readers have changed their interests. In this light the historian must interpret the rise to popularity of Arthur Schopenhauer, who had first published in 1818, but who began to be read only after 1850. Schopenhauer reversed the tenets of the philosophers of the early nineteenth century in two ways: first, in that he took Will rather than Reason as his ultimate reality; and second, because he regarded the universe as ethically barren, or a domain of evil. Man can escape from this unhappy realm only through art.

From Schopenhauer's influence came Richard Wagner's effort to draw the arts together (as the scientists were synthesizing the sciences) with a theory of *Gesamtkunst*, and along another line Nietzsche's development of the concept of the will-to-live into the concept of the will-to-power. There had been other philosophers who helped to swing the axis of philosophy from the problem of reason to the problem of will. It was Stirner (*The Ego and His Own*) who had taught Herzen to conceive individualism as egotism; previously Herzen had been more interested in the bearing of individualism on the problem of knowledge.[20] And the only important metaphysician on the continent, Lotze (*Microcosmos,* 1856-64) racked his brain to devise a system that could let the scientists have their world of cause and effect, and still leave room for the free will of man. The problem of the freedom of the will was no longer what it had been in the age of the Puritans, when a lonely individual stood in the presence of an omnipotent God; in only a few significant documents of the day is this variety of fatalism explored—Fitzgerald's translation of Omar Khayyam (1859) and Tolstoi's *War and Peace*. The determinism that seemed to challenge any possibility of significant individual freedom was the social determinism of men like Taine, the economic determinism of Marx and the classical economists, and the physical determinism of men like Büchner and Moleschott.

When the Walrus and the Carpenter took their memorable walk

[20] Thomas G. Masaryk, *Spirit of Russia* (Jena, 1913), I, 401.

along the beach in 1867, the Walrus wept for the oysters and sympathized deeply, yet he acted in accord with the iron laws of the Dismal Science:

> With sobs and tears he sorted out
> Those of the larger size.

In *Erewhon*—so Samuel Butler reported in 1871—the people regarded moral lapses as misfortunes deserving of sympathy, and were ruthlessly intolerant of ill health—a scheme which exposed Victorian inconsistency by reversing it.

The poets shared with the satirists a distrust of the machine. De Vigny, for instance, depressed by the thought of the fatality of physical and physiological law, recorded his feelings in verse:

> La Science
> Trace autour de la terre un chemin triste et droit
> Le Monde est retrecé par notre expérience
> Et l'équateur n'est plus qu'un anneau trop étroit,
> Plus de hasard. Chacun glissera sur sa ligne
> Immobile au seul rang que le depart assigne
> Plonge dans un calcul silencieux et froid.

A third-rate poet like Turner could not in 1868 write a poem on the steam threshing-machine without troubling his mind over this problem of his age:

> I thought of mind and matter, will and law
> And then of Virgil.

Butler preserved the people of Erewhon from this pessimism by a strict law forbidding the use of machines.

For the deepest contradiction that underlay the culture of the time was what a philosophical mind could soon perceive between the mechanical universe symbolized by the steam-engine and the world of free individuals, assumed as an axiom of the whole philosophy of liberalism. The liberals as allies of science set out to make a temple for freedom even while science was proving that freedom was impossible.

Of the giants of literature who dealt directly with the problem of the will, Hebbel and Ibsen were the greatest. Hebbel drew his dramatic material from all ages, but his theory of tragedy from his own. For Hebbel the essence of tragedy was not trespass and punishment, but inescapable conflict between protagonists of whom both are right. And Ibsen, after his great disappointment that Norway-Sweden had yielded to the imposing power of Austria and Prussia and had failed to succor Denmark in the war of 1864, came back to put into dramatic form the types of the weak will and the strong, Peer Gynt and Brand, in 1866 and 1867.

For the universe so elaborately mapped by science, whose immutable laws were so amply proved by irrefutable evidence, was in the end incredible, and men could not sustain their faith in it to the end. The romantic impact carried over into the age of realism principally in the form of the worship of the Hero; idealistic preconceptions survived in an age of materialism chiefly as a faith in the power of Will.

For the risings of 1848 had been essentially mass movements, impersonal, anonymous. That had been their power and their weakness. It became a commonplace to speak of the "madness" of the crowds. The failure of the movements not only discredited the philosophy and the romantic idealism in which they had lived, but created everywhere a yearning for leadership. Erich Brandenburg has collected a corpus of poems in which Germans of all political complexions called out for a hero to lead them.[21]

The radical poet Herwegh wrote, "Give us the man . . . who will break a road for Freedom through Europe"; the conservative Geibel, "Oh, Fate, give us a Man . . . who will command the Times"; the aristocrat Count Strachwitz, "Let there be a time of heroes after the time of cryers and scribblers. . . . When the Gordian knot is ready, let God send an Alexander"; while the Swabian Georg Fischer sang:

Komm, Einzger, wenn du schon geboren,
Tritt auf, wir folgen deiner Spur!
Du letzter aller Diktatoren,
Komm mit der letzten Diktatur!

It will be seen that this age of mechanical natural law attributed to the men who became its leaders the power of molding destiny and making nations.

[21] Erich Brandenburg, *Die Reichsgründung* (Leipzig, 1922), I, 343.

Chapter Four

THE CHURCH AND THE SECULAR DOGMAS

I. CHURCH AND STATE

THE ROMAN CATHOLIC CHURCH entered the 1850's in close collaboration with all the dominant elements of society, and was left in 1871 standing isolated and alone. This transition was associated with every one of the principal currents of change, intellectual, economic, and political.

Alexis de Tocqueville analyzed, with his usual acumen, the place of the Church in society in the early 1850's:

> The return toward faith and toward those who profess it, which we have witnessed since the Republic and which has not surprised any save those who do not reflect, has not depended and does not depend upon the influence of this or that man or even of this or that government. . . . This return has two general causes: (1) the fear of socialism which produces momentarily upon the middle classes an effect analogous to that which the French Revolution produced upon the upper classes; (2) to the government of the *masses,* which for the present at least gives back to the Church and the landowners an influence which they have not had for sixty years.[1]

Politically, the return of the Roman Church as a bulwark of society against revolution was marked by the negotiation of numerous concordats: with Spain in 1851 and 1859, Austria in 1855, Württemberg in 1857, Baden in 1859, and with half a dozen Latin-American states between 1860 and 1863. These concordats carried out the policies Consalvi had laid down in the era of the Holy Alliance: they conceded to the state a right to intervene in the appointment of the higher clergy, and in return exacted as much as the bargaining power of the Papacy could achieve in the way of special privilege within the state, control of book censorship and education, canon law, marriage, separate penal system for the

[1] A. de Tocqueville to M. de Corcelle, Sept. 13, 1851, *Œuvres Complètes* (Paris, 1866), VI, 178.

clergy, protection of church property and monastic foundations. The most complete of these concordats was the one with Austria in 1855, in which the Papacy won every point. In France no new concordat was necessary, but the alliance of the Second Empire with the clericals was the foundation of the first decade of the reign of Napoleon III.

By 1871 the whole picture had changed. The Austrian concordat had been denounced (1867), a *Kulturkampf* loomed in Germany and Switzerland, in France the Second Empire had moved from clericalism to liberalism and was then succeeded by the wholly anticlerical Third Republic. The states of the Church had been lost, the kingdom of Italy had seized Rome, and the Pope was a prisoner in the Vatican.

Meanwhile there reappeared the breach between religious thought and the fashionable thought habits of the non-clerical intellectual class that eighteenth-century liberal philosophy had opened and early nineteenth-century reactionary philosophy had partly closed. But this time science rather than philosophy stood out most clearly as the antagonist of religion, giving intellectual nourishment to anticlericals everywhere. The revival of Thomist philosophy, which was destined in the last quarter of the century to give the Catholic Church an impregnable intellectual citadel, was then only in its infancy. Joachim Pecci, the future Leo XIII, was Archbishop of Perugia. In 1858 he founded the Academy of St. Thomas, from which the whole revival was to spread.

In the nineteenth century during the last years of the pontificate of Pius IX the attitude of the Church toward the non-clerical world was almost exclusively one of negation and resistance.

II. INTERNAL TENSION IN THE CHURCH

The increasing tension between the Church and the modern world was accompanied by tension within the Church. One party, with gifted leaders everywhere—Acton in England, Montalembert in France, Döllinger in Germany, Strossmayer in Austria—believed that the Church could accommodate itself to a philosophy of freedom. The liberal Catholics in France were the heirs of Lamennais. They wanted freedom within the state, not control of the state, nor the use of the machinery of the state for religious purposes. They would have accepted Cavour's slogan of "A free Church in a free State."

In England, Germany, and Croatia, where Catholicism confronted heretics and schismatics of the Anglican, Lutheran or Greek Orthodox faiths, the idea of liberal Catholicism was associated with the hope that a basis of understanding could be found with those who had strayed from the fold, and that ultimately they might be brought back into communion with a larger and more generous Church of Rome. Newman, who had moved from the Anglican to the Catholic faith as a result of his historical studies, and Döllinger, the greatest Church historian in Germany, saw that the study of history need not weaken faith—as Renan and Seeley seemed to be weakening it—but might bring Christians closer together by carrying them back to their common ground in history. A congress to explore these ideas met at Malines in 1864.

These liberal Catholics, with their suspicion of the state, their willingness to collaborate with other Churches, their confidence in free association, might be called ecclesiastical federalists, as Proudhon and the mutualist social reformers were economic federalists. And they suffered the same fate at the same time.

For liberal Catholicism had no foothold in the Vatican. Pius IX had learned his lesson when he was driven from Rome by the revolution. When he returned to the Vatican he was not in a mood for compromise with any kind of liberalism. He fought Piedmontese secular liberalism with all the weapons at his command and regarded the liberals within the Church as heirs of the conciliar party of the fifteenth century. He made it his policy to build up the Church by building up its machinery of centralized administration. A move in this direction was the restoration of the hierarchy in England and the Netherlands.

The Jesuits became a kind of government party within the curia. They founded the *Civiltà Cattolica* as the organ of their party in the Church and of the Church in lay society. While liberal Catholics were dreaming of a reunion of faiths and conversion of sceptics and Jacobins, the Pope's entourage was planning to guarantee the centralized control of the Church by securing the adoption of the dogma of papal infallibility.

The direct attack from the Vatican upon liberal Catholicism was made in 1864 in the Encyclical *Quanta Cura,* with its appendix, a *Syllabus of the Principal Errors of our Time.* The *Syllabus* listed as errors all the varied turns of policy and doctrine that offered a working basis for liberal Catholicism. There were eighty items in the *Syllabus* and the last was expressive of the spirit of them all. It declared, citing an Allocution of 1861, that it was an error to teach "that the Roman pontiff can and ought to reconcile himself to and agree with progress, liberalism, and modern civilization."

III. THE VATICAN COUNCIL

The plan to call a general council of the Church, inviting Protestant and Eastern Churches to be represented, and to proclaim therein the dogma of papal infallibility, was matured from 1864 to 1869. When the Council met in the Vatican, only Roman Catholic bishops attended, and of them the great majority were of the centralist or ultramontane party, favorable to the dogma of infallibility.

Under the circumstances, the dogma was a gesture of separation from the state, for it challenged the supremacy of political authority. It implied that a relationship of church to state—a relationship as old as Western European civilization—would be redesigned, not as a harmony of a free church in a free state, but as a conflict of an authoritarian church with an authoritarian state.

Though liberal thought in Europe regarded the proposed dogma as an affront to progress and freedom, as a return to something very much outworn and discarded in European culture, it must be admitted that this attitude was in part the result of a misconception of what was taking place in European society. The liberals thought that their state was a giver of liberty; they did not weigh the fact that it was also a taker of authority. The modern state might, in the plenitude of its power, grant to individuals great zones of freedom that had been closed off in earlier states, but on the other hand it assumed in its doctrine of sovereignty an infallibility, an unchecked supremacy, which earlier states had not assumed.

The omnipotence claimed by the modern state threatened the Church in its internal government and in its universality. Priest and bishop under the old régime had possessed vested interests in their posts. Their sharing in the product of an agrarian economy, their various privileges, had been part of a general fabric of agricultural organization and political privilege. The clergy of the new order was becoming a salaried bureaucracy, subject to the same kind of control from above that was effective with the civil bureaucracy. The Concordat of 1801 had marked a turning point in this respect, and the agrarian reforms that abolished the relics of feudalism usually had the effect of putting the priests on a salary.

Who would control the clergy? Church and state could coöperate in this control as long as the state, in fear of revolution, was driven to seek the aid of the Church in maintaining its own authority. This was the policy of "throne and altar," of which the last example was the Austrian Concordat of 1855. But what would happen when the states lost their fear of revolution, when, as in the 'sixties, they made terms with it or even embraced it? Might not the Church, under such conditions, lose its international character? The dogma of papal infallibility was a response to the political conditions of the nineteenth century, as the papal decree of 1075 against lay investiture was a response to the political conditions of the eleventh century. And like the decree of the eleventh century, it implied a conflict with powerful forces, cultural and political.

The opponents of the dogma in the Council did not defend state authority against the Church, but they dreaded the isolation into which the dogma would force them. Newman wrote of the discouragement to the English ritualists who, though they might never themselves become Catholics, "were leavening the various English denominations and parties (far beyond their own range) with principles and sentiments tending toward their ultimate absorption into the Catholic Church." And Darboy, Archbishop of Paris, asked in a great speech in the Council:

> Will personal and independent infallibility serve to rouse from their graves those perished Churches on the African coast. . . . Will it be easier for our brethren, the Vicars-Apostolic, to bring the heathen, Mahometans and schismatics, to the Catholic faith if they preach the doctrine of the Pope's sole infallibility? Or will the proposed definition

perhaps [induce] . . . the Protestants and other heretics to return to the Roman Church and lay aside all prejudices and hatred against it.[2]

When, on July 18, 1870, the Council solemnly proclaimed the dogma that the Roman pontiff is infallible when speaking *ex cathedra* on matters of faith and morals, the Church turned away from collaboration with the nineteenth-century national state and from conciliation with schismatics and heretics.

On the next day, the war between France and Prussia began, sealing the triumph of the national state in Europe. When, three months later, the Italian army breached the wall at Porta Pia and entered the city, it immured in the Vatican a firm-fleshed and quiet old man whose established spiritual authority was greater than that of those great popes of the Middle Ages who in their day had deposed kings and crowned emperors. The liberal Catholics, save for a few in Germany, submitted.

IV. EDUCATION

Foremost among the fields in which Church and State were in conflict were those of education and family law. In each of these matters certain cross-currents were evident which must be examined.

The immediate consequence of the reaction to 1848 was a tendency to give education, especially primary education, more completely into clerical control. Frederick William IV was willing to sabotage the Prussian school system if necessary to bring his people back to God. In 1849 he gave a fatherly scolding to a convention of masters of teacher-training colleges:

You and you alone are to blame for all the misery which was last year brought upon Prussia. The irreligious pseudo-education of the masses is to be blamed for it, which you have been spreading under the name of true wisdom, and by which you have eradicated religious belief and loyalty from the hearts of my subjects and alienated their affections from my person. This sham education, strutting about like a peacock, has always been odious to me. I hated it already, from the bottom of my soul, before I came to the throne, and, since my acces-

[2] Johann I. von Döllinger, *Letters from Rome on the Council* (London and N. Y., 1870), p. 829.

sion, I have done everything I could to suppress it. I mean to proceed on this path without taking heed of anyone, and indeed, no power on earth will divert me from it.[3]

In the spirit of this complaint, the curriculum, not of the Prussian lower schools alone, but of the teacher-training colleges as well, was reduced to the barest essentials—the three R's and the catechism. A candidate for teacher training was required to know fifty hymns, eighteen psalms, the stories of the Old and New Testaments and the catechism. In Catholic France, the reaction had a similar effect, for the Falloux Law of 1850 permitted the establishment of elementary schools under clerical control, and the Austrian concordat of 1857 gave control of education to the clergy.

Though there was no clerical reaction in England as on the Continent, the vested religious interests in education were a constant obstacle to the development of general education, and were not surmounted until the Education Acts of 1870 and 1871 bought off religious opposition.

England was the last of the western European states to establish a national school system. Since the establishments elsewhere long antedated 1852, and were integrated with the administration, the decline of clerical control of the schools merely followed the general decline of clerical influence in the government. When Austria repudiated the Concordat in 1867, when the Prussian government lost its fear of the people after 1871, and when the French state passed into the hands of anti-clericals, the increased secularization of education followed as a matter of course.

In secondary education, which was of the highest importance to the middle classes because it was the starting-point of professional and official careers, the conflict between the principles of lay and clerical control was supplemented by a conflict between science and the humanities in the curriculum. The Falloux Law was a compromise which gave control of primary education to the clergy, but reserved secondary education to the French state. The curriculum

[3] Friedrich Paulsen, *German Education Past and Present,* translated by T. Lorenz (London, 1912).

of the French secondary schools was "bifurcated" in 1863 between science and letters. Science was given a place in the Austrian secondary curriculum in 1849, but in Prussia and England this was delayed until after 1870. Prussia, however, compensated for this deficiency in her secondary school system with a strong array of technical high schools.

Though the decade of the 1860's was a time of intensive self-consciousness on the part of all nationalities, the problem of the language of instruction did not occupy the place it later acquired as a focal point of controversy between nationalities. Only in Schleswig was the cause of an oppressed nationality primarily associated with a grievance over language of instruction.

V. THE FAMILY

It was a leading grievance of the Church that the family was being withdrawn from its jurisdiction. The evidences of this withdrawal are found in such things as the spread of legislation on civil marriage and divorce (as in Austrian legislation of 1867, and the English divorce law of 1857, which took divorce cases out of the ecclesiastical courts and the Italian Code of 1871). But the tempo of change in the family institution was such that twenty years' time made little difference. The family was probably the European institution that changed least between 1852 and 1871.

Le Play, the French sociologist, thought the French family was disintegrating before his eyes because of the inheritance laws that required the equal division of estates. He advised Napoleon III to have these changed to permit a family to maintain its roots in its homestead. Let one son inherit the paternal estate, and let the savings accumulated by the family be distributed among the rest. No steps were taken to carry out his recommendation. The most important change in family life imposed by legislation was undoubtedly that which came in Russia in the train of the emancipation of 1861, which made it possible for the adult members of serf families to escape from the jurisdiction of the patriarchal family head. Greenfield has noticed that the dissolution of a similar patriarchal peasant family unit in northern Italy was practically completed by 1848 without the intervention of special laws.[4]

The whole period was marked, both on the Continent and in England, by a dominant ethic of respectability. Under the Second Empire, the group that set the style was the official class; in England the court and the middle class.

How is the historian to explain this interesting and widespread phenomenon of nineteenth-century "respectability"? The aristocracies had lost their privilege of caste, and the metropolis had not yet granted the privilege of anonymity. Men had received freedom and equality; women were still in a state of legal tutelage. The women of the working class had gone to work in the textile mills and were going to work in the telegraph offices, but the type of office girl had not developed and the working class was not assimilated to the middle class in standards of dress or habits of thought.

The aristocracy and the upper middle classes had come to dress alike. Women's fashions for the middle classes were well devised to accommodate a caste devoted to idleness and child-breeding. The fashion plates of the era were singularly devoid of any pictures of garments in which the wearers were not physically helpless. The well-hooped skirt concealed pregnancies in a way that conformed to the conventional reticences of the time.

The very adventurousness of scientific and economic thought may have had as its consequence a stiffening of the traditional element of morality. In France during the Second Empire the Church itself offered a framework for respectable and conventional morality; in England conditions were reversed and respectable morality offered a place for the Church.

A standard of taste which was no longer Puritan but merely prudish was evident in literature. Flaubert was prosecuted in 1857 for corrupting the youth with *Madame Bovary*, and in the same year Lord Campbell introduced his obscenity bill in the House of Lords to prohibit "works written for the single purpose of corrupting the youth and of a nature calculated to shock the common

[4] Kent R. Greenfield, *Economics and Liberalism in the Risorgimento* (Baltimore, 1934); *Accounts and Papers. Land Tenure. Europe* (27), 1870, V. 67, Part II, Reports, p. 30.

feelings of decency of any well-regulated mind." Baudelaire was fined three hundred francs in the same year for *Les Fleurs du Mal*. The procurateur found obscenity in the lines:

> Je sucerai, pour noyer ma rancœur,
> Le népênthès de la bonne ciguë
> Aux bouts charmants de cette gorge aiguë
> Qui n'a jamais emprisonné de cœur.[5]

Swinburne escaped with nothing more serious than the denunciation of his fleshly paganism by the critics.

Another very significant indication of a changing moral code may be found in the decline of dueling. There were duels in German politics in the 1860's, and dueling was still a part of the code of the gentleman, but the life was going out of the institution. *Oakfield*, or *Fellowship in the East*, a novel by W. D. Arnold, published in 1855, treats of this theme as other social-grievance novels attacked other evils of the time.

The two most conspicuous domestic relations cases were those of Countess Hatzfeld—which made Lassalle's fortune and reputation—and the aftermath of the intricate case of Mrs. Norton which gave Meredith his material for *Diana of the Crossways*. Both cases caught public opinion in a quandary. On the one hand there was evident injustice to a woman, and on the other hand a threat to the system which imposed legal subordination upon women.

The movement for emancipation of woman had not reached the forefront of social conscience, though Frederika Bremer was preparing the way in Sweden, and John Stuart Mill was clearing the ground in England with his essay on *The Subjection of Women* (1869). The issue came up under the head of legislation on married women's property. A royal commission sat on this subject in England in 1867-68, and heard with surprise the testimony of British manufacturers that a custom giving women control of the purse was developing in the British working population, and the testimony of Americans that

> It is contrary to the American idea that any part of the wife's fortune should be used to contribute towards the support of the family. A

[5] P. Dufay, "Le Procès de 'Fleurs du Mal,'" in *Mercure de France*, April 1, 1921.

man ought to be, and is considered to be, clever enough, at least, to be able to support his family without calling upon his wife.[6]

On the Continent, the influence of the Napoleonic Code continued the tutelage of married women without modification until the last decade of the century, but criticism of the Code in this respect appeared in the 'sixties. In 1866 a group of eminent men, including Jules Favre, Jules Simon, Jules Ferry and Henri Brisson, all republicans, joined to study the revision of the Code, and agreed that "Republican democracy is right in inscribing in its program of reform the total revision of the relations between men and women in marriage and in demanding equality."[7] An English statute in 1870 gave women increased control of their property.

Women were slowly making their way toward higher education and the professions. Though Tennyson in *The Princess* (1847) mocked them, they gained admission in 1869 to Cambridge, where Girton College was founded for them. Duruy offered them special courses in 1867, and in the same year, when Dmitri Tolstoi, Russian minister of education, refused them admission to the university, the faculties arranged special instruction for them.

VI. THE SECULAR DOGMAS

As the breach of the Catholic Church with the dominant secular forces approached the dimensions of a schism in civilization, it was evident that there were in Europe a number of organized systems of ideas, each of which stood outside the Church, and yet laid claim to the kind of loyalty or enthusiasm which the Church itself had always demanded. First among them was what Croce has called "the religion of liberalism"—a legacy of the eighteenth century. Its political and economic program had become definite by 1852: in politics liberalism meant constitutional government, that is to say, a mechanism by which a majority in parliament controlled the administration. In economics, liberalism meant *laissez-faire* policies such as free trade and the abolition of political control of business. In ethics, it meant humanitarianism on the one hand, individualism on the other. When Auguste Comte in his last years turned toward

[6] C. M. Fisher of Vermont in *Report of Select Committee*, 1867-68.
[7] Louis Fiaux, *Le Femme, le Mariage, et le Divorce* (Paris, 1880).

the formulation of a "religion of humanity" it was not, as some thought, a repudiation of his positivism, but a logical completion of liberalism. Leo Tolstoi was also thinking of a new humanitarian religion. On March 5, 1855, he entered in his diary:

> Yesterday a conversation about Divinity and Faith suggested to me a great, a stupendous idea, to the realization of which I feel I am capable of devoting my life. This idea is the founding of a new religion, corresponding to the present development of mankind, but purged of dogmas and mysticism—a practical religion, not promising future bliss, but giving bliss on earth.[8]

Despite its high ethical content, the ideal world of liberalism was a mechanical world. It was a world in which things were set to regulate themselves by automatic controls. A liberal of 1789 did not even understand responsible government; he thought of political liberalism as a compound of such elements as "the rights of man" and popular sovereignty. He even believed that "the people" expressed a "general will." A liberal of the mid-nineteenth century fixed his attention upon the parliamentary mechanism. He was in many cases suspicious of expressions of the general will as Napoleon used them in the plebiscites. The touchstone of liberalism in government was for him the device by which a ministry resigned when it could not command the majority of the parliament, and the administration of the state passed to those who had the confidence of the representatives of the people. This was the design of political machinery that England exported along with the design of steam engines in the nineteenth century.

Nationalism was another great secular dogma. It was the product of a long course of evolution, and yet it took in the middle of the nineteenth century a form in harmony with the spirit of the times. Its significance as an all-European movement was laid before the public by Napoleon III's exposition of the principle of nationalities. This principle, as Napoleon interpreted it, was a device for legitimizing by plebiscite cessions or conquests of territory. It did not concern itself with the internal development of a national culture, nor was there any place in it for the principle—sponsored by the European Congress of Nationalities in the 1920's—that nationalities

[8] *The Private Diary of Leo Tolstoi, 1853-1857* (New York, 1927), 144.

should be allowed to organize as cultural corporations independently of territorial bases. There was in it no clear appreciation of what the twentieth century found to be one of the most difficult of nationality problems—that of the national minority. It was a simple, clean-cut principle that opposed itself to the principle of legitimacy as a basis for European public law. As interpreted explicitly by Palácky, and implicitly by most publicists, the principle meant that a nationality—*i.e.,* the totality of all individuals speaking the same language—was a kind of corporate personality, which had interests, desires, and rights. Foremost among these was an interest in and a right to a territorial state, with state frontiers coinciding with national frontiers.

In a brilliant critique of European politics, Francis Delaisi has suggested that modern nationalism is essentially an agrarian myth. Certainly this is true of the territorial aspects of nationalism. The nation is like a peasant on a farm; his land has its fixed and just boundaries. The neighboring peasants may seek to deprive him of his soil, or unjustly withhold from him that soil to which he has a right.[9] The simple imagery may lead to grossly fallacious conclusions. It seems, none the less, to have appealed to many agrarian populations that had become politically conscious. Among the lower classes resistance to the dogma of nationalism did not find a foothold except to a limited degree among the urban proletariat, where nationalism rivaled international socialism.

Many were the appeals that nationalism could present to an individual. Where foreign soldiers walked the streets, as in Germany in the time of the first Napoleon, or Milan in the time of Cavour, resentment against the foreigner furnished a motive. Where exiles, involuntary expatriates from Poland or Italy to London, or voluntary migrants from the countryside to the city, reflected upon the scenes of their youth, a nostalgic sentiment fed nationalism. When the members of an organized hierarchy, military or civil, came to identify themselves with a certain territory and nation, their interests and national interests came to seem identical. When the ambitious sons of middle-class families found that their mother tongue was a detriment to their advancement in the schools or the profes-

[9] Francis Delaisi, *Political Myths and Economic Realities* (London, 1927).

sions, they strove for a régime in which the knowledge of their mother tongue would be an advantage rather than a detriment. And in all probability the idea of the nation as a super-personal entity embodied in its people and its land furnished a recourse for millions of distressed personalities worried by insecurity or depressed by frustration. Membership in a nation offered to the individually powerless person a satisfaction of the yearning for power, to the unfortunate a transfer of the blame and burden of his misfortune. In this respect nationality was indeed a secular substitute for religion. As Carlton Hayes has brilliantly demonstrated, nationalism became a cult. It took over elements of ritual that the Church had established in European consciousness, giving new content to an old form.[10] The twentieth century has seen, in its Fascist and Nazi manifestations, how far the cult character of European nationalism could be developed.

The period from 1852 to 1871 was a transition period for nationalism. The romantic cultural nationalism of the first half of the century was yielding to a nationalism allied to *Realpolitik*. Just as liberalism came to a focus on political mechanics, so nationalism came to a focus on territorial facts. The secular dogmas of the age of realism were elaborated with special vigor in their mechanical and materialistic aspects.

This general truth was equally applicable to the dogma of socialism, which became "scientific" rather than "utopian." It has been shown that socialism concerned itself with the redistribution of material commodities. But its materialism did not stop there. In the hands of Karl Marx, the authentic dogma of socialism became a materialistic metaphysics.

All of these secular dogmas were in some measure opposed to the Church; all of them developed at the same time certain features that were imitative of the Church. Henri de Man has done for socialism what Carlton Hayes has done for nationalism in showing how much it borrowed from the Church, how much it made use of the forms that the Church had established.[11] Caussidière's *Let-*

[10] Carlton J. H. Hayes, *Essays on Nationalism* (New York, 1926); also H. W. Lasswell, *World Politics and Personal Insecurity* (Chicago, 1935).

[11] Henri de Man, *The Psychology of Socialism* (London, 1928).

ter to Marianne (1856) was not a parody, but a significant illustration of the transposition of symbols, for Marianne was the socialist and republican Virgin

> Thou art our Queen, thou alone shalt reign by the Grace of God and the Will of the People . . .
> Virgin of Liberty, deliver us from kings and popes! . . .
> Virgin of Equality, deliver us from aristocrats. . . .[12]

Both socialism and nationalism held before their adherents the prospect of a new world seen in a vision no less inspiring than Augustine's vision of the City of God. Both were at work on their martyrology and hagiography, much of which has been perpetuated by later historians with the greatest fidelity. And both of them included in their authentic teaching the pervasive assumptions of materialistic science. Nationalism became a cult of national interests, socialism of class interests.

When Mazzini, a Quixotic champion of the idealistic nationalism of 1848 in an age that repudiated it, denounced "the exclusive cult of material interests," he found himself in strange company. For Pius IX was listing among the *Principal Errors of our Time* the view

> that no other forces are recognized than those which reside in matter, and which . . . are summed up in the accumulation and increase of riches by every possible means and in the satisfaction of every pleasure.

In this protest against the materialistic basis of the secular dogmas there was no definite prophecy, but rather an intuition that the world would not rest peacefully upon them.

In the short span of twenty years the Church had fallen from first to last place in European leadership. The secular dogmas that triumphed against it in those decades were destined to stand for the remainder of the nineteenth century and into the twentieth as its most pitiless and persistent rivals.

[12] Alexandre Zévaès, "Les proscrits français en 1848, et en 1851 à Londres," *Revolution de 1848* (Paris, 1923-24), V. 20, 366.

Chapter Five

THE LAND AND THE PEOPLE

I. POPULATION

THE POPULATION of Europe in the middle of the nineteenth century was approximately 266,000,000. One-fourth of this population lived under the sovereignty of the Tsar of Russia, one-fourth in the German-Hapsburg state-complex of central Europe (the German Confederation and the lands of the Hapsburg monarchy), 36,000,000 lived in France, 28,000,000 in the United Kingdom. The population was to increase by some thirty million during the twenty years following 1852, a gain of about eleven per cent. The rate of increase was lower than that of the preceding twenty years, and lower also than that of the twenty years that were to follow. The curve of rising population was in this era temporarily flattened out. This temporary reduction in the rate of population increase stands in marked contrast to the rates of increase of economic and financial activity. The great indices of production, trade, and finance, exhibit in this period an acceleration greater than that of the preceding twenty years, while population lagged behind.

Perhaps for this reason the problem of population was not the haunting specter that it had been during the preceding generation. The changed attitude can be noted in both England and France. In 1869, in the first comprehensive discussion of emigration that Parliament had staged for twenty years, the influence of the ideas of Malthus, so evident in earlier debates, was entirely absent. Instead, the rise of the level of wages and of the standard of living of the laboring classes was emphasized, and the value of a large population in the accumulation of capital was stressed. Articles in the *Royal Statistical Journal* noted with gratification that the English population was increasing more rapidly than that of France, and deplored the evidence in certain localities of an actual decline in the population. The record of the discussions in the Political Economy Club of England reflects also this declining fear of over-population. The population problem was the subject of five discussions between 1835 and 1846, but not once between 1846 to 1876.

The ideas of Malthus had been popularized in France throughout the first half of the century. In 1851 the Academy offered a prize for a book on the happy results of the limitation of population. But a change in the attitude toward large families appeared in the 'sixties. In April, 1857, after the census, Davergne, in the *Revue des Deux Mondes*, urged attention to the slow increase in the French population. In the 'sixties, the renewal of war dangers brought about an uneasiness in the presence of the rapidly-growing German population, and when the German Empire was founded with a population exceeding by five million that of France, it became generally recognized that the object of French public policy should be to increase, not restrict, the growth of population.

The dynamics of population growth is still one of the most disputed points of social science. It seems clear, however, that the rate of population growth in any area must be the resultant of three factors: a birth rate, a death rate, and a rate of migration. Although Europe's population increased throughout the nineteenth century, these three components entered differently at various periods into the total result. Making allowance for the very imperfect state of vital statistics, it seems probable that throughout the first half of the century a high birth rate was the decisive element in the increase; the death rate fell but little, and emigration had not reached the proportions of a mass movement. In the last quarter of the century the birth rate was falling and emigration was taking place on a colossal scale, but a declining death rate more than made up for the reduction in fecundity and the effects of migration. Between the era of the rising birth rate and the era of the pronounced fall in the death rate lay this third quarter of the century in which mass emigration began.

In 1852 France and Ireland were experiencing that fall in the birth rate which was by 1880 to be normal for all western Europe. The decline in the Irish birth rate was probably a result of the dislocation caused by the famine and resulting emigration; it proved to be only temporary; but the fall in the French birth rate, threatened since 1814, proved permanent. The Scandinavian birth rate reached its heights in the early 'fifties; England and Germany their peak year in 1878, after which a steady decline took place.

Sociologists are not agreed as to how far changes in the birth rate are the result of social conditions, of rational individual control, or of some cyclical change in the fecundity of the race. Statisticians must always correct a crude birth rate to take into account the age distribution of a population. It is often said that the birth rate of France succumbed to the influence of the inheritance provisions of the Code Napoleon because these compelled equal partitioning of estates among all the children of a family, and hence brought the peasantry to the two-child family system. In Russia, on the contrary, repartitional tenure in the villages gave additional land to the prolific family; the English poor-relief system rewarded the parent of large broods; and in Ireland the peasant-tenant had no property to bequeath to heirs. These conditions may or may not have affected the birth rate. The influence of contraceptive techniques is more easily traced. They were spreading through France during the first half of the century. In 1842 Bishop Bouvier of Le Mans informed Pope Gregory XVI that he was powerless against them, and that to continue to teach that they were a mortal sin would drive his flock from the confessional. The Curia Sacra Poenitentiaria thereupon gave the decision that *coitus interruptus* is a sin for the man, but not for the woman.[1] German and English middle and upper classes developed the use of contraceptive techniques in the later decades of the century. In the 1850's the difference between the social standards of France and England in the matter of child-rearing was so pronounced that Queen Victoria, in planning her visit to Paris in 1855, took only two of her children, lest the visit should give rise to jokes about the *ménage Anglais*.[2]

II. MIGRATION

While Europe in the two decades after 1852 was adding thirty million to her own population, she was sending five and one-half

[1] A. Grotjahn, *Geburten-Rückgang und Geburten-Regelung* (Berlin, 1914), 206.

[2] Cowley to Clarendon, *The Paris Embassy during the Second Empire*, ed. Wellesley (London, 1928), 79.

million overseas, mostly to the United States. The period after the 'forties was a new era in the emigration movement. Prior to this, emigration had been in distinct waves, the result of local or temporary conditions. The distinctive feature of the emigration of the middle and later nineteenth century was that certain dislocations in economic structure—not necessarily involving increased misery—shook loose huge masses of the population at the time when the idea of a new life in America, with land, opportunity, and political freedom, was presented to them as a complete and happy picture. The annual volume of emigration was about three hundred and fifty thousand in the quinquennium 1851-1855, dropped to two hundred thousand in the following decade, and rose to about four hundred thousand by 1871. The crests of the migration waves came in the early 'fifties, about 1870, and again in the 'eighties. The emigrants of the 'fifties and 'sixties were predominantly peasants from Germany, Scandinavia, and the British Isles; the South European emigrants did not leave the Continent until later; in the late 'sixties about a hundred thousand Italian peasants were crossing the frontier every year, but this was a temporary short-distance migration into France; only fifteen per cent of the Italians who left their native soil in the 'sixties remained permanently in exile.

The cause of emigration, and its place in the whole fabric of social history, is complex and insufficiently known, but a few leading facts stand out. Irish emigration, which predominated in the early 'fifties, was the result of famine and land-tenure discontents. It reached its peak in 1854, six years after the famine, and then continued for decades, fed by the passage money sent back by relatives in America, and stimulated by political hatred. Only in 1869 did the mid-century emigration from Great Britain equal the emigration from Ireland. German emigration had been a normal flow into Russia in the days of Alexander I, but Nicholas shut off that outlet in 1826. The impact of cotton upon the domestic linen industry, and some of the consequences of crop failures and agrarian reform drove German peasants from their homes in the early 'fifties. Along the Baltic shores, in Mecklenburg and Sweden, the transition of agriculture to commercial export grain farming displaced many of the cotters by a process that was in effect an extension of the great European inclosure movement to these areas. In England and Scandinavia, prevalence of the principle of primogeniture, the inheritance laws and customs, sent the younger sons of substantial families to seek their fortune across the seas. The political refugees from the storms of 1848 were conspicuous, but numerically unimportant in the stream of emigration.[2a]

The emigration wave of the late 'sixties differed somewhat from that of the early 'fifties in the spirit by which it was actuated. The element of distress with home conditions was greater in the early phase, the element of land-hunger and of hope for a better life in America was more important in the later. Besides, the perils of the voyage were reduced in the intervening years, making the ocean crossing less formidable. After 1864 the majority of emigrants from the British Isles went by steamer. Propaganda for America was spread not only by letters, but by the active encouragement by immigration boards set up by the various states of the American Union, the activities of American consuls, and the advertising of the steamship companies. Immigrants provided the cargo necessary to fill out the return freight to America, for the ships brought bulky raw materials and grain to Europe and took lighter manufactured goods on the westward voyage. The Homestead Act of 1862 also influenced the stream of migration. It was translated into Swedish by the American consul at Bergen. In 1864 the United States government, following the precedent established by some of the states, created a commissionership of immigration and legalized the introduction of contract labor. The periodical and newspaper press of the Continent discussed the "America fever," and the governments came, by 1870, to look with increasing disfavor upon this current which was draining the best blood across the sea. There was a canvassing of the possibility of holding this population by colonization projects, a plan that came to life only when the demographic need for it had passed. For, before the growing antipathy toward emigration led to any controlling measures, the rising industrial cities in the north and west had absorbed the stream.

[2a] Marcus A. Hansen, "The Revolutions of 1848 and German Emigration," *Journal of Economic and Business History,* II (1930), 630-658.

III. THE MOVEMENT TO THE CITIES

In England the movement to the cities reached such proportions that an absolute decline in the rural population took place after 1861, despite the fact that population in the country as a whole was still growing rapidly. This decline was associated with the change in the source of food supply. English wheat imports were fourteen million cwt. in 1851 and rose to forty-four million in 1871. In France, during the twenty years before 1851, the cities took four-fifths of the national increment of population; in the twenty years from 1851 to 1871 they took eleven-twelfths. The movement to the cities came later in Germany. In 1852, seventy-one per cent of the population of Prussia was rural, and the increase in population during the following two decades was distributed between city and country in the ratio of two to one. As compared with migration to the cities, migration across the seas was a mere trickle.[3] Out of every seven persons added to western Europe's population, one went abroad, and four or five to the cities.

The movement to the cities received its legal recognition in the general relaxation of restrictions on the right of domicile. Only in the 1860's was internal migration and settlement rendered free to all in central Europe. The Austrian communal laws of 1861, the Swiss legislation that put into effect the commercial treaty with France in 1866, and the law on domicile enacted by the North German Confederation in 1867 are landmarks on this legislative road.

The development of the rôle of the great city—industrial as in Essen, commercial as in Bremerhaven or Shanghai, financial and commercial as in London and Paris—marked a change not only in the location of population, but also in the whole organization of economic life. The term "metropolitan economy" has been coined by Professor N. S. B. Gras to describe the economic organization in which financial control is established in the metropolis, while the actual operations of industry are moved out to the lower-rent regions of the hinterland. The movement of people to the cities

[3] A. F. Weber, "The Growth of Cities in the Nineteenth Century, a Statistical Study," *Columbia University Studies in History, Economics and Law,* XI (1899).

was a sign of the triumph of metropolitan economy in Europe. But this movement is only half the story. The other half has to do with the development of financial controls, and that will be told in the next chapter.

IV. LAND TENURE IN EUROPE

Although cultural primacy lay with the urban population, and the most important social problems after 1871 were presented by the industrial cities, the great majority of Europe's people remained on the soil. But even there they felt the impact of the growth of the new financial and economic structure. The universal money-economy drew them into its network, equating ownership with investment, labor with wages.

In France, more than half the cultivated land was farmed by share-croppers, less than half was in the hands of peasant proprietors with holdings averaging nine acres. These peasants limited their families and saved money in the form of gold. The war indemnity of 1871 drew them into the market for government bonds and taught them to invest in securities.

In England, 2,250 persons owned half the inclosed land. They rented it in large farms to tenants who hired agricultural laborers to do the work. It was only in these decades, according to Clapham, that the money derived from the rent-rolls began to flow into company shares.

In the administration of Irish landed property, it was a grievance of long standing that the owners regarded their estates as a source of revenue, and assumed none of the responsibilities for the welfare of the tenantry that were concomitants of English landholding. The most modern financial methods of exploitation were combined with the most unscientific methods of cultivation. The Irish tenant rented on yearly lease, retained no property right in improvements, and had no recourse against eviction or rent-raising if the landlord was able to make a more profitable deal. This was the rack-rent grievance. The tenants raised grain and livestock for a money crop in which to pay rents, and lived on potatoes. English economists were troubled by the evidence that the system of untrammeled property right and free contract coincided with such extensive distress in Ireland, and by the end of the 'sixties parliament became willing to give the Irish tenant more rights against the landlord, though the transition to peasant proprietorship in Ireland did not come until a later era.

In central Europe and Scandinavia the remnants of serfdom, especially the right of a landlord to exact labor from a tenant in payment for land, were disappearing. The revolutions of 1848 destroyed them in the Hapsburg realm and in those of the German states that had not previously put an end to them, although some of the nobles were protesting even in the 1850's that the abolition of their right to the labor of their peasants was a violation of the Act of the German Confederation. Emancipation was usually, not always, followed by the consolidation of scattered strips into compact farms. In Norway the cotters, or *husmaend* class, who paid for their land in labor, gradually melted away, being drawn off by migration to the cities or overseas.[4]

While the peasant was being relieved of his service duties, and having his obligations commuted into a fixed money charge, the landlord was being drawn into the net of finance through mortgage financing and the export grain trade. Gustav Freytag, in his best seller of the 1850's, *Soll und Haben,* writes the story of the German noble who is drawn to disaster when he mortgages his estate to invest in a sugar factory. The panic of 1873 in Austria and Germany caught a host of the great landholding investors.

Not only the wealthy landlords, but even the ruling princes, were occupied with the standardizing of their proprietary rights. From 1830 to 1860 there were continuous disputes in the small German states over the division of property between the private estate of the princely family and the public domain.

Another pressure upon the landholders to enter the money economy system was imposed by the weakening of the system of entail, which had served to protect the landed estate of a family, but also to withhold it from sale. In Italy the entail was abolished (1866-1870), and elsewhere made easier to break.

The position of a noble landholder was by no means always one

[4] The husmaend class fell from twenty-six per cent to fifteen per cent of the country population between 1848 and 1875.

of prosperity. In Poland and Hungary there was a class of poor squires who were almost a noble proletariat. In southern Italy the effect of the Napoleonic laws of inheritance had been to cause the noble families to keep together, farming their common heritage as a kind of corporation, squeezing all they could from their property, but not finding prosperity.

In central Italy, the position of the landlord was unfavorable in the period before the *Risorgimento*, because the prevailing *mezzadria* system fixed rents by custom and made the sustenance of the tenant family a first charge on the land. If the crops were poor, the landlord suffered; in Ireland it worked the other way. The Italian system made for a conservative peasantry and a liberal nobility. When the Church lands were seized by the Kingdom of Italy, they were bought up by the landlord class and farmed in a more capitalistic way. Cavour himself, with his rice-growing at Leri, was one of an important class of large landholders in northern Italy who farmed their estates with hired labor. Silk culture was one of the principal industries that drew the northern landholders into the net of finance.[5]

Land tenure in the Ottoman Empire had undergone great changes since 1830 in the breaking up of great estates. About one-third of the land was government or religious endowment land, two-thirds under a usufructuary form of private ownership, subject to labor dues and enforced cultivation. One of the very few points upon which Richard Cobden and Stratford Canning agreed in their attitude toward the Eastern Question was that Turkish land tenure should be altered to resemble more nearly the English system of unrestricted ownership. Cobden thought there was a fortune to be made in Turkish real estate on this basis. But the Ottoman Empire did not enter the western investment system as completely as the investors desired.

When Rumania broke away from Turkish law, the changes in land tenure were very advantageous to the large landholders. One of the effects of Turkish suzerainty had been to prevent the growth of an all-powerful landlord class, but the political emancipation of

[5] K. R. Greenfield, *Economics and Liberalism in the Risorgimento* (Baltimore, 1934); W. K. Hancock, "Italian metayage," *Economic History,* I (1928), 368-384.

the Danubian Principalities brought with it the political supremacy of the landholders. Throughout the early nineteenth century the peasant dues and services had been increased. The first occasion on which the *boiars* forming the national *divan* or parliament were allowed to legislate was used to transform their usufructuary title into full ownership of their land.

The Rumanian reform of 1864, while it formally emancipated the peasants, left them with holdings insufficient for subsistence and reintroduced their labor servitudes in practice by means of laws on agricultural contracts. At the same time the landlords were released from all obligations to the peasants, and many of them obtained land which was by ancient right common to the peasant villages.[6]

East Prussia, under the Prussian laws of 1806, and the Baltic shores to the eastward under Russian decrees of 1816 to 1819, had been transformed from serf economy to the system of great estates farmed by hired labor through the juridical device of emancipating the serfs without giving them any land. This was not the most common practice in emancipation. In general the trend in all changes in land tenure systems was toward freeing the peasants from servile obligations, giving them land on long-term payments, and granting the landlords compensation for losses. This was the pattern followed in Russia in 1861 and in Poland in 1864.

V. EMANCIPATION IN RUSSIA

By far the largest of these operations by which agrarian land tenure was brought into line with the requirements of a universal money economy was the great reform of Russia. It was called an emancipation, for it had its intellectual foundation in that complex of ethical ideas which the nineteenth century associated with such words as "freedom," and "liberation." The writers and critics of the 'forties and 'fifties created an atmosphere favorable to the reform. The effect of Turgenev's *Memoirs of a Sportsman* (1852) in arousing opinion in Russia has been noted. *Uncle Tom's Cabin* was translated into Russian in the year after its publication in America.

[6] D. Mitrany, *The Land and the Peasant in Rumania* (London, 1930).

Baron Wrangel records an episode which must have taken place in the 'fifties, when he was about ten years old:

> One day we were sitting quietly on the terrace listening to the reading aloud of *Uncle Tom's Cabin*, a book which was then in fashion. My sisters could not get over the horrors of slavery and wept at the sad fate of poor Uncle Tom.
>
> "I cannot conceive," said one of them, "how such atrocities can be tolerated. Slavery is horrible."
>
> "But," said Bunny, in her shrill little voice, "we have slaves too."

There followed an argument on the difference between serfs and slaves, in which the governess explained that

> "Slaves, my dear children, are negroes torn from their native country and from their families, and so you can understand that they are very wretched. Serfs are people of the same religion and race as their masters, living in their own country and among their own people, only they are attached to the soil. Do you understand?"[7]

The argument with the governess went on as the children, with irresistible logic, observed that their serfs were bought and flogged, like Uncle Tom. The story illustrates the tension under which the cultivated classes of Russia were working in receiving humanitarian ideas from the west, while maintaining serfdom.

Under this tension there had arisen in the 'forties the class of the "repentant noblemen." In the next decade the impact of a more vigorous attitude was felt. From London Alexander Herzen's *Kolokol* (*The Bell*) hammered away at the weaknesses of the Russian system, and in the universities there appeared the "*raznochinsti*," or men of no class, sons of petty nobility, of small merchants and clergy, dissatisfied, unable to find a place in the existing society, and ready to listen to and aid in developing the sentiment for a fundamental change of the existing order. The members of the famous Petrashevsky Circle of 1849, in whose arrest and condemnation Dostoyevsky was seized, exhibited the characteristics of this new social class. Thenceforth through the century they continued to form the "intelligentsia," the revolutionists of all kinds, who continually "went forth to battle, though they always fell."

[7] *Memoirs of Baron N. Wrangel, 1847-1920* (London, 1927).

The weakness of the economic and financial system of which serfdom was the basis was revealed in the Crimean War. It was evident that serfdom, as it then stood, would not provide the financial sinews necessary for a modern state. The discrediting of the government increased the danger of revolution. The number of peasant risings requiring military action for their suppression had increased decade by decade through the century, and Alexander II drew a sound conclusion from the evidence when he warned the nobility of Moscow in 1856 that "it is better that it come from above than from below."

And quite apart from the danger of serfdom to the state, there were evidences that the system was not even sound and profitable from the landlord's point of view. The governess of the little Wrangel children missed the important point in contrasting Russian serfdom with American slavery when she failed to observe that the American slave was worked on a great plantation, under the owner's discipline with the owner's tools while the Russian serf lived in a highly organized little village, supported himself by working his strips of the village lands, and then rendered service to his master by cultivating with his own plows and draft animals the master's field, or paying to the master annually a sum of money (*obrok*) fixed by agreement.

There had been a movement in Russia to shift the agricultural system toward the plantation type of servile labor, not hired labor as on the Baltic coast. Wilkins, one of the foremost agricultural experts in Russia in the 'thirties and 'forties, advised the landowners to turn the serfs out of their holdings, equip the estates with the necessary stock, and force the serfs to work entirely on the landowner's account. In the southwest, the Ukraine and the western provinces something of this nature was taking place prior to the emancipation, for the eviction of peasants from village lands increased despite government hostility.

Favorable to the transition toward plantation farming was the development of the export grain trade, particularly in the southern black-soil belt. In the eighteenth century the Russian exports had been principally flax, hemp, iron, timber, and tallow. In the nineteenth century the rise of new techniques put an end to the Russian iron export, and wheat became predominant. When crops were poor in western Europe in the late 'forties, they were good in Russia, and the general rise in the price level in the 'fifties added to the possibility of profitable grain farming for export. But the Russian landlord was ill-equipped to take advantage of this opportunity. He did not own the tools and stock with which his land was worked, but depended upon the peasants for these. His nearest approach to capitalist farming was to reduce as much as possible the proportion of land farmed by the peasants on their own account, and increase as much as possible the amount they farmed for him with their own tools and horses in fulfillment of their labor duty (*barschina*).

In the black-soil area there were prospects of profitable farming of this kind, but in the forest zone in the north the land was poor, and the serf owner generally preferred to leave as much as possible to the serf, fixing an annual *obrok* payment, and letting the serf earn the money as he might—by farming or by cottage industry. In the forest-zone provinces land with serfs attached sold at a premium of twenty-nine per cent to fifty-two per cent; in the black-soil belt, where export grain farming was possible, the premium was only five per cent to twenty per cent. These figures indicate that serfdom as such was not so great an asset to the land where Russian agriculture was developing and expanding as to the land where its expansion was limited by natural condition. These figures also reflect the greater actual density of serf population in the black-soil region.

The ebbing vitality of the institution of serfdom is indicated further by the great extent to which the Russian landlord had mortgaged his human possessions. On the eve of the emancipation, two-thirds of all the private serfs had been mortgaged by their masters to state institutions for loans totaling four hundred million rubles, or more than half the market value of these serfs at the prices then prevailing. And this estimate does not include the loans from private sources for which the landlord paid a higher interest. Finance had already commuted into money terms half of the value of private property in serfs, before the emancipation decree forced the commutation of the remainder.[8]

The preparation of the emancipation decree took six years. It began with Tsar Alexander's address to the nobility in Moscow in March, 1856—while the congress in Paris was ending the Crimean War. There followed the appointment of a secret committee at the end of the year, and the petition of the Lithuanian nobility in August, 1857, for permission to liberate their serfs. An imperial rescript in November, 1857, empowered the nobility of certain of the provinces to draw up projects "for the amelioration of the conditions of the peasants." Then came the appointment of a new committee—the so-called principal committee—and of a statistical committee, and in February, 1859, the formation of two elaboration committees to work up the material received from the provinces, which was finally given into the hands of the principal committee. A final draft was ready for the council of state in January, 1861, and the emancipation decree followed in February. This sequence is interesting because it offers a contrast to the course of events in the United States, where a federated democracy had before it a political problem of similar difficulty, but lacked the political device of autocracy and the machinery of administrative centralization. The two situations were equally loaded with dynamite; one of them was ended without rebellion.

The Tsar's comment to Bismarck in 1861 after the decree had been promulgated, and while the Civil War was opening in America, is suggestive:

> In the whole interior of the country the people see the Monarch as the paternal and absolute lord given them by God; this sentiment which has almost the force of a religious belief is wholly independent of the personal attachment of which I may be the object. . . . To abandon the fullness of this power with which my crown is invested would be to undermine the prestige which dominates the nation. The profound respect with which the Russian people, with an inner sentiment, surround the throne of the emperor cannot be divided; I would do nothing but diminish governmental authority without compensation if I would cause to participate in it any representatives whatsoever

[8] G. T. Robinson, *Rural Russia under the Old Regime* (London and N. Y., 1932).

of the nobles or of the nation. God knows what would come of the affair of the peasants and the landlords if the authority of the Emperor were not sufficient to exercise a dominating ascendency.[9]

The intent of the emancipation decree was to accomplish three interdependent objectives: to free the serfs without creating a landless agrarian proletariat, to give land to them without destroying the economic and social position of the landlord class, and to preserve as the foundation of Russian society the highly organized village commune.

In practice this meant that the key points in the emancipation program were the distribution of acreage between landlord and serf, the scale of compensation payments to the landlord, and hence of redemption payments by the peasants, and the fixing of responsibility within the peasant organization for the collection of the redemption money.

The two most typical situations controlling the distribution of acreage and the scale of redemption payments were those of the fertile black-soil area in the south and the less fertile areas in the north. In the former the landlord wanted to keep as much land as possible, in the latter he wanted to sell the peasant as much land as possible. The basic valuation was established by capitalizing at six per cent the current annual peasant payments. In the infertile areas this usually exceeded the rental value of the land, for there the landlords had been collecting from some of the side earnings of the peasants. The application of the decree was left in the hands of "mediators," a temporary class of officials chosen from among the more liberal landlords. Within the terms laid down by the decree of emancipation, it was generally the landlord interest that prevailed. It left the landlords holding some of their land and receiving the interest on government bonds, while it left the government collecting the money from the peasants. This completed the transition to money economy.

There were many different classes of peasants whose situations required special arrangements in liquidation—thirty categories of state peasants, the crown peasants, and the Cossacks, and the "court-

[9] *Bismarck, Die Gesammelten Werke*, edited by F. Thimme (Berlin, 1924-35), III, 184.

yard people" or domestic servants. Some of the state peasants were freed in 1857, and the Polish peasants not till 1864. The Polish peasants received the most favorable terms because the government wanted to break the power of the Polish landlords. The courtyard people received nothing—they were freed, and drifted to the cities to form a proletariat. The most extensive peasant situation to which the emancipation decree applied was that of the village commune, made up of households and holding its land in separate strips under two systems of tenure, repartitional and hereditary. Where hereditary tenure prevailed, the share of a household in the village land was fixed; where repartitional tenure existed, the land was redistributed periodically according to the number of working hands in the village.

The weight of opinion interprets the statutes of emancipation as having assigned the allotment to the household as a collective, with each member having the right to share in the common use of the allotment. The household, in turn, was subject to joint responsibility—for taxes and for redemption dues. In case of default, individual members of the household might be put to compulsory labor. The land and agricultural equipment and the side earnings of the group were under the control of the household, though the juniors were permitted to establish separate households within the village, even against the opposition of the patriarchal head of the household.

The principle of joint responsibility of the village for the redemption payments made it difficult for the householder to get rid of his allotment if it were a burden or to sell it if it were an asset. Thus the personal mobility of the peasant was still restricted, by the authority of household and village commune, just as it had previously been restricted by the authority of the landlord.

VI. RUSSIAN EMANCIPATION AND THE EXPANSION OF EUROPE

The restrictions upon freedom of peasant movement that remained in Russia after the emancipation were of special interest in view of the existence of a vast frontier of territory in the east and south into which a peasantry might have expanded had it been free to move. Repartitional tenure favored large families in the same way that French inheritance laws favored small families; the peasant population was increasing rapidly, and yet the possible safety valve of emigration was little used. Less than a thousand peasants a year went into Siberia as free emigrants in the decade following emancipation, and most of these went illegally. The government did not encourage emigration, which would have ruined the bargaining position of the landlords by drawing off the labor surplus. In 1866 special regulations for the colonization of Transcaucasia were made, offering homesteads of one hundred and thirty-five acres. The principal colonizers were the religious dissenters (as in seventeenth-century America), but the numbers were not sufficient to affect the population pressure at home.

By this negative policy on colonization Russia withheld from the world what would have been an experiment in the single tax on a stupendous scale, for the title to the Siberian and Transcaucasian land remained in the crown, and all tenures (save for a few special grants) were on a rental basis with rents paid to the state and periodically readjusted. Most of the peasants who emigrated to Siberia were content to be squatters.[10]

The agrarian problem in Russia must take its place in a picture which includes the agrarian situation along that whole overseas area and frontier fringe which a world-wide division of labor was setting up as a source of raw materials for Europe. Wherever European economy touched open land, it encountered a labor problem, which it tended to meet by imposing restraints upon the movement of labor. In the absence of restraints, the bargaining power of labor was so great that it could prevent that concentration of wealth in the hands of a ruling class that was deemed necessary for the maintenance of the social order. This problem had been met in Russia in the sixteenth and seventeenth centuries by imposing upon the *pomestchiki* (a kind of frontier squire) certain political duties, and giving him authority as tax collector over the free peasants. Then, to keep the free peasants from moving out from under him, they were bound to the soil.

In the overseas colonies, the situation was different because it

[10] Vladimir Sineokow, *La Colonisation Russe en Asie* (Paris, 1929); A. A. Kaufman, *Pereselenie i kolonizatsiia* (St. Petersburg, 1905); *Aziatskoi Rossiia* (a three-volume geographic work published by the Russian government).

was necessary not only to hold labor power on the land, but in many cases to import it first and then hold it. Convicts and indentured servants from Europe and slaves from Africa provided this supply of bond labor. When slave labor became associated with the plantation system of land exploitation in the production of goods for the European market, the resulting economic complex showed great tenacity, but it did not survive its contemporary Russian servile system. Russian serfdom and colonial slavery had risen together and they fell together.

Slavery was abolished in the English colonies in 1833; in the French in 1848; in Argentina in 1853; in Venezuela in 1854; in Peru in 1856; in the United States in 1862-65; in the Dutch East Indies in 1859-69; and in Brazil in 1871-88. When the English started railway building in India after 1858, they were able to make the emancipation of slaves effective there, because they could give jobs to the freedmen.

In regions where plantation economy had not established itself, other changes took place. In Quebec (1854) and New York (1846), the last relics of the French seigneurial and Dutch patroon systems were discarded. Then in the administration of the public domain in Australia and the United States the principle of free selection, by which a homesteader could get title to a small farm by occupying the land, was enacted under pressure of the smaller farming class (New South Wales, 1861; United States, 1862; Victoria, 1863).

In neither Australia nor the United States had the law kept abreast of events. The pressure of populations moving on to new land was something elemental and irresistible. The American squatters (who were small farmers) and the Australian sheep men moved out on the public domain with or without authorization. In South Africa the Boers moved out of English jurisdiction when the English freed their slaves in 1833, and began their last great trek into the Transvaal country in 1848. The movement of the farmers to new land was supplemented by a stream of miners to the goldfields of California in 1849 and of Australia in 1850. The gold in turn fed the great economic machine of which they were a part.

In China, as in Europe, there was probably a rapidly increasing population in the nineteenth century. Some estimates have it that the population increased from eighty to four hundred million in the eighteenth and nineteenth centuries.[11] The increase is of little moment so far as the history of western Europe is concerned except for its possible bearing on the mooted problem of population growth. For if population increased simultaneously in western Europe and China, many of the suggested explanations of European population growth must be discarded. It is sometimes said, for instance, that the conquest of disease raised Europe's population. In China the ravages of disease were increased rather than diminished in this period, for the British imported Asiatic cholera from India to China during the opium war of 1840.

To the study of European history the history of China affords a control. The relations were so slight that the two histories ran their course independently until the last part of the century. The political pressure of the west was felt along the coast and there was some commercial and missionary penetration. The coolie trade of the 'fifties and 'sixties helped to fill the place in Europe's overseas economy left vacant by the abolition of slavery and the slave trade. But the social and economic history of China was still largely independent of that of the west. And yet there were some interesting parallels. The Taiping Rebellion, which engulfed all southern China in turmoil from 1851 to 1864, was in some of its aspects an agrarian movement of a peasantry distressed by population pressure. The open country of Manchuria was for China, as Siberia for Russia and the Mississippi Valley for the United States, a zone of possible population expansion. But Russia and China alike closed these open spaces to immigration. Chinese emigration to Manchuria, like Russian emigration to Siberia, was merely a clandestine trickle.

The frontier land of northeastern Asia, though not a field of population expansion till the twentieth century, was none the less an area of political expansion. In 1858-60 Muraviev, governor of eastern Siberia, obtained from China the cession of all land north of the Amur River.

In India, western economy penetrated more effectively than in

[11] Victor A. Yakhontoff, *The Chinese Soviets* (New York, 1934); H. F. McNair, *The Chinese Abroad* (Shanghai, 1926). For discussion of the problem of Chinese population see *International Migration, National Bureau of Economic Research* (New York, 1929), I.

China. The East India Company had come to base its economy, like that of the despots it replaced, on the collection of land taxes. But in organizing the collection of taxes it had carried to the east the British conception of land tenure. The *zemindar* class—a class of tax collectors—had been transformed at the end of the eighteenth century into a class of landlords owing a tax to the company and free to exploit the peasantry. Western plantations did not appear until the late 'thirties. The preservation of order in India was in the hands of a small white army and a large army of native troops officered by the English. A number of causes of social and political unrest combined to precipitate in 1857 a mutiny of these native troops. The mutiny shook the East India Company out of its position and led to a great increase in the penetration of western economy into India, especially in railway construction. Plantation economy spread at the same time. And something was done in the Bengal land act of 1859 to protect the peasantry from the exactions of the *zemindars*.

VII. CONSPECTUS OF EUROPEAN ECONOMY IN THE FREE TRADE ERA

What a marvelous spectacle is furnished by this international economy that western Europe was launching. Europeans were distributing themselves about the world as if for some great common task. Some went to Australia to raise wool, others went to the city to weave it, and still others to America to raise the wheat that would feed the city. No one held back; all did what was necessary to join in the stupendous enterprise, and the marvelous money mechanism regulated all. There was free movement of goods, free movement of peoples! How long would it last?

Examine the compromises that underlie it and inquire how far they are stable. The English are exporting their factory system, either ready-made as machinery, or in the form of investment loans or in the form of ideas. When it is rooted on foreign soil, it will demand protection in Germany, France, the United States. All European farm labor is now at last free labor, but the European farmer must bid against the mill for his hired man, and compete with the soil of the American prairie and the Ukraine. He will soon have his back to the wall and demand protection. Then there will be an end to the free movement of goods. Moreover, when labor has abandoned the low-level security of the villages for high-level insecurity of the city, there will emerge a "problem of unemployment" which will cause resistance to the free movement of peoples. The international economy will not last forever. But it hums with power while it lasts.

Meanwhile, like a breaking monsoon, there runs eastward over Europe, westward over the United States, the line that divides agriculture from industry, separating the zone of production of raw materials from the zone of production of finished goods. As regions which have through their whole history been agricultural feel the wind of trade setting in the new direction, the whole balance of social forces is altered. They are then said to be confronted with the decline of the aristocracy, the rise of the business man, the triumph of liberalism, the victory of the money power. In those regions people of the middle class speak with greater self-confidence. The Landtag deputy Vincke demands of the king that the Prussian officer corps be opened to commoners; and Schmerling overrides the high Austrian aristocracy.

All parts of the scene are related to each other. Cavour put some of them together in 1858 when he defended the principle of free emigration in the Piedmontese chamber by proving that it was not responsible for the decline in the price of land:

> Among us before 1848 industry was much less developed than today; far fewer of the upper classes devoted themselves to commerce and industry. It is even true that in Piedmont, when a merchant or manufacturer had amassed some capital, he used at least a part of it to buy land to raise his social standing. (Interruption: that is true.) It is natural that under those circumstances the price of land would rise relative to other properties. But it is no longer so."[12]

The monsoon was passing over Piedmont. It was moving through central Europe. The political crises in which the new national states were born took place in the midst of this shift from agrarian to industrial economy, when industrial organization was in its international phase.

[12] C. B. de Cavour, *Oeuvre parlementaire du Comte de Cavour* (Paris, 1862), 475.

Chapter Six

THE WORLD OF BUSINESS ENTERPRISE AND INDUSTRIAL RELATIONS

I. THE INDEX OF MATERIAL PROGRESS

THE WORLD of business enterprise is a world of commodities, fixed capital, and means of payment. Statistical information is not sufficiently complete to permit more than an approximation of the dimensions of this world from 1852 to 1871, but a few figures can be cited to give an indication of its extent and its relation to the preceding and succeeding eras. A generation that has learned to read its economic fate in the form of charts of business activity will find the statistical information inadequate, indeed, but none the less useful, for it establishes very clearly the place of the twenty years following 1850 as a critical point in the expansion of modern economic activity.

If world trade be calculated in dollar volume and plotted on a sheet of cross section paper with time intervals of twenty years from 1830 to 1929, the resulting curve will show that trade doubled itself approximately every twenty years. The series, 2, 4, 8, 16, 32, 64, comes very near to the actual estimated figures for world trade in billion-dollar units and in twenty-year intervals.[1] The year 1850 was near the beginning of a period in which the expansion of international trade proceeded in a geometric progression. These geometric progressions are notorious for their ability to carry a quantity to astronomic dimensions. This runaway course was in its early stages in 1852.

Production of commodities, foods, textiles, metals, and fuels shows an astonishing continuity of growth from 1850 to 1913. Though the actual production of commodities (except textiles during the Amer-

[1] These estimated figures are 1.75 (1830); 3.6 (1850); 9.4 (1870); 15. (1890); 42. (1912); 68. (1929). In 1933 the figure fell back to 24.

ican Civil War) deviated only slightly from the secular trend, price levels, on the contrary, showed wide variations.[2] They rose sharply to 1857, dropped, and recovered until 1873. The increasing production and exchange of products were brought into line with an expanding money economy by a great increase in the stock of monetary gold, which more than doubled from 1852 to 1871,[3] and by the invention and spread of credit devices that made each ounce of gold serve for a greater number of monetary transactions.

The economic institutions of the nineteenth century were keyed to this tempo of expansion. Since the expansion was more rapid than the rise of population, the amount of goods per person in the world was constantly increasing. It has been noted that the increase in Europe's population from 1852 to 1871 was somewhat below the normal rate of increase for the century; the figures for world trade indicate that foreign trade was, on the contrary, increasing more rapidly than normal between these dates. The "normal" increase (doubling every twenty years) would have brought world trade in 1871 to the total of 7.2 billion dollars; actually it reached the total of 9.4 billion dollars. Even when these figures are corrected to allow for rising price levels, the fact remains that these were runaway decades in a runaway century of expansion.

II. CORPORATION FINANCE AND THE INVESTMENT MARKET

The main thread of economic history, apart from the sheer increase of all factors on a quantitative scale, was a rearrangement of property interests made possible by the extension of the corporation form of ownership and the widening of the investment market. The property of the wealthy classes at the opening of the nineteenth century was still principally landed property. By the close of the nineteenth century property interests were more commonly represented by securities. The conversion of title to industrial property into the form of company shares and bonds had profound effects on the social and economic structure of the Continent. It was this

[2] Carl Snyder, "On the Structure and Inertia of Prices," *American Economic Review*, XXIV, 1934, 187-207.

[3] 63,000,000 ounces, or 2.2 billion dollars, in 1852; 134,000,000 ounces, or 4.6 billion dollars of 1934 weight, in 1871.

conversion that ended the long-standing conflict of agrarian with business interests.[4]

From Adam Smith to John Stuart Mill the economists had held that the joint stock company was by its nature inefficient as a unit of business management for the same reason that government was held to be inefficient. Nevertheless, resort was had increasingly to this business device in the first half of the century, because it offered such great conveniences in the accumulation of capital for new ventures. But the commercial law of Europe, except in the Netherlands and the Hanseatic cities, did not offer much encouragement to this form of enterprise. A special act of government was necessary to incorporate a company, and, ordinarily, a company organization imposed upon all stockholders unlimited liability for debts of the company. The owner of a single share of stock could have his whole estate taken from him in a liquidation. Bulwer-Lytton in *The Caxtons* described the unhappy consequences of this element of company law.

Railroad building was an ideal form of enterprise for the development of company organization practices, because no railway could be built without an act of government to permit condemnation of land. Therefore the chartering of railway companies was not greatly held back by the need for a special act of government in each case. The same act that granted the right to condemn land could authorize a charter. And into the charters of railway companies there was easily inserted a provision limiting the liability of the stockholders to the amount of their shares. The limited liability feature made it safe for an investor to risk something in a railway venture without risking his whole estate. The financial technique popularized in railway building was then extended to industry and banking by the English statutes of 1855-62 and the French laws of 1863-67. The essence of these company laws was that it made incorporation possible without special act of government, and shifted some of the risk of industry from investor to creditor. For this latter reason, the new company law was denounced in London as a

[4] H. Sée, "Zur Rolle des Finanzkapitalismus im Zeitalter des Hochkapitalismus," *Weltwirtschaftliches Archiv*, XXXIII (1929), i, 561-573; M. Nordmann, *L'Entreprise par Actions et la Législation* (Paris, 1919); A. Leist and H. Nipperday, "Die Moderne Privatrechtsordnung und der Kapitalismus," *Grundriss der Sozialoekonomik*, IV, 1.

"rogue's charter," but it rapidly worked its way into business use. France and Germany preceded England in developing corporate ownership of big business, because the English business world was well established on the basis of individual ownership. But in the late 'sixties even the English family business enterprise began to shift over to the new form of organization, which not only facilitated the division of property interests among members of a family, but also made it possible for a declining family enterprise to pass its losses over to the investing public by incorporating, selling shares, and getting out from under.

The extension of corporate enterprise created a supply of securities. The demand appeared at the same time. After the turn of the century, the revenue from the English rent rolls began to flow into company shares. The middle classes learned to buy them. The widened market for investment paper was felt not only in industry and commerce, but also in the government bond market. Governments began to resort to national subscriptions in raising money. In 1854 France and Austria embarked simultaneously on this financial course. A five-per-cent loan at ninety-five brought a half billion gulden to the Austrian treasury in 1854 from bonds sold in denominations as low as twenty gulden. The French loans of 1854 and 1855 brought into the market a total of half a million subscriptions. The flotation was described in the press as "the universal suffrage of capital." Cavour used this method in raising funds for the war with Austria in 1859, when the Rothschilds held him up for exorbitant terms. The securities, both of the states and of corporate industry, found a ready market on the stock exchange. These were the great days of the Paris *bourse*. In England, the "stock exchange joined the House of Commons as an institution upon which the common hopes and fears of the enfranchised classes centered."[5]

The democratizing of the capital market and the extension of security flotation were accompanied by changes in banking institutions. The most important of these innovations were investment banking and deposit banking.

A group of one-time St. Simonian socialists were the apostles of

[5] L. H. Jenks, *The Migration of British Capital to 1875* (New York and London, 1927), 132.

investment banking. Isaac and Émile Pereire, who had talked in the romantic era before 1848 of the moral power of credit, were close to the inner circles of the Second Empire. They secured from Napoleon a charter for the *Crédit Mobilier* in 1852.[6] The fundamental idea of the *Crédit Mobilier* was the sale of shares to the public and the use of the invested money in company flotation. The idea succeeded so well that imitators sprang up immediately, not only in France, where the Rothschilds founded the *Crédit Foncière*, but all over Europe. An apostolic band of one-time St. Simonians became promoters everywhere. The shift from Utopian dreaming to daring business adventure was the counterpart of the general change of outlook in Europe after 1848. Investment banking reached England in the early 1860's. One of the leading innovators was Junius Morgan, of George Peabody and Company, who helped to float the International Financial Society, Ltd. in 1863. The investment banks and finance companies helped in the promotion of all kinds of enterprises, but the principal objects of investment were railways.

Deposit banking and discount banking expanded short-term credit as investment banking of the *Crédit Mobilier* type extended long-term credit. Discounting of notes was a well-established banking function. It remained the basic instrument in the financing of foreign trade. But within a financial community another practice grew up. A borrower would no longer make out a note and have it discounted; he would go to his banker and have a loan credited to him as a deposit, and then draw upon it by check. He could use securities as collateral for the deposit. In this way the expansion of long-term credit served to expand short-term credit. Moreover, the customary ninety-day notes discounted by the banks were often extended and reëxtended until they became in effect long-term loans.

Along with the new finance companies and investment banks that appeared in England in the 'sixties, there appeared a host of new discount banks whose function it was to operate this part of the credit machinery. Walter Bagehot noticed a change in commercial practice that accompanied this development of banking. He distinguished between the Old Trader and the New Trader. The Old

[6] J. Plenge, *Gründung und Geschichte des Crédit Mobilier* (Tübingen, 1903).

Trader took pride in doing business with his own money, the New Trader worked with borrowed capital.

While long-term credit was building railways, steamships, and factories, and short-term credit was financing the movement of raw materials and manufactured goods in increasing quantities, the steady influx of gold from California and Australia broadened the metallic base of financial operations. "We are accustomed to see the remedy for each financial difficulty in the arrival of a shipload of Australian gold," said a witness testifying before the English bank commission.[7]

III. FREE TRADE AND INTERNATIONAL MONEY

The frontiers of business enterprise were greatly extended by the principle of free trade, with its corollaries, free labor, and free migration. When Cobden proved, in a great speech in March, 1845, that even the landed interest of England would profit by free trade in corn, Sir Robert Peel crumpled up his notes and said to a colleague, "You answer him, for I cannot." From that day to the Black Friday that began the panic of 1873, free trade was in the ascendant as the guiding star of economic policy.

The doctrine was taken over intact, as formulated by the English economists, and preached on the Continent. The Great Exhibition in London in 1851 was interpreted as a harbinger of the era of universal free trade. The decade of state-making in the 'sixties was in fact the high point of the free-trade movement in Europe. The first impetus came from Cobden in the repeal of the corn laws in 1846, the second initiative came from Michel Chevalier, another one-time St. Simonian who had attached his fortunes to those of the Second Empire. Michel Chevalier was really the principal author of the so-called "Cobden treaty," the Anglo-French commercial treaty of 1860 which launched the free-trade movement in international politics.

French tariff policy in the early 'fifties was not alone protective; it included many absolute prohibitions against importations. In 1852 Napoleon tried to reorganize the tariff system, substituting

[7] A. Sombart, *Wirtschaftsleben im Zeitalter des Hochkapitalismus* (München and Leipzig, 1928), I, 192.

protective tariffs for prohibitions; but the protest from chambers of commerce and groups of manufacturers was so loud that he gave up the attempt. It was at the time of this tariff agitation that Michel Chevalier opened his long and fruitful correspondence with Cobden. A second tariff-reform effort in France failed in 1856. The strength of the protectionist party in the French *corps législatif* made it impossible to reform the tariff by the normal legislative process. Chevalier proposed, therefore, in 1859 that the tariff reform should be accomplished by means of a commercial treaty, which the emperor could promulgate of his own authority, and which might be sweetened for French public opinion by bringing about a reduction of the English import duties on wine at the same time that the French industrial market was opened to English competition.

Cobden's first response to Chevalier's proposal of a commercial treaty was not encouraging. Cobden had always argued that a nation benefited by free trade, regardless of the policies of other nations. If France would consult her true interests, she would reduce her tariffs, treaty or no treaty. He wrote to Chevalier (September 13, 1859):

> . . . I feel no present solicitude for an extension of our foreign trade in so far as the material or pecuniary interests of this country are concerned. We have as much to do as we can accomplish. It is very difficult to manage matters with the working classes owing to the great demand for their labor. I am afraid we shall have "strikes" in all directions, and if we are to have any sudden and great expansion of demand from abroad, it would probably throw the relations of capital and labor into great confusion. Therefore, I repeat, we have no necessity for opening new markets in France or elsewhere with a view to promoting our material prosperity, ***the only limit to which is the supply of labor and raw material.***[8]

But the political possibilities of the treaty appealed to Cobden because it seemed to be a means of promoting the conciliation of England and France, whose relations were somewhat strained at the moment in consequence of the Italian War. This aspect of the treaty appealed equally to Napoleon, who empowered Michel Chevalier

[8] A. L. Dunham, *The Anglo-French Treaty of Commerce of 1860 and the Progress of the Industrial Revolution in France* (Ann Arbor, 1930).

to work out with Cobden the details of a low-tariff treaty of commerce.

When the treaty was signed on January 23, 1860, it served to sustain Anglo-French amity through the tension occasioned by the French annexation of Savoy and Nice in March, and even more to give heart to the doctrinaire economists all over Europe who had been preaching free trade along with political liberalism. The impact upon French industry was softened by an imperial loan of forty million francs to aid manufacturers in bringing their equipment up to date.

The negotiation of tariff reduction treaties followed for the next eight years. Bismarck used the free-trade movement in his conflict with Austria for the hegemony of Germany. He negotiated a low-tariff treaty with France and forced the *Zollverein* states to accept it in a renewal of the *Zollverein* in 1864.[9] Cavour, in holding English sympathy for the Italian cause, frequently resorted to the argument that Austria was protectionist and Piedmont a free-trading country. The free-trade movement, much as it seemed to imply the divorcing of commerce from political control, was itself a political implement of no mean utility in international affairs.

It is none the less a paradox that the great national states of the nineteenth century, with their ample internal trading areas, should have been born into a world of free trade; and the small national states of the twentieth century into a world of high protective tariffs. Free trade was a doctrine of peace in an era of war. Back of the success of the free trade principle lay the fundamental fact that the European continent was establishing its peculiarly nineteenth-century position as a region drawing raw materials from other areas and converting them into finished products. Free-trade policy was a great synthetic intuition drawn from the observation of this fact. As the steam-engine led to the doctrine of thermodynamics, so railroad and steamship fostered the doctrine of free trade and made it seem for a time the self-evident basis of an enlightened economic policy.

In the late nineteenth and early twentieth centuries there ap-

[9] E. Franz, *Der Entscheidungskampf um die wirtschaftspolitische Führung Deutschlands (1856-1867)* (Munich, 1933).

peared to be a conflict between the idea of imperialism and the idea of free trade. This conflict was absent from the politics of the 'fifties and 'sixties. When the British and French opened war on the Chinese Empire in 1858 and made a treaty in 1860, they did not seek to carve out for themselves spheres of influence or zones of privileged exploitation. They required that the Chinese government should open additional ports to world trade and reduce the tariff to five per cent—a rate low enough to satisfy any free-trade economist. The opening of Japan on American initiative in 1855 was followed by a round of commercial treaties which established a low-level tariff on European goods imported into Japan. The commercial treaties of this era, whether negotiated by equals in Europe or imposed by force or threat of force in Asia, contained the unrestricted most-favored-nation clause, which rendered all tariff reductions granted in any subsequent commercial treaty with another state applicable to the commerce of the prior signatory state. The most-favored-nation clause always operated to lower tariffs, never to raise them.

The falling away from free-trade principles began in the United States with the Morril tariff of 1861, in which the Republican party redeemed its pledge to the Pennsylvanian ironmasters, and was continued when the French Third Republic reversed the free-trade policies of the Second Empire in 1871. It was continued when the depression of the 'seventies called forth everywhere a demand for the protection of the home market.

Corresponding to the ideal of free trade in commodities was the ideal of standardization of means of payment. England was on the gold standard, France on a bi-metallic standard, most of the German states and Switzerland on a silver standard, Austria and Russia on paper. The taler, which had become legal tender throughout the customs union in 1838, received wide currency in the treaty of 1857 which made it legal tender in Austria. But the actual state of the coinage remained confused. North Germany used the taler, south Germany the gulden, the Rhineland the franc, Hamburg used silver, Bremen used gold. To add to the confusion, a host of banks of issue sprang up in the smaller German states, each profiteering on the circulation its notes received beyond its state frontiers. When Prussia in 1856 excluded these bank notes from the kingdom, the action helped to prepare the way for the panic of 1857.

Reform of the coinage was constantly demanded by the German mercantile classes. And as the free-trade movement took hold, monetary reform came to mean not merely standardization within Germany, but on a world basis. The German economic congress of 1867 and the German trade congress of 1868 voted for adhesion to the French franc standard. The Diet of the North German Confederation in 1868 passed a resolution calling for a system of currency that would "as far as possible pave the way towards a universal system comprising all civilized countries."

Meanwhile in the lands that were more completely within the French zone—Switzerland, Belgium, and Italy—a monetary union was formed. By the treaty of 1865 the Latin monetary union made the French five-franc piece the controlling coin in these four states, with a gold-silver ratio of 15½ to 1. Greece joined the Latin monetary union in 1867, giving the drachma the weight of the franc. Rumania conformed to the standard. An Austrian monetary commission in the same year voted for entering the universal monetary system, and in England a royal commission voted (February 18, 1868) to reduce the gold weight of the sovereign to equal the gold weight of twenty-five francs. In 1869 the statistical congress at The Hague voted to state values for statistical purposes in units of ten francs, nine-hundred fine gold.

The world monetary conferences that met in 1867 recommended the gold standard and found that the principal obstacle to further standardization of coinages lay in the different policies adopted toward the two monetary metals in different lands.[10] The influx of gold from California and Australia, and a drain of silver to India to pay for railway construction after 1857, had made gold a cheap metal and silver an expensive one. The silver subsidiary coins had sometimes tended to disappear. The problem of maintenance of subsidiary coinage rather than the problem of regulating price levels governed the discussion of monetary metals in this era. Europe was

[10] H. P. Willis, *History of the Latin Monetary Union* (Chicago, 1901); Karl Helfferich, *Money* (London and N. Y., 1927); J. L. Laughlin, *A New Exposition of Money, Credit and Price* (Chicago, 1931).

not far from a universal coinage in the late 'sixties. Then came the Franco-Prussian War.

The war indemnity made it possible for the new German Empire to reform the currency and go from a silver to a gold basis. But an aroused nationalism dictated that the weight of the new German gold mark should be just not divisible into the French five-franc piece or the British sovereign.

The same considerations of commercial convenience that made the standardization of the metallic weights of coins desirable called for standardization of laws on bills and notes. This problem, like the monetary problem, had been formulated in the German and Swiss confederations prior to 1848 in efforts to secure uniformity of legislation among the various German states and Swiss cantons. In 1862 the Swiss *Bundesrat* ordered the drafting of a uniform law for the cantons. The English National Association for the Promotion of Social Science took up the question of world standardization in 1863, and the Paris *Société de Législation Comparée* in 1869. The effect of the French moratorium in 1870-71 upon British banking was severe enough to stimulate a further demand for the standardizing of law on credit instruments, but all the spirit had gone out of plans for international action by 1871.[11]

IV. THE ENTREPRENEUR, THE INVESTOR AND THE STATE

The great *condottieri* of business were the promoters. At their best they were engineers like Thomas Brassey and Morton Peto, who had built up highly integrated railway construction organizations which they had to maintain by a continuous series of railway contracts. At their worst they were stock-market riggers who learned the technique of preying upon the investor's desire for easy money. They learned the tricks of corporation finance; they organized construction companies and railway companies at the same time, controlling both and letting one milk the other. L. H. Jenks writes of the English finance company entanglement of the 'sixties:

> The multiplicity of company names scarcely concealed the feat of self-levitation which railway finance was attempting to perform. Barned's banking company bought shares of the Joint Stock Discount Company.

[11] F. Meter, *Das Weltwechselrecht* (Leipzig, 1909).

The Joint Stock Company owned the Contract Corporation, a concession-hunting concern. The Contract Corporation owned Smith, Knight and Company, an incorporate contractor. Each of these organizations was involved with the contractors Watson and Overend in the Irish railways and with McHenry in his road.[12]

The morale of business sank in the presence of these opportunities for money-making. At the same time, opportunity opened to men without inherited wealth to get into the game. Samuel Smiles was a great prophet of opportunity. His book, *Self-Help,* which appeared in 1859, sold 20,000 copies immediately and rivaled Darwin's *Origin of Species* in influence. It was a forerunner of a countless number of success books. It preached a new message to the working classes. Hannah More in the early years of the century had told the workingmen to be content with their lot and to fill well the place to which God had appointed them. Smiles exhorted them to rise and win fortunes for themselves by "application and perseverance" (in chapter iv) and by "energy and courage" (in chapter viii). In chapter vii he practically promised them a peerage, and in chapter x he explained how the right use of money is the test of wisdom, and self-denial a high virtue. His chapters fairly reek with moral advice, but say nothing of corporation finance.

The business world was full of other examples of success and the means of attaining it. After the crash of bankruptcies in 1873, one of the Austrian barons who was caught in it said significantly to the trial court in Vienna: "One does not build railways with moral proverbs." In 1862 the Paris financier, Mires, stood trial in connection with the collapse of his little empire. The procureur charged him with having appropriated five million francs of investors' money. He replied that he had given the money away in presents and that, if pressed, he would divulge the names of the recipients. The court did not ask him to give the names, which were believed to be very close to the top of the French political world. Mires was acquitted, and a few weeks later issued a prospectus of a new financial undertaking, claiming that he was the greatest financier in the world, that he had once saved Spain's public credit, and that he was

12 L. H. Jenks, *Migration of British Capital to 1875* (New York and London, 1927), 260.

now offering securities in the amount of two hundred million francs to be used in a loan to a certain unnamed state. The new investing public was indeed a rich field of exploitation.

The key to the relations of private enterprise with political authority in this runaway era of expansion was not only freedom of business enterprise, but also aid to business enterprise by the state. In railway-building the state always appeared as one party to the transaction, and the entrepreneur drove as hard a bargain as he could. In England he got no more than the right to condemn land and float a company, but in France he secured the aid of the state in selling shares, and sometimes the use of state credit. The Second Empire saved the entrepreneurs vast sums by guaranteeing railway-bond interest, and this type of state aid was invoked throughout Europe. In the more remote areas, in the Balkans, the Ottoman Empire, and overseas, the promoters expected to receive a guarantee of profits upon every kilometer built; a railway concession that was a mere permission to build was not enough. In the United States public land was used for subsidy, in India a claim on the land tax revenues. The promoters of the Grand Trunk Railway tried to get a British guarantee to the Canadian railway and ended up by giving a Canadian state guarantee to the British investor. It was in this kind of bargaining that the corruption of public officials by the promoters entered most deeply into business practices. The strategy of the entrepreneur required the private ownership of profits together with the socialization of losses.

The financial complex of which concession-hunting and company promotion was a part included also the marketing of the bonds of the states that lay outside the European source of investment capital. The more remote the state and the more shaky its financial position, the greater was the risk to the investor and the profit to the promoter. The Ottoman public debt was pyramided rapidly in the 'sixties from the foundation laid by the financial necessities of the Crimean War; the building of the Suez Canal helped to make Egypt a financial vassal of Europe; public finance in Mexico was a field in which the Swiss banker Jecker and Napoleon's half-brother, the Duc de Morny, expected to make a great killing in 1861; and when the panic of 1866 weaned the British investors from finance companies, they turned to the government-loan business where speculative profits were equally high and opportunities for market-rigging by the promoters equally great. In 1868 the Corporation of Foreign Bondholders was organized in England to protect these government-loan investments. In general the expansion of government loans kept pace with the general expansion of finance and trade. The public debts of continental Europe rose in twenty years from nine to twenty billion dollars.

While state credit sometimes helped promoters to sell bond issues at a lower rate of interest than would otherwise have been possible, and state guarantees against loss were a form of private property brought into existence by the concession-hunter, the most conspicuous success of business enterprise in the socialization of loss appeared in connection with labor policies. The shift from agriculture to industry, the drift of population from countryside to city, and the dissolution of relatively stable relationships of master and servant, landlord and serf, in favor of the instability of the industrial wage bargain increased the proportion of the working population that was subject to periodic unemployment. Rural poverty and relief, rural unemployment, was a thing of long standing, to which institutions had adapted themselves. The large-scale unemployment in the urban industrial centers that came with the financial crisis of 1857, or resulted from the cotton famine of 1863 was relatively new. The entrepreneurs had no difficulty in getting society to underwrite their labor overhead. This situation developed almost without protest. When John Ruskin, in his essays *Unto This Last*, suggested that an employer had a moral duty to provide sustenance for unemployed labor even to the limit of bankruptcy, the editors of *Cornhill's Magazine* discontinued the publication of the series because of the protest of outraged readers. The entrepreneur had obtained limited liability not alone against creditors, but against labor as well.

The rôle of the state as the protector, subsidizer, and guarantor of industrial and financial capitalism corresponded to its earlier rôle as the special protector of the interest of the agricultural class. The types of privilege that had been associated with the great landed aristocracies were undermined by the principle of equality before the law, and the family as the normal corporate holder of property received a severe blow in the movement of legislation away from primogeniture and entail. Much of the difficulty over married women's property laws was the result of the shift from landholding to shareholding as the normal way of possessing wealth, for legislation relating to property in land usually protected women's rights. While the family corporation was declining, the business corporation was growing. And just as in the past, certain families had expected and received special legal privilege, so certain business corporations became the recipients of special legal privilege. The agrarian aristocracy had never been backward in claiming state aid; the propertied class that came into existence with the merger of the aristocracy and bourgeoisie in the net of shareholding was not less forward in its claims.

V. THE FIRST WORLD CRISIS

The four years from 1852 to 1856 were years of unprecedented expansion. The establishment of the reactionary governments in Europe reassured property-holders that the danger of revolution was over, and thus led them to bring their money out of hiding. The new gold from California and Australia, and the new credit resources, increased the monetary supply. Commodity prices rose rapidly; wages followed at a distance; the durable goods industries boomed; there was money even in real estate. A new era was opening, and business optimism was so great that politics were forgotten.

Then in 1856 there were signs of the turn of the cycle of business activity. From June, 1856, to May, 1857, the shares of the *Crédit Mobilier* dropped from 1,980 to 1,300, the stock of the *Darmstadt Kredit-Bank* from 240 to 105. German financial structure was shaken by the exclusion of non-Prussian bank notes from circulation in Prussia (September, 1856). The commodity price level in America, which had risen forty per cent, turned downward. The signal for a general deflation might have come from anywhere; in this case it came from America. On August 24th, 1857, the Ohio Life Insurance and Trust Company in Cincinnati closed its doors; this was a signal for a general collapse. The financial panic hit New York on October 13th, and reached northern England and Scotland almost simultaneously in a holocaust of bank failures and bankruptcies. Moving along the worn channels of trade, the panic pressed eastward and reached Hamburg and Paris in November.[13] As the panic drained the gold from the reserves of the Bank of England and the Bank of France, the discount rate was advanced repeatedly until it stood for two weeks at ten per cent in France for ninety-day paper.[14] The Bank of England was forced to issue notes beyond the limits of the legal reserve established by the Bank Act of 1844. The crisis passed its acute phase in England and France in November and December of 1857, but its repercussions extended to Moscow and Odessa and the coast cities of Latin America. It was the first world crisis and the first crisis that struck simultaneously at raw materials, industry, agricultural products, and the products of the tropics.

> Princely fortunes were reduced overnight to nothing, and commercial houses that had stood without shaking through three generations of war and revolution and in whose offices the non-payment of an acceptance was unheard of, toppled as if uprooted by a gale . . . thousands of bankruptcies followed upon each other in the course of a month; hundreds of thousands of laborers were left without work or wages.[15]

Revival came quickly after 1859. Then the promotion era of the 1860's marked by the advent of the finance companies in London, led to another severe crisis in 1866, but the crisis of 1857 was the classic of the nineteenth century for its severity, intensity, and spread.

The experience of the crisis of 1857 may have contributed materially to the revival of political agitation and the yearning for national solidarity in central Europe, and thus to the founding of the national states. For it emphasized to the business and working class alike that the new economic order brought insecurity along with profits, losses along with wealth. The history of capitalism has always been written as the history of profits, and no one could deny the elemental force of the profit motive in launching Europe on its great course of economic expansion. But it might equally be

[13] H. Rosenberg, *Die Weltwirtschaftskrisis von 1857-59* (Stuttgart und Berlin, 1934); H. Wätjen, "Die Weltwirtschaftskrise des Jahres 1857," *Weltwirtschaftliches Archiv*, XXXVIII (1933), II, 356-367.

[14] G. Ramon, *Histoire de la Banque de France* (Paris, 1929), 269.

[15] "Die Verkehrskrisis des Jahres 1857," *Preussische Jahrbücher*, I (1858), 97 ff., cited in H. Rosenberg, *op. cit.*, 133.

written as the history of losses, of successful deflations, of disappointed hopes. John Stuart Mill was the first economist to offer risk as an explanation for and justification of profits. Among the great number of companies that were floated, only the exceptional one survived permanently. Of thirty-one thousand companies launched in Great Britain from 1846 to 1884, only nine thousand were still alive at the latter date.[16] From time to time in the history of European economy there have been large-scale liquidations of property. The land confiscations of Charles Martel, the liquidation of the property of the Templars, the taking over of Church and monastic endowments by secular authorities in the sixteenth century —all involved a large-scale shifting of property rights, with losses to some individuals and profits to others. The periodic liquidations that have marked the development of capitalistic institutions, if contrasted with these earlier liquidations, had a much smaller revolutionary impact on society, but their effect upon individuals was not less drastic. There is a certain symbolic significance in the fact that the legal step that launched the corporation form of ownership on its course was something that related to bankruptcies, not to profits.

To the extent that the teaching represented in England by Samuel Smiles reached the working classes and taught workmen that they might by enterprise gain fortunes, the number of personal failures in Europe was increased; for though some of the working class might succeed, by far the greater number of the entrants in the race for wealth were foredoomed to failure. The extension of the capitalistic spirit to the working class added to psychic insecurity as effectively as the extension of industrialism added to economic insecurity. And for those who failed in the economic struggle after having become infected with the virus of ambition, what recourse remained? How were they to reëstablish an equilibrium in their personalities? Was not their camp an ideal recruiting-ground for socialism and nationalism, which could explain failure in terms of the iniquity of an economic or political system, or shift attention from the meager self to the great super-personal entities such as the proletariat or the nation? The ethic of an acquisitive society is

[16] Gustav Schmoller, *Principes d'économie politique* (Paris, 1905), II, 559.

thin enough when it comes to filling the lives of those who succeed. What does it have to offer to those who cannot be victors in the deadly struggle it inspires?

VI. CAPITAL AND LABOR IN THREE ECONOMIC SCENES

The economic world lay in three great zones. At the center was the island of Britain, where the process of industrialization was pretty well carried out; then there was the surrounding radius, including France, Germany, northern Italy, and the eastern United States, where industrialization was in rapid progress; and finally there were the great agricultural areas and frontier fringes from which raw materials were drawn—Russia, Rumania, South America, Australia, and the western and southern United States.

The flow of capital investment and the organization of enterprise varied with the economic scene. In the early 'fifties English railway contractors invaded western Europe, built railways partly with English and partly with local capital, sold out to operating companies and moved on. After 1857 the current of English interest shifted to the frontier and raw materials zones. The Sepoy Mutiny created a demand for railways in India, and the English government was generous in providing support by guarantees based on the Indian tax yield. America also drew English capital in that era. Meanwhile, France and the rest of western Europe was not only continuing the railway building work, but retooling industry to meet the competition to which the free-trade treaties opened it. Iron production was shifting from charcoal to coke, weaving from hand to power. This was the era of the finance companies in England. Then, when the English money market shifted to government bonds after 1866, the great promotion boom hit Germany. In general the corporation and industrial bank played a larger part in the introduction of capitalism into France than into England, and a still larger part in Germany.

English investments in India and other outlying zones resulted in a change in the type of control. The English investor could not sell out to local capitalists, but continued to use his financial control to supervise management. That type of organization which English finance developed for overseas expansion Germany developed for home investment as well. Export of capital from England came to an end in 1874; thereafter British investment was expanded by reinvesting foreign earnings.[17]

This variation in economic scene and in the rôle of corporation finance in economic development is of great importance in connection with the development of the opposition of capital to labor.

For while the agrarian and business propertied classes were closing their long feud and joining hands as a group of stock and bondholders, the rift was widening between labor and capital. In the course of this shift in the terrain of social conflict, the chronic opposition of employer to employee became institutionalized in labor unions and socialist parties. But before the institutionalized opposition crystallized, there was some hope that the working class might be brought in on the ground floor of expanding industry, and that there might be a merging of the interests of owner and workman.

The doctrinal and institutional developments that implemented the alignment of labor against capital had two roots: in the bargaining tactics of the labor unions and the political program of social reform. When the classical economists abandoned their wages fund theory, following John Stuart Mill's recantation in 1869, they gave their blessing, previously withheld, to the tactics of the labor unions. When the Marxian class-struggle and surplus-value concepts triumphed over the varied proposals for the application of principles of co-partnership, European socialism became committed to an attitude of conflict for which the bloody events of the Paris Commune of 1871 offered a symbol and an illustration.

The principal types of doctrine and program that mark the development of the social and labor problem from 1852 to 1871 are exemplified in six leaders of thought and action: John Stuart Mill, heir to the tradition of classical economics and utilitarian radicalism; Ferdinand Lassalle, the meteoric German labor leader of the early 'sixties; Proudhon, whose doctrines of credit, productive copartnership, and decentralization of authority penetrated the whole French labor movement; William Allen, the architect of the modern

[17] According to Jenks between 1854 and 1874 about $15,000,000,000 of British capital was exported; in the same period reinvested earnings amounted to $50,000,000,000.

trade union; and the prophets of protest, Karl Marx and Henry George.

Marx, Mill, and Allen had England as their scene. They looked out on a world where the factories were built and the chimneys smoking. All three of them concerned themselves with the means for increasing the share that labor would secure from the operation of the existing plant. Marx proposed that labor should take possession of the plant; Mill and Allen proposed that labor should improve its power of bargaining with the owners of the plant. In 1848 Mill's only proposal for increasing the bargaining power of labor was depopulation; let labor reduce its numbers, and the law of supply and demand would increase its value to the owners, and give each laborer a larger share of the "wages fund." In 1869 Mill conceded that collective bargaining could also operate to increase the share of labor. Allen showed how collective bargaining could be organized efficiently. Both Mill and Allen took the existence of the plant and its ownership by the capitalists as a fixed condition of their problem; Marx assumed the existence of the plant and demanded that the ownership be changed. The Marxian doctrine was not adapted to a scene (like that of Russia in 1917), where the process of industrialization was only in its early stages, and the plant that a proletarian dictatorship would seize did not yet exist.

In France and Germany, the industrial plant was only in process of building. The exportation of machinery from England had begun only in the 'thirties. Essen was a town of nine thousand in 1849; it grew to fifty thousand by 1875. The sky of the Ruhr was not yet overhung with a pall of smoke when the German labor movement began. Schmoller's statistical calculations designate 1858 as an interesting turning-point in German industrial development.[18] Up to 1858 the number of artisans and the number of shops were increasing; after that date the number of shops was diminishing, though the number of artisans increased at an accelerated rate. The late 'sixties and early 'seventies are known in German economic history as the *Gründungs Ära*, when German big business got its start.

In France the hand-loom weavers were still fighting the power loom in the time of the Second Empire. In this scene the labor prob-

[18] Gustav Schmoller, *Zur Geschichte der Deutschen Kleingewerbe* (Halle, 1870).

lem could be presented, not in terms of expropriation, but as a problem of letting labor participate in the exploitation of steam power. Since British capital was invading both France and Germany in the 'fifties, and credit expansion was financing big business, it was not illogical to conceive the accumulation of capital as the result of credit operations rather than savings. These were the basic ideas of both Proudhon and Lassalle; both proposed that credit for building productive plant be granted to the laborers who would work in the plant when built. Thus did economic program reflect economic scene.

In their political thinking Marx, Lassalle, and Proudhon each proposed to reverse the conditions of his own environment. Proudhon, living in centralized and authoritarian France, proposed extreme decentralization and democracy. Russians like Kropotkin and Bakunin, who came from a similar political environment, fell in easily with this anti-authoritarian element of Proudhon's thought. Lassalle, on the contrary, against the background of the extreme decentralization of the German Confederation, was favorable to centralized state authority provided it be democratically controlled and exerted in the interests of the working class. And Marx, with English administrative decentralization and parliamentary government before his eyes, had a political ideal of centralized authority and dictatorship.

In the agricultural and frontier zone the most pressing social problems of the 'fifties and 'sixties had to do with institutions of servile labor on the one hand, and the appropriation of natural resources, especially land, on the other. There were problems of land policy in Australia, New Zealand, and the United States; slavery in North and South America; and serfdom (which combined a land problem with a slavery problem) in Russia. The slavery and serfdom controversies gave rise to no social doctrine of lasting importance. The most original system of social thought that reflected the conditions of this economic scene was that of Henry George, who published in 1871 his pamphlet on land policy, the forerunner of his book *Progress and Poverty*, as the *Communist Manifesto* was a forerunner to *Das Kapital*.

How does the single tax of Henry George compare with the

scientific socialism of Marx? Whereas Marx concerned himself with the surplus value that labor puts into commodities and does not receive back as wages, George fixes his attention upon the appropriation of the unearned increment in the value of land which society contributes but does not collect. His scene is one in which wealth is obtained by appropriating natural resources rather than by sweating labor in factories. How does George compare with Mill? Where Mill, reflecting on the experience of the rate-ridden landlord who destroys cottages on his estate in order to relieve himself of Poor Law obligations, associated an increasing population with increasing misery, George, with boom towns before his eyes, associated it with increasing prosperity. And how does George compare with Allen? Where Allen took for granted the wage bargain as the central fact of economics, George had before his eyes the vision of a world of freeholding peasants and townsmen.

VII. THE NEW TRADE UNIONISM IN ENGLAND

William Allen was not a theorist: he was a professional trade-union secretary. He wrote no books. His legacy to the world was a type of trade union that took advantage of three generations of labor experience. His Amalgamated Society of Engineers, founded in 1851 by the merger of existing unions, became the "New Model" of the trade-union world.

The Amalgamated, as organized by Allen, was first of all a craft union of skilled labor, not a general or industrial union. It balanced centralized control with local initiative by leaving the funds in charge of the secretaries of the locals, but controlling expenditures from the center by rigid rules. It collected substantial dues—a shilling a week—and used them for insurance benefits and strike relief. There was no secrecy, no ritual, no aspiration toward a beautiful and distant ideal. The objectives were immediate, and yet not petty. On January 1, 1852, all the members of the Amalgamated refused to work overtime; the employers replied with a national lockout, and the fight was on. Though the strike was lost, the Amalgamated emerged with its organization unshattered.

The great strikes of the nineteenth century are milestones marking the development of the sentiment of labor solidarity. Class consciousness is more the result of labor warfare than its cause. The next great English strike took place in London in 1859, when the carpenters demanded the nine-hour day. The English employers were at this time rejecting everywhere the principle of collective bargaining, but among the middle-class humanitarians labor began to receive some sympathy. John Ruskin had the issues of the London builders' strike in mind when he wrote the series of essays, *Unto This Last,* which, as has been noted, affronted the readers of *Cornhill's Magazine.* Strangely enough these essays, with their attack upon the fundamental tenets of *laissez-faire* economics, were destined to be felt in England sixty years later in a rebound from India, for they exercised a powerful molding influence upon the mind of Mohandas Gandhi. At the time they were written they served only to reveal how deeply the public was committed to *laissez-faire* orthodoxy, and the régime of competition rather than social duty.

Labor itself accepted the principle of conflict. The London carpenters fought their strike to a draw, and then organized their own Amalgamated on the model of the engineers, to give battle to the employers on the open field of bargaining power. The effect of the strike was to set all England to organizing Amalgamated unions.

The new unionism was politically active, but not in a revolutionary sense. William Allen and his colleagues mobilized the political influence of labor upon concrete legislative issues arising in parliament. When a court decision threatened the stability of the Amalgamated type of union by refusing protection to funds deposited with local secretaries, a legislative remedy became a necessity. Meanwhile the employers, frightened at the growing strength of the Amalgamated unions, made an effort to hold them in check by law. In 1867 a royal commission investigated trade-union practices. The careful leadership of the London Junta of trade-union secretaries, the pressure exerted by the inter-craft trade-union councils in the industrial centers, and the political power given to the artisan class in the Reform Act of 1867 resulted in a favorable Trade Union Act in 1871. This Act legalized union activities and protected their funds, but left them vulnerable in picketing tactics. The pattern of labor organization for England was none the less quite clearly marked out by 1871. An aristocracy of labor organized in craft unions was determined to force the employers to recognize collective bargaining and grant favorable terms. The laboring class, equipped with the franchise, had constituted itself an interest group to secure favorable legislation from parliament. The whole labor program was based on existing property and political institutions, and on carrying on economic and political conflict according to the accepted rules.

VIII. LABOR AND SOCIALISM IN GERMANY

While England was the country in which trade-unionism and interest-group politics were most completely developed as the form of the labor movement, Germany became the land of the perfected Marxian socialist party, with trade unions as subsidiary factors. The German labor movement went through four phases after 1852, before it crystallized in this form about 1875.

The first phase was the Schultze-Delitsch era of self-help coöperation among the artisans and small business men. Schultze-Delitsch was the Samuel Smiles of Germany; like Smiles he appealed to his hearers to be frugal and save, that they might later enjoy comfort. But, unlike Smiles, he taught that savings should be pooled, and organizations of consumers and producers formed. In this respect his program resembled somewhat the coöperation movement that had made its first conspicuous success in the enterprise of the Rochdale Pioneers of 1844. Schultze-Delitsch got many of his ideas from England. In 1860 there were two hundred thousand members of his coöperative societies. He believed that the pooling of savings would create funds sufficient to launch productive enterprises owned by the artisans collectively. The new European experience of large flotations of securities among small investors made his plan seem practicable.

The second phase was the Lassalle era, from 1862 to 1868. Lassalle formulated the labor program of state-aided production associations and universal suffrage. He argued from the "iron law of wages" that labor could not save enough out of its earnings to equip itself with industrial plant, and must therefore have the help of the state. Lassalle's Universal German Working Men's Association had a membership of about five thousand when the leader was killed in a duel in 1864. In 1868 the third phase opened with the organizing of labor unions on the English model. Schweitzer, heir to Lassalle's leadership, organized some of them as a wing of the socialist movement, and simultaneously rival organizations, the Hirsch-Duncker, non-political unions appeared. In 1870 Austrian legislation permitted labor unions. But German labor did not duplicate the economic and political complex that had developed in England. Instead it found itself entering the fourth phase—the conflict between the heirs of Lassalle and the disciples of Marx for control of the political socialist movement. In 1869 August Bebel, who had first entered the labor movement as an adherent of Schultze-Delitsch, and Wilhelm Liebknecht, who had started as a follower of Lassalle, formed the German Social Democratic Party, the first authentic Marxian party in Germany. The two wings of the socialist movement did not merge till the Gotha Congress of 1875. It was all the easier to draw the two wings together because Marx and Lassalle agreed in their confidence in centralized political authority.

IX. FROM MUTUALISM TO THE COMMUNE

In France, as in Germany and England, there took place a healing of the rift between industrial capitalists and agrarian aristocracy, and a crystallizing of the opposition of the laboring class to the owning class, but the evolution exhibited certain differences due to the political situation. In France the owning classes were brought together, not alone by the opening of the investment market, but also under the banner of the Church, which seemed to offer them protection against the danger to property that the socialism of 1848 had threatened. And the French labor leadership did not separate economic from political and religious questions. The Parisian radical, whether a laborer or a member of the professional class, thought of the Republic as the new social order, and reserved his bitterest hatred for the clergy rather than the owners of property.

The labor movement as such was completely benumbed by the reaction after 1848; all that survived and developed in the 'fifties were the mutual insurance groups, which had the friendly assistance of Napoleon III.

Trade unions had been illegal since 1791. There had been in the

1830's a kind of romantic secret trade unionism, the "compagnonnage" of wandering journeymen like the contemporary German *Brüderschaft.* But trade-unionism English style was undeveloped. In 1862 two events took place to give French unionism a start. When a number of striking printers were convicted of belonging to a trade union, the Emperor pardoned them. And then, at public expense, a delegation of laborers was sent to England to see the Exhibition of 1862. The French workmen reached London in the middle of the fever of union organization that had followed the carpenters' strike of 1859, and brought home some ideas of the possibilities of collective bargaining with employers. There followed in 1864 the repeal of the law against trade unions. Thereupon the practical education of French labor in trade-union organization and tactics began. The two institutions that developed were the *Chambre syndicale*, the local association comparable to the English trades-union council, and the *société de résistance*, the collective bargaining unit.

The two lights of radicalism in France under the Second Empire were Blanqui and Proudhon. Blanqui was a Jacobin; his constant thought was of revolutionary tactics, his aim to seize the state. In this respect and in this respect only did he bear any resemblance to Marx. His program was not so much pro-labor as anti-clerical and anti-Imperial. He had no patience with utopias of any kind. His vision reached forward to a great day on the barricades, and not much beyond that. Proudhon was the intellectual, the critic of society, economic and political. The substance of his economic program—the mutual productive society—was so much a commonplace of the social thought of his time that it received the approval of Napoleon III and John Stuart Mill.

The political side of his thinking was more original. Before 1848 he called himself an anarchist, afterwards he began to call himself a federalist, but always he regarded the strong, centralized state as an unnecessary consequence of an imperfectly arranged social order. He did not ask, like Lassalle, for the aid of the state to reach his economic goal. He would dispense with interest and rent, and thereupon the new social order would take form of itself. Marx always regarded Proudhon as a petty bourgeois, and so indeed he was. For the French labor world through which his ideas penetrated had not accepted the status that Marx assigned to the proletarian. The French artisan wanted to rise and advance himself in a way that Samuel Smiles understood. He was thinking of individual opportunity. This is shown by the fact that the principal practical demand of French labor under the Second Empire was for free, universal, and secular education.

If it was England that taught the organized opposition of labor to capital on the basis of existing institutions, and Germany that based this opposition on the vision of a future society, it was in France that the lesson of violence was most completely taught. It was in this country, where both in fact and in doctrine the class distinction between proletariat and bourgeoisie was least clearly drawn, that the most tragic chapter of Europe's social history was written: the armed resistance of the Paris Commune to the national government of France at the close of the Franco-Prussian War in 1871.

This resistance began in patriotic exasperation against a defeated government, and in republican suspicion of a monarchist National Assembly. Paris felt that it had been sold out to the victorious Prussians, and would next be sold out to a returning monarchy. The emotions that launched the Commune on its resistance were patriotic and republican, not proletarian and socialist. The immediate grievances that precipitated the rising were three: the ending of a moratorium (which embarrassed small business debtors), the project for dismissing the members of the citizens' National Guard, and the attempt to remove some cannon held by the National Guard in Paris. These were not the special grievances of a labor class. In the course of the insurrection there was put together a hodge-podge policy that drew something from Blanqui and something from Proudhon. The commune of Paris appealed to the other communes of France for a decentralization of government. This was pure Proudhon. The leaders seized hostages, especially members of the clergy, threatened to execute them as a measure of reprisal in the civil war. This was pure Blanqui. The nearest thing to a socialist measure that emerged from the Commune was a provision for limiting night work in bakeries.

The massacres of hostages and communards that marked the crisis of the civil war, the desperate destruction of property, and the merciless repression set a new standard for savagery in the nineteenth century. It was from this violence, and not from any element of program or quality of leadership, that the Commune drew its meaning in European history. The Commune became a symbol of the socialist class struggle; Karl Marx and Adolphe Thiers, apologists of vanquished and victors, agreed in imputing to it that character.

X. THE FIRST INTERNATIONAL

There was still another forum in which the social problem was increasingly clarified in a Marxian sense: that was the International Working Men's Association, founded in London in 1864. When it began it was a stage set for the coöperation of almost any radical or labor leaders, from Mazzini with his idea of nationalism and republicanism to the English trade unionists who wanted continental laborers to refuse supplies to strike-breaking English employers. Marx contested the leadership with Mazzini when it began, with Bakunin when it ended. This transit is a significant indication of the crystallizing of European radicalism in a form that accepted the centralized state as a means of action, separated the conflict of labor and capital from other conflicts, and reconciled itself to a philosophy of conflict.

The congress of the International Working Men's Association, held at Geneva in 1866, voted for the reconstitution of Poland, the abolition of standing armies, and the general arming of the people. The Lausanne Congress in 1867 voted to work for a democratic franchise and to support the cause of international peace. The followers of Proudhon tried to keep the International away from political action because they did not want to subject themselves to prosecution by the Second Empire. Then Napoleon's police began an attack on the Proudhonists, and in 1868 large-scale republican and Proudhonist propaganda began. At the third congress at Brussels in 1868, the problem of peace was again in the foreground. It was voted that, although the principal cause of war is economic and its cure requires socialism, yet workers can help discourage wars by strikes. Private property had been respected in the congresses of 1866 and 1867; communist ideas won out for the first time in Brussels in 1868. The congress voted for community ownership of railroads, arable lands, forests, canals, roads, telegraph and other means of communication. The French délegates opposed agrarian communism, but were voted down. Prior to the Brussels meeting the International was a society for mutual defense of labor interests, for raising wages, and other reforms. After Brussels, it looked toward the suppression of the wage system. In 1869 at the Basle congress, the rift between the Bakunin and Marx factions opened. Bakunin tried to capture the society from within. While Marx wanted an organization to capture political power, Bakunin worked for a loose federal organization to stimulate insurrections and thus dissolve authority. Bakunin was in some measure an heir of Proudhon because, like Proudhon, he detested the centralized state. And the program of Marx was an advance upon the program of Lassalle in somewhat the same way that Bakunin's ideas differed from those of Proudhon; for Lassalle had wanted to accept the help of the state, while Marx saw no future save in the capture of the state. There was, therefore, an advance toward rigor and violence all along the line.[19]

When in the congress of 1872 Marx expelled Bakunin from the International, socialism was doing no more than to take the same road that nationalism had just been taking. Like nationalism it posited the centralized state as the natural form of political society. And whether the social problem was stated by trade unions to employers who had not yet learned to accept collective bargaining, or by socialist parties to a world that had just witnessed the commune, the problem seemed to be reduced—like the problem of international relations after the Franco-Prussian War—to a great common denominator of warfare and violence.

In Russia the revolutionary party did not occupy itself with the problems of capitalist economy, but rather with political liberalism and agrarian reform. Herzen's influence over the revolutionary party faded soon after the abolition of serfdom. The Polish revolution cut a deep chasm between the revolutionists who would have

[19] G. M. Stekloff, *History of the First International* (London, 1928).

worked with the Poles and the reform party in Russia that combined liberalism with Russian nationalism. Moreover, Herzen belonged to the generation of 1848; the nihilist movement among the Russian revolutionists, satirized by Turgenev in *Fathers and Sons*, found Herzen in the ranks of the fathers. With the decline of Herzen's influence Chernyshevski became the next in the true line of descent of the Russian revolution. His organization, *Land and Will*, was set up in 1862 with a central committee in Petersburg and branches in the provinces. Its object was to destroy autocracy and convene a national assembly. When Chernyshevski was imprisoned he wrote his influential novel: *What is to be done?* offering a program of producers' coöperatives not unlike the program of Proudhon. The third in line of descent was Nechaiev, whose organization of terror was the subject of Dostoyevski's novel, *The Possessed*. He appeared in Moscow in 1869 with an elaborate scheme of terrorist organization, an endless chain of "fives." His movement collapsed when he arranged the assassination of one of his own followers. From Herzen and Chernyshevski to Nechaiev the transition was not unlike the movement from Proudhon to Bakunin—a drift in the direction of violence.

XI. CONCLUSION

Railway building was the pacemaker of economic life. It extended the market area for commodities, reached new zones of supply, and served as a training-school for corporation finance. The new ownership and credit institutions that came to life brought both branches of the propertied class together, and set apart the unpropertied class, thus defining what became the underlying social scheme of Europe. To the complex of corporation finance, investment and politics in the camp of business enterprise, there corresponded the complex of trade-union and socialist organization in the camp of labor. The counterpart of the free-trade treaty system was the International Working Men's Association.

In respect of the development of business life, the European culture area was a unit. Its internal political frontiers counted for little in the spread of technology, of business institutions, of attitudes and ideas. Even in the relations of politics to economic life, the state was not the only political unit that played a part. Local governments, not states, took over the labor overhead of business in times of unemployment; international society or groups of states established many of the conditions of trade and finance. The international expansion of business, coming at a time when the control of business by the state was not in favor, seemed to point the way toward the development of a stronger international society, a more pervasive cosmopolitan spirit, than the preceding decades had seen. Yet in fact political events moved in precisely the opposite direction, toward the reduction of the authority of international society and an intensifying of nationalism rather than cosmopolitanism. This fateful turn of events presents the problem that will be examined in the remaining chapters of this book. Yet it may serve a purpose to call to mind two elements in European culture that ran counter to international and cosmopolitan tendencies. One of these was realism, which involved the repudiation of the whole system of sentiments and myths with which international society had in the immediate past been inspired. To materialism in natural science and economic thought and to realism in the world of æsthetics, there corresponded *Realpolitik* in the sphere of diplomacy. The other element was psychic; the nostalgia and insecurity born of the very conditions of expansion and movement that gave international economic life its vast dimensions. In examining the conditions under which the national states of the mid-century were organized, the historian is constantly impressed by the coexistence of a highly idealistic enthusiasm for national unity and a cold-blooded disregard of high principles in political action.

Realism and nationalism seem in some ways to be contradictory; they stand to each other as logic to emotion, as knowledge to life. It has been suggested in an earlier chapter that the secular dogma of nationalism was defined in a way that made it intelligible to worshipers of hard facts, and in this respect it belongs in the same thought-world with realism. But it also offered to its devotee something that would carry him away from a world too hard and factual. Like hero-worship it responded to human needs not satisfied by science and mechanism, needs that were all the more insistent as the kaleidoscopic changes of the business world were reflected in the experiences of the millions in terms of insecurity.

Chapter Seven

THE POLITICS OF REACTION

1. THE SOLIDARITY OF THRONES

IN THE 1850's as in the 1920's, men looked back across a great divide. What had happened before the revolutions of 1848 was remote, *vormärzlich* (pre-March), as the world before 1914 came to be known as "pre-war." The revolutions of 1848 had exhibited a double quality: first, they were democratic and national in object; and second, they were romantic and idealistic in manner. With the failure of the revolutions, both qualities were discredited—both their democracy and their vain idealism. The reaction to the revolution, therefore, had a double character which can be summed up in the two words *absolutism* and *realpolitik*.

The reaction against democracy, popular sovereignty, or mob rule came first. It was the immediate reaction, it was what everybody saw. In 1854 the great historian, Leopold von Ranke, was giving lessons in history to the King of Bavaria. At the end of the course the king asked the historian to state the "fundamental tendency of our time" and von Ranke replied that it was "the conflict between monarchic and popular sovereignty, with which all other conflicts are connected."[1] The publicists and statesmen of the day, whether they wrote pamphlets from an exile's lodgings or moved in the circles of the royal courts, agreed with Ranke that the great problem of government lay in the adjustment of the relations of peoples to their monarchs, not of peoples to each other, nor of state to state. Upon this great issue it seemed that an international union of monarchs opposed an international union of democratic leaders.

The monarchs did, in fact, constitute a union, for intermarriage had merged into one all the ruling families of Europe. All the wearers of crowns were near relatives of each other. The Tsaritsa

[1] The lectures are reproduced in L. von Ranke, *Weltgeschichte* (Leipzig, 1881-1888), IX, 233-244.

was the sister of the Prussian King; the Prussian Queen was the sister of the Austrian Empress-Mother Sophie and aunt of the young Emperor Francis Joseph. Victor Emmanuel of Savoy was the son of a Hapsburg mother and married a Hapsburg wife, though in due time he sealed an anti-Hapsburg policy by giving his daughter in marriage to a Bonaparte. While the trouble was brewing in the 'fifties and 'sixties between Denmark and Germany over the Schleswig-Holstein settlement, Queen Victoria's eldest daughter married the Prussian Crown Prince and her eldest son a Danish princess.

When, in the 1850's, the forty years' peace was finally broken, it required, except in Italy, the hand of a strong minister or the pressure of an abnormally excited population to induce one member of this family to despoil another. And on the question of monarchic against popular sovereignty, they all tended to think alike, and to see the political world moving of necessity between the poles of autocracy and democracy, having no other orbit.

Was it possible to compromise between popular and monarchic sovereignty? Upon this point the sovereigns did not agree. The parliamentary mechanism to which liberals pinned their faith seemed to be such a compromise. The English were even more proud of it than of their industrial inventions. Its working parts had been explained on the Continent by Benjamin Constant, and its merits preached to Continental powers by Palmerston. Belgium and Piedmont furnished small working models of it.

Many circumstances seemed to justify the confidence felt by the English in their machinery of government, for England had enjoyed comparative quiet while Europe was in uproar. The English democratic movement had produced nothing more violent in 1848 than a monster Chartist petition to parliament, and had subsided without dragging down with it the intellectual leaders of English radicalism, because these had not committed themselves to its cause. The air of England did not become spoiled, like the air of the Continent, for such social romanticism as the Pre-Raphaelite movement; the English poet laureat lived comfortably on a government stipend, while the leading poet of France lived in exile. England escaped the reaction as she escaped the revolution. Tennyson, in the *Ode on*

EUROPE
IN 1852
Scale of Miles
0 100 200 300 400
ATLANTIC OCEAN
NORTH SEA
SCOTLAND
Glasgow
Edinburgh
Belfast
IRELAND
Dublin
Stockton
Newcastle
Liverpool
Manchester
Hull
Sheffield
Birmingham
ENGLAND
London
Amsterdam
HELIGOLAND
(British)
HOLSTEIN
KINGDOM
NORWAY
Christiania
KM. OF DENMARK
HANOVER
NETHERLANDS
Brussels
BELGIUM
GERMAN
CONFED
Amiens
Paris
Seine R.
Metz
Strasbourg
WURTEMBERG
BAVARI
Munich
FRENCH EMPIRE
Nantes
Loire R.
Neuchatel
(To Prussia)
SWITZERLAND
TYROL
Lyon
Rhone R.
Turin
LOMBARDY
VENETI
Po R.
PARMA
MODENA
Genoa
Florenc
GR. D. OF TUSCANY
PAP STAT
KINGDOM OF SARDINIA
CORSICA
Rome
SARDINIA
KINGDOM OF PORTUGAL
Lisbon
KINGDOM OF SPAIN
Madrid
BALEARIC IS.
MEDITERRA
GIBRALTAR (Br.)
Ceuta (Sp.)
Melilla (Sp.)
Algiers
MOROCCO
ALGERIA
Tunis
TUNIS
Palermo
10
0
10
50
40
MANHATTAN DRAFTING CO. INC., N.Y.

20
30
40
GD. D. OF FINLAND
St. Petersburg
Volga
R.
Stockholm
BALTIC SEA
Moscow
RUSSIAN EMPIRE
Dvina
R.
Vilna
Königsberg
Danzig
Vistula
R.
Warsaw
KINGDOM OF POLAND
50
Dnieper
R.
GALICIA
AUSTRIAN EMPIRE
Pressburg
Budapest
TRANSYLVANIA
MOLDAVIA
Agram
Danube
WALLACHIA
R.
DOBRUJA
BLACK SEA
BOSNIA
SERBIA
HERZEGOVNIA
MONTE NEGRO
BULGARIA
OTTOMAN EMPIRE
Adrianople
Constantinople
Bosporus
40
RUMELIA
Salonika
Yannina
Dardanelles
Smyrna
GREECE
Athens
MOREA
Messina
CYPRUS
CRETE
MALTA
(Br.)
20
SEA
30

the Death of the Duke of Wellington (1852), a poem that reverberated to the political issues of the 1850's as Kipling's poetry echoed the ethical ideas of the age of imperialism, did not hesitate to describe the English government as "the one true seed of freedom sown between a people and their ancient throne." And he meant just that! He meant that all other political systems had somehow missed the mark.

In the royal family of Europe, there was one group which believed that the liberal compromise between popular and monarchic sovereignty would work. This was the family of Coburg. The marriages of this house had been remarkably successful in bringing Coburgers close to many thrones. Among the children and grandchildren and great-grandchildren of Franz-Friedrich Anton of Coburg and his wife, the Princess Augusta of Reuss-Ebersdorff, were included the Queen of England and her Prince-Consort Albert, King Leopold of Belgium, the consort of the Queen of Portugal, the Crown Princess of Prussia. Duke Ernst II, who kept the old family homestead at Coburg and Gotha, came near to taking the Greek throne in 1862. The Bulgarian throne ultimately went to a Coburger. The Coburg empress, Charlotte, was caught in the tragedy of Mexico, and went mad while trying to win help for her Hapsburg husband, Maximilian.

Victoria and Albert labored in England to protect the parliamentary compromise from the danger that royal authority would be completely extinguished. When Palmerston persisted in sending out foreign office mail without showing the drafts to the Queen, the Queen helped to force him out of office, and for a few months in 1852 it was thought that his political life was over. However, he bounded back into office the following year.

Among the princes of the German Confederation, the Coburgers were influential as sponsors of liberal government against absolutism. In the 1860's, Duke Ernst, in Gotha, and Queen Victoria's son-in-law, the Crown Prince, with the latter's brother-in-law, the Grand Duke Frederick of Baden, worked together for a reform that would set up a liberal central German government.

The Coburgers were willing to accept parliamentary government, but they were still sensitive to the natural opposition of peoples and monarchs. Queen Victoria's letters are full of disparaging references to democracy, and in 1853 she argued against a plan to put Lord John Russell in the cabinet without portfolio on the ground that "a man independent of office might consider himself independent of the crown also, and postpone its interests to popular requirements."[2] Russell had to tell the Queen that the ministers did not distinguish anyway between their duty to the Queen and their duty to the country.

The solidarity of monarchs in the reaction of the 'fifties was not an alignment merely for the protection of interests. It was part of a political conception of a high order, which combined rational ideas of monarchic duty as they had been defined in the era of the enlightened despots with the religious and historical-sentimental imagery that had emerged in the decades of conservative romanticism.[3] It was associated with the alliance of throne and altar, the European treaty system, the idea of legitimacy, the faith that right principles are a part of the natural world of politics. It had struck deep roots in European culture at a time when people believed that the ethical world and the natural world were identical, and when "modern ideas" ran toward the Church rather than away from it. The realistic atmosphere of the 1850's was unfavorable to the perpetuation of this political principle.

II. NEW MEN FOR OLD

In the 1920's, when the world was trying to settle into the stride of peace with the aid of the League of Nations, it was not uncommon to distinguish what were conceived to be two kinds of statesmen and two kinds of statesmanship—the new and the old. Ray Stannard Baker gave a classic form to this distinction when he interpreted the Paris peace conference as a conflict between the New and the Old, with Wilson and Clemenceau as protagonists, respectively, of these two principles. What immediately impresses the historian who examines the political and diplomatic literature of the 'fifties and 'sixties is the evidence of a similar tension, even a similar vocabulary, but with this difference, that the "new" spirit of

[2] Greville, *Memoirs*, ed. H. Reeve (London, 1911), VII, 44.
[3] H. Ritter von Srbik, "Der Ideengehalt des 'Metternich'schen Systems'," *Historische Zeitschrift*, CXXXI, 1935, 240-262.

Bismarck's time was very like the "old" spirit of the Paris peace conference, and the men and policies that were called "new" eighty years ago bear some resemblance to those that are more recently called "old."

A sign of the passing of the older line of statesmen was the death of the Duke of Wellington in September, 1852. The Iron Duke was not only, in Tennyson's resounding phrase, "the last great Englishman," but also one of the last great Europeans. Sir Hamilton Seymour, British ambassador to St. Petersburg, who himself belonged, according to Baron Brunnow, to "the old school of British diplomacy, incomparably superior to the new,"[4] scanned the international horizon at the end of 1852 and observed that Europe was in danger from lack of European leadership, because there was "no one like the Duke of Wellington or Prince Metternich enjoying the confidence of all the courts."[5]

It was Palmerston, the demagogue whose foreign policy was the pattern for all late nineteenth-century jingoism, who took over the great place in the public eye left vacant by the death of Wellington. The time was one of uncertain issues and personal feuds in English politics. The great issues of the Corn Laws had been fought out, the new problem of franchise extension was not yet ripe. Two new men achieved prominence in English politics in 1852. When in February Lord Derby, an old wheel horse of English politics who had started out as a Whig and ended as a Tory, organized a ministry of second rate or untried men, he included among them the brilliant and unprincipled Benjamin Disraeli, who then took his first cabinet post as chancellor of the exchequer. It was Disraeli's first budget that opened his life-long feud with William Ewart Gladstone, who was then shifting from the Conservative to the Liberal side, and whose faith in God and mastery of the multiplication table were destined to make him the paragon of English statesmen of the Victorian era. Gladstone's attack of Disraeli's budget brought down the Derby ministry in December, 1852, and the

[4] F. de Martens, *Recueil des traités et conventions conclus par la Russie avec les puissances étrangères* (St. Petersburg, 1898), XII, 274.
[5] V. Puryear, *England, Russia, and the Straits Question, 1844-1856* (Berkeley, 1931), 205.

cabinet of nonentities was succeeded by a cabinet of all the talents, with Gladstone succeeding Disraeli at the exchequer.

In France, the men of the era before 1848—Thiers and Guizot—slipped into the quiet life of the scholar. Their passing was not even noticed in the brilliance of the rise of Louis Napoleon, who was both a first-class politician and a dreamer. He drew his great power over the people from the glamor of his uncle's name, but his political writings as pretender and his strategy as president served him as the mere name alone would never have done. Taking advantage of a widespread fear of anarchy, he rallied to his support the Church and the army, the agricultural and the business classes. The peasantry that Millet painted, the piety his paintings so often have as their theme found in Napoleon a protector. He also had something to offer the poorest classes, whose misery caused the panic of the property-holders. He had written a pamphlet on *The Extinction of Pauperism* advocating great reclamation projects to give every impoverished Frenchman a place on the soil. He was both a Frenchman and a European; he had fought in a Carbonaro army in the Italian revolution of 1831, and his dreams of a new France and a new Europe were generous, like the ideas of 1848. In his character and situation there were the mingling of elements that seemed contradictory—the union of popular sovereignty with despotism, the symbiosis of the mystical political idealism of the age that was passing away with the harshness and opportunism of the age that was at hand. On the fateful December 2, 1851, he stepped out of his rôle as constitutional president of the French Republic to become an unconstitutional dictator. He used the army to break up the legislative assembly and crush resistance in the streets, and then asked the people to ratify his acts and empower him to make a new constitution for France. The people gave their ratification by a vote of six and a half million to a few hundred thousand. The doctrinaire democrats in exile cried that the election was a fraud, but in fact it is incontrovertible that the great majority of the French people were well pleased with Napoleon. To the half-democracy of the plebiscite he added a half-socialism by surrounding himself with a group of one-time St. Simonians. Until the 1920's it was the fashion of historians to belittle this strange man. English thought knew him as a "despot"; his countrymen charged him with responsibility for making changes in the European political map disadvantageous to France, and for the final and unpardonable fault of allowing himself to be defeated. A Europe which has completed the national revisions of the map that he outlined and revived something of his technique of dictatorship on a broad popular base is in a better position to understand the Man of December.

The difference in outlook between the old generation and the new was most clearly revealed in the politics of the Austrian capital. There Metternich was replaced by Schwarzenberg, the aristocrat who despised aristocrats, and who impressed all who came in touch with him with his strength of will and his cynical contempt for his fellow men. He had become minister-president in 1848 when Austrian power seemed to lie in ruins. Step by step he had recovered the fortunes of the dynasty, consolidating every achievement as he went along. Under his ministry a constitution, promulgated by the sovereign for the whole Hapsburg realm, launched "New Austria" as a centralized state. Hungarian resistance he crushed with Russian aid, and then held all political opposition in check by nineteen regiments of well-disciplined political gendarmerie. With his power firmly established in the whole Hapsburg realm, he turned in 1850 to build up Austrian hegemony in Germany, manœuvered Prussia into an impossible political and military position, set the stage to crush her as he had crushed Hungary, and then satisfied himself with merely diplomatic triumph at Olmütz. This was no longer the statecraft of Metternich in which it had been an axiom that diplomacy is a technique that cannot permit itself a triumph. Schwarzenberg's *Machtpolitik* was destined to turn German politics into such a naked struggle for power as had not been known since the time of Frederick the Great. His political ideal was to give permanent structure to Hapsburg hegemony in central Europe, and he was moving toward this with a steady stride when he was suddenly stricken down by apoplexy, and the hand of death removed him in April, 1852.

Metternich perversely refused to die, although his day was passed. He lived on until 1859, sometimes influencing policies directly and sometimes indirectly through younger men like Rechberg, whom he had trained in office, or through older men like the Baron Kübeck who wormed his way into the confidence of the Emperor in 1851. The politics of the Austrian court came, therefore, like the personality of the French Emperor, to be a mingling of the older spirit and the new. It displayed the weaknesses of both and the advantages of neither.

And what of the fair-haired youth who had been taken away from his studies to become Emperor at the age of eighteen? He had not known the ferment of the 1840's nor its issues, but he had known the horrors of 1848, and he never forgot that the army had saved the dynasty. He understood only the simplest political ideas, like that of a benevolent sovereign acting through ministers and officials of all kinds to bring happiness to all his people. He had an ardor for detailed and painstaking labor that was to make him the greatest bureaucrat of a great bureaucracy. But he lacked imagination; the lessons Schwarzenberg taught him he learned only in part.

It was fateful for Europe that the political technique of Schwarzenberg, so imperfectly continued at the court of Vienna, should have been learned so well by the young man who, at the time of the great Austrian's death, was starting his diplomatic career as Prussian delegate at the German federal assembly at Frankfurt. Otto von Bismarck entered upon this service in 1851 with a prejudice against all forms of liberalism so deeply rooted that he was prepared to coöperate with Austria in working to entrench the reaction in Germany.

At the court at Berlin the spirit of the older generation dominated. Frederick William IV, like Pius IX, was completely cured of all leanings toward liberalism and returned to an extreme mystical conservatism in which he was encouraged by a clique of devout Lutherans and legitimists who surrounded him—among them Leopold von Gerlach, who had helped to bring Bismarck forward.

Bismarck declared many years later in his memoirs that he had learned *Realpolitik* from Schwarzenberg, and that when he was at Frankfurt he kept some sentiment favorable to Austria until he saw copies of the Olmütz dispatches which convinced him that Schwarzenberg's policy had been indeed as it was reputed—to humiliate Prussia and then to destroy her. In Bismarck's own correspondence from the early Frankfurt period the drift into antagonism with Austria can easily be traced; in November, 1851, the harsh note begins to appear, and in January, 1852, he utters for the first time the threat that if Austria goes too far in the policy of developing the centralization of authority in the Confederation, Prussia will secede. But when he went to Berlin at this time he was disappointed to discover that Berlin regarded his Frankfurt disputes as "a mere bagatelle."[6]

The points at issue in Bismarck's Frankfurt years will be analyzed later. They had to do with an Austrian effort to develop the German Confederation in the direction of a federal system. His dispatches year after year constantly expatriated on the subtle ways in which Prussian sovereignty was threatened by the growth of all-German institutions, and constantly gave warning against the mischief of a policy of sentiment. When Manteuffel, the Prussian minister-president, a hard-working and unimaginative bureaucrat, spoke of German interests in 1854, Bismarck countered with the argument that "German interest was just a pretense used by a single state to designate what it wanted from another."[7] In 1876 he would say the same thing about Europe: "I have always heard the word Europe in the mouth of some one who wanted something from another which he dared not ask on his own account. . . .[8] As the years passed his attitude became more and more independent of the theoretical conservatism of Berlin. He proposed and carried a recognition of the coat of arms of 1848—the German rather than the Austrian eagle—as the seal of the Confederation, thus for the first time using the legacy of 1848 against Austria. And in 1857 he was writing to Gerlach that the policy of sentiment was "an exclusively Prussian possession in which there is no reciprocity of any kind," and advising that Prussia increase her influence among the German states by threatening them with a Franco-Prussian alliance. Whatever he may have been in these days, he was certainly no "German" patriot.

[6] *Bismarck, Die Gesammelten Werke* (Berlin, 1924-35), I, 127.

[7] A. O. Meyer, *Bismarcks Kampf mit Österreich am Bundestag zu Frankfurt* (Berlin, 1927).

[8] *Die Grosse Politik der europäischen Kabinette* (Berlin, 1922-1927), II, 88, 92. Quoted by A. O. Meyer.

The best of Bismarck's biographers utters a warning against all over-simplified expositions of the many-sided character of this remarkable man.[9] He was no shallow materialist, no mere Machiavelli. He felt terribly the contradiction of the divine order with the rule of blind force. The old Protestant piety to which he came as a youth meant much to him throughout life. He did not, like Gladstone, write essays on religion; nor find in it, as Lincoln did, a form in which the highest political purposes could be stated to a people; but when he left his estate at Varzin in July, 1870, to go to the warlike atmosphere of Berlin, two days before he edited the Ems telegram to start the war with France, he underlined in his desk calendar the text, *Blessed are the Peacemakers.*

In his early Frankfurt days he impressed all his colleagues with his industry and ability, but one of them described him in 1852 as being "more of a theoretician," while Count Thun was "a more practical man." The reason for this judgment lies, no doubt, in the nature of the cause Bismarck was learning to defend in Frankfurt —the anti-Austrian interpretation of the juridical character of the German Confederation.

In Piedmont as in Prussia a constitution was inherited from the years of revolutionary disturbance, but the Piedmontese constitution had been retained in its original liberal form, and was administered in a thoroughly English sense, with a ministry responsible to a parliament. In November, 1852, Count Camillo Benso di Cavour became for the first time prime minister. He had the solid capacities of Gladstone and a flair for diplomacy unexcelled by his contemporaries. He had been a journalist and a student of agricultural problems, and knew how to manage not only public opinion, but also finance.

At the close of the Crimean War, Cavour moved toward a secret but secure alliance with the revolutionists who were drifting away from the Mazzinian camp. He maintained close contact with La Farina, who was organizing Italian patriots in a National Society. "Come and see me whenever you like," said Cavour, "but come before dawn so that no one will recognize you. If I am asked ques-

[9] Erich Marcks: "Handschriftliche Materialien zur Geschichte Bismarcks in den 50 er Jahren," *Historische Zeitschrift*, CXLIV (3), 1931, 492-508.

tions in the chamber I shall deny you like Peter and say 'I know him not.' "[10] Schwarzenberg, Palmerston, Napoleon, and Bismarck repudiated some of the implications of the solidarity of monarchs against peoples, but Cavour repudiated all.

The most influential court at which the old policies survived in 1852 was the Russian court. Tsar Nicholas I, then in his fifty-fourth year, was close to the generation of the Congress of Vienna, and was loyal to many of its ideas. He retained as chancellor the aged Nesselrode, a holdover from the Congress itself. The other leaders of Europe were younger, except Palmerston. Schwarzenberg was fifty-two, Napoleon forty-four, Cavour forty-two, Bismarck only thirty-seven. Palmerston, though sixty-eight years of age, was still a boy. To him politics and diplomacy provided sporting events, played to the cheers of the British public; while to Nicholas they were a responsibility to God; to Napoleon, they offered the fulfillment of the destiny of his name; and to the others they were the instruments in the inevitable struggle among states for power. *Realpolitik*, the "new" politics of the 'fifties, contrasted with the politics of Metternich's day as realistic literature contrasted with romantic literature, as the ample synthesis of science contrasted with idealistic philosophy. It was not derived from realism in science nor in literature; it had its independent roots in the political and military experience of Europe; and yet it conformed to the larger cultural pattern.

III. THE SOLIDARITY OF PEOPLES

The change in the spirit of politics was equally evident in the democratic camp, where the leaders of 1848 were beginning to pass from the scene. By 1852, all those who had led the "people" against the "despots" had been given the choice of abandoning their principles or their homes. Some, like Kopp the great Alsatian chemist, who went into chemical manufacturing in England, turned to business and forgot politics. Others, like Pagenstecker, once a member of the Frankfurt assembly, wrote off their experiences in their memoirs. "The sad events of the years 1848, 1849, and 1850 completely cured me of my idealism."[11] The liberal jurist Bach passed

[10] A. J. Whyte: *Political Life and Letters of Cavour, 1848-1861* (London, 1925), 230.
[11] Erich Brandenburg: *Die Reichsgründung* (Leipzig, 1922), I, 375.

over from the revolutionary government in Vienna to the reactionary ministry of Schwarzenberg, and made it a point to attend mass conspicuously. Those who persisted in revolutionary aspirations and activities saw the world move away from them.

Each of the successive crises and calamities in the course of the revolutions had sent its quota of refugees streaming into exile. All roads led to London, for only the most innocuous and inactive were permitted to remain in Brussels or Switzerland, whither many had at first repaired. The refugee colony of London numbered several thousand, democrats and socialists of all nations, meeting together on the common ground of poverty and defeat, and making for themselves a world of illusion in which they kept up not only the petty quarrels left them by their brief day of power, but also some of the great phrases by which their lives had been shaped. French socialists and democrats who had fought each other across the barricades in the June Days now reproached each other across the table in a tavern kept by one of their number. The adherents of the different leaders competed like hotel runners for each new fugitive arriving on the Channel boat. Alexander Herzen, who arrived in London in August, 1852, has left a pathetic picture of their spiritual bankruptcy:

> They point to one event, the end of some event, they think about it, they go back to it. Meeting the same men, the same groups—in five or six months, in two or three years—one feels terrified: the same arguments are still going on, the same personalities, the same recriminations, only the furrows drawn by poverty and privation are deeper, jackets and overcoats are shabbier; there are more grey hairs, and everything about them is older and bonier and even more gloomy . . . and still the same things being said over and over again.[12]

But despite their spiritual discomfitures, they still spoke at times that great language of political idealism which was destined to go into obscurity with them and not to reappear as a living program for Europe until the days of Woodrow Wilson. Mazzini organized his Central Democratic Committee to lead the union of peoples against the union of monarchs, and drafted for it an exalted creed broad enough to comprehend all the radicalisms of the day.

[12] Herzen, *Memoirs* (London, 1926), IV, 168.

We believe in a social state with God and the law at its summit, the People, that is to say the free and equal citizens, at the base, progress for its norm, association as its means, devotion for its baptism, genius and virtue for torches to light the way.[13]

The thought that free peoples should present a common front to autocrats was not a new one, but in London it had a new setting. The Germans, Poles, Italians, and Frenchmen, even while they might be losing touch with conditions at home, worked constantly upon each other. They helped each other in relieving the distress of their fellow exiles and in raising money. Mazzini would ask Kossuth for help in soliciting funds from wealthy sympathizers; Kossuth would offer to sell half a million of Mazzini's one-franc revolutionary bonds to the Americans. The standard ritual of the many commemorative meetings and celebrations included the representation of as many nationalities as possible. And a standing point of dispute was the precedence of one country over another in revolution: should the great movement be started in France, Italy, or Hungary, or even in Greece or Spain? In this world of fantasy and conspiracy nationalism and internationalism dwelt together, surrounded by mists of democratic rhetoric. And the cause of the solidarity of peoples seemed to find a natural expression when the fugitives in London reached out their hands to the great democracy across the Atlantic.

In those days the American ear was tuned to the rhetoric of 1848; it was still sensitive to the repercussions of that glorious month of February which had brought almost simultaneously the treaty with Mexico and the revolution in Paris, the extension of American territory in the New World and American principles in the Old. There was a political interlude in which a few of the grand old men of American politics moved off the scene—Calhoun in 1850, Webster and Clay in 1852—and during this time the plight of the European democrats caught the imagination of the American public. The attitude toward European monarchs was no longer defensive, as in the days of the Monroe Doctrine, but truculent and challenging. In 1850 Secretary of State Webster sent the Austrian

[13] Zévaès, "Les proscrits français en 1848 à Londres," *Revolution de 1848* (1923-24), XX, 358.

government a note phrased like a stump speech, asserting that the democratic principle had given the American nation a territory beside which the possessions of the House of Hapsburg were "as a patch on the earth's surface."[14] In 1851 an American warship fetched Kossuth, chief public enemy of Austria, from his asylum in Turkey. In 1852 Kossuth toured America, holding mass meetings everywhere and seeking to convert American enthusiasm into money, arms, or help for the democratic cause in Europe. A faction of the Democratic party took the name of "Young America" and sought to make political capital out of the Kossuth madness by advocating American intervention in Europe in the cause of democracy; and while Kossuth was in America, the revolutionary exiles in London entertained a curious bargaining proposal.[15] Orense, leader of the Spanish Republicans, asked Mazzini in April, 1852, to transmit to the Americans through Kossuth an offer of the island of Cuba in exchange for aid to be given the Spanish revolutionary cause.

When Franklin Pierce was elected President in 1852, the Young America group was able to dictate appointments to key positions in the diplomatic service from which it could deal with the European democrats. John O'Sullivan, editor of the *Democratic Review*, and author of the doctrine of manifest destiny, took the Lisbon post; Pierre Soulé, a Frenchman born, but exiled by the Bourbons as a revolutionist and naturalized an American, went to Madrid; and George Sandars, who had once sold some old army muskets to Mazzini, took the London consulate. In 1853 it seemed that a flock of republican agitators had descended upon Europe in the guise of American diplomats. And Marcy, the new secretary of state, although out of sympathy with Young America, made his own gesture toward flaunting the principles of American democracy in the faces of the European monarchs when, in the spring of 1853, he advised all American representatives to appear at court functions so far as possible "in the simple dress of an American citizen."

[14] M. Curti, "Austria and the United States, 1848-1852," *Smith College Studies in History*, XI, 3 (1926).

[15] J. W. Pratt, "The Origin of 'Manifest Destiny'," *American Historical Review*, XXXII (1927), 795-798; M. Curti, "Young America," *American Historical Review*, XXXII (1926), 34-55.

Through 1853 and early 1854 the American consulate at London and the American legation in Madrid were headquarters for revolutionary groups. It was at a dinner given by Consul Sandars that Garibaldi met Kossuth for the first time. It was there, and in the presence of the American Minister Buchanan, that a toast was drunk to the future alliance of the peoples of Europe and America. The consulate helped the exiles with their passport difficulties, and on one occasion a certain Victor Fronde, an adherent of the Ledru-Rollin group of French republicans, secured a passport as a bearer of American diplomatic dispatches and used it to carry to conspirators on the Spanish border an instruction to arrange the assassination of Napoleon III. Fronde's report was sent back to Ledru-Rollin under the protection of the seal of the American legation.[16] But Marcy in the state department was distressed at these improprieties and vetoed the policies of Young America. Nevertheless, Kossuth did not hesitate to guarantee to circles of conspirators in Italy immediate American recognition if they would only have the courage to rise.

This alliance of peoples was short lived. Within two years all hope or prospect of collaboration between the European democrats and the Americans had dissolved. The fantasy lived longest in Madrid, where Soulé, even in the summer of 1854 was bargaining with the Spanish revolutionists for the cession of Cuba, but in the autumn of that year, while the allied troops were beginning the siege of Sebastopol, the American diplomats from the courts of Spain, France, and England met at Ostend to formulate a policy in relation to Cuba. Their decision, the famous "Ostend Manifesto" of 1854, turned definitely away from collaboration with the revolutionists, and advised a straightforward offer to purchase the island from the Spanish government, and failing that, a possible resort to a war of conquest. The international solidarity of the democrats was going the way of the solidarity of the monarchs, who were by that time involved in the Crimean War.

From time to time there were risings and outbreaks, especially in Italy, but it became increasingly evident as the 1850's advanced that the exiles in London had ceased to lead any powerful popular

16 Amos Ettinger: *The Mission to Spain of Pierre Soulé* (New Haven, 1933).

forces on the Continent. A few of these men—Garibaldi, Karl Marx—were still to have a rôle to play in history, but most of them passed into the twilight in company with their ancient enemies, the statesmen of the school of Metternich.

IV. THE CENTRALIZATION OF THE MODERN STATE

Political history of the nineteenth century, following the interests of the publicists of the time, has devoted its attention far more closely and systematically to the history of legislative authority than to the history of administration. If the political organization of a parliamentary state be conceived as a cycle it appears that a people elects representatives, the representatives make laws and maintain in power a ministry, and the ministry, acting within the limits of its authority by means of an administration, returns upon the people the consequences of their lawmaking. It is evident that the last segment of this cycle has been accorded a much smaller place in modern European history than the first. The experience of the twentieth century has brought about a decline of confidence in parliaments, and is bringing about a corresponding shift in interest toward administration, though it must be confessed that political science has been more forward than history in shifting the focus of interest.

The history of administration includes a variety of subjects, such as the development of practices of appointment, tenure, promotion, and pay in the civil service, the allocation of functions, responsibilities, discretionary powers among the agents of the government, with more or less specialization and more or less latitude for local variation. The agents of the central government may be an unpaid local magistracy combining executive and judicial functions or a hierarchy of career men shifted from post to post and dependent for tenure and promotion on the fidelity with which they execute orders received through channels from above. The posts in administration may be the virtual monopoly of a number of dominant families, or may be open to any individual talent through a system of education and competitive examination. Compared with the history of parliamentary government the history of administration seems at first to be a complex mass of uncoördinated details. Yet it is *par excellence* the history of the European state. The "state" that Bismarck served was a state embodied in an administration alongside of which the "nation" was to him a nebulous and theoretical construction. The decisive rôle of nationalism in the nineteenth century was the product not only of its connection with territoriality, but also of its relations with this state machine. The nineteenth century witnessed a development of this machinery that may prove far more significant than the contemporary development of parliamentary institutions.[17]

Even while Ranke was confirming to the King of Bavaria the generalization that the fundamental problem of the day was the conflict of monarchic with popular sovereignty, a keener mind than his saw in the politics of the time a deeper reality, a more pervasive trend. Alexis de Tocqueville saw the conflict of thrones and peoples as an incident, and underlying it all the relentless march of the centralized state toward the realization of its omnicompetent claims and the establishment of an irresistible government apparatus. He reexamined the history of the first French Revolution, and in 1855 published in a monumental work his conclusion that the Revolution had not broken with the policies of the kings, but had rather fulfilled them. Not popular sovereignty, but centralization had been the achievement of revolutionary France, and as he looked out upon the Europe of 1855, he observed the same movement under way, as the monarchs

> all endeavor, within their own dominions, to destroy immunities and abolish privileges. They confound ranks, they equalize classes, they supersede the aristocracy by public functionaries, local franchises by uniform enactments, and diversities of authority by the unity of a central government.[18]

The political history of almost every country in the third quarter of the century showed something of this mechanizing or centralizing of the governing process. Just as the secret political police was a special development of the first half of the century, so an acceleration in the improvement of administration marked the

[17] W. Jellinek, *Verwaltungsrecht* (Berlin, 1928); F. J. Goodnow, *Comparative Administrative Law. An Analysis of the Administrative Systems, national and local, of the United States, England, France, and Germany* (New York, 1903).

[18] A. de Tocqueville, *L'ancien Régime et la Révolution* (Paris, 1856), I, chap. ii.

second half, and in this improvement the period of the reaction was a time of maximum change. The early 'sixties were more given over to experiments in federalism and provincial autonomy; the late 'sixties to parliamentary government, extended suffrage and military reorganization. The great day of administration was the authoritarian era of the early 1850's. Therefore, the story of developments in administration throughout the third quarter of the century may be included in a history of the politics of reaction without unduly distorting the account.

When a movement that takes centuries in its stride is observed in a scale of decades, there may appear a variety of seemingly disconnected events, each arising in a different environment from different immediate causes, and bearing no apparent relation to the others because the relationship is not contained within the narrow term of years. So it is with the development of the state apparatus in this quarter-century. Russia improved her law courts; England her police; The German Confederation, Austria, and England took measures to simplify their substantive law; England concerned herself with the problem of bringing her system of primary education nearer to the Prussian in completeness; Austria and Prussia sought to bring their local government nearer to the French model. Everywhere the corps of officials and the body of instructions under which they worked were expanded. On the technological side these changes were accompanied by the railroad and the telegraph. Francis Joseph was the first monarch to make a habit of using the telegraph for communications of all kinds. Politically they responded in some regions to the demand for protection from the menace of anarchy as it had been revealed in 1848 or as it threatened in Russia after 1855, in others to the need for new public services. In Austria during the 'fifties the ground was prepared for them by a liberal constitution and they were carried out in the name of autocracy; in Russia during the 'sixties they were prepared by an autocrat and carried out as a liberal reform. Even in Japan, where nothing in the background was related to anything in Europe, the forms of European administration (but not of parliamentary government) were taken over in their entirety in the revolution of 1867.

As de Tocqueville implied, it was France that had led the way in the development of the mechanically centralized administration, with an orderly ministry at the top dividing the affairs of state rationally among coördinate offices, and a state apparatus that touched each citizen in a standardized way through the prefect of the department and the appointed officials of the commune. England had worked out parliamentary government, central Europe had evolved a marvelous complex of provincial autonomies and confederative relationships, and Russia had exceeded all other states in her reliance upon the military establishment for purposes of civil government.

First among the political developments of the era of reaction was the sweeping victory of the French administrative system in Austria, and the rejection of the English parliamentary system in France as in all central Europe except Piedmont. The new formations crystallized suddenly in December, 1851, in the French *coup d'état* and the Austrian Sylvester Patent, a document issued by Francis Joseph on St. Sylvester's Day (December 31, 1851), declaring the semi-liberal constitution of 1849 null and void, and setting up new regulations in its place. On January 14, 1852, Louis Napoleon also set up his new regulations in the document that became the constitution of the Second Empire. Both these great states, France and Austria, entered the year 1852 with the foundations of authority newly planted at the center.

The two new autocracies were compelled to set themselves against two different kinds of resistance. In France there was the possibility of parliamentary resistance at the center; in Austria of provincial resistance at the extremities.

Napoleon III made few innovations in the territorial administration of the country. He gave to the prefects a more complete power of appointment, and held them responsible for controlling the voting in the elections to the *corps législatif*. According to de La Gorce a type grew up, the "prefect of the Second Empire," active, often doing good, but inclined to suspect everything that did not come from himself.[19] Never in the history of France did the members of the civil service enjoy a higher social position than during

[19] Pierre de La Gorce, *Histoire du Second Empire* (Paris, 1894-1905), I, 83.

this period. The administration was the foundation of the Second Empire; its legislature was hardly even a façade. In filling the lacuna at the center left by the dissolution of the legislative assembly, Napoleon had to exercise great care. He could not dispense entirely with an elected legislature. He therefore retained a *corps législatif*, but gave it very few powers. It could debate, without publicity, only upon texts laid before it, and had no power to amend or initiate. The power to initiate was left with an appointive senate, and the principal duties in preparing or amending legislative drafts fell to the council of state, a hard-working body that he picked out of comparative obscurity and restored to the brilliant place it had occupied in the system of the First Empire.

In Prussia the changes in administration were changes in emphasis rather than design. The liberal constitution brought with it a French-style ministry and a parliament with powers that did not define themselves till the constitutional crisis of 1862. The ministry, under the presidency of Robert Manteuffel, tightened the system of local government, bringing it nearer to the French model. Prussian local government had inherited from the era of Stein a resemblance to the English system of local autonomy; the crown appointed a *Landrath* from among three candidates presented by the people in each district. Under Manteuffel's ministry the participation of the people in the nomination was refused, and the nomination of burgomaster and Landrath transferred to the crown. These appointed magistrates nominated all local officeholders down to the parish beadle. Circulars forbade the officials to entertain political opinions contrary to those of the ministry. Thus the Prussian system came closer to the French.

In the English central government there persisted anomalies in the distribution of functions such as French administration had long abolished; but in England such evidences of the true continuity of political development were not only tolerated, but cherished. Thus the control of the army was divided among five independent offices: those of the secretary of war, the secretary of state for war, the ordnance board, the commander-in-chief, and the home office. There was friction among them, and wasteful incompetence, but reform was not forthcoming until the Crimean War revealed the weakness.

In the development of a civil service England made rapid steps in the 1850's and 1860's to bring her institutions up to the level of the French. In local affairs the "stipendiary" official, salaried out of the local rates, was replacing the volunteer magistrate, while in the central government the civil service examination was replacing patronage. In 1853 the members of parliament still monopolized the patronage, but recommended their favorites through the "patronage secretary" of the treasury. The appointments were made on the basis of political considerations. The candidate qualified by passing an examination and undergoing a period of probation, after which he took his place in the famous circumlocution office satirized by Dickens in *Little Dorritt*, along with the other members of the Tite Barnacle tribe. In 1853 the Macaulay report laid down the principles to be followed in examinations for the Indian service. Through the later 'fifties and 'sixties the examination system worked its way into use, pressed on by public exasperation at official incompetence in the Crimean War and by the increasing need for well-qualified men in the consular and colonial services. In 1870 an order in council laid down the rule of open competitive examination as the normal method of entrance into the permanent service.

At this time the French were using competitive examinations after special training in schools that prepared for each public service; the Germanic countries were using a qualifying examination based upon the university course in law; and the Russians were using no examination at all. The English system took up the competitive principle, like the French, but without the technical link between the educational system and the civil service that was established on the Continent. The higher education in England did not train for the civil service; it continued to train "gentlemen," and the civil service adapted itself to the university. The examinations were set in the subjects that were taught, rather than the subjects that were needed. So it came about that the English offices were staffed with a class of gentlemen more highly qualified in Greek and Latin prosody than could be found in the public services of any other country.

V. THE BACH SYSTEM

It was in Austria that the mechanizing of administration reached its zenith. The new Austrian autocracy was the product of two successive changes. The first was a liberal revolution of 1848-49 that destroyed local privileges and set up a central ministry in the French style, with the expectation that it would be responsible to a parliament; this was followed by the autocratic revolution of 1849-51, which salvaged all the advantages of the simplified ministerial system at the center and the leveling of juridical obstacles in the country, but left no place in the system for the representatives of the people. Although the constitution of 1849 provided for the calling of a central parliament, no measures had been taken to call it, and all the legislation from 1849 to the day of the Sylvester Patent had been issued "provisionally," as if pending the calling of this parliament. Now the Sylvester Patent closed out every prospect that a parliament would be called. This left no embarrassing lacuna to be covered by subterfuge as in France. Never in Hapsburg history had there been a central diet representing all the Hapsburg lands.

To aid in the preparation of legislation, there was established a council of state, with functions not unlike those of the council of the same name in Paris. It scrutinized drafts of laws, and offered advice to the sovereign. A fronde of old-line aristocrats and bureaucrats led by Baron Kübeck tried to give it a rôle more important than that of the ministers, and almost succeeded at the time of Schwarzenberg's death, but was checked by the industry of Alexander Bach.

The council of state, as a body possessing such powers as these, turned out to be a somewhat ephemeral tool of the absolutism of the 'fifties. Members of the ruling dynasty sat in it; it was a latent rival of the ministry, and showed some possibility of becoming a fifth wheel in the administration. In Prussia it had been established in the time of Frederick William but abolished in 1848; an unsuccessful attempt was made to revive it in 1852.[20] In Piedmont it dated from 1831, it was consultative until 1859, and then by decree was

[20] Bismarck, *Gedanken und Erinnerungen* (Stuttgart, 1898), II, 271.

given the function of a supreme court of administrative justice.[21] In France it had lived between the First and Second Empires as an administrative court, and to this rôle it returned under the Third Republic. In Austria after 1860 it grew into a parliament, but in the 1850's Austria felt no need of a parliament. All her political energies went into the building up of the French type of territorial administration over the varied populations of the Monarchy. This system, confirmed in the Sylvester Patent, came to be known as the Bach system.

The character of the Bach system may be evaluated by contrasting it to the arrangement in existence prior to 1848. In all parts of the Hapsburg Monarchy prior to that time the masses had been under the immediate patrimonial jurisdiction of the landed nobility. In all the crown lands except Hungary, that is to say in Bohemia, Moravia, Tyrol, Styria, etc., the imperial government had kept its hand on administration by means of a system of inspection and control, of which the territorial unit was the circle, and the administrative agent the *Kreishauptmann* (chief of circle), a genial tribune whose activity in protecting the peasants left a lasting tradition of official kindliness in the Austrian civil service.

In Hungary the administration had not been centralized; Joseph II had tried it but had failed. It remained, therefore, in the hands of the elected authorities of the *comitat*, dominated by the higher nobility. The reform movement of the 'forties, led by Széchenyi, Eötvös and Kossuth, had, in the name of Hungarian unity, attacked the autonomy of the *comitats*, and had, in the name of liberal democratic principles, assailed the privileged status of the high nobility. Reform laws built up the power of the Hungarian parliament as against the *comitats*, and of the smaller landed gentry as against the higher nobles. Thus a centralized parliamentary state was developing in Hungary to match the centralized administrative state that functioned throughout the rest of the crown lands. In neither part of the Monarchy were the masses in direct contact with the government.

When the revolutions of 1848 freed the serfs and destroyed

[21] A. C. Jemolo, "Il Consiglio di stato tra il 1848 e 1865," *Rivista di Diritto Publico e della Publica Admistrazione in Italia,* XXIII (1931), 440-449.

domainal jurisdictions, they brought the masses for the first time into active political life. The supreme problem of the Monarchy was to provide a channel by which this activity could be guided toward a sense of citizenship in the Hapsburg Empire. After several transitional experiments, the Bach régime undertook to solve the problem by extending the administrative state downward until it touched all the people, and outward to include all the Hungarian lands, where the older constitution was declared forfeited by rebellion. Since circle and *comitat* were units too large for such direct administrative contact, the district (*Bezirk*), roughly one-sixth the size of the circle, became the primary administrative unit. The extension of the administration in this way required so many officials that it became necessary to economize by combining administrative and judicial functions.

These district officials, who were combed out of the German and Bohemian crown land offices and spread over the Empire, were loyal, honest, tyrannical, and in their small way efficient. They would be sent down to some little backward village in Hungary to teach an almost illiterate staff the rudiments of official paper work. They struggled to keep their tax collecting and recruiting from falling in arrears. They labored in the midst of hostility, suspicion, and incompetence, for the displaced aristocrats whose functions they had usurped despised them as parvenus, and the population detested them as foreign meddlers. Often they were ignorant of the language of the district to which they were sent.[22] The minister of interior kept a firm hand on them, prescribing their clothes, and even the cut of their beards. The type was not peculiar to the Hapsburg Monarchy; it was the type of servant to which the modern state inevitably resorted whenever it could not entrust local government to the free action of the residents of a district. Wherever, as in Schleswig where Danes ruled Germans, or in Hungary where Germans ruled Magyars, a language barrier intervened between the official and the populace, the hard mechanical character of the system was seen at its worst.

All the way from the monarch at the top to the humble subject

[22] *Acht Jahre Amtsleben in Ungarn.* Von einem K. K. Stuhlrichter in Disponibilität (Leipzig, 1861).

at the bottom, the Bach system provided an unbroken chain of administrative instances. Nowhere in the system was there a foothold for a legal opposition. The diets of the crown lands went out of existence, the ancient constitution of the Kingdom of Hungary was declared forfeited by rebellion, and all that remained in the provinces were certain "consultative committees" made up of representatives chosen by the merchants, nobility, large landholders, and peasants to interpret their respective interests. These were the vestigial remnants of the old organs of provincial autonomy as the Napoleonic *corps législatif* was a remnant of the old legislative assembly. In its completeness, the centralization of the government of Austria was a *tour de force* unparalleled in nineteenth-century history. And the young man of twenty-one who assumed the vast responsibility of guiding this machine did not even know how unprecedented, how revolutionary, were the powers it gave him. Throughout the Empire his will was the sole source of law, his initiative supreme in the directing of policies. When Schwarzenberg died, Francis Joseph appointed no one in his place, but undertook himself to preside over the Council of Ministers.[23]

VI. LOCAL GOVERNMENT

England was historically the land of decentralized local government. The parish and the county were the historic units, the preservation of order and relief of the poor the principal responsibilities. In the course of the nineteenth century the pressure of demands for new public services increased the number and variety of the territorial units of local government, but without altering their fundamentally autonomous character. The Poor Law of 1834 authorized the creation of Poor Law Unions of parishes and introduced the principle of centralized supervision. In the 'fifties, 'sixties and 'seventies health districts, police districts, and finally school districts were organized throughout the land. The sanitary district was the political district in which the demographic facts of English urban concentrations of populations were first recognized. The central government was slowly drawn in as inspector and supervisor of

[23] J. Redlich, *Das Österreichische Staats- und Reichsproblem, Geschichtliche Darstellung der Inneren Politik der Habsburgischen Monarchie von 1848 bis zum Untergang des Reiches* (Leipzig, 1920-26), I.

local initiative. The change was continuous throughout the century, but one of the landmarks was the act of 1871, which established a local government board to supervise the activities of local government.

While the English local government system moved slowly toward centralization, a reverse movement toward decentralization and greater communal autonomy was getting under way on the Continent early in the 'seventies. The liberal tendencies in the French Empire led in 1866-67 to an extension of the functions of the elected departmental and municipal communes, and the Third Republic in 1871 allowed a committee of the departmental council to supervise the prefect. The Prussian system was altered in 1872 to leave more authority in local hands. When the Bach system collapsed in 1860, Schmerling reorganized Austrian local government in the spirit of autonomy, with freely elected officials charged with local duties. The shift was due in part to the influence of Rudolf von Gneist, who stands with Montesquieu and Benjamin Constant as a great interpreter of English political institutions to the Continent. Where Montesquieu had taught separation of powers and Benjamin Constant the system of ministerial responsibility, von Gneist preached the ideal of "self-government" by unpaid volunteer officials, under restraints imposed by the supremacy of the law, as enforced by an independent judiciary. The ideas of von Gneist led in central Europe not only to an increase in local autonomy, but also to the development of administrative law as a system controlling the action of bureaucrats.

In Russia, too, there was a movement toward local autonomy in the 'sixties, for that decade was the great era of the Russian *zemstvo*. The significant changes in Russian administration took place in consequence of the fundamental agrarian reform. The emancipation edict of 1861, like similar Austrian legislation in 1848, required the setting up of some local authority to fill the place left vacant when the serfs were released from the power of their owners. In the Russian administration four semi-independent systems coexisted at that time. The oldest was the military network of garrison regiments, under cover of which the civil bureaucracy had grown up. In 1817 Alexander I had set apart some of this force as a political gendarmerie, and in 1826 Nicholas had added a secret political police, the famous "third section" of the chancellery. The political gendarmerie and the third section worked together. The civil administration was independent of the army, but ordered with equal precision in a hierarchy of ranks, through which the civil servant rose, normally one grade every three years, to the highest offices of the state. The civil administration reached the people through the governor of the province and the district police office. The peasants had their own economic organization—the village commune and the canton or *volost* under their own peasant elders. All three of these coextensive systems were left intact by the emancipation edict, and the peasant organization was even strengthened. But there was another unit which the emancipation decree dissolved—the landholders' estate—a unit for purposes of tax collection and recruiting, in which the serf owner had maintained a petty responsibility which was now taken from him.

During the period of liquidation, while the lands were being divided between estate owners and peasants, "mediators," appointed from among the liberal landholding gentry, not only interpreted the emancipation decrees, but also fulfilled some of the functions of local government. The temporary arrangement in which they participated was dissolved between 1868 and 1874. In the meantime, Alexander in 1864 set up a permanent organization in its place, providing for local government and the administration of justice.

Under the ukas of 1864, local government initiative was vested in district and provincial *zemstvos* or councils, elected by peasants and gentry. In 1870 similar provisions were made for the setting up of urban councils. These local bodies received authority over schools, hospitals, bridges, roads, and similar matters, but had very little money to work with. It must be noted that in Austria and in Russia the system of free elective local governing bodies was not organically tied up with the bureaucratic machine, a situation which led in both countries to tension between the popular organs of local government and the agents of the central authority.

The Russian courts prior to 1864 were staffed with untrained magistrates, arranged in a multiplicity of jurisdictions through which endless appeals could be carried, and conducted in complete dependence upon the administration. Alexander in 1859 set a committee to work to plan a judicial reform. As the next years passed and the winds of liberalism blew with increasing force over Russia, the project came nearer and nearer to the best standards of western Europe. As finally proclaimed by the Tsar in 1864, the reform provided for an independent judiciary, with judges irremovable and separate from the administration, and juries to decide questions of fact. The courts were given their own bailiffs to enforce judgments, to render them fully independent of the police. Elected justices of the peace were to replace the police officials in deciding petty criminal and civil cases. The number of instances of appeal was reduced, and an effort made to bring trained legal talent to the bench. For a time the new judiciary took jurisdiction over some political causes from the third section.[24]

What the great reforms accomplished in the modernizing of Russian administration was brought about in central and southern Italy during the same decade as a consequence of the unification of the peninsula, and in Rumania and Serbia by the efforts of Alexander Couza and Michael Obrenovič. The publicists and politicians whose eyes were fixed upon the antithesis between parliamentary and despotic rule were often unaware of the magnitude of the changes in administration.

VII. THE ARMIES AND THE ADMINISTRATION

The armies of Europe gained great prestige from the events of the period from 1848 to 1852, but not as heroes defending the soil of the fatherland against foreign invaders. Their laurels came to them for their services in protecting the established order against subversion, and even though in a few instances this involved crossing a frontier, they emerged from the conflict as victors in a civil, not an international, war. Never was there a time when the armies of Europe seemed to be more completely given over to the function of maintaining order and less committed to the task of settling disputes between states.

In the military establishments of Piedmont, Prussia, and England,

[24] Comte Jean Kapnist: *Code d'organisation judiciare de l'Empire Russe de 1864* (Paris, 1893); Isaak Urysohn: *Das Verbrechen des Hochverrats im russischen Strafrecht geschichtlich und dogmatisch dargestellt* (Breslau, 1906), 23, 97.

in the early 'fifties, there were improvements intended to prepare for the contingency of a foreign war. But the most important innovations in these years were to be found in the relation of the army to the administrative apparatus of the state—as in the Austrian regiments of political gendarmerie, organized as a force to suppress sedition. Throughout central Europe measures were taken to define in legal terms the rôle of the army in the preservation of internal peace.

It was the established practice of governments from the most remote times to resort to the army to suppress internal disorders, but under the old régime of royal prerogative, and in the absence of a highly developed administrative system with minute rules, the practice required no special legal definition. In the eighteenth century the Germanic countries introduced a special military court procedure of *Standrecht* for times of civil disturbance. But the pattern of modern continental legislation was prepared in France. And wherever on the Continent citizens received constitutional rights, or civil administration was harnessed rigidly to its duties and powers, the old practices of military intervention were required to undergo a juridical baptism and be born again. To meet this need the governments of France, Austria, and the German states borrowed from international law the conception of the state of siege.

It was well established in international law that the commander of a garrison in a beleaguered city in time of war may take measures of precaution against resistance or treason within the gates, and assume for this purpose full police jurisdiction over civilians. During the great French Revolution a legal fiction had developed in France—that seditious areas nowhere near a theater of war might be proclaimed in a "state of war" or if the danger was extreme, in the more rigorous "state of siege." In the one case, the military authorities were to coöperate with the civilian; in the other, to supplant them. The device was upset by the court of cassation in 1832, but reëstablished by the legislative assembly of the Second Republic in 1849. Napoleon III made use of this law to achieve his *coup d'état*, imprisoning under its terms the legislators who had voted it.

The corresponding legislation in Austria dates from 1849,[25] a provision for the suspension of civil rights; in Prussia from 1849 and 1851; and in the other German states from the same era. The innovation was not the use or granting of extraordinary powers to the army, but the defining of the powers that were granted.[26]

In Russia the need for a legal definition of extraordinary police and military powers developed more slowly. A "state of siege" was proclaimed in Poland in time of peace in 1862, and extraordinary powers defined by ministerial decree in connection with strikes in 1870 and 1871, but the full systematic development of the Russian law did not take place till 1881. And in the meantime the other jurisdictions on the Continent had amplified their rules, departing from the simple fiction of a state of siege by distinguishing between a mild and rigorous use of it. This distinction appeared in Austrian law in 1868 in connection with the suppression of the nationalist agitation of the Czechs, and in Germany as a part of the drive against the socialists in 1878. It was included in the Russian *ukas* of 1881.

England did not enact comprehensive laws for emergency powers in time of crisis until 1920, but throughout the mid-century she had in Ireland a problem of government not unlike that which troubled the Austrians. The army was regularly used to protect the polls in general elections in Ireland[27] and some exceptional law applying to the island was on the statute book most of the time. From 1848 to 1856 the *crime and outrage (Ireland) act* ran on by annual renewals; it was followed by the *peace preservation (Ireland) act* till 1871; and then the severe provisions of the *protection of life and property (Ireland) act* gave the police of a "proclaimed" area the right to imprison suspects without trial.

There was always latent in the relation of the army to the civil service a possibility of bitter antagonism. In Poland and in Italy the occupying army seemed to be a state within a state, using its

[25] Austria had actual war on her hands and was introducing a civil rights code, therefore her legal provision was for a suspension of civil rights; and Austrian jurisprudence knew *Ausnahmegesetz* instead of *Belagerungszustand*.

[26] C. M. Clode, *The Military Forces of the Crown: Their Administration and Government* (London, 1869); T. Reinach, *De l'État de Siège. Étude Historique et Juridique* (Paris, 1885).

[27] See speech by the Earl of Cardigan, Hansard, CXXIV, 30.

own system of courts, levying charges upon cities for revenue purposes, and exasperating the population with military cruelties. A controversy over the respective spheres of action of army and civil government was chronic in Poland. In Austria it was disastrous. The army was very reluctant to yield the powers it was exercising under the state of siege in the 1850's. It contrived to prolong this situation in Italy and Hungary until 1854. The rivalry was intensified and collaboration made more difficut by the action of the Emperor in withdrawing the portfolios of army and police from the council of ministers, so that these matters were in his immediate charge and the war ministry ceased for a time to exist. The general adjutant of the army would not even discuss his budget with Finance Minister Bruck. "What a thing costs we know as well as you; it is your business to get the money."[28] This system wrecked Austrian finance, and foreshadowed the paralyzing rivalry of the twentieth century between ministry and general staff.

By 1871 the European armies had changed greatly in purpose and structure. The rôle of the army as a suppressor of sedition had been eclipsed by its rôle in international war. And of the two principal types of army organization—the *cadre* army with a reserve mobilized in war and the long-term professional army,—the former had triumphed. This *cadre* system was an invention of Austria during the Napoleonic wars. It was imported into Prussia in 1814, and combined with a militia system by which the reserves, having passed through army training, entered the *Landwehr*, a kind of local militia under elected officers. The *Landwehr* had some resemblance to the French national guard. The revolutions of 1848 proved that the *Landwehr* was politically unreliable and the mobilization of 1850 that it was of little value from a military point of view. For this reason the Prussian Prince-Regent and his adviser, General von Roon, proposed to change the rôle of the *Landwehr* and make military service at once more universal and more professional. The army reform led immediately to the great constitutional conflict in Prussia, and ultimately to imitation by other states. France and Russia, which had used the long-term enlistment system, revamped

[28] Walter Rogge, *Österreich von Világos bis zur Gegenwart* (Leipzig & Wien, 1872-73), 295.

their army organization to bring it into line with the Prussian model (1871-1878). The Hapsburg Empire extended its conscription system (1868). Meanwhile, railroads had altered mobilization methods and weapons had been improved. Victory in war had been proved profitable, and the political foundations of the armed peace had been laid.

Army, administration, parliaments, and the unified law codes were the four organs of state centralization. They marched on together. Absolute monarchy as such did not necessarily imply centralization. It was increasingly evident in Europe that monarchic sovereignty was not quite the same thing as state sovereignty. Austin in England and Bluntschli in Germany helped to complete the transfer of this sovereignty concept from the personality of the monarch to the impersonality of the states. The state was very much more than the patrimony of the ruler. When Bismarck defended the rights of Prussia against the German Confederation in the diet at Frankfurt, when Cavour asserted the right of the Piedmontese state to subject the clergy to the lay courts in defiance of the Church, these statesmen were concerned with the sovereignty and omnicompetence of a territorial state, not with the relation of a monarch to a people. The same change in emphasis and meaning appeared as the attention of the army was diverted from the maintenance of thrones to the defence or extension of state frontiers. This institutional development in political society—whether it came in the parliamentary, administrative, or military organ—had the effect of making the boundaries between states stand out clearly and distinctly. The state gathered its forces behind its frontiers.

What might be seen in administration as the leveling process that revoked the special functions and privileges of noble landholders, what appeared in jurisprudence as the extension of the principle of equality before the law, in the army as universal military service, in the legislative branch of the government as the spread of the modern parliament, all these changes had a common denominator in the completion of the shift from personality to territoriality as the foundation of political society.

To illustrate: the cleric in Piedmont could no longer, after the Siccardi laws of 1850, claim for his cloth a special legal position in criminal action; an Englishman could not, after the bankruptcy act of 1861, expect to come under a special kind of law in bankruptcy proceedings;[29] the Saxon and Székler inhabitants of the same comitat in Transylvania could no longer, after the change in law from 1848 to 1868, maintain their old separate non-territorial national political organizations, but had to merge in a common citizenship. Political rights and duties were becoming the uniform resultants of domicile within a given territory. Was it then surprising that nationality itself should become a territorial concept?

The secular dogmas of liberalism and nationalism were in line with the actual development of government when they dealt with the mechanical and material basis of politics. Just as the socialists and the classical economists unconsciously agreed with each other in their assumptions regarding the primacy of the commodity and the potency of the automatic forces of the market or of the class struggle in economic life, so the liberals and the bureaucrats, the leaders of nationalities and the ministers of non-national states were all in accord in their underlying belief that political mechanics, whether bureaucratic or parliamentary, and territorial frontiers, whether they enclosed national or non-national states, were the basic realities of politics.

[29] Prior to 1861 there was one bankruptcy law for merchants, another for non-merchants in England.

Chapter Eight

THE CONCERT AND THE CRIMEAN WAR (1852-1856)

I. FEDERATIVE POLITY IN EUROPE

In primitive languages there will often be found a paucity of words with broad meanings. There will be a word for spearing-fish-through-the-ice, but none for fishing, a word for hunting-deer-with-bow-and-arrow, but none for hunting. The historian finds a similar limitation in some parts of the vocabulary of political science. The descriptive vocabulary seems to be built around the concept of sovereignty. The many structures which do not conform to the pattern of the centralized and sovereign state are given a variety of names, such as federation, confederation, *Bundesstaat, Staatenbund,* personal union, real union, amphyctyony, concert, states-system, league, entente, and alliance.

Corresponding to the constitutional law fiction of absolute state sovereignty there stands the international law fiction of absolute state equality, in terms of which dependencies, protectorates, autonomous republics, dominions, semi-sovereign states, spheres of influence, and great powers appear only as exceptions to a norm. There is no word that searches for an element common to these formations. The word "state" serves to hold in focus every political fact that divides occidental political society into its mutually hostile groups, and to blur over the facts that would yield another reading.

The state concept has served, moreover, to obscure some of the significance of the change from the monarchic to the popular state, in respect of both international and internal law. State sovereignty was territorial, monarchic sovereignty personal. Roscoe Pound has rightly charged that

> Nineteenth century historical thinking tended to keep international law in the net of the personal duties of personal sovereigns transformed into the personified duties of personified peoples. It discouraged all

creative thinking toward devising means of reconciling the activities and harmonizing the interests of states.[1]

When Voltaire wrote history in the eighteenth century, he could start with the assumption that Europe is a republic; when Hans Kelsen and Alfred Verdross expound jurisprudence in the twentieth century, they can portray the world's legal fabric as a unity in which different political societies—whether states, provinces, communes, or cities—enjoy different degrees of self-determination under one great common law.[2]

Twentieth-century political thinking has also developed a doctrine called "pluralism," which emphasizes the self-determining character of institutions such as churches, labor unions, and business corporations, which exercise authority not derived from the state. From the pluralist standpoint, society is normally federative in structure and the anomaly is the claim of the modern state to omnipotence and omnicompetence.

There were many men in the mid-nineteenth century whose thought flowed into this federative pattern. Otto von Gierke, from whose monumental work on German corporative law the critics of sovereignty have drawn their inspiration, published his first volume in 1868. A whole generation of pamphleteers campaigned in the 'fifties and early 'sixties for the federative reconstruction of Europe. Among them were Constantine Frantz in Germany, Franz Palaćky in Bohemia, Giuseppe Ferrari in Italy; they were the heroes of a lost cause, and events closed over their heads.[3] They were of the same family as mutualist socialists like Proudhon, who gave way before the state-centralist socialists of the Marxian school. They had points of contact with Döllinger, Acton, Strossmayer, who opposed centralization in the Church. Proudhon championed what he called "Federalism," not only in the economic sphere, but in the

[1] Roscoe Pound, "Philosophical Theory and International Law," *Bibliotheca Visseriana,* 1923, I, 87.

[2] Hans Kelsen, "Les rapports de système entre le droit interne et le droit international public," *Académie de Droit, Recueil des Cours 1926* (Paris, 1927), IV, 231-331.

[3] Waitz: *Wesen des Bundesstaats,* 1853; Frantz: *Quid Faciamus Nos* (Berlin, 1858); F. Palaćky: *Oesterreichs Staatsidee* (Pragüe, 1866); P. Proudhon: *Le Féderalisme* (— -1860). These are high points in an extensive literature. See also Nicolas Bourgeois: *Les théories du Droit International chez Proudhon. Le Féderalisme et la Paix* (Paris, 1927); Monti, *L'idea Federalistica del Risorgimento Italiano* (Bari, 1922) gives an estimate of Ferrari.

political sphere as well. In a pamphlet on federalism in 1860, he warned the Italians that a centralized state would destroy liberty. Acton was almost alone among English thinkers in his appreciation of the insufficiency of ordinary liberal political ideas for the solution of the intricate problem of nationality. In 1860, when Francis Joseph was trying to federalize the Monarchy, Acton wrote:

> The problem presented to the government of Austria is higher than that which is solved in England because of the necessity of admitting national claims. The parliamentary system fails to provide for them, as it presupposes the unity of the people. Hence in those countries in which different races dwell together, it has not satisfied their desires, and is regarded as an imperfect form of freedom. It brings out more clearly than before the differences it does not recognize, and thus continues the work of the old absolutism, and appears as a new phase of centralization. In those countries, therefore, the power of the imperial parliament must be limited as jealously as the power of the crown, and many of its functions must be discharged by provincial diets, and a descending series of local authorities.[4]

In this and the following chapters the expression "federative polity" will be used as a term intended to deprive the sovereignty concept, whether personal or territorial, of preëminence in the language of political history. It is to be taken as opposite in its implications to such concepts as "sovereignty" and "power." The use of the expression does not imply that sovereignty and centralization were lacking in decisive importance in European politics; it serves only to designate the alternative pole of political orientation. Professor Merriam, in analyzing the power concept, writes:

> It is not infrequently found that political relations flow on most smoothly when juristic exactness hibernates, when the question of ultimate authority is not too sharply raised . . . and why should not political twilight be recognized as a useful reality as well as the sharper rays of high noon?[5]

This "twilight zone" of the juridical theory of the state is the

[4] J. E. E. Dalberg Acton, *The History of Freedom and other Essays* (London, 1907), 296-297.

[5] C. E. Merriam, *Political Power. Its Composition and Incidence* (New York and London, 1934), 54; see also R. Emerson, *State and Sovereignty in Modern Germany* (New Haven, 1928).

high noon of a theory of European polity as a whole. The jurists have labored to make fine distinctions between *Bundesstaat* and *Staatenbund*, federation and confederation, regarding them as anomalous political forms. The expression "federative polity" is here presented as a concept covering both *Bundesstaat* and *Staatenbund*, federation and confederation, which are assumed to be normal. The Concert of Europe, the German Confederation, the British Commonwealth of Nations, the League of Nations, are examples of federative polity. The realization of federative polity is, like the realization of centralization and sovereignty, a matter of degree. The complete realization of the full claims of sovereignty leaves only anarchy between sovereign states; the complete realization of federative polity leaves no sovereign organization anywhere. Neither ideal has been completely realized in European politics, but Europe has at one time been nearer to the one pole, at other times nearer to the other pole.

If the expression *federative polity* be used in this broadest sense, and if the distinction between the personal sovereignty of a monarch and the territorial sovereignty of a state be kept in mind, the political structure of Europe in the mid-nineteenth century must be described as predominantly federative.

There were, to be sure, two political patterns on the Continent—the one furnished by France, the other by the Germanic states. In France and four other states (Spain, Portugal, Piedmont, and Greece), sovereignty was undivided. One monarch ruled by one title over one territory. In such a state a republic could succeed a monarchy, a monarchy replace a republic, and the powers of the people, acting through parliaments, could be extended or contracted without introducing territorial difficulties. But most states of Europe more nearly resembled the Germanic model.

In some cases one sovereign ruled over several territories by different titles and by different laws (*e.g.,* Norway-Sweden, Denmark-Schleswig-Holstein, Russia-Poland-Finland, the Austrian states-system before 1849). In such states any transfer of powers from monarch to people brought immediate territorial complications, for it became necessary to decide whether the "sovereign people" of a region like the Hapsburg Monarchy should be a conglomeration of all inhabitants united in one body-politic, or a series of separate units, the Hungarian people being sovereign in Hungary, the Bohemians in Bohemia, and so on.

Elsewhere princely powers were held subject to external limitations, as in Serbia, Wallachia, Moldavia, those Italian states that were treaty-bound to Austria or policed by armies of occupation, the German states, and those part-German states (Austria, Prussia, Denmark, Netherlands), some of whose territory was within the German Confederation and some outside it.

The federative principles exemplified in the politics of central Europe were very close to the principles of diplomacy that had sustained the international system of the great powers. These two sets of principles had lived together and they both went down together. The contrast between the French unitary state and the Germanic states-system was paralleled at the international level by the contrast between the dictatorial imperialism of the first Napoleon and the collaborative methods of the great Austrian chancellor, Metternich. The victory of the grand alliance in 1815 had entrenched in European practice the coöperative techniques of coalition, especially on the part of the Austrian, Prussian, and Russian courts.

The peculiarity of the language of political science has made it difficult for the historian to do justice to the states-system of Metternich, for the organization of the five great powers (Russia, Austria, France, Britain, and Prussia, in order of population), with all its rich content of loyalties, ideals, traditions, and interest alignments, is portrayed in juristic terms as a bare alliance-treaty group, formed among equal states by the second treaty of Paris for the purpose of maintaining the territorial provisions of the Vienna settlements and keeping the Bonapartes off the French throne. Yet these treaties, as they were amplified by the admission of France in 1818 and tested in crises like those over the policy of intervention in Italy and Spain, or the creation of Greece and Belgium, amounted to a European constitution.

The unwritten constitutional law of Europe expanded and enriched the meaning of two fundamental concepts of diplomacy:

concert of Europe and *balance of power.* To these concepts many different meanings have been attached. Sometimes they are understood psychologically, as if they were descriptive of two attitudes, conciliatory and truculent, and then appraised as if one were the special instrument of peace, the other of war. But *balance of power* in 1852 did not mean (as it meant in 1914) a balanced alignment of hostile states against each other; it meant rather that no state could obtain aggrandisement without the consent of the others. This was the precise definition given by Lord John Russell in the debate on the militia bill in 1852. It was a conception which, in the field of European relations, resembled the arrangement between Slave and Free States in the American Union, by which additions to the tier of slave states were balanced by additions to the tier of free states. The concert was the instrument by which the five powers gave their consent to the acts of a state. Not until the 1860's did Europe see great territorial changes take place unratified by a conference. If the expression *balance of power* referred to a territorial situation, the term *concert of Europe* referred to a legislative authority and a conference procedure.

The German Confederation was like a small corporation embedded in a great one. Its executive powers were exactly like those of the concert; it could and did on occasion authorize a member state to send an army to enforce its will over a recalcitrant population (Holstein and Hesse). In German jurisprudence this was called *federal execution*; in European jurisprudence, a similar procedure had been called in Metternich's time intervention or interposition.

Neither the conference procedure of the concert, nor semi-parliamentary procedure of the diet of the German Confederation excluded the tensions of rivalry, the flux of alignment and realignment, nor the isolation of one member by the others. Among the shifting alignments of the great powers certain groupings and antagonisms were more stable than others. In the Iberian peninsula English influence was aligned against French; in Italy, French against Austrian; in Germany, an Austro-Prussian combination overawed the middle states before 1848, and Austria with the middle states isolated Prussia after 1850. For Europe as a whole the three eastern courts were often grouped against France and England, where the political atmosphere was more liberal. Sometimes England was isolated, sometimes France. This was the European system as it had survived forty years of peace. Authority was arrayed in a continuous series of instances from the European concert at the top to the patrimonial landlord at the bottom. German Confederation and European concert in the nineteenth century, like British Commonwealth and League of Nations in the twentieth, reflected each other, each challenging the assumption that there is no intermediate ground between complete independence and complete subjection. The political experience of the Germanic states-system was rich in precedents to serve an international society. The political institutions of Europe were not made subject to the tragic prejudice that the independence of states and the maintenance of international order are antithetic.

Yet somehow, in the 'fifties, the great monument began to crumble. It was in some way undermined or thrown out of equilibrium. It came crashing down, and from the ruins emerged in the next decade the new national states of Italy and Germany, and the international system of the armed peace.

II. DISRUPTIVE FORCES IN THE CONCERT

The concert was still in working order in 1852, when a conference at London was deciding upon the succession to the Danish crown and liquidating the dispute between the Schleswig-Holsteiners and the Danes. "Europe," acting through the five powers, decided that Prince Christian of Glücksburg should succeed to the Danish throne on the death of the childless Frederick, and that the rights of the Schleswig-Holsteiners, under the crown, should stand unimpaired. Neither the constitutional law of the Danish state nor the house law of the Danish royal family was final as to who should rule in Denmark. That was a matter for Europe to decide, and Europe, through the concert, decided it. Twelve years later, another London Conference deliberated vainly on the same Danish question, and proved itself powerless. What had intervened between 1852 and 1864?

One disruptive event was the establishment of the Second Empire in November, 1852. The four powers that won at Waterloo had pledged themselves in the name of the most Holy and Indivisible Trinity that the family of Bonaparte should be perpetually excluded from supreme power in France. When Louis Napoleon seized supreme power in December, 1851, his *coup d'état* not only destroyed the constitution of France, but challenged the constitution of Europe. How would the challenge be met?

Palmerston on impulse, Schwarzenberg in expectation of reward from Napoleon, and the Tsar out of his hatred for republics and championship of the cause of order, gave recognition to the *coup d'état*. The Tsar wrote a kindly letter expressing the hope that Divine Providence might aid his "great and good friend, the Prince-President, to close the era of revolutions in France." It was possible to reconcile this recognition with the terms of the treaty of 1815 on the ground that a mere Prince-President did not possess "supreme power" in the sense that a legitimate autocrat possessed it. But what if Napoleon should change his title to that of Emperor?

The Tsar examined this prospect from the standpoint of a romantic legalism that made small things loom large. He thought it would be possible to recognize even an Emperor Louis Napoleon as a transitory personal exception, without receding from the treaties of 1815 or acknowledging the existence of any such thing as a Bonaparte dynasty in France. Notes circulated from court to court through the spring of 1852. Schwarzenberg, with his tongue in his cheek, agreed and proposed that a successor to Napoleon should also receive the benefit of transitory personal recognition. This was the point reached in April, when death removed the great Austrian from the scene. When, in November, Napoleon confronted Europe with his new title, the principle of legality so jealously guarded by the Tsar was seen to hang by a thread. In the Tsar's opinion, it would be possible to recognize a "Louis Napoleon, Emperor of the French," but if the title assumed were "Napoleon III" the numeral would imply the existence of a dynasty, from which it would follow that the Bourbons who signed the treaties of 1815 were usurpers:

What becomes of the territorial boundaries? . . . All public law is undermined or at least called in question, and Europe will no longer know upon what principles she exists.[6]

When Napoleon refused to admit the force of the Tsar's juridical metaphysics, and persisted in using the name Napoleon and the numeral III, the Tsar resorted to one final gesture in which a stalwart championship of the vestiges of European legality merged with an expression of personal vanity. He refused to address the new emperor as "my brother," after the custom of the family of monarchs, but continued instead the presidential salutation "great and good friend." Napoleon backed down, accepted the credentials of the Russian ambassador in this form, and then took occasion, in January, 1853, to reply to Nicholas' snub. In announcing his betrothal to Eugénie de Montijo, he referred to himself as "a man carried by the force of a new principle to the exalted level of the old dynasties." The new principle was the principle of the plebiscite, and beyond it lay the principle of nationality. Though a short war scare followed, Europe quickly showed a disposition to accept at their face value Napoleon's assurances that "The Empire means Peace."

And yet it came about within two years that the great peace was broken and that great powers fought each other for the first time since Waterloo. It was a strange war, indeed, arising haphazard from a series of trivial causes, and fought in an out-of-the-way corner of the world, where it did not greatly interfere with more important affairs. The war in the East not only broke the spell of peace, but let loose two new forces of movement which, together with Napoleon's "new principles," destroyed the foundation of the concert. The new forces were the Prussian fear of losing great-power status, and the change in Russian foreign policy that made Russia after 1856 a revisionist power.

III. "CIVIS ROMANUS SUM"

The issue that gave rise to the Crimean War, while trivial in itself, was illustrative of a general development of international law and

[6] A. M. Zaionchkovskii, *Vostochnaia Voina, 1853-56* (St. Petersburg, 1908-13), I, 242.

politics. This development can be understood if contrasted with the international politics of the Metternichean age, for the European states, while perfecting their internal administrative systems, began to reach out to exert authority over, and give protection to, individuals outside their frontiers.[7]

The doctrine of extradition, and the network of treaties applying to it, was then in the first stage of vigorous growth. In Europe the controversy over the surrender of Hungarian fugitives on Turkish soil served to clarify the doctrine, especially the distinction between political and non-political offenses in the matter of extradition. Related to the doctrine of extradition was the so-called right of asylum. Demands were made upon Belgium, Switzerland, Piedmont, and even England to expel revolutionists from their soil or to suppress their activities. When Metternich attacked revolution on foreign soil he intervened to overturn revolutionary governments; but Schwarzenberg was trying to extend police power over individuals through the international system. The American Union was being strained at the same time by the fugitive-slave law, which permitted agents acting under federal law to pursue individual slaves into the free states. England was sending her navy to enforce against individual ship captains the laws and treaties suppressing the African slave trade. To these efforts to pursue individuals on foreign soil there was conjoined a corresponding effort to protect them. In 1853 an American warship in the harbor of Smyrna threatened to fire upon an Austrian warship in demanding the surrender of the Hungarian refugee, Martin Koszta, who had taken out American citizenship papers. These controversies resembled the issue raised during the Napoleonic wars over the impressment of seamen, but in some ways they were more far-reaching, especially when it became a matter not alone of protecting the persons of citizens abroad, but of protecting their property as well.

The controversies over the protection of the property and privileges of individuals on foreign soil foreshadowed the juridical techniques of late nineteenth-century imperialism. It was only in 1848 that the British foreign office formulated a policy calling for diplomatic

[7] E. C. Stowell, *Intervention in International Law* (Washington, 1921).

intervention on behalf of the English holders of defaulted foreign bonds. The principle was stated with Palmerstonian thoroughness:

> . . . If the Government of one country is entitled to demand redress for any one individual among its subjects who may have a just but unsatisfied pecuniary claim upon the government of another country, the right so to require redress cannot be diminished merely because the extent of the wrong is increased, and because, instead of there being one individual claiming a comparatively small sum, there are a great number of individuals to whom a very large amount is due.[8]

Here was the principle that would take the English and French into Mexico in the 1860's, and into Egypt in the 1880's, and form an important link between world finance and world politics in the age to come. Cobden feared that the principle would make England the bum-bailiff for European creditors everywhere.

Far more striking was the dramatic statement of the principle of property protection abroad made in 1850 by this same Palmerston, who, fighting French influence at the Greek court, had made use of the pecuniary claims of Englishmen to embarrass a Francophil Greek cabinet. When affairs came to a crisis, he sent the British fleet to blockade the port of Piræus to force the payment of the padded claims of one Don Pacifico, a Jewish merchant who happened to have been born on British soil. When attacked in parliament for this free use of the fleet in a small matter, Palmerston replied with one of the greatest speeches of his political life, proclaiming the right of a British subject to say *civis Romanus sum* in whatever land he might be, "confident that the watchful eye and strong arm of England will protect him against injustice and wrong." The Blue Books of the 1850's indicate how often the watchful eye and strong arm were called upon to do their work. In 1856 Fong Ah Ming at Canton, owner of the lorcha *Arrow*, with a claim upon British protection much slighter and a cause less just than Don Pacifico's, furnished the occasion for the second Anglo-Chinese war.

The principle could also be used against England. In 1853 an American warship bombarded and fired the British port of Greytown on the Mosquito Coast because the citizens refused to pay for damages they had done to the property of Vanderbilt's Acces-

[8] *British and Foreign State Papers* (1852-53), 385-386. Circular of January, 1848.

sory Transit Company. Cavour, in 1853, was making political capital of the protection of the property of naturalized subjects of Piedmont against sequestration by the Austrian government. At the same time the Austrian government, partly to please its own Slavic subjects and partly to increase its influence over the Christian populations of the Balkans, was intervening in Constantinople to protect the political rights of the Montenegrins, while the French and Russian governments interfered on behalf of the religious privileges of the Latin and Orthodox Churches.

IV. THE QUESTION OF THE HOLY PLACES

The question of the Holy Places as raised by French diplomacy in 1850 was significant in its triviality—that an affair so small should wreck the concert was an evidence that the new generation of statesmen was not able successfully to manipulate the political machinery devised by the old generation. The question began as a defense of clerical interests by France; became a question of prestige between France and Russia; then in March, 1853, a Russian juridical experiment in the possibility of using the protection of the subjects of a foreign state as a means of controlling its government; in April it became a conflict between English and Russian diplomacy over balance of power and Turkish sovereignty, in which the element of force gradually supervened over the element of conciliation and direct action over European mediation. Then came the moment when public opinion, in September at Constantinople, in December at London, forced the hands of governments. And finally, the last word that forced the issue between peace and war was an instruction to the fleet in the Black Sea. It required thirteen months to move from ultimatum to war—a transit the twentieth century learned to make in as many days.

The controversy which was to have such curious repercussions originated over the use of the buildings which mark the reputed sites of the birth of Jesus at Bethlehem, his vigil in the garden of Gethsemane, and his burial at Jerusalem. In these places the priests of all Christian sects sought to worship. Chateaubriand has left a vivid description of their joint occupancy of the Church of the Holy Sepulchre in Jerusalem. He saw them "niched like pigeons"

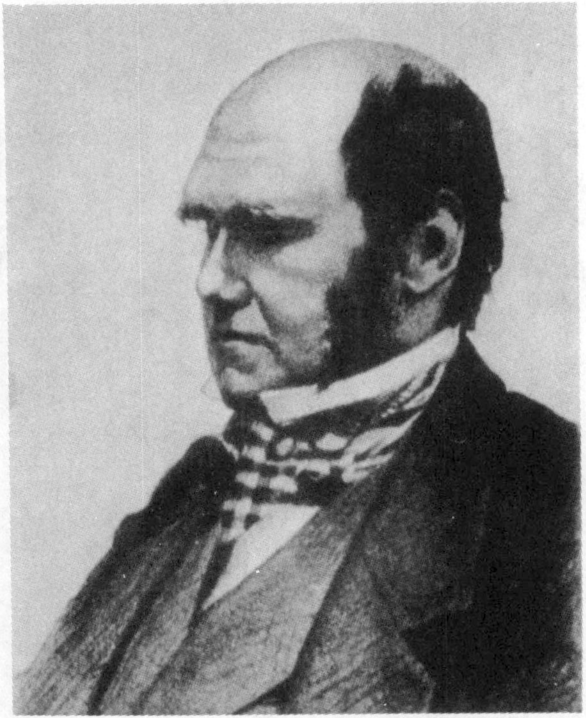

1. Charles Darwin

2. Michael Faraday

Leaders in Natural Science

3. Herbert Spencer

4. Richard Cobden

The Science of Society and Political Economy

5. Ferdinand Lassalle

6. Karl Marx

Founders of Socialism

7. Charles Dickens

8. William Makepeace Thackeray

9. Gustave Flaubert

10. Ivan Turgenev

Masters of the Realistic Novel

11. Richard Wagner

12. Giuseppe Verdi

Leaders of the World of Music

13. La Source (Ingres, 1856)
Classical Idealism

14. La Source (Courbet, 1868)
Realism

15. Daumier portrays the battle of idealist and realist

16. Satirizing a Courbet painting in the Salon of 1869

The cartoonist satirizes: "It is our duty to warn the painter of Ornans that if he continues along this line, the most docile cows will refuse to enter his landscapes. See the poor animals on the right! Are they suffering from an inflammation? Yes or No? Too much air, my deat master, too much air!"

The controversy over realism in art

17. The Wrestlers (Courbet)

18. The fright of the custodian of the exposition at the prospect of receiving a picture by Courbet

The controversy over realism in art

19. Courbet's Atelier and School (1855). (Detail)

20. MANET, DEJEUNER SUR L'HERBE (1863)
The Impressionist School in Art

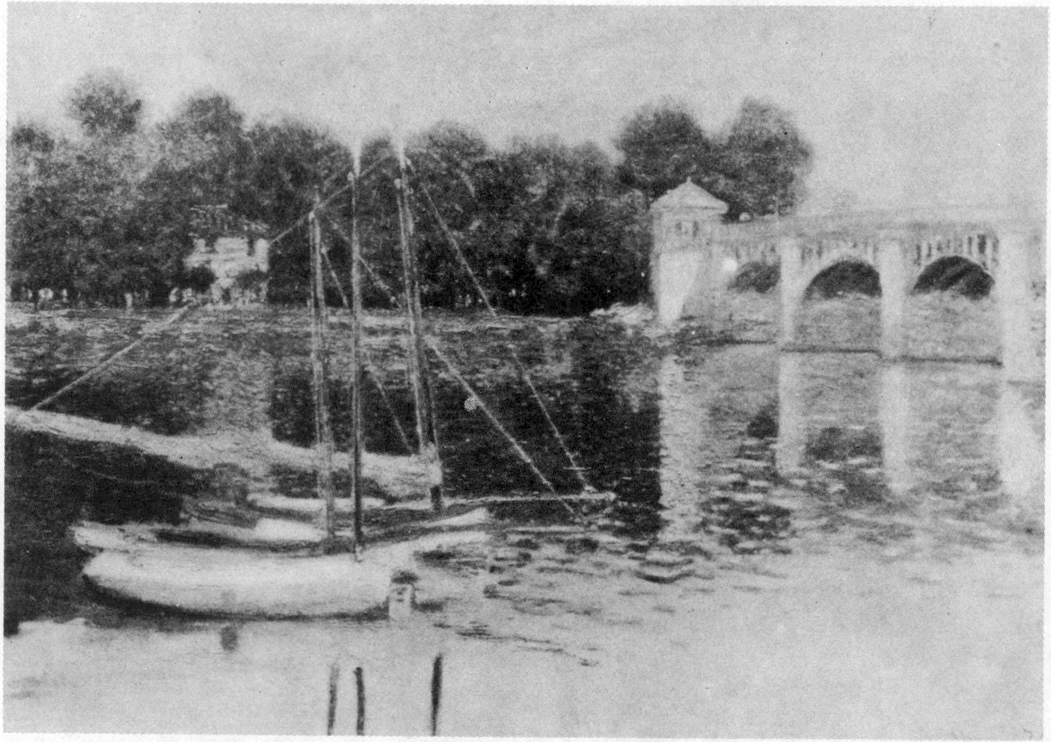

21. Monet: Argenteuil
The Impressionist School in Art

22. Rodin: Man with a Broken Nose
Realism in Sculpture

23. Jules Cheret
Poster Art

24. King Cophetua and the Beggar Maid
National Gallery, London

Pre-Raphaelite Art. Burne-Jones

BOL. ARM
NUX VOMICA
RED LEAD
SAND
THE USE OF ADULTERATION.

25. Poisoned Food

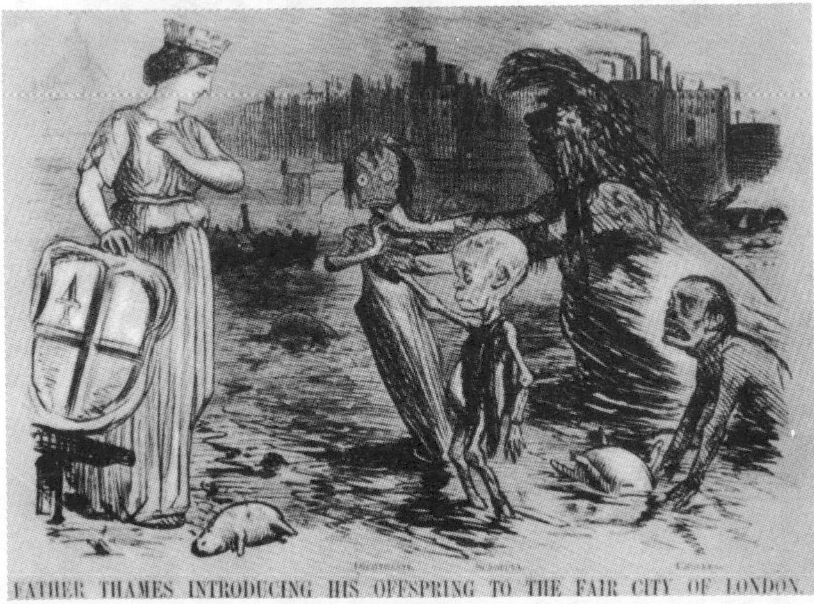
FATHER THAMES INTRODUCING HIS OFFSPRING TO THE FAIR CITY OF LONDON.

26. The Cholera Epidemic

The retreat from Laissez Faire because of public health—
Adulteration and Sanitation

27. RAILROADS: PIERCING THE ALPS AT MT. CENIS (1871)
Technology and Construction

28. THE LAST SHOVEL OF EARTH AT SUEZ (1869)

29. CEREMONY AT OPENING OF SUEZ CANAL

Technology and Construction

30. The Atlantic Cable: Paying out the Cable from the "Great Eastern"

31. Limited Liability *(Punch)*

Magistrate: "Prisoner, you hear what the policeman says, that you and some ten or twelve other boys not yet in custody were seen in the act of demolishing a street lamp; now what have you to say for yourself?"

Prisoner: "So please Yer Worship, as there was more nor ten of us engaged in this transaction, why I pleads limited liability."

Guter Wille für die That.

32. Sale of Government Bonds to the Public

"Children, our state needs money; now you must show confidence and subscribe for as much of the loan as you can."

"Mr. Magistrate, you are right, and I will subscribe twenty gulden."

"Bravo! You may pay half now."

"But, Mr. Magistrate, I would prefer to stay in jail for the whole twenty gulden."

The Development of Finance Capitalism

THE KISS OF PEACE: A NEW MODE OF RIGGING THE MARKET

33. Subsidies and Concessions in France

34. Subscribing to the Austrian Public Loan of 1854

The Development of Finance Capitalism

35. Soldiers Voting

36. Civilians Voting

Democracy: The Plebiscite in France

37. Nationalism: The Plebiscite in Italy

38. William Ewart Gladstone

39. Francis Deak

40. Adolphe Thiers

41. Camillo di Cavour

Leaders of Parliamentary Liberalism

42. King William I of Prussia

43. Queen Victoria of England

44. Pius IX

45. Emperor Francis Joseph of Austria

Four Sovereigns

46. Dr. Dollinger

47. Baron Beust

48. Bishop Strossmayer

49. Pierre Joseph Proudhon

Defeated Protagonists of Federative Polity

50. Prince Couza of Rumania

51. King Victor Emmanuel

52. Prince Michael Obrenovich of Serbia

Princes of Rising Nations

53. Bismarck in 1850

54. Bismarck in the 'Sixties

Bismarck, hero of Realpolitik

55. Napoleon III in 1848

56. Napoleon III in 1871

The Vanquished European

57. A Street in Sedan during the Bombardment
The Dénouement of Violence

58. THE SIEGE OF PARIS—THE BALLOON POST
The Dénouement of Violence

59. Execution of Communards, 1871
The Dénouement of Violence

60. The Breached Wall at Porta Pia where the Italian Army Entered Rome
The Dénouement of Violence

above the arcades, and through all the chapels and places underground, "rendering their chants at every hour of the day and night." He heard "the religious organ of the Latins, the cymbals of the Abyssinian priest, the voice of the Greek cantor, the wails of the Coptic monk"[9] mingled together. He saw only a mysterious confusion, and did not know that every part of the vast and shadowy edifice was the subject of definite rights and particular servitudes. The same was true of the Tomb of the Virgin in Gethsemane, and the Church of the Nativity in Bethlehem. The Latins in 1850 were complaining that in all three of these places the Greeks had systematically, generation after generation, encroached upon them, claiming to share where the Latins had sole right of ownership, and holding on to exclusive possession where the Latins had a rightful share. In the Church of the Nativity at Bethlehem the conduct of the Greeks had been particularly outrageous. There, from time immemorial, the Latins had maintained in the holy lamp-lit grotto an altar and a silver star. The Greeks had gained possession of the main door of the church, then gradually worked down the nave past the chapels served by the Armenians and the Latins, until they finally sought to usurp the grotto itself, the site of the Nativity. In 1847 their intrusion had reached a point of audacity that called for punishment. While Greek and Latin pilgrims were rioting in front of the church, a Greek stole the star of Bethlehem and carried it away from the site of the manger. An investigator, Eugène Boré, outlined these grievances to the French government and proposed that they be remedied by an appeal to the treaty of 1740, which gave France an ill-defined right to protect the Roman Catholics in the Ottoman Empire. Boré proposed that the French Republic "in recurring to the traditional policy of the Crusades would serve the cause of the Church and increase our preponderance in the world."[10] The treaties would compel favorable action at Constantinople, and the fleets assure prompt execution in Palestine. For the next two years, till February, 1852, the French did not cease to harass the Porte with threats of naval action on behalf of Latin rights in the Holy Places.

9 Chateaubriand, *Itinéraire de Paris à Jerusalem* (Paris, 1855), IV, 235-236.
10 Eugène Boré, *La Question des Lieux Saints* (Paris, 1850), 272.

Russian influence at Constantinople had been diminished by the successful defiance the Porte had given to the demand for the surrender of the Hungarian refugees. In championing the cause of the Greek Church against the Latin, Russian diplomacy sought to revive its prestige. In February, 1852, the Porte undertook to effect a compromise between France and Russia by recognizing the Latin claims to share in disputed sanctuaries, while denying all claims for exclusive possession. Acting under this decree, the Turks gave a key to the Church of the Nativity to the Latins. Then on December 22, 1852, Franco-Turkish provocation reached the limit of Russian endurance. On that day the Latin patriarch received from the Turkish officials the key to the main door, passed through it with great ceremony, and replaced in its lamp-lit grotto the silver star of Bethlehem.

In the presence of this humiliating diplomatic defeat, the Tsar laid out a vigorous policy. Since France had threatened with a fleet, Russia would threaten with an army, and on January 3 Russian troops moved toward the border of the Danubian Principalities. Since France had claimed rights under a treaty, Russia would stretch the meaning of the old treaties of Kainardji and Adrianople to cover a right to protect the Greek faith in Turkey. The Christian population of Turkey, as well as the European powers, must be made to realize the magnitude of Russian influence at Constantinople. To accomplish this result, the chancellor, Nesselrode, suggested the sending of a special and extraordinary mission.

But what if the mission should fail? The flow of the Tsar's thought in response to that question, as he worked out his eastern policy in late December, 1852, or early January, 1853, is revealed in a rough but logical outline in his own handwriting, a succinct statement of the Russian aspect of the Eastern question in all its possibilities.[11] What he proposed to do if the mission failed to yield a diplomatic victory was to go to war with the Turks and partition their empire among England, Austria, France, and Russia. He assumed the coöperation of all the powers except France in the liquidation of the empire, but was prepared to allow France a

[11] A. Zaionchkovskii, *Vostochnaia Voina, 1853-56* (St. Petersburg, 1908-13), I, 357-358.

share in the proceeds. He was prepared, in other words, to use the machinery of the concert and to preserve the principle of the balance of power. An agreement with Austria dating from 1833, and one with England from 1844, pledged these powers to confer with Russia on common policy if the dissolution of the Ottoman Empire should be threatened. Acting under this latter agreement, the Tsar began, in the middle of January, 1853, to unfold his policy to Sir Hamilton Seymour, suggesting a discussion of the succession to the Turkish territories.

In reporting this conversation to his government, Seymour argued enthusiastically that

> a noble triumph would be obtained by the civilization of the nineteenth century if the void left by the extinction of Mohammedan rule in Europe could be filled up without an interruption of the general peace, in consequence of the precautions adopted by the two principal governments the most interested in the destinies of Turkey.[12]

V. THE ORIGINS OF THE CRIMEAN WAR

The Tsar's special commissioner, Prince Menshikov, arrived in Constantinople in February, 1853, with instructions to settle the question of the Holy Places in Russia's interest and to demand as clear a treaty right to protect the communicants of the Greek Orthodox Church as France had to protect the Latin Christians. Thus Russia would use on an unprecedented scale, as a device for exerting political influence abroad, the interesting technique of protecting individuals on foreign soil.

The prince had no more than begun operations at Constantinople when Lord Stratford de Redcliffe (Stratford Canning) arrived on the scene as British ambassador. Stratford harbored a Palmerstonian sentiment against autocracy. One of his great ambitions was to reform the Ottoman Empire in a liberal sense, introducing equality of religions and substituting the concept of citizenship for the bond of religion. He helped Menshikov to settle the question of the Holy Places; thereafter the demand for the right to protect Greek Orthodox Christians stood out alone. Stratford could not but oppose it, for it not only threatened the development of modern citizenship

12 Puryear, *England, Russia and the Straits Question, 1844-1856* (Berkeley, 1931).

in the Turkish Empire, but gave Russia rights that would have disturbed the balance of power in the east. Though the Turks and the Russians and Stratford's first biographer, Stanley Lane-Poole, have, for different reasons, exaggerated the degree to which Stratford worked for war, there is no doubt that he helped to bring about Menshikov's diplomatic defeat.[13] According to the Tsar's plan as it had been elaborated before the mission was sent, the diplomatic defeat must result in military action.

It is fascinating to watch the slow succession of motions by which the great powers approached a war. In June, 1853, the French and English fleets came into Besika Bay off the Dardanelles—a gesture, nothing more. In July a Russian army occupied the Danubian Principalities—merely a pledge to be used to force Turkish concessions. Then the concert swung into action. Count Buol brought the French, British, and Prussian ministers to find a formula of compromise. The Vienna conference adopted the text of a note framed to conceal in ambiguities the extent of the Tsar's legal interest in the protection of the Orthodox Church. The Tsar agreed that if the Sultan would sign the note as drafted in Vienna, and send it to him by a special ambassador, he would regard the incident as closed. But when the draft note arrived at Constantinople, Stratford disloyally failed to use his influence to secure its acceptance; rather he lent tacit approval to the Porte in refusing to accept the note without some amendments.

It required a rigorous mind like that of Lord Stratford to see in the refinements of drafting that separated the Vienna note from the Turkish modifications the difference between the maintenance and destruction of Turkish sovereignty. Vienna proposed, for instance, that the Turks should "remain faithful to the *letter and spirit*" of previous treaties; Constantinople replied that they would "remain faithful to their *stipulations*." The Tsar refused these amendments. The diplomatic system of Europe was foundering upon small differences in phraseology, for the note as drafted at Vienna would still have remained open to a variety of pro-Turkish interpretations, and even the text as modified at Constantinople

[13] Harold Temperley, "Stratford de Redcliffe and the Origins of the Crimean War," in *English Historical Review*, XLVIII (1933), 601-621; XLIX (1934), 265-297.

would not have excluded possibilities of Russian encroachments. But by September it was evident that Vienna diplomacy had failed, and events moved toward war between Turkey and Russia.

Meanwhile the war spirit was rising in Constantinople. The Moslem mob was excited. There was talk of a Holy War. The Russians had to be expelled from Turkish soil! In October the Sultan declared war, and with that the French and English fleets raised anchor and moved up through the Straits to lie before Constantinople. Then weeks elapsed before there was any fighting. Finally, on the last day of November the Russian Black Sea fleet, armed with the latest naval guns, annihilated a Turkish fleet at anchor in the harbor of Sinope. The news, relayed to London, aroused the British public to a boiling passion against Russia. And still the great powers were at peace.

The reply of France and England to the "massacre" of Sinope was a proposal to send their fleets through the Straits into the Black Sea with instructions to "invite" any Russian warships there encountered to return to their home ports. Meanwhile, Buol had revived the Vienna conference in a new attempt to doctor up the "note" of the preceding summer. But Stratford substituted his own initiative for that of Vienna; he formulated for the Turks the demand that the Russians should evacuate the Principalities, that Turkey should be admitted to the concert as a great power, and that aid to Turkey take the form of help in modernizing the Turkish government rather than protection for Christians. When Vienna accepted this proposal from Constantinople, it left the Tsar isolated and angry. The issue had shifted from the "note" to the evacuation of the Principalities and was rapidly shifting again to the naval question in the Black Sea. For on January 3, the French and English fleets entered those waters, and the Tsar, when he drew from the foreign offices at London and Paris the clarifying statement that the fleets would permit Turkish warships to sail from one Turkish port to another, but refuse the same liberty to Russian vessels, broke off diplomatic relations.

Napoleon made a last-minute appeal for peace in a personal letter to the Tsar on January 29, 1854, but the contest had gone too far. Diplomacy was now occupied with forming the alliances for the war, and especially with the rôle to be played by the Austrians and Prussians. The Tsar tried in vain to win from them a pledge of armed neutrality and succeeded only in drawing from Vienna some disagreeable hints about the occupation of the Principalities. At the end of February came an ultimatum from England and France, demanding that the Russian army be withdrawn from that region; on March 12 the alliance of the two western powers with Turkey; and on March 28, 1854, the declaration of war.

VI. THE WAR AND THE WAR AIMS

Though the war was declared in March, 1854, the fighting in the Crimea did not begin until September. Meanwhile the question of the occupation of the Principalities was taken out of the field of dispute by the action of the two German powers. Austria, carrying Prussia in her wake with an alliance treaty, demanded that the Russian army be withdrawn from its position.[14] The Tsar reluctantly complied in July, and an Austrian army of occupation took over the territory, to hold it for the duration of the war. An Anglo-French expeditionary force appeared at Varna in June to drive out the Russians, but the Russians had already gone. Without even seeing the enemy the expeditionary force lost a fourth of its numbers through sickness. After more than a year of crisis, the tough old system of organized international comity had finally yielded sufficiently to permit a war, but there seemed to be nothing to fight for and nowhere to fight.

In September, 1854, seven months after the declaration of war, the English and French armies finally found a place to fight. They arrived in force before the Russian naval base at Sebastopol, and laid siege to it. The siege lasted a full year, giving Tolstoi, who was there, and Tennyson, who was not, an excellent occasion to admire the heroism of man, but revealing to a horrified public almost every conceivable kind of military and administrative incapacity. The inefficiency of the European military establishment was merely the counterpart of the bygone efficiency of its diplomatic establishment. It had not been customary for European peoples to live in a panic of fear that at any moment a hostile army would cross the frontier.

[14] K. Borries, *Preussen im Krimkrieg (1853-1856)* (Stuttgart, 1930).

In 1871 there would be better armies, and people would be more conscious of the need of them.

The diplomacy of the war indicated with increasing clarity that the Tsar was isolated and "Europe" was against him. In August, 1854, before the armies went to Sebastopol, the four powers agreed at Vienna upon Four Points as a basis of peace—four points in which traces of the original dispute were barely discernible. One point was derived from the original controversy over the extension of a protectorate to Christians; the Tsar must renounce his pretensions, and agree to coöperate with Europe in fostering Turkish reforms. Another point was developed from the defunct issue of the occupation of the Principalities; the Tsar must renounce any claim to an exclusive right of intervention there, and share his influence with Europe. Another point: the revision of the régime of the Straits seemed to have emerged from the naval episode in the Black Sea. The fourth point was the freedom of the Danube. On November 18 Russia accepted these four points as a basis of peace, and Count Buol sought to re-convene the Conference at Vienna.

Yet the war went on, and its diplomacy became a diplomatic revolution. For Austria, with Prussia reluctantly dragging behind her, moved to an alliance with the Western Powers. The critical debates in the Austrian cabinet took place on November 17 and 19, at the very time that the Tsar was accepting the four points.[15]

In Russia the effect of Austrian policy was to create an antagonism that persisted, fed by frequent renewals, as long as these two empires lasted. And in the Prussian ministry there was planted the distinct impression that Prussia's independence and freedom of action as a great power were being undermined.

It is only too well established in European experience that the scars of war can be healed over more easily than the scars of a dictated peace. Therefore the course of the war aims of the western powers is as important as the course of the war. Throughout the year 1855 the British foreign office built up ever more crushing peace terms to be imposed on a defeated Russia. The war had been undertaken, so far as the British were concerned, in the name of the principle of balance of power; the British war aims may have preserved

[15] Gavin B. Henderson, "The Diplomatic Revolution of 1854," *Amer. Hist. Rev.*, XLIII, October, 1937, 45-46; "The Eclipse of Lord John Russell," *Cambridge Hist. Journal*, V, 1, 1935, 60-86.

the balance of power in the territorial sense, but they destroyed the basis of the concert, because they made Russia an enemy rather than a protector of the *status quo*. The additional terms written into the claims of the allies during the year 1855 called for the surrender of Russian territory in Bessarabia and the permanent restriction of Russian naval power in the Black Sea.

When it became evident that Austria would not fulfill its alliance duties to the western allies, France and Britain made the circle of the secondary states and secured Piedmont as a full partner in January, 1855, and Sweden as a secret ally in November of the same year. In March, 1855, Nicholas died; in September Sebastopol fell; and in December peace terms were once more under discussion. Alexander II consented reluctantly to the cession of Bessarabia and to naval limitation in the Black Sea, and a congress met in Paris in March, 1856, to complete the peace.

VII. THE CONGRESS OF PARIS

Never had war been fought with more deference to the requirements of trade. The British board of trade ruled that an English merchant might legally import Russian goods if he purchased them in a neutral country. A prize court decision allowed a subject of the British Protectorate of the Ionian Isles to trade with the enemy.[15] British orders in council allowed Russian ships six weeks of grace in which to load at any British or colonial port and return to Russia immune from capture. A Russian loan, to pay interest on Russian bonds was floated on the London market during the progress of the war with the permission of the English government. There were also friendly gestures in the relations of Russia and France. When diplomatic relations were broken, the Tsar gave the French minister, Castelbajac, a decoration as a parting gift. While the war was going on, the French government invited Russia to participate in the Exposition of Industry and the Arts.

The contrast with the Napoleonic wars was all the more noteworthy because in those wars England and France had held radically opposed views of belligerent rights at sea, and between them had squeezed out almost all neutral commerce. But now their fleets

[15] H. A. Smith, *Great Britain and the Law of Nations* (London, 1932), I.

were coöperating, the free-trade spirit was alive in England, and consequently the French and British principles were combined in an opposite sense, giving to commerce the benefit of the rules of both nations rather than harassing it with the restrictions of both. The two governments, at the moment of declaring war on Russia, issued identical declarations that they would observe the rule (taken from French practice) that free ships make free goods, as well as the rule, previously championed by England, that non-contraband neutral property would be respected on enemy ships. Another paragraph of the declaration implied that the right to impose a blockade could only be claimed if the blockade were established with adequate force—no paper blockade—and a fourth section promised that no letters of marque should be issued to privateers. These principles were now codified and adopted by all the great powers as the Declaration of Paris.

Almost every one of the peace terms agreed upon at Paris seemed to reaffirm the authority of Europe as against the independent action of any single power, and give further precision and extension to the collective responsibility of the five great powers. Article VIII gave Europe the specific right to mediate between the Porte and any power in any dispute. Article XXIII established among the powers a general right of mediation. Other articles gave Europe a mandate to supervise the national autonomy of Serbia and the Principalities under the suzerainty of the Sultan. Another article made the four powers guarantors of the Ionian Isles under the protection of Britain. The provision for the free navigation of the Danube and the neutralization of the Black Sea increased notably the range of international jurisdiction, as the Declaration of Paris limited belligerent rights in time of war.

Then the moment came, on April 8, 1856, when the congress, in consequence of the assiduous agitation of Cavour, allowed the discussion of "The Italian Question." Lord Clarendon, having been educated by Cavour in Italian politics, used strong language to condemn the bad government of Naples and the Papal States, and to protest against the continued presence of Austrian troops throughout central Italy. Cavour spoke with moderation, arguing that the presence of Austrian troops in Italy maintained a state of things contrary to the Treaty of Vienna and threatening to the balance of power. The brief discussion had no immediate practical consequences except to raise the prestige of Piedmont as the champion of Italian against Austrian interests. Historians of the *Risorgimento* have not failed to interpret this episode as a great step toward the making of the Kingdom of Italy, and so perhaps it was. But the writer of European history must emphasize the difference between the procedure of discussion in a European congress with all the great powers present and the procedure of piecemeal wars and bargains by which the Kingdom of Italy was ultimately created. This was not, after all, the first congress to deal with the Italian question, but the last, for in form at least Cavour, like Metternich, spoke deferentially about the Vienna settlement, even though he spoke in the presence of the new alignment of powers that had issued from the wreck of Austrian diplomacy in the Crimean War.

VIII. THE END OF EQUILIBRIUM AND MONARCHIC SOLIDARITY

The new alignment that emerged from the Crimean War was not a mere continuation into the period of the peace of the wartime alliances. Prussia, the recipient of a tardy and grudging invitation to sit in the congress, became even more sensitive than before of her imperiled great-power status. The collaboration of France and England continued actively in the Far East, where the two powers moved into a war with China; France on behalf of the protection of missionaries, and England on behalf of the privileges of traders. But on the Continent the friendship of Napoleon and Alexander, and the diplomatic collaboration of France and Russia, were dominant from the Paris Congress of 1856 to the Polish Insurrection of 1863. The defeat of Russia had lowered her military prestige, and thus served in some measure to clear an old obstacle from the path of European development, but even more significant than the defeat of Russia was a change in her policies that almost amounted to conversion. Nicholas' resentment at Austrian ingratitude in 1854, his death in 1855, leaving the throne to a reforming monarch, and the retirement of the aged Nesselrode in 1856 marked the gradual release of Russian policy from the dogmas of the sanctity of the settlement of 1815 and the perpetual solidarity of monarchs against peoples. For the treaties of 1856 became for Russia what the Vienna treaties were for France. Napoleon could write to the Tsar Alexander in 1858: "You wish to change in part the Treaty of Paris; I would change in part the treaties of 1815."[16]

There remained in 1857 no great political force irretrievably committed to the preservation of things as they then stood. Vienna sought the consolidation of central Europe, London the spread of the constitutional system of government, Paris satisfaction of the principle of nationalities, and St. Petersburg the revocation of the Black Sea clauses and the restoration of Bessarabia.

Just as Nicholas while planning in 1853 the partition of the Turkish Empire had drawn up a new map of the Ottoman territories, so Napoleon in 1854 began his map-making. In March of that year he corrected the proofs of a pamphlet on the *New Map of Europe*, and in December, 1855, while he was working upon England to restrain the rising British war aims, he proposed that if the war were to be continued it should be made the occasion of the complete revision of the map of Europe, with Poland reconstituted and the Italian question settled. This prospect frightened the British government into some moderation, but nevertheless the peace terms provided for the cession of territory by a great power to a young nationality. The cession of Bessarabia in 1856 was the precursor to the cession of Lombardy in 1859. The revision of the map of Europe, though in a small way, had actually begun.

If the revision were to be carried further, under what auspices and in the light of what principles would it be conducted? Would it take place under the authority of Europe in congress assembled or by the separate action of the different states? Would it defer to the principle of the balance of power or the principle of nationality? Would its motive force lie in the policies of governments or the activities of revolution? The diplomacy of the Crimean War period furnished precedents and opened the way for development in any of these conflicting directions.

The clearest breach with the past would be the alliance of monarchs with the revolution. Such an alliance had actually entered the

[16] Albert Pingaud: "Un projet d'alliance franco-russe en 1858," *Séances et Travaux de l'Académie des Sciences Morales et Politiques, Compte Rendu,* LXXXVIII (1928), 155.

mind of Tsar Nicholas in the first year of the Eastern crisis. He proposed in May, and again in November, 1853 to proclaim

> the real independence of the Moldo-Vlachs (Rumanians), the Serbs, Bulgarians, Bosnians, and Greeks, letting each one enter into the possession of the country it has inhabited for centuries, governed by a man chosen by themselves from among their own nationals.[17]

Nesselrode dissuaded his master from taking this step, but an insurrection had nonetheless broken out in Epirus in the spring of 1854, and Mazzini, anxiously watching from Switzerland and hoping that the European revolution would spread westward from the Balkans, definitely aligned himself with Russia against France and England. On the other hand, some of the exiled revolutionists, especially Poles and Hungarians, went to Constantinople to help the Turks against the Russians. In the final months of the war, when Napoleon was frightening the English by suggesting operations in Poland, the collaboration of western allies with Polish revolutionists was a distinct possibility. The lines that seemed so clearly drawn after 1848 between peoples and monarchs were vanishing.

The principle which the congress seemed most clearly to confirm was the one which in fact was to prove least stable in the ensuing years—the principle of all-European action through the instrumentality of congresses. In the crises of the succeeding decade, when territorial questions were at stake, congresses would be called and would not meet, or would meet and do nothing of significance. And in the final crisis of 1871, when territory in the heart of western Europe changed hands, there would be no meeting of diplomats to give European ratification to the annexation. In the fifteen years that followed the Congress of Paris, Europe went marching along toward the nadir of anarchy. But on the way it passed through a strange experience which, if a name must be found, can be called the crisis of federative polity.

[17] F. de Martens, *Recueil des traités et conventions* (St. Petersburg, 1898), XII, 344.

Chapter Nine

THE CRISIS OF FEDERATIVE POLITY (1857-1858)

I. THE ERA OF FEDERATIVE EXPERIMENTS

THE DISTURBANCE of equilibrium in the concert was followed by stresses in the subordinate elements in Europe's federative structure. But it did not become clear immediately that the federative principle would be sacrificed. Rather it seemed for a time that it would be expanded and utilized to bring the whole European system into adjustment, not only with political forces, but with economic forces as well.

In the seven years following the Congress of Paris, there came experiments in confederation, federation, and autonomy—that is to say, in federative polity—over the whole central European area, from the Baltic to the Black sea, and from the Rhine to the great Russian plain. Political experiments, reform projects, and diplomatic adventures in the years 1857 to 1863 tested the potentialities of federalism at all juridical levels, from the provincial to the all-European. In the summer of 1858, Wallachia and Moldavia received from the European concert a federal constitution as the United Principalities; in the summer of 1859 the armistice of Villafranca decreed a paper Confederation for Italy; in the autumn of 1860 Francis Joseph attempted a federal reorganization of his monarchy; in the spring of 1861 Tsar Alexander experimented with autonomy in Finland and Poland. The movement to reform (rather than to destroy) the German Confederation reached its climax in 1862 and 1863, at the time when Bismarck's advent as minister-president alienated the liberals from Prussian leadership and Francis Joseph brought the *Grossdeutsch* movement to a climax in the Frankfurt congress of princes. King Frederick of Denmark, who had tried many experiments in an effort to fit common parliamentary institutions to a complex of crown lands that had no other bond of union than his own royal sovereignty, came at last in March, 1863, to that fateful Patent that led directly to the German-Danish War.

At the diplomatic level there were projects of confederation of many kinds, sponsored with varying degrees of authority. The proposal for a Scandinavian Confederation rose above the stage of mere literary agitation when King Oskar of Sweden-Norway offered an alliance to Frederick VII of Denmark in February 1857. The Russians schemed persistently for a Christian confederation in the Balkans. In 1860 Gorchakov asked French consent to a Balkan Confederation as the price of Russian permission to annex Nice and Savoy; in 1862 at the height of the controversy over the Serbian demand for the evacuation of Belgrade by the Turkish garrison, Napoleon approved a Russian project for such a confederation. Prince Michael Obrenovič of Serbia, most statesman-like figure of his whole dynasty, gave further development to the plan, which was not scotched till his assassination in 1868. Napoleon III in his frequent fantasies of political geography would fill great areas with confederations and the pamphleteers carried them everywhere. In 1861 Gorchakov showed Bismarck a "future map of Europe" from a French source in which the whole area of the Continent was divided between Iberian, Gallic, Italian, Greek, Austrian, and German confederations. Some of the same ethnic-geographic situations which in the 1920's gave rise to projects of "regional pacts" under the League of Nations suggested to the publicists of the mid-nineteenth century plans for confederations within the framework of the concert.

Meanwhile the authority of the European concert was put to its most severe tests. It had failed to avert war in the east in 1854, but had succeeded in reëstablishing peace. It failed again to avert war in 1859, and this time did not even sit in at the peace-making. It was invoked in vain in 1860 to settle the Italian question. And just as Pope Boniface in the fourteenth century expanded papal claims while the substance of his authority was dissolving, so the institution of the European congress was invoked to meet issues of increasing magnitude while its powers were diminishing. The crowning gesture was Napoleon's proposal, in November, 1863, to entrust to a European congress the complete revision of the Vienna treaties and the redistribution of territory. This vast extension of the authority of the concert was not accepted by diplomacy; the agenda of 1863 was referred instead to the arbitrament of war. And this same year was the year of Gettysburg, the turning-point in the history of American federalism.

The bloody denouement of nationalism in Europe leaves the historian with the unanswered question: why was the nineteenth century unable to maintain or develop, either in Europe or in America, those political systems in which the location of paramount authority is left indefinite? Even the American Union saved at Gettysburg was in this respect no longer the same as that which the fathers brought forth upon the continent fourscore and seven years before. Government of the people, by the people, and for the people survived the Civil War in America, just as monarchic government survived the civil war of 1866 in Germany, but in both cases the fine balance of the federative compromise was ended, in America by the triumph of the unionists, in Germany by the victory of the Prussian secessionists. In both cases the conflict itself was preceded by a challenge to the authentic and traditional basis of federative polity. In the United States the triumph of the unionists preserved federalism in North America; in Germany the triumph of the secessionists sacrificed it in *Mitteleuropa.*

The history of these events has come down to us charged with the atmosphere of the period in which they took place. Historians have written as if it were self-evident that the Europe which matured in 1871 was a sound political establishment. The historians' verdict echoes the triumphant propaganda of the time, and conforms, moreover, to the profound thought-patterns of the age, with their corroding self-contradictions. When the historical narrative suggests that Italy and Germany came into being as the inevitable product of the irresistible forces of nationalism, and were at the same time artfully created by the extraordinary political gymnastics of two incredible "makers of history," Cavour and Bismarck, this contradiction merely exemplifies the standard nineteenth-century dilemma of mechanistic determinism and free will, where science-worship and hero-worship were in conflict. When the nationalist historians

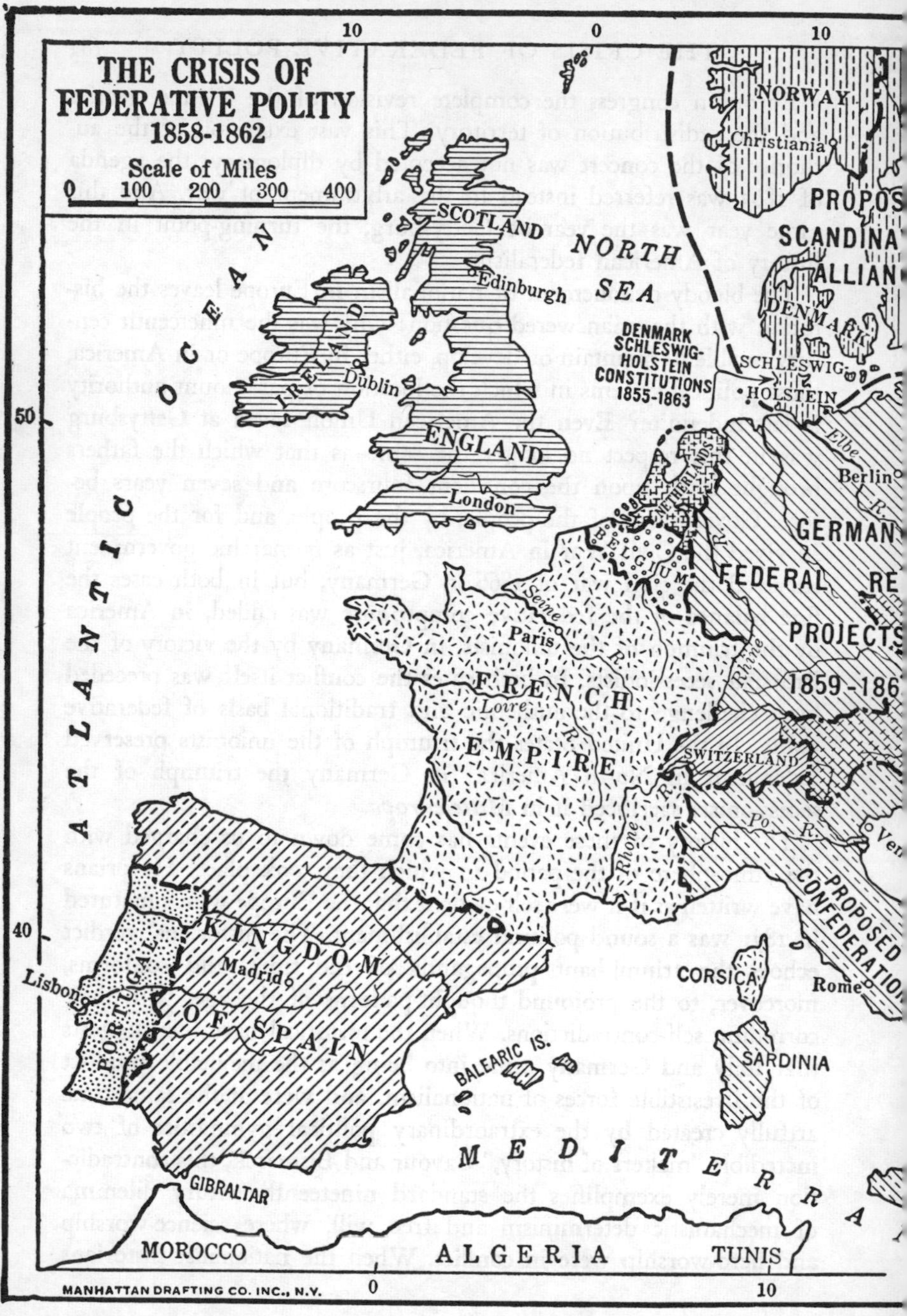

MANHATTAN DRAFTING CO. INC., N.Y.

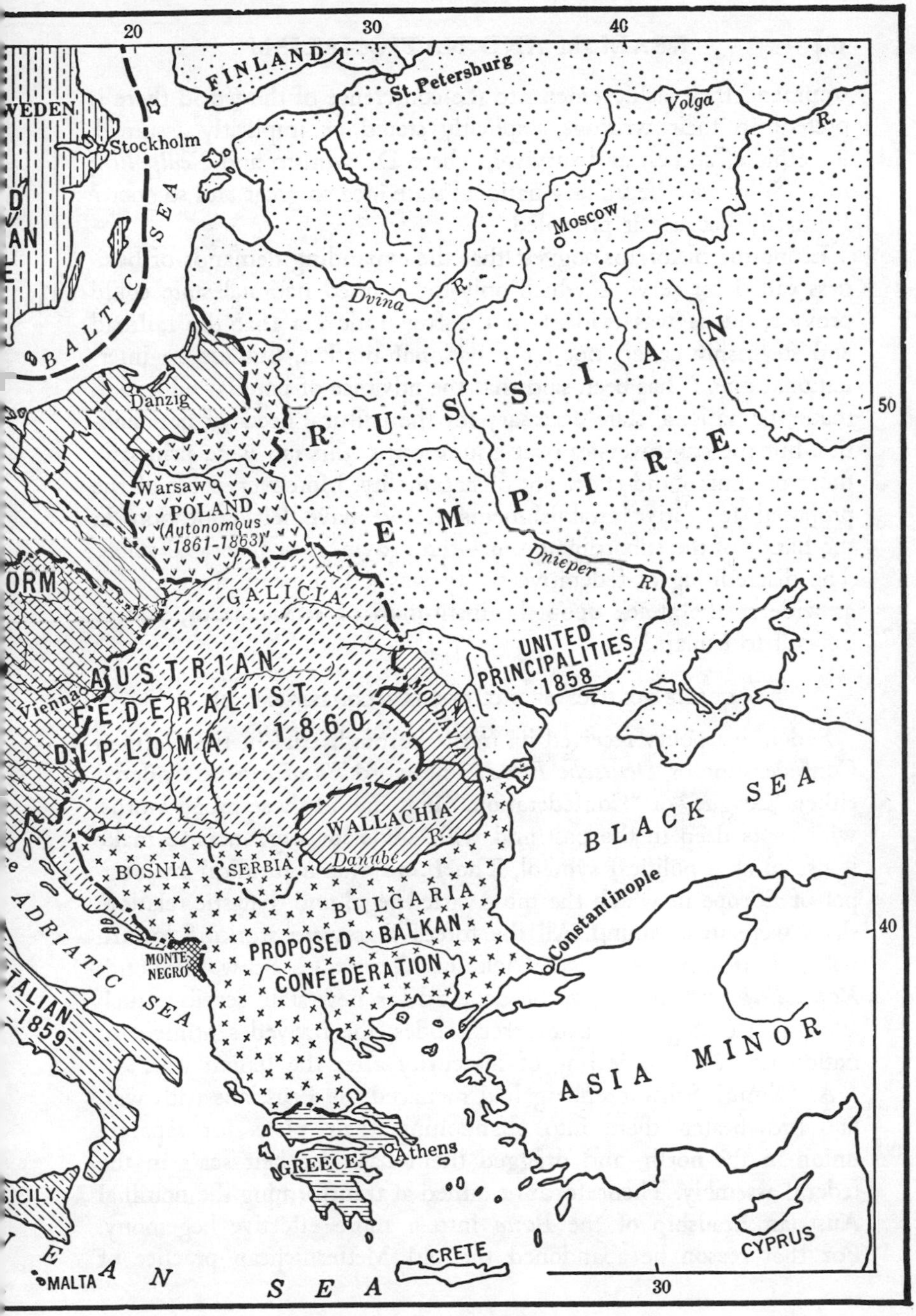

20
30
40
FINLAND
St. Petersburg
Volga
R.
WEDEN
Stockholm
BALTIC SEA
Moscow
Dvina
R.
RUSSIAN
EMPIRE
50
Danzig
Warsaw
POLAND
(Autonomous
1861-1863)
ORM
GALICIA
Dnieper
R.
UNITED
PRINCIPALITIES
1858
AUSTRIAN
FEDERALIST
DIPLOMA, 1860
Vienna
MOLDAVIA
BLACK SEA
WALLACHIA
Danube
R.
BOSNIA
SERBIA
BULGARIA
PROPOSED BALKAN
CONFEDERATION
Constantinople
40
MONTE
NEGRO
ADRIATIC SEA
ITALIAN
1859
ASIA MINOR
GREECE
Athens
SICILY
CRETE
CYPRUS
MALTA
SEA
30

commend these achievements to the conscience of the world there is present in their writings, explicitly stated or implicitly assumed, the ethic of success and survival, where Darwinism and *Realpolitik* meet. Why was the unitary national state idea so great and so good? Primarily because it prevailed.

Economic historians suggest that the expanding demands of business called for services which only the unified national state could provide, but it was evident in the free-trade era that the railroad and steamship called, not for a national market, but for an international one. It has been said that the advance of popular education made the national state necessary for the cultural needs of nationalities, but the controversies over education in this era were primarily those of church and state, not of nationality. Moreover, most of the proposed federative establishments would have left education in the hands of the subordinate unit—the provinces or federated states. The discrediting of federative polity was a European phenomenon as wide as the attack upon the institution of servile labor, and as difficult to explain.

II. THE POLITICS OF THE GERMAN CONFEDERATION

Federative polity received its most thorough trial in the German Confederation or *Deutsche Bund*. The word *Bund* can be rendered either "League" or "Confederation." It is one of those broad words, with roots deep in the past and with sufficient vagueness to make it useful as a political symbol. The *Bund* was a juridical melting-pot of Europe in which the most varied legal and dynastic relationships were to be found. All the forces that were working toward political readjustment were felt in Germany: Schwarzenberg's *Realpolitik* and its legacy, the demand for new state services, such as unified coinage and commercial codes, the revived sentiment of nationality, and the feeling of insecurity after the Italian war.

At Olmütz Schwarzenberg had menaced the Prussians with war, had browbeaten them into abandoning their plans for separate union in the north, and dragged them back to their seats in the federal assembly. Thenceforth he aimed at transforming the nominal Austrian headship of the *Bund* into a more effective hegemony. For that reason he abandoned the old Metternichean practice of consulting Prussia in advance before carrying business through the confederate assembly (*Bundesversammlung*), a practice that had given the Prussian government a virtual veto right in confederate affairs. He built up a majority of middle and small states, capable of outvoting Prussia in the assembly, and thereby forcing her into the position of an ordinary German middle state, despite her quality as a great power. The politics of the *Bund* in the 1850's turned on the issues of the power of a majority to coerce a minority in the assembly, and the interpretation of the fundamental law of the *Bund* as constitutional rather than international law.

In the reaction period the Austrian drive to tighten the *Bund*, develop the majority powers, and treat the Confederate Act as constitutional rather than international law, had the help of the reactionary party throughout Germany. But young Bismarck, though himself completely in sympathy with reactionary principles, engineered Prussian opposition to Austria. The issue was defined in the confederate assembly in the matter of the German fleet. A majority voted to levy an assessment to maintain the fleet. Prussia challenged the vote on the ground that this was a question requiring unanimity. The Austrian president of the assembly, the jaunty and tactless Count Thun, tried to ride roughshod over Prussian objections. His conception of majority powers tended to transform the confederate assembly into a simple legislature for Germany. Acting under the letter of the Confederate Act, he claimed that the majority could decide its own competence. Here was a principle which, if unchallenged, would have given the *Bund* great powers of growth.

Bismarck resisted with relentless zeal. When Thun tried to secure some money to maintain the fleet by mortgaging the ships to the Rothschilds, Bismarck warned the bankers against making the loan. Count Thun complained bitterly that he "could have cried like a child over the shame to our common Fatherland" when he heard that "a German government, member of the *Bund*, would drag into the mire the authority and reputation of the *Bund* by protesting a confederate ordinance to a Jew."[1]

[1] A. O. Meyer: *Bismarcks Kampf mit Oesterreich am Bundestag zu Frankfurt (1851 bis 1859)* (Berlin & Leipzig, 1927), 78.

Bismarck won out on the question of the fleet, which was then sold at the auction block. Thenceforth whenever he found a rule or custom based on the theory that the assembly was the legislative organ of a sovereign body, or anything more than a mere conference of diplomats, he attacked it ruthlessly. He demanded, for instance, that the order of precedence at formal dinners be changed, and the practice of voting by proxy altered. On small affairs and large he built up his reputation as a die-hard doctrinaire, often muttering threats of secession and irrepressible conflict. Doubtless he could have been bought off with the old "veto-right" of Metternich's time, but since he failed to gain that concession, his service at Frankfurt was one long filibuster against the development of confederate authority.

Schwarzenberg supplemented his forward policy in the confederate assembly with an attempt to force the inclusion of Austria in the customs union. In 1852 he obtained from the South German states an agreement that if Prussia refused protective tariffs and the inclusion of Austria in the union, they would secede and form a new union with Vienna. The economic *Mitteleuropa* was within reach when the great prince died. Count Buol failed to follow up the advantage; he sent a business man, Baron Bruck, to carry on the customs negotiations in Berlin. Bruck brought back only a commercial treaty and a promise that Austrian inclusion in the customs union would be reconsidered in ten years. When the ten years were up, Bismarck, risen from the Frankfurt post to the Prussian minister-presidency, easily kept the Austrians excluded.

During the Crimean War Count Buol obtained by treaty with Prussia and by act of the confederate assembly the assurance of protection for the non-German parts of the Hapsburg realm, and even for the Austrian army of occupation in the Danubian Principalities. But neither Prussia nor the Confederation would follow Austria into an offensive war against Russia, nor mobilize their armies except for the defense of the *Bund*. The treaty and the confederate decree giving protection to non-German Austrian territory lapsed after the Crimean War, before the Italian crisis broke. It was evident, however, that with proper political preparation a defensive military *Mitteleuropa* could be brought into existence in time of crisis by the machinery of the Germanic states system.

During the 'fifties the *Bund* devoted a good part of its energies to purely reactionary measures, such as the revision of too-liberal constitutions and the extension of press censorship. In this it resembled all Germanic legislative bodies, even the little provincial diets of the Prussian provinces. But some more constructive tasks came to it. When the national democratic elements of the revolution of 1848 had been swept away, there remained a few utilitarian elements that could be taken over by the reaction. A ministerial conference at Dresden in May, 1851, voted that common action ought to be taken throughout the *Bund* on patents, coinage, commercial law, maritime law, and insurance, as well as weights and measures. The confederate assembly did not wholly ignore this legacy of problems, even in the era of reaction. In 1852 it found time to bring up a patent law, and in 1855, on Bavarian initiative, considered a plan to unify commercial law throughout the Confederation.

The Prussian position was hostile to all lawmaking by the *Bund* itself. On press censorship Bismarck was willing to have the *Bund* set up norms to which the separate states might conform, but not to establish a confederate press law. Prussia preferred the procedure of special agreements among individual states for special purposes. The customs union was the most shining example of this device. Another was furnished in the matter of domicile by the *Notheimatsverband*. In 1851 the representatives of ten states met at Gotha to prepare a general German law on domicile. They drafted a multilateral treaty on the subject. By 1860 it had been accepted by all states except Denmark and the Netherlands, and in 1861 the confederate assembly voted to have it redrafted as a decree of the *Bund*. When the Bavarian project for a unified commercial code came up, strict consistency with Prussian policy would have called for Prussian opposition, but Bismarck persuaded his government to compromise in order to avoid odium. Prussia consented to the project on condition that the commission set up to draft the new law code should not be an organ of the confederate assembly, nor hold its meetings at Frankfurt. The commission was appointed; it met at Nürnberg in 1857 for the work on the commercial code, moved to Hamburg to draft the maritime code, and in 1861 made its report. Austria together with almost all the other German states adopted this basic law, which carried the *Bund* farther in the direction of unified legislation than the American Union had gone.

In the late 'fifties there were demands for further services of this kind. An all-German economic congress met in 1857, a trade congress in 1858, and a welfare congress in 1861. There was also the all-German congress of jurists. Quietly, without pressing the issue of sovereignty or majority power, the confederate assembly proceeded to take care of the government functions pressed upon it. It set up commissions on the law of bills and notes, on coinage, and on weights and measures. The procedure was not unlike that which in the twentieth century came into use in the drafting of international labor legislation.

While the *Bund* was using this procedure, on the border line between international and internal legislation (as martial law and intervention were on the border line between international and internal police action), the international world was beginning to assume new functions and to create new organizations presaging the later development of international administration. The International Statistical Congress, beginning in 1851, made efforts to standardize the practices of the statistical services of the European states. An unofficial committee in August, 1863, prepared resolutions on the rights of neutrals to aid the wounded during war, and an official diplomatic conference in 1864 redrafted these at the Geneva Convention, establishing an international agency, the Red Cross, for humanitarian service in war time. The Telegraphic Union of 1865 blazed a new trail, to be followed ten years later by the Postal Union. The Latin Monetary Union in the 'sixties met with international action a complex currency situation created by a changing ratio of gold to silver. The free-trade movement of the 'sixties was meanwhile bringing into existence a network of tariff conventions with the unconditional most-favored-nation clause, which had the effect of subjecting more and more of the general tariff-rate structure to a control expressed in international conventions. In the days of Metternich both the German *Bund* and the collectivity of European states had taken as their chief field of coöperation matters relating to police; now they were organizing coöperation in new fields, thereby assuming new functions. As the new tasks were imposing themselves upon national and international agencies alike, the question seemed open as to what distribution of labor would be made between them.

The national historians have adjudged the German confederate assembly an utterly inefficient body, and so it must seem if its tempo is compared with that of modern government. So also did the parliament that replaced it seem to be when compared with twentieth-century dictatorships. But alongside the Russia of Nicholas I or the Austria of Ferdinand the *Bund* was not conspicuously ill-equipped with legislative machinery. Projects lay buried in its committees for years, as the Polish law code lay for a generation in the hands of a committee of jurists in St. Petersburg. Efforts to reform it were ineffectual, but so were Metternich's efforts to improve the central government at Vienna. Law cases dragged on interminably before the assembly of the *Bund*, but the same complaint was made of the English chancery before the reform in English procedure. When the demand for new services appeared, it seemed that the German confederative system functioned with reasonable effectiveness, but only on one condition: it could work effectively only so long as concrete legislative proposals could be considered on their merits, without involving the question of supremacy within the Confederation. Whenever it seemed that sovereignty or primacy in the *Bund* was at stake, the whole machine became deadlocked. Such a deadlock was reached in 1863, in the development of the plan for a common code of civil procedure.

But in 1860 the whole setting of the German question had been changed by the Italian War, which created a new feeling of insecurity (thus increasing the interest that Germans took in the military functions of their government), revived a vigorous nationalist movement, and directed attention more toward military than economic objectives. And the military problem was of all problems the one least capable of separation from the question of supremacy or primacy in the *Bund*.

The nationalist movement in Germany was of course much deeper than the mere demand for services; it was perhaps even deeper than an interest in defense. The secular dogma of nationalism had been long in growing. Its effective history is not confined to the literary and philosophical expounders of its tenets, from Herder down, but must take into account the responsiveness of masses to it. The masses had been aroused to excitement during the period of French hegemony, when they could see on the streets foreigners speaking a language they could not understand. In the quiet Biedermeyer period that followed they responded more to such issues as the religious question of mixed marriages in the Rhineland. The popular liberalism of the pre-March era was organized as a movement of religious dissent—the *Lichtfreunde* movement.[2] But 1848 and again 1859 found nationalism taking hold of the people. The speculation is here advanced that it may have been the insecurities of the new economic order, especially as they were accentuated in the crisis of 1857, that gave the renewed stimulus to the momentous form of self-transcendence that nationalism offers to an individual.

III. THE UNITED PRINCIPALITIES

While the German *Bund* was feeling its way toward an extension of its functions, the great powers were setting up on the lower Danube a federal state with legislative and executive organs not unlike the German. When the principalities of Wallachia and Moldavia had become, in consequence of the Treaty of Paris, a mandated area under the supervision of the great powers, the guardians found it hard to agree upon a form of government for their ward. Should the two principalities be united or maintained in separation? Russia wanted them united so that they might be strong enough to resist Austrian penetration; Napoleon was eager to comply with the popular demand for union and to apply on the lower Danube the Napoleonic idea of the principle of nationalities. The Austrians and Turks, in opposing the Franco-Russian plan, made the mistake of arguing that the population did not desire union. The Russians countered by proposing an election. Thus at the suggestion of the most autocratic of the European governments the plebiscite appeared as a device for settling territorial problems, just

[2] H. Rosenberg, "Theologischer Rationalismus und Vormärzlicher Vulgärliberalismus," *Historische Zeitschrift*, CXLI (1929-30), 497.

as it had appeared as a method of settling constitutional problems in France.

The principle of nationalities and the procedure of the plebiscite began in this way their short but glorious career. They appeared together in the Danubian Principalities in 1857 and 1858, in the Italian states in 1860, 1866, and 1870, and in the Ionian Isles in 1863 as a means of legitimating a change of sovereignty. It seemed for a while that they were to become a part of the public law of Europe, and that no territorial change could be valid without them. In the making of Italy no congress of the great powers was used to ratify what the plebiscites had confirmed. The story of the breakdown of the plebiscite principle in the making of Germany will be told in another chapter. For the present it is sufficient to trace the use of the plebiscite on the Danube.

In July, 1857, an election was held in each Principality, but the Turkish authorities, by force and fraud, secured a vote against union. Walewski, Napoleon's foreign minister, then demanded that the elections be canceled and new ones held. He formed a bloc with Sardinia and Russia to insist on cancellation. Prussia joined forces with him, thus openly entering the lists against her German colleague in the *Bund*. Failing to secure satisfaction, Napoleon broke off relations with the Porte. England, partly because of the persistent intriguing of Lord Stratford de Redcliffe, stood by the Turks and Austrians. The Crimean alliance was broken and war threatened. Napoleon met the situation by paying a visit to Queen Victoria and Prince Albert at their summer residence at Osborne. Clarendon and Palmerston came down from London, Persigny and Walewski arrived with the Imperial couple from France. The sovereigns and ministers, after a few days of conversation, reached a compromise between the French policy of union and the Anglo-Turkish policy of separation. They agreed to annul the fraudulent elections and permit the people to express their desire for union, but to limit the union to the compromise form of a federative bond between the two Principalities.

The conversations leading to the settlement were not recorded, but it is certain that Albert and Napoleon had long political talks together, and that Albert, with his stolid and thorough German mind, well crammed with all the facts of current politics, was familiar with the measures then being taken in Germany to satisfy practical demands for common political services without sacrificing the sovereignty of the separate states. The agreement reached by the French and British seemed like an attempt to transport to the Danubian environment the contemporary Germanic scheme:

> The two provinces shall have similar organic institutions and while retaining their separate governments, they shall have a common system in regard to all matters, civil and military, to which such a community of system can advantageously be established.
>
> Such arrangements would include a coinage which should pass current in both provinces, a tariff that should be the same for both, a customs union, and the absence of any customs duties on goods passing from one province to the other, a provision that decrees of courts of justice in one province should have force against persons who might have withdrawn from that province to the other, and a common system of military arrangements for the defense of the two provinces.[3]

New elections in the Principalities resulted in an overwhelming victory of the unionists. The *divans* (assemblies) of Moldavia and Wallachia adopted identical programs calling for union and independence under a prince chosen from one of the European royal families. A conference of the powers then convened in Paris to draw up a constitution that would carry out the Osborne Compromise by giving the "United Principalities" a federative relationship rather than a union. The constitution as finally adopted by the powers on August 19, 1858, provided for each province its separate government with legislature, ministry, and prince, and gave control of the common affairs of the two provinces to a central committee and a supreme court. The central committee, composed of four delegates from each legislature and four representatives appointed by each prince, was given the task of unifying the law codes and supervising customs, money, weights, measures, and communications. Its duties, in other words, were those which the German confederate assembly was beginning to assume for the German *Bund*. The armies of the Principalities were to be coördinated but not

[3] Prince Albert's memorandum of August 9, 1857, quoted in part in T. W. Riker: "The Pact of Osborne," *American Historical Review*, XXXIV, 1929, 242.

united, except in cases of emergency. An inspector, appointed alternately by each prince, was to certify that training and equipment in both armies were kept to a common standard. The flags were to be different, but each staff was to carry a blue pennant as a symbol of union.

The system was vitiated from the start by the action of the two new legislatures. They both elected the same man as prince. Colonel Alexander Couza, upon whom this honor was thrust, had not been in the forefront of politics in the Principalities; he was a compromise candidate and a dark horse. He turned out to be a man of unsuspected ability, who preserved the external appearance of a languid and lecherous oriental prince while quietly occupied with a forceful and far-reaching political correspondence. His election sabotaged the new confederate constitution. Within three years he secured recognition as prince-for-life over both provinces, and received permission to appoint a common ministry for both. The constitution of 1858 did not strike roots in the country to which it was transplanted from German soil. The experiment was closed out not only by the nationalist movement in the Principalities, but also by the French victory in the Italian War of 1859. The constitution was doubly European rather than national: it had its end and its beginning in the high diplomacy of the powers, and it has served in history only to illustrate concretely what European statesmen meant by confederation or federal union at the time they all expected to see the Italian question solved by that device.[4]

IV. SWISS NATIONALISM AND THE NEUCHÂTEL CRISIS

In 1857 the political spotlight fell for a short time upon Switzerland, the Confederation that had been fortunate enough to complete its mid-century reorganization early in 1848, before the reaction set in. Under the new constitution the Swiss received some of those services that the Germans were demanding of their confederate assembly ten years later, notably unification of weights and measures and coinage. The high political tension that accompanied the spirit of Schwarzenberg elsewhere in Europe was absent from Switzerland. Had it been present the new constitution might well

[4] T. W. Riker, *The Making of Rumania* (Oxford, 1932).

have proved unworkable, for it made no provision for breaking a deadlock between the executive committee and the assembly, and left to unwritten comity the arrangement that in choosing seven councilors from twenty-two cantons, representation should always be given to all three nationalities, to both religious faiths, and to the two great cantons of Berne and Zürich. Since the army remained in the hands of the separate cantons, there was no clear-cut establishment of paramount power anywhere. The scheme worked because it was run in a business spirit, not in the spirit of *Realpolitik*.

The business class was the ruling class: railway politics furnished the dominant issues in the 'fifties. Adolf Escher, the wealthy patrician of Zürich, planned a railway empire to the profit of his own city. Staempfli, a man of the people and a journalist, resisted with a rival plan, which would have benefited the western cantons and his city of Berne. Escher had behind him the great financial power of the Crédit Mobilier and a strong political position. He signed the articles of the Northeastern Railway three times, once as head of the government of Zürich, once as member of the federal council, and again as president of the railway company. Staempfli fought Escher with the power of the press. With the *Berner Zeitung* he rallied opposition to the railway king in the assembly, which voted to forbid the construction of Escher's projected railway in the canton of Vaud because it would have competed with the line projected by the canton of Freiburg. Vaud denied the competence of the federal authorities. When Escher brought in French money, Staempfli obtained a large loan from the Swiss treasury. It was federal rights against cantonal, Berne against Zürich, demagogue against patrician, public control of railways against private, and Swiss capital against French.

Then suddenly a comic-opera revolution in the city of Neuchâtel precipitated a crisis which ended the factional strife, brought out all the latent national loyalty of the people, and gave them a chance to disentangle themselves from embarrassing foreign connection. The characteristic elements of the mid-century state-making process were present, but in miniature. There was a territorial entanglement to be straightened out, for the King of Prussia was sovereign prince of the free canton of Neuchâtel. There was a conflict of monarchic with popular sovereignty, for the revolution of 1848 had broken with the King to establish a popular government in the canton. There was also a collision of international with national authority, for the new Swiss constitution of 1848 guaranteed popular government in the cantons, while a protocol signed by the powers at London in May 1852, recognized the sovereign rights of the Prussian King in Neuchâtel. Beyond that there was a surge of militant patriotism among the people.

In September, 1856, a storming party of two hundred royalists attempted a *coup d'état.* They seized the castle of Neuchâtel and ran up the Prussian flag. The day after their exploit they were captured and imprisoned. King Frederick William intervened for their release, and appealed to the powers on the basis of the London protocol of 1852. When diplomatic methods failed, the Prussian government decided, on December 2, 1856, that the time had come to make reprisals by occupying Swiss territory. Prussian officers were sent to Württemberg and Baden to prepare the way for the marching Prussian columns. The Swiss federal council replied to threats of war by calling for a general mobilization of the cantonal armies. Amid tremendous popular enthusiasm the cantons responded to the military appeal, men flocked to the colors, children collected money and clothing for the cause, employers paid the wages of their workmen who went with the army. Party strife was forgotten, and the last scars of the *Sonderbund* War were healed in this military-national demonstration. A similar passion was to sweep the Italian peninsula two years later.

The powers resorted to the machinery of the concert to keep the peace, while Austria made use of the machinery of the *Bund* to hold down Prussia. Count Buol declared that Prussia would have to obtain from the confederate assembly permission to march her troops through the South German states. Eventually, at Napoleon's invitation, a conference met in Paris in March, 1857, to devise a settlement. Europe asserted her authority; the royalists were released, and the King of Prussia surrendered his sovereignty over the canton.

There remained to be cleared up one more anomaly in the relations of Switzerland to the system of national states. This was the presence in Italy of hired regiments serving the Neapolitan Bourbons under the Swiss cantonal flags. The Italian war of 1859 put an end to this situation, for the Swiss federal council, after a Swiss commander in papal service had allowed his men to sack the city of Perugia, forbade the practice of placing Swiss regiments in foreign service. Thereafter Swiss subjects entering a military career abroad acted as individuals and abandoned the flag and law of their country.

Both by virtue of the extent of territory involved, and because of the profound repercussions on other states, the unification of Italy was the turning-point in the history of European federative polity. The remarkable thing about the developments of 1859 and 1860 in Italy was not so much the destruction of the system of 1815 as the fact that the new Italy arose as a unitary state rather than as a confederation. This process must now be examined in detail.

Chapter Ten

CONFEDERATION AND UNITY IN ITALY (1859-1860)

I. THE CONFEDERATIVE PROGRAM IN ITALY

THE IDEA OF CONFEDERATION had been present in Italian statecraft for more than a generation, not as an exotic political invention, but as a seemingly inevitable alternative to the situation established in 1815. It was accepted both in the conservative and in the liberal camps. Metternich tried to organize an Italian Confederation modeled on the German in 1816. The anti-Austrian liberal party built up by Gioberti in the 'forties was committed to the principle that federation was the "ideal and perfect government"[1] for Italy. In the reform era just prior to the outbreaks of 1848, the three newly liberalized and constitutional states, Piedmont, Tuscany, and the Papal States, entered into the preliminaries of a customs union agreement as a step toward a liberal confederation, while Austria organized a political combination of despotic states by means of protectorate treaties with Parma and Modena.

When the storm broke in March, 1848, it seemed for a moment that there would be general coöperation of Italian princes against Austria, and that this must end in a free Italian federation under the presidency of the Pope, but the vision faded quickly. The war of Charles Albert in the Lombard plains did not result in any step toward the establishment of all-Italian institutions; there was no Italian constituent assembly as in Germany. But when the reaction returned to Italy in 1850 plans for a confederation reappeared as an adjunct to Schwarzenberg's central European power-policy. Representatives of the Pope and of the central Italian rulers conferred in Rome on a project drafted by the Tuscan minister, Baldasseroni, for an Italian Confederation with a common army to preserve order. Naples, at this juncture a champion of Italian

[1] Vincenzo Gioberti: *Del primato morale e civile degli Italiani* (Bruxelles, 1848), II, 61.

independence of Austria, proposed that the confederation exclude Austria and open the door to Piedmont. Despite Neapolitan opposition the papal and central states bound themselves in a preliminary treaty to develop the Baldasseroni plan. The only concrete achievements resulting from this initiative were a postal union and a railway convention.

Napoleon, too, worked on plans for Italian confederation. In 1856, as part of the preparation for the Congress of Paris, he drew up a project for an Italian Confederation modeled on the German *Bund*.[2] In 1857 Archduke Maximilian, in an effort to conciliate the people of Lombardy and Venetia, conceived a scheme for incorporating Romagna with the Austrian domains, giving Parma and Modena to Piedmont, and forming an Italian Confederation under the Pope. Neither Austria nor Naples, neither the Pope nor Napoleon, neither Cavour nor even Mazzini were wholly antipathetic to the idea of confederation. Each would have accepted it upon his own terms.

II. POLITICAL ALIGNMENTS IN ITALY

In the Italy of the 'fifties the political alignments were those standard for the time throughout Europe: liberals with a scientific outlook on life, a free-trade bias in economics, and a hankering for free speech were lined up against the "Codini" (so-called from the powdered wigs of the old régime), the partisans of absolute monarchy and clericalism. Factional hatreds as bitter as those that sent Dante out of Florence harried the liberals into exile or imprisonment in most of the Italian states; from Piedmont the bishops rather than the liberals went into exile. The sectarians of Mazzini were nowhere allowed to come into the open. Even the smaller towns had their liberal Capulets and reactionary Montagues. In the Kingdom of Naples they would fight over precedence in church processions. The cause of Italian solidarity was fed by this factional strife, for each party welcomed support from partisans in other states. The reaction was willing to make an Italian Confederation to defend authority; the liberals saw in the national movement a

[2] A. Pingaud, "Napoléon III et ses projets de confédération italienne," *Revue Historique*, CLV (1927), 333-336.

useful ally. The national cause was something they could use in Lombardy against the Austrians, in Sicily against the Neapolitans, in Naples against the Bourbons, in Rome against the Pope. Under these circumstances any Italian state that would declare itself solidly liberal became automatically the leader of a party throughout the peninsula. This was the destiny of Piedmont.

How did it happen that Piedmont, once the home of the most reactionary clericalism in Italy, became the head of the liberal faction? When the little huntsman-soldier king, Victor Emmanuel, with his marvelous mustaches and his brusque ways, assumed the crown laid down by Charles Albert on the battlefield of Novara, he did not abandon the constitution of 1848. He was held to this purpose by the staunch and honorable Massimo d'Azeglio, his prime minister. Grand Duke Leopold of Tuscany had the opportunity to share this leadership, but sacrificed it when he made use of an Austrian army of occupation. Because the terms of the Piedmontese constitution, prescribing equality before the law, made it necessary to close out the special courts and jurisdictions of the Church, the mere adherence to the constitution entailed a bitter battle with the clericals. This battle was won in 1850 with the Siccardi Laws, abolishing ecclesiastical courts. Hostility to Austria, never absent since the war of 1848, flared up anew in 1853 when the military government of Lombardy sequestered the property of Lombard exiles living in Piedmont. Because Turin was the resort of liberal exiles from all the other states, her intellectual and political society developed an Italian character. But the great statesman whose leadership replaced d'Azeglio's in 1852 was not so much dreaming of Italy as working for Piedmont.

Nineteenth-century nationalism, like twentieth-century socialism, had many adherents who favored it as a remote ideal but not as an immediately practical objective. For instance, there was King William of Prussia, who as late as 1860 told Napoleon he did not expect to live to see German unity. Of Cavour in the 1850's it is not easy to say when he shifted his direct objective from the cause of Piedmont to that of Italy. In his youth he had daydreamed of "waking one morning a directing minister of the Kingdom of

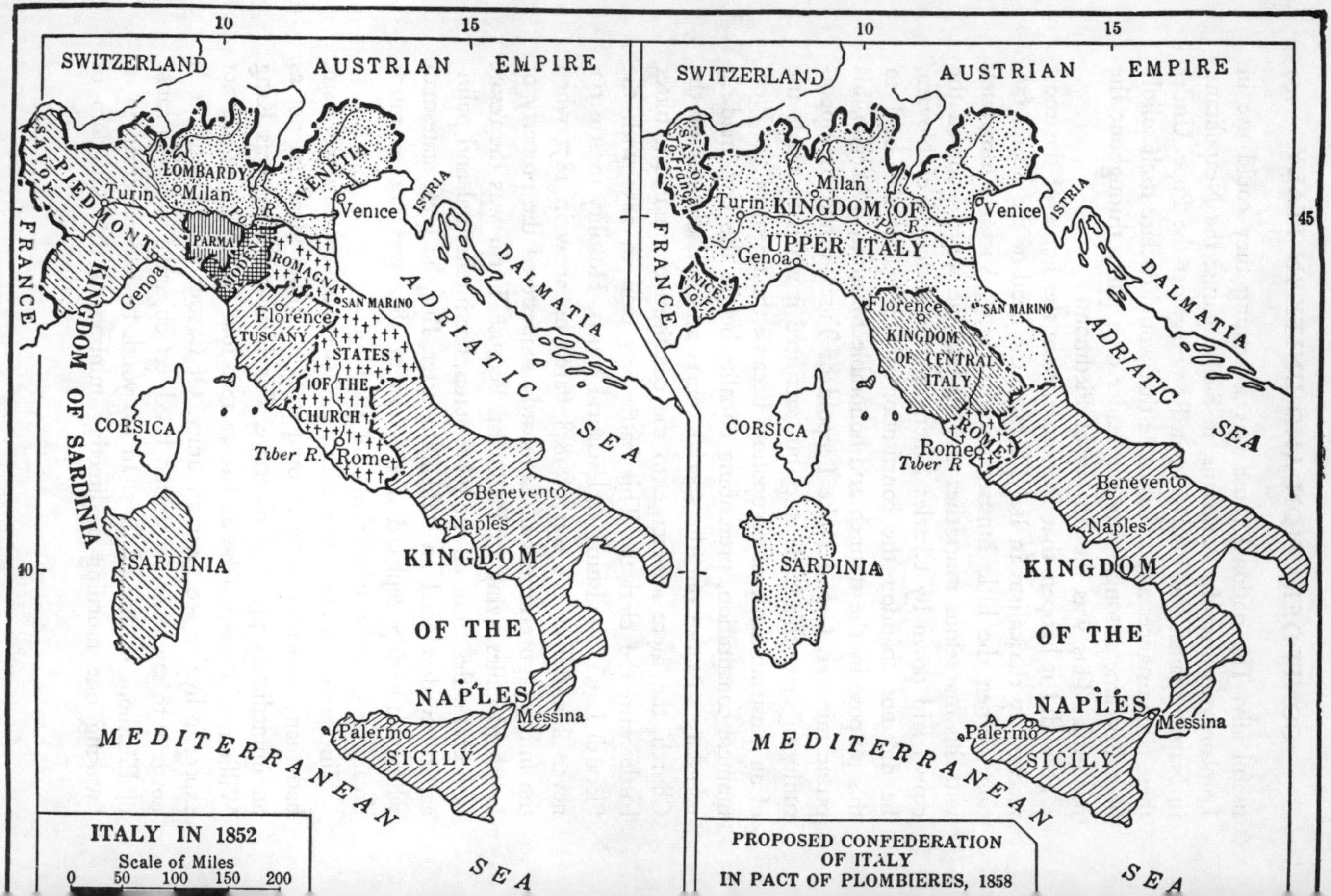
ITALY IN 1852
Scale of Miles
0 50 100 150 200
SWITZERLAND
AUSTRIAN EMPIRE
FRANCE
SAVOY
PIEDMONT
KINGDOM OF SARDINIA
LOMBARDY
VENETIA
PARMA
MODENA
ROMAGNA
TUSCANY
STATES OF THE CHURCH
SAN MARINO
Turin
Milan
Genoa
Venice
Florence
Rome
Tiber R.
Po R.
ISTRIA
DALMATIA
ADRIATIC SEA
CORSICA
SARDINIA
KINGDOM OF THE NAPLES
Benevento
Naples
Palermo
Messina
SICILY
MEDITERRANEAN SEA
10
15
40
PROPOSED CONFEDERATION OF ITALY IN PACT OF PLOMBIERES, 1858
SWITZERLAND
AUSTRIAN EMPIRE
FRANCE
SAVOY To France
NICE To Fr.
KINGDOM OF UPPER ITALY
KINGDOM OF CENTRAL ITALY
ROME
SAN MARINO
Turin
Milan
Genoa
Venice
Florence
Rome
Tiber R.
Po R.
ISTRIA
DALMATIA
ADRIATIC SEA
CORSICA
SARDINIA
KINGDOM OF THE NAPLES
Benevento
Naples
Palermo
Messina
SICILY
MEDITERRANEAN SEA
10
15
45

PROPOSED CONFEDERATION OF ITALY AT ARMISTICE OF VILLAFRANCA, 1859

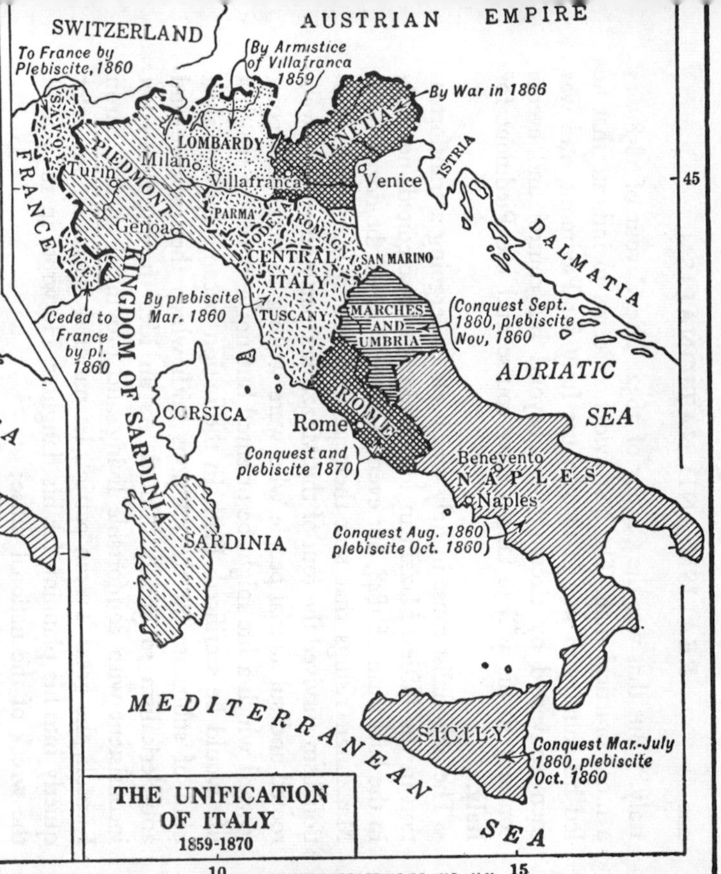

THE UNIFICATION OF ITALY 1859-1870

Italy."[3] But that was the Cavour of 1832. The Cavour of 1858 was a more practical man. The best evidence seems to indicate that he led his country to war in 1859 to use Italy for Piedmont, and was then converted by circumstances beyond his control and events contrary to his will to take a new course and use Piedmont for Italy.

The nationalist cause in Italy was itself undergoing a transformation in the 'fifties. Mazzinian leadership was discredited, not only in the backwash of 1848, but even more because of the dozen futile Mazzinian risings that sent their participants to martyrdom. Nationalism survived the rout of the Mazzinian party among the well-rooted and substantial people who were willing to make it a point toward which a life might be oriented but not a cause for which a life would be sacrificed. Faith in the nation became for liberals a kind of substitute for the religious faith which their science and anti-clericalism so greatly diluted. As an ideal it was found not inconsistent with comfortable living and provincial loyalty. Baron Ricasoli, the great Tuscan patriot, let national considerations enter quietly into his planning for his daughter. He wrote in 1850, amid the wreck of the national cause:

> Happy or unhappy, good or ill, I hold it to be a principle that one can have only one fatherland. Therefore I am educating Betta for her own country, Italy. She is free to marry or not as she chooses, but if she marries, it must be in Italy, to an Italian, and if possible a Tuscan.[4]

The stress of extraordinary circumstances could spread this ideal among the masses who did not read books, were not well-to-do, and had no leisure. It could enlist some of the clergy to it and even rally to it a peasantry that enjoyed the security of favorable land tenure. But for the most part nationalism was a petty luxury of a part of the aristocracy and the upper middle and professional classes. That their sympathy with the national ideal acquired political strength was due to the activities of a few strong leaders who broke away from the Mazzinian influence, and found a formula upon which moderate liberal nationalists could unite.

[3] Letter of October 2, 1832, Chiala, *Lettere edite et inedite di Camillo Cavour* (Torino-Napoli, 1884), I, 280.

[4] *Lettere e documente del Barone Bettino Ricasoli* (Firenze, 1887), II, 116.

The leaders were Daniele Manin, hero of the Venetian rising of 1848, Giorgio Pallavicino, a Lombard noble, and the Sicilian La Farina. These three founded the National Society in 1856, with the rallying cry, "Victor Emmanuel, King of Italy." This was a formula which might unite monarchists, federalists, and unitarians with the solid liberals of the peninsula, and drag into the movement the tired Mazzinian republicans. Manin explained that the formula was not to be too strictly interpreted.

> It is not necessary that all of Italy should be immediately united under the House of Savoy; it would be sufficient to justify the title if a goodly part of it should be, for the title was held in that way by the Lombards, the Franks, and the First Napoleon.[5]

Cavour first cultivated the National Society because it furnished an underhand means of thwarting a Muratist movement in Naples, a movement he dared not oppose lest he offend his ally Napoleon, but wished to scotch lest it should make Naples rather than Piedmont the focus of French Italian policy. He always sought to use rather than to serve the movement. The ideals of Manin he described as

> always a little Utopian. . . . He wants the unity of Italy and other nullities, but none the less in a practical occasion all this might be useful.[6]

Cavour as leader of the liberal faction in Piedmont found in the "moderate" nationalist movement a natural ally against the conspiracies of Mazzini's sectarians, the pressure of the Piedmontese clericals, and the hostile policies of Austria and her satellites in the Peninsula.

While Cavour was nursing Piedmont's position as the moral leader of liberals and nationalists, he maintained a foreign policy natural under the circumstances, unfriendly to Austria, friendly to France. He took no large initiatives on the European stage, but responded appropriately to the proposals of others. Upon a British invitation he brought Piedmont into the Crimean War. When his

[5] Conversation with Nigra, January, 1857, in *Il Carteggio Cavour-Nigra* (Bologna, 1926), I, 22.

[6] Cavour to Ratazzi, April 12, 1856, in Chiala; *Lettere edite et inedite di Camillo Cavour* (Torino-Napoli, 1884), II, 429.

hope of getting from the victory some territorial gain in central Italy or Sicily was disappointed, he made the best of his failure and wrote off the whole costly war investment as a contribution toward Piedmont's moral position. How far this particular increment of prestige contributed to Piedmont's success four years later is an open question.

III. THE PACT OF PLOMBIÈRES

The decisive initiative in the resurrection of Italy came from Napoleon III in the spring of 1858. He took over a threefold plan suggested in the entourage of his cousin Jerome. According to this plan the fifteen-year-old Princess Clotilde, daughter of Victor Emmanuel, should be given to Jerome in marriage, France should make war on Austria in alliance with Piedmont, and at the ensuing peace Piedmont should be given territorial compensations and made into a Kingdom of Upper Italy. The outline of the plan was conveyed to Cavour early in May, confirmed by the Emperor himself to Cavour's secret agent on May 9, elaborated for ten weeks in ciphered correspondence behind the backs of the accredited diplomats, and sealed as a bargain in an interview between Napoleon and Cavour at Plombières les Bains on July 20, 1858.

In this meeting at Plombières it seemed that two men could pick up all the threads of history and hold them for a moment in their hands. The long thought of Napoleon on the future of nationalities passed on that summer morning from dreaming toward action. Back to that interview can be traced not merely the making of Italy and Germany, but the readjustment of the whole political structure east of the Alps and Rhine. In the Eastern question and the Crimean War Europe had drifted; in the Italian question and the war of 1859 it was set on a course deliberately plotted, although the conspirators could not have foreseen how far the course they were setting would ultimately carry toward the bankruptcy of the confederative reorganization of Europe that Napoleon had in mind, the hypertrophy of national statehood, and the triumph of international anarchy.

The reconstructed Italy agreed upon at Plombières was to be a confederation "on the model of the German Confederation,"[7] made up of four states. The Pope was to be president and ruler of the territory immediately surrounding Rome. An Upper Italian Kingdom was to be constituted of the Austrian provinces, the duchies of Parma and Modena, and the Papal Legations. This realm of eleven million inhabitants was to be Piedmont's reward. Across the Alps the territories of Savoy and Nice were to be surrendered to France as Napoleon's reward, while across the Apennines from the Kingdom of Upper Italy was to rise the Kingdom of Central Italy, formed by adding to Tuscany the papal provinces of Umbria and the Marches. The boundaries of Naples were not to be changed.

This plan for the future constitution of Italy was a natural objective; ingenuity and imagination were required, not in projecting the structure of the new Italy, but in finding a pretext for war. Despite the precedent of the Crimean War and the strains thereby introduced into the European system, it was not easy in 1858 to break the peace.

Not often have the annals of European diplomacy recorded so clear a "war-plot" as that which Cavour described in his letter to his King:

> The Emperor began by saying that he had decided to support Sardinia with all his forces in a war against Austria provided the war should be undertaken for a non-revolutionary cause, and could be justified in the eyes of diplomacy and even more in the eyes of the public opinion of France and Europe.
>
> The search for this cause presented the principal difficulty. . . .

Cavour proposed that a war might be made out of an Austrian violation of a customs treaty, and then suggested that the illegitimate extension of Austrian influence in the Peninsula might be developed into a ground for war, but Napoleon objected that the commercial treaties were too small an affair, and that while his own troops were at Rome he could not protest the presence of Austrian troops at Bologna.

> My position was becoming embarrassing [continues Cavour's letter],

[7] Cavour to Victor Emmanuel, July 24, 1858, Chiala, *op. cit.*, II, 566-567.

for I had nothing further to propose. The Emperor came to my aid and we put our heads together and went through the whole map of Italy looking for this cause of war which was so difficult to find. After having traversed without success the whole Peninsula we arrived almost with certitude at Massa and Carrara, and found what we had sought with such ardor. . . . We agreed that we could provoke an address from the inhabitants to Your Majesty asking your protection, and even annexation to Sardinia. Your Majesty would not accept the rendition of territory, but taking note of the address would champion the cause of these oppressed peoples and address a haughty and threatening note to the Duke of Modena. The Duke, strong in the support of Austria, would reply with impertinence, whereupon Your Majesty would occupy Massa and the war would begin.[8]

The next ten months were spent in preparations for war and in engineering its provocation. For a time the whole enterprise hung on the decision of little Clotilde, for the King did not wish to force a marriage upon her. The suspense ended in mid-September when there was relayed to Cavour a "textual quotation" from the lips of the "dear little girl":

I told papa to have Prince Napoleon come here and if he is not actually repulsive to me I have decided to marry him.[9]

Then the diplomatic field had to be cleared. The verbal Plombières pact had to be put into treaty form. The signing took place in January, 1859. Then Russia had to be squared. This was accomplished by a treaty signed on March 3, 1859, by which French support for a revision of the Treaty of Paris of 1856 was traded for Russian approval of the revision of the treaties of 1815 as they touched Italy.

Although rumors of impending war circulated among the diplomats throughout the winter, Count Buol, with magnificent hauteur, discounted them all. On December 9 he told the Prussian envoy:

That he was accustomed with the coming of every winter to hear of the misery of the poorer classes, and so it had been for a long time

[8] *Il Carteggio Cavour-Nigra* (Bologna, 1926), I, 104.
[9] *Il Carteggio Cavour-Nigra*, I, 148.

the fashion to prophesy a war, especially an Italian War, for every spring.[10]

Even while Buol was indulging in this characteristic sarcasm, Cavour was refining his war plot. The Austrian government played into his hands with a decree establishing a conscription system in Lombardy and Venetia. This promised a better war pretext than misgovernment in Massa and Carrara. Cavour explained his new plan in a letter of December 13: he would let it be known that deserters fleeing from conscription would be harbored in Piedmont; nationalist agitators would organize a flight of hundreds, perhaps thousands, of deserters; Austria would then demand their extradition and Piedmont refuse:

> the levy of conscripts will take place in March, the deserters will come to us in April, the disagreement with Austria will then begin and can be carried on in such a way that the rupture will come in May.[11]

In January, 1859, the war plans began to come into the open. Napoleon hinted at trouble in a greeting to the Austrian ambassador at the New Year's reception; Victor Emmanuel ten days later told an applauding parliament that his government would not be insensitive to the "cry of anguish" from the subjects of the other Italian princes; the word was passed down the line in the National Society to prepare for great events; the marriage of Prince Jerome and Clotilde advertised the close alignment of France with Sardinia. On February 2 the pamphlet *Napoleon III and Italy*, which had been written under the Emperor's direction soon after the Plombières meeting, was published to inform the public of his plan for a free and confederated Italy.

IV. THE TEST OF THE GREAT POWER SYSTEM

The war scare called forth intensive action by three agencies: the concert, the *Bund*, and Italy. The concert moved to Europeanize the Italian question and prevent war. In the *Bund* there arose the question of the terms upon which there could be reëstablished the military defensive *Mitteleuropa* that had been set up during the

[10] *Die Auswärtige Politik Preussens* (Oldenburg, 1933), I, 99. Flemming to Schleinitz, December 9, 1859.

[11] *Il Carteggio Cavour-Nigra*, I, 240.

Crimean War. In Italy it was a question whether the revolutionary movement which Cavour was stimulating could be held in hand and delicately synchronized with diplomatic developments, for if a popular revolution should take the wrong course, appear in the wrong place, or occur at the wrong time, it would destroy the favorable diplomatic constellation of French aid and Russian benevolence.

From the moment when France and Russia aligned themselves diplomatically against Austria, the two remaining powers, England and Prussia, became the restraining and mediating agencies. England worked within the framework of the concert, and Prussia partly within the framework of the *Bund*.

The British government led off in February with direct mediation between Vienna and Paris. English suggestions developed by the end of March to the point where the basis of discussion was an evacuation of Italy by French and Austrian troops alike, and the establishment of a confederation (excluding the Austrian provinces) to take over the duties of preserving order that had been performed by the armies of occupation. This scheme was not unlike that which had been put forward by Naples as an amendment to the Baldasseroni plan of 1852.

So effective was the response of diplomacy to the threat of war that Napoleon hesitated to go ahead with the fulfillment of his Plombières agreement. Cavour sensed the untoward and unexpected efficacy of the "conspiracy of peace" that threatened to block his plans. But he went ahead with war preparations. In February he floated a loan of fifty million lire. When the Paris bankers refused him accommodation except on exorbitant terms he turned to the Italian investors, and sold Piedmontese war bonds in Milan and Livorno. Just as the Russians were able to use the London money market during the Crimean War, so Cavour was able to raise a war chest in the prospective enemy territory.

With the money safely provided, he pushed ahead with military preparations. On March 9 the King's proclamation called the Sardinian reserves to the colors. A few days later a decree appeared establishing a corps of volunteers which was rapidly filled up with fugitives dodging conscription in Lombardy, according to Cavour's plan.

While these provocative measures were being carried out in Italy, the diplomatic scene shifted. The procedure of British mediation was traversed by a Franco-Russian proposal to convoke a congress —a proposal that no power dared refuse. Thenceforth the subject-matter of negotiation among the powers shifted from the terms of an Italian settlement to the terms upon which the congress should meet. And among these terms those which gave rise to greatest contention were Cavour's demand that Piedmont be admitted to the congress on the same footing as the great powers, and Buol's demand that Piedmont should immediately demobilize the royal army and dissolve the volunteer corps.

This crisis brought out more clearly than any previous one the curious effect of the cadre army system upon the processes of diplomacy. The long-term professional French or Russian armies could be moved toward a threatened frontier or could accumulate special stores and equipment for war purposes without the derangement of civil life within the state and without the bellicose repercussions abroad that accompanied the transition of a cadre army from a peace to a war footing. For a nation with a cadre army, like Piedmont, the decision to call up the reserves involved an irrevocable commitment for the duration of the crisis. While the people of the German *Bund* were clamoring for mobilization, Cavour by mobilizing threw down the gauntlet, and Austria, a month later, by mobilizing, picked it up.

Cavour realized that mobilization placed him in a position from which he could not withdraw without disaster; the popular movement he was raising against Austria would turn upon him and destroy him if he were unable to feed it with a war. And word was coming from Paris that Napoleon, under pressure of diplomacy and public opinion, was ready to abandon the war plan. Cavour hurried to Paris at the end of March to warn his Imperial accomplice that it was too late to draw back. He threatened that if Piedmont were left in the lurch Victor Emmanuel would abdicate, and he, Cavour, would emigrate to America and there publish documents to prove that Napoleon himself had instigated the war plot. This desperate intervention was apparently effective. Napoleon forbore for the time being to clamp down on Piedmont, and this forbearance permitted Cavour to resist the pressure of London and Berlin for the demobilization of the army. When the time finally came on April 18 that Napoleon, unable to hold out longer against Europe, called upon the cabinet of Turin to accept demobilization, the delay had sufficed to give Austria a chance to make a crucial error.

The Italian crisis broke upon Vienna at a moment when German affairs were taking a new turn. Prince Regent William of Prussia, replacing his mentally ailing brother at the head of the state, had inaugurated a so-called "New Era" in November, 1858. He had dismissed the reactionary Manteuffel ministry, made a bid for the support of the liberal party in Prussia, and laid down a generous German policy. "In Germany," he declared to his new ministry on November 8, "Prussia must make moral conquests." This meant that an end would be put to the long filibuster at Frankfurt, that an effort would be made to work with Austria rather than against her, and that support would be given to the development of utilitarian improvements in the *Bund*. Piedmont had made "moral conquests" in Italy; now Prussia would make them in Germany.

The Piedmontese war-scare put this program of the New Era to a most severe test, for the German public raised a patriotic outcry for mobilization in defense of Austria. The Prussian cabinet faced the political dilemma that resistance to this patriotic call would mark the Hohenzollerns as chronic marplots and obstructors in Germany, while compliance would make them an Austrian cat's-paw. Moreover, there was the chance that mobilization in Germany would divert the war from the Po to the Rhine.

The new cabinet, after a period of internal tension, approved the policy of Foreign Minister von Schleinitz, which was to draw a sharp distinction between Prussia's capacity as a great power and her quality as a member of the *Bund*. While she would patriotically perform her strict duties within the *Bund*, she could not permit a majority of the confederate assembly to dictate her conduct as a great power.

This position gave critical importance to the articles of the Vienna Act of 1820 which defined the obligations of members of the *Bund* in the event of war. These articles had been carefully drawn to render the *Bund* powerful for defense, but impotent as an instrument of aggression. Articles XXXVI and XXXVII stated the principle that injury to any member of the *Bund* harmed the whole *Bund*, but that the duty of members was to refrain from actions that might provoke trouble. Article XLVII provided that if a member should be attacked on a frontier outside the territory of the *Bund* (such as Lombardy) the confederate assembly would decide by majority vote whether the attack endangered the safety of Germany. An affirmative vote obligated all members to give aid. The Prussian cabinet knew that Austria could get this majority vote whenever she asked for it. Therefore Prussia announced in advance that if the vote were taken without her consent, she would stand on her capacity as a great power and refuse to be bound by it.

But this did not mean that Prussian aid would be withheld under all circumstances from Austria, nor that the *Bund* as a military defensive organization was of no account. The Austrian minister to Prussia repeatedly informed Buol that Prussian aid would be forthcoming if Austria were clearly the victim of an attack. Let Austria carefully avoid aggression, and the resources of all Germany would be thrown in the balance on her side.

But Francis Joseph was provoked by Cavour's obstinacy into taking a fatal initiative. On April 7 he ordered Austrian mobilization, and within the next two days decided that the best way to clear the air was to force Sardinian demobilization with a short and conclusive military expedition. It was to be an *"Einmarsch in Sardinien"* like the *"Einmarsch in Serbien"* of 1914. As in 1914, it was necessary to consult in advance with Berlin. Archduke Albrecht was sent with a memorandum along the same road that Count Hoyos was to take fifty-five years later. The Albrecht memorandum explained the Emperor's purpose to send Piedmont

> an ultimatum to disarm in a few days, and in case after a few days there should be a refusal from Turin, the Austrian army would invade Piedmont in order to compel disarmament. This would not be war but

the enforcement of a right, for under the circumstances the Austrian Army would immediately withdraw and seek to retain not even a village.[12]

Prince Regent William, unlike his grandson, gave no blank check to Vienna. He insisted that Austria should use the instrumentality of the congress to settle the Italian question. But if war should come by French aggression, after Austria had made full use of pacific procedures, then, the Prince Regent agreed, Prussia would sponsor a war-vote in the *Bund* and two armies would form, one under Prussian command on the Rhine, the other under Austria in the Black Forest. Thus, despite Count Buol's many errors in judgment since 1852, Austria was in a strong legal, political, and military position. If the French and Piedmontese attacked Lombardy, the response in Germany would immediately shift the major theater of war to the Rhine, and there the imponderable forces of nationalism would have worked for Austria. If, on the other hand, diplomatic methods prevailed, there was every chance that the revolutionary movement in Italy would get out of hand and ruin itself as well as Cavour.

It seemed that at the very moment when the Archduke was concluding his pact with the Prince Regent, the concert was taking control of the crisis. During the night of April 18, telegrams were brought to Cavour showing that Napoleon was letting him down, and joining the other powers in demanding that Piedmont disarm and demobilize. Cavour exclaimed, "Now there is nothing for me to do but to put a pistol to my head and blow out my brains." On the morning of the 19th the Sardinian ministry reluctantly yielded to Europe and agreed to disarm.

But even as the concert made good its authority and as the *Bund* established its ability to stand as a defensive bulwark against an aggressor power, Austria put herself into the position of an aggressor. Francis Joseph on his own responsibility, acting on the advice of his military adviser, Count Grünne, and without Buol's knowledge, ordered the dispatch of the ultimatum to Piedmont. On April 20 the news flashed through all the capitals that Piedmont had

[12] *Die Auswärtige Politik Preussens,* I, 421.

yielded and that Austria was now provoking a war. Thus the Plombières pact bore fruit, but only with the aid of its victim.

V. VILLAFRANCA

The Austrian ultimatum was for the Italian cause "one of those lucky turns of the lottery that arrive only once in a century,"[13] and yet it was only the first of a series of similar accidents.

The first of these accidents, arising from the normal hazards of war, was a major defeat for Cavour, the Armistice of Villafranca. In six weeks of fighting the French and Piedmontese forces had driven the Austrians out of Lombardy and won two pitched battles, Magenta and Solferino, but despite these successes Napoleon was worried. There was dissatisfaction at home, the Germans were arming on his flank, and Cavour was double-crossing him in central Italy. Immediately after Solferino he asked for English mediation, and when he could not get the London government to recommend his pet confederative settlement to Austria, he sent an officer across the lines with a white flag to negotiate a truce. Francis Joseph, despite the Prussian mobilization, could get no assurance that Prussia would help in the reconquest of Lombardy, and was therefore inclined to peace. At nine o'clock on the morning of July 11 the two monarchs met, and in an hour's conversation agreed upon the outlines of a preliminary peace. Austria was to give up Lombardy, an Italian Confederation was to be formed under the presidency of the Pope, and the rulers of Parma, Modena, and Tuscany, who had been expelled from their states by their peoples during the war, were to be restored to their thrones, though not by force.

Napoleon had developed his plans for an armistice and peace without giving more than a hint to Victor Emmanuel. Cavour, busy with administration in Turin, knew nothing about it till the news arrived that the truce was an accomplished fact. Then he dropped everything and took a train for the front, arriving on the morning of the 10th to learn that the two Emperors were to meet on the morrow to decide political terms. Almost mad under the strain, he sought out his King and the two had a frightful session. Cavour

[13] D'Azeglio to Cavour, April 27, 1859, in P. Matter: *Cavour et l'Unité Italienne* (Paris, 1927), III, 185.

demanded that Victor Emmanuel continue the war alone if France made peace—an insane demand. He broke down and stormed until the King turned his back upon him and left the room. Then came the news of the actual preliminary peace terms. They seemed to Cavour a complete defeat, since by organizing a confederation in the Peninsula with Austria a member they confirmed rather than ended Austrian hegemony. Cavour resigned and left the political field.

The war was over and Cavour was out of the way. It was only at this point that the nationalist movement, so famed in the annals of the nineteenth century for its state-making potency, became the determining factor in Italian politics. Its field of operations was central Italy. The National Society had fomented revolutions there just as fast and just as far as safety permitted. The risings began in Tuscany in April. The Florentine liberals gave their Grand Duke, "Papa" Leopold, a chance to join the war against Austria, and when he refused sent him and his family into exile. It was a genial revolution in the town; the young wits among the Liberals amused themselves by calling at the houses of the die-hard conservatives to say, "Papa will not be home for dinner." But there was some fear that out in the country the peasantry might make trouble in favor of the Duke.

As the Austrian army retired along the Po the revolutions followed close at its heels, sweeping through Parma, Modena, and Romagna. They did not extend southward into the Marches because Perugia, after declaring for the national cause, was barbarously sacked by a regiment of Swiss soldiers in the service of the Pope. As the excitement of the spring continued the nationalist fever caught hold of the masses. The new Garibaldi hymn with its stirring refrain "Get out of Italy, O foreigners!" was sung by great crowds. But although Victor Emmanuel appointed commissioners to organize the liberated territories for war effort, their contributions to the war against Austria were disappointing. Especially in Tuscany war activity lagged.

Villafranca brought the liberal nationalists of central Italy for the first time to a spirit of desperation. With the prospect that Austria would remain dominant in Italy and the dukes return to their domains, it seemed that 1859 would be again what 1849 had been. Some of the liberal leaders resigned themselves to the probability of a life of exile; all of them were spurred to activity. Nationalism became for them a matter of life and death. Central Italy had raised no army to fight the Austrians, but it quickly recruited thirty thousand men to keep the dukes from returning and to protect Bologna from the fate of Perugia.

In the fanatical nationalism that ensued the autonomist party in Tuscany disappeared. This party had been strong enough during the war to resist the maneuvers of the National Society and to maintain itself in the Tuscan provisional government. The liberals of Florence did not then intend to make Tuscany a province of Piedmont. But after Villafranca the fusionists had everything their own way, for fusion with Piedmont seemed the only asylum from the certainty that the conservatives would turn the tables on the liberals, and the danger that the returning dynasty might inaugurate a cruel reaction.[14]

Thus the Villafranca terms had the curious effect that while they set up a confederation as the agreed program of European diplomacy in Italy, they destroyed its Italian national foundations. It became odious to Piedmont because it meant Austrian rather than Piedmontese hegemony; it appeared menacing to the Tuscans because it was coupled with the return of their Grand Duke. In the critical winter of 1859 the Italian national movement was compelled to array itself against European diplomacy as the Swiss and Rumanian national movements had done in 1857 and 1858. The nationalist cartoons of the time portray most unsympathetically a fussy little old woman named "Diplomazia." "Diplomazia," of course, expected to settle the Italian question in a congress, for which the

[14] A. Monti, *L'idea federalistica del risorgimento italiano* (Bari, 1922); A typescript seminar paper by J. B. Sirich is the only comprehensive study of the Italian pamphlet literature, especially of E. Alberi, *La politica Napoleonica e quella del governo Toscano* (Paris, 1859); *La Toscana durante la guerra dell'indipendenza* (Florence, 1859); *Luigi Napoleone dopo il 11 Luglio 1859* (Florence 1859); *La Maison de Lorraine* (Paris, 1860); C. Busi, *Governo e Riforme in Toscana* (1859); A. de Gori, *Confederazione* (Florence, 1859); A. de la Forge, *La guerre, c'est la paix* (Paris, 1859); G. Montanelli, *L'impero, il papato, e la democrazia in Italia* (Florence, 1859); See also L. G. de Cambray-Digny, *Carteggio politico di L. G. de Cambray-Digny* (Milano, 1913); E. Poggi, *Memorie storiche del governo della Toscana nel 1859-1860* (Pisa, 1867); R. Delle Torre, *La evoluzione del sentimento nazionale in Toscana dal 27 aprile 1859 al 15 marzo 1860* (Roma, 1915).

call went out in November, and to impose a confederate constitution on the Peninsula.

The nationalists bent all their efforts to present Europe with a *fait accompli*. In all four insurgent areas, Parma, Modena, Tuscany, and the Romagna, constituent assemblies met in August to vote their independence of the old sovereigns and to elect Victor Emmanuel their King. When it was clear in November that the King could not accept, they elected the Prince of Carignan, a member of his family, as regent. And when Napoleon would not let the Prince officiate in Tuscany, they accepted a Piedmontese emissary, Boncompagni, as a vicar of the regent. They formed a military league with a common army. And meanwhile they preserved order.

Although the strict letter of the peace preliminaries and the final peace that was signed at Zürich ran against them, the diplomatic situation was not unfavorable to the central Italian nationalists. Lord John Russell committed England to the policy of non-intervention, which meant that the Italians could do as they pleased. And Napoleon exhibited increasing disloyalty to his bargain with Francis Joseph. By December the French Emperor had reached the point where he was willing to antagonize the clericals in France for the sake of the Italian subjects of the Pope in Romagna. On December 22 the semi-official pamphlet, *The Pope and the Congress,* appeared on the Paris newsstands, expounding the proposition that the Pope should surrender his territories (except Rome) and build up his spiritual sovereignty. The pamphlet made the congress impossible because it showed that Napoleon would not stand by his treaty commitment to have central Italy restored to its legitimate authorities. Thus once again, as in April, the supreme agency of the European concert was set aside. Instead of a congress there was to be a round of independent bargaining.

VI. THE PRICE OF UNITY

In January, 1860, Cavour resumed office as prime minister, convinced that Villafranca had proved an unexpected blessing. He had not anticipated at the time of his resignation how the disintegration of international authority could make a dead letter of the treaty of peace, nor had he foreseen the stability of the national movement in central Italy. He returned to power with a tougher conscience and a bolder policy than before, and immediately announced to Europe that he must carry out the annexation of central Italy. Upon what terms would Napoleon permit this annexation to take place?

On February 2, in a letter to Victor Emmanuel, Napoleon named his terms: Piedmont might annex Parma and Modena, and retain the Romagna under Piedmontese administration but subject to the nominal sovereignty of the Pope. Tuscany could be given to a younger member of the House of Savoy as the nucleus of a Kingdom of Central Italy. Of such a territorial arrangement confederation would be the natural result. The liberals who had rallied to the national cause would be protected, and Austrian hegemony would be ended in central Italy. This much Napoleon would permit without demanding any territorial compensation.

For the outright annexation of Tuscany to Piedmont a price would have to be paid, the cession of Nice and Savoy to France. Cavour and the King could choose between a liberated and confederated central Italy without sacrificing territories to France, and an enlarged Piedmont paid for with two provinces. Cavour seems not to have hesitated in making his choice. He chose to surrender Nice and Savoy in order that the political form of the liberated region should be the unified national state of the French type, rather than one of those state systems, impotent for aggression, exemplified in German politics. In defending before his parliament the cession of Nice and Savoy, he never alluded to the alternative. His biographers have concurred in this silence, and have given the impression that there was no way of saving the national cause in central Italy save by sacrificing Nice and Savoy.

Why did the choice seem so natural at the time? Was it not that Cavour and the King took it for granted that the supreme object of statecraft was not a merely liberal and national state, but rather a "powerful" state? And confederations were not believed to be strong. The French ambassador, Persigny, pointed the moral clearly in justifying against British objections the taking of Savoy and Nice:

If we now want Savoy, it is because Italy, instead of contenting herself with a federative organization, seeks centralization as a powerful state.[15]

If Villafranca had undermined the confederative plan for Italy, Cavour's choice in February overturned it. The decision contributed greatly to the feeling of insecurity in Germany, for the French annexations in the Alps seemed to foreshadow further annexations on the Rhine. Thus the failure of the confederative program in Italy prepared the way for a further disintegration of the international system. Meanwhile Italian nationalism moved forward.

The social-psychological phenomenon of a mass-movement, responsive to some dominant symbol, exalting the spirits of whole populations and moving them to the greatest efforts and the most generous sacrifices, has so often been recorded in history that its appearance in Italy in the years 1859-60 should arouse neither wonder nor critical doubt. "Italy and Victor Emmanuel" had become a symbol of the highest psychological value because the National Society had propagated it, the war against Austria had dramatized it, and the seven months' tension after the unfavorable armistice had brought its meaning home to whole populations in terms of living hopes and fears and interests deeply vested in the new régime. The pressure that had been generated during the long period of waiting in central Italy was sufficient, by the spring of 1860, to burst out even beyond the wide dimensions of the politics of Cavour. Central Italy voted almost unanimously for union with Piedmont in the plebiscite held in March, and then sought new fields to conquer.

VII. GARIBALDI IN THE SOUTH

Cavour had always repudiated the tactics of popular mass revolutions; the Mazzinians, on the contrary, had always believed in them. Cavour expected to get results by diplomatic action on the international stage, reinforced by stable government at home; he used Mazzini as a bogey to scare the other governments into letting him do as he wished. The Mazzinians, never having forgotten that in the five days of March, 1848, the populace of Milan had expelled

[15] In De La Gorce *Histoire du Second Empire* (Paris, 1894-1905), III, 207. Cf. Chiala, *op. cit.*, IV, xxx-xxxi, for Napoleon's letter of February 2.

an Austrian army from the city, thought that this operation could be repeated any time and anywhere if only the right preparations were made. Neither calculation proved correct. The people of central Italy did not contribute by mass risings to the expulsion of the Austrians, nor did the population of Sicily respond *en masse* to the summons of Garibaldi. But the mass movement that was evoked *after* the liberation in central and northern Italy overleaped its home frontiers and contributed its force to the revolution in Sicily and Naples. This contribution was made through Garibaldi; it could have been made through no one else.

Of the typical romantic figures of 1848, with their faith in democracy and their political incompetence, their generous idealism and their sense of drama, Garibaldi alone took a decisive part in the nation-making process of 1860. He abandoned Mazzinian republicanism to accept service under the King in 1859, but in all other things he was still a man of 1848—still faithful to democracy and the efficacy of mass action, still contemptuous of the combinations of high international politics.

His exploits as leader of a volunteer corps in the war against Austria had added to the prestige of his name and surrounded him with a group of loyal followers who could always constitute on a moment's notice the nucleus of a private army. In November, 1859, during the period of tension, he had commanded the forces of the military league in central Italy, but had shown his political irresponsibility by planning an invasion of the papal Marches. Recalled in the nick of time from this project, he had shown further political naïveté by lending his name to the machinations of an anti-Cavourian clique in Piedmontese politics. Out of it all he had come with a new asset, the "Million Rifles Fund." The name of the fund itself was a program, and the money flowed in. The King himself was a large contributor. With men, money, and prestige, Garibaldi in the spring of 1860 had become an independent force in Italian politics—an incalculable force which might easily have been ruinous to the Italian cause.

There were four possible objectives for this professional guerilla fighter: Venetia, Rome, the Kingdom of Naples, and the County of Nice. To attack Venetia meant war with Austria; to attack Nice or Rome meant trouble with France. With characteristic disregard of these perils Garibaldi made plans in April for a raid on Nice to prevent cession to France, and on his way to Sicily mounted an attack against Roman territory. But fortunately for the Italian national cause he was diverted at the last moment from Nice, and his lieutenant Ziambachini made a complete fiasco of the attack on Rome, with the result that the test of Garibaldi's political and military strength came in the place where it involved the least risk of international complications, namely in the island of Sicily.

When Cavour had completed the annexation of central Italy he took some time to feel his way toward his next move. It seemed that an alliance of Austria, Naples, and Rome was forming to win back the papal territories. Cavour made an offer to Naples to partition Italy and share hegemony. Let King Francis break with Austria and the Pope, adopt the national cause and the liberal constitutional policy, recognize Victor Emmanuel's title to Romagna and compensate himself by taking Umbria and the Marches. There was little probability in the spring of 1860 that Naples would accept the offer, and Cavour seems to have hoped that it would be rejected. For he was following carefully the possibilities of a revolution against the Bourbon dynasty and hoping to gain by it.

The island of Sicily was the most favorable starting-point for a rising against the Bourbons, for it was traditionally hostile to the Neapolitans. The sentiment of hostility to Naples was a real bond of solidarity between peasant and large landholder, priests and people. Although both the Mazzinians and the National Society had revolutionary contacts in Sicily, the natural and traditional objective of a revolution there was the independence of the island rather than unification with the Peninsula. The victory of Solferino caught the imagination of the citizens of Palermo sufficiently to bring their revolutionary spirit up to date. But to the peasants of Sicily—as indeed of the whole Bourbon kingdom—the cult of national patriotism, as it was understood in the north, had no meaning. They could not understand, much less read, the language in which the ideals of nationalism were defined. They hailed Garibaldi, when he arrived, with an enthusiasm that was as much superstitious or religious as liberal and national, and they naturally interpreted his political program in terms of their nearest needs and most immediate grievances. They wanted the salt tax abolished, the domain lands distributed to them, the price of bread reduced, and work provided for all.

Garibaldi, who knew the practical requirements of guerilla fighting if not those of high diplomacy, had given his word that he would lead an expedition to Sicily if and when the people of the island gave the signal by a general rising. This they did not do. But a young Mazzinian, Rosalino Pilo, set out in March, 1860, to stir one up. He happened there upon the disintegrating relics of a small-scale rising that had been engineered by a committee in Palermo. By promising that Garibaldi would soon appear, Pilo kept the squads of peasant-brigands from fading away, and sent word north that the revolution was in progress.

Upon receiving this news, Garibaldi opened headquarters in Genoa; the National Society shipped to him from its stores some heavy boxes labeled "books"; he filled a war chest from the Million Rifles Fund, and rapidly recruited a little army of a thousand of the best youth of north and central Italy. After a period of wavering and hesitation he embarked his army on two steamships, stopped *en route* to launch the little subsidiary expedition against Rome, landed at Marsala on May 11 under the noses of three Neapolitan warships, and proclaimed himself dictator of the Island.

Cutting through the back country, he met and defeated a force of Bourbon soldiers, outwitted the only competent Bourbon commander into leading his column off on a wild-goose chase, maneuvered his way through the hills back of Palermo, and on May 27 entered the town, which the incompetence of the defenders quickly put into his hands. Under his leadership a thousand determined men, equipped with fifteen hundred muskets and a chest of money to hire peasant-bandits as auxiliaries, and aided to some extent by a sympathetic populace in the city, overcame a royal army twenty thousand strong. Palermo had risen in revolt before this time, and would rise again; in 1866 the city would even rise against that "Italy and Victor Emmanuel" for which the crowds cheered in the Garibaldi days. But the nineteenth century would never again see amateurs overwhelm a professional army, nor a populace successfully rush to arms. Garibaldi would try again at Aspromonte and Mentana. The Poles would try in 1863, the French in 1870, Paris in 1871, but never with a chance of success.

The Bourbon military establishment, like the Austrian, had been strengthened since 1848 for the purpose of preserving order within the kingdom. Ferdinand had gained his nickname "Bomba" by tactics as relentless as those of Cavaignac in Paris or Windischgrätz in Austria in dealing with rebellious civilians. The young King Francis inherited an army of a hundred thousand men. Its effectiveness had been reduced in June in consequence of the Swiss order putting an end to foreign-service regiments, for the four Swiss regiments in Neapolitan service mutinied when they were compelled to surrender their cantonal flags. Garibaldi's success in Sicily disheartened the army, and then the King himself took a step which demoralized it. On May 30, while Garibaldi was negotiating the truce preparatory to the surrender of Palermo, a crown council at Naples decided upon a fundamental change in system. The Kingdom should go liberal, adopt the red-green-white national flag, have a constitution, and take up the Piedmontese offer of Umbria and the Marches—perhaps even concede the loss of Sicily. When this decision was put into effect in the decree of July 25, it discredited and disheartened the friends of the dynasty, filled the government with liberals who were eager to betray the King, and allowed a free press an unrestrained license to undermine Bourbon authority. The repressive system of the Bourbons, built up to protect the throne against the very forces that were attacking it, was jettisoned in the midst of the crisis in the expectation of an understanding with Piedmont.

VIII. CAVOUR'S REALPOLITIK AT ITS ZENITH

Cavour had been driven by circumstances into many deceits and subterfuges, but never before had he revealed so callous a conscience as he showed at this time. While pretending to negotiate with the reformed Neapolitan court, he bent every effort to provoke a revolution against it in the city of Naples in order to forestall and double-cross Garibaldi, all while letting the Italian patriots think he was supporting the great guerilla fighter, and telling Napoleon that he was not supporting him. Cavour's agents in fomenting Neapolitan revolt were less successful than Rosalino Pilo in Sicily. The subjects of the Bourbon King were disgustingly apathetic to the opportunity to rise and overthrow the dynasty. They were willing to wait for Garibaldi.

This was something that Cavour feared, for the dictator's prestige had risen so high that his name was replacing Victor Emmanuel's as the symbol of the Italian national cause. And the Mazzinians were becoming increasingly influential in the Garibaldi camp. On August 20 the dictator crossed the Straits of Messina, and led his army of red shirts, now greatly reinforced from the north, toward Naples. The resistance of the Bourbon army collapsed before him; his journey was a triumphal march. Francis obligingly withdrew from his capital, and Garibaldi hurried on by train with a few companions to take possession of the city on September 7. It was his announced intention to proceed next to Rome, and there, on the steps of the Capitoline, turn over a liberated Italy to Victor Emmanuel.

The dangers to Cavour's policies inherent in the situation were two: that Garibaldi should bring the Italian nation into conflict with France by attacking Rome; and that he should acquire more prestige than the dynasty and turn the national movement over to the Mazzinians. Both these possibilities were, for different reasons, distasteful to Napoleon as well as Cavour. And meanwhile Pope Pius had been alienating the Emperor's sympathies by his political intransigence, by the encouragement he gave to the clerical enemies of the government in France, and by an effort he was making to get out from under French protection by organizing a Catholic army to defend and reconquer his domains. The new papal army, largely officered by French legitimists, was placed under the command of General Lamoricière, an outspoken enemy of the Bonaparte dynasty. Cavour brought all these elements of the situation together in his last and most daring political combination, the invasion of the Marches.

On August 27, while Garibaldi was moving up toward Naples, two agents of Cavour obtained an audience with Napoleon at Chambéry. They explained that it was too late to stop Garibaldi short of Naples, and too late to keep him from attacking Rome unless King Victor Emmanuel's army should intercept him in the Marches. An insurrection in these provinces was imminent, anyway. The King would destroy Lamoricière's army—at this Napoleon smiled—but would keep Garibaldi out of Rome. Napoleon accepted the plan, according to one account with the words "do it but do it quickly."[16]

On the day Garibaldi entered Naples, Cavour precipitated the invasion of the Marches with an ultimatum to Rome. In September the royal army swept through papal territory, destroying Lamoricière's forces at Castelfidardo, and giving the city of Rome a wide berth as it moved on toward Naples. There was a sharp crisis in Garibaldi's camp as the Mazzinians worked to prolong the dictator's authority by deferring the inevitable annexation to Piedmont. Cavour's agents, working for immediate annexation, prevailed. The plebiscites took place in October; only about ten thousand in the whole kingdom voted against annexation. The Marches and Umbria were annexed in the following month, despite the assurance Cavour had given Napoleon that he would allow a European congress to determine their fate. Napoleon broke off relations with Piedmont, and the Tsar called at Warsaw a meeting of the monarchs of the old Holy Alliance to discuss measures to be taken against such provocative conduct in Italy. But nobody intervened and Cavour and his King went right ahead. On a glorious November 7 the King and Garibaldi rode together into Naples, sealing the union of north and south and bringing together the fruits of the two master-techniques of the Risorgimento: the romantic mass leadership of Garibaldi and the Machiavellian *Realpolitik* of Cavour.

The annexations in the south had marked the end of confederation in Italy. Its last defender was Giuseppe Ferrari of Milan. The other federalists—the Tuscans like Montanelli and Alberi—had all come into the fusionist fold, but Ferrari in a last-stand speech in the Turin parliament in October, 1860, raised his voice against an Italian settlement that would subordinate to so backward a city as Turin great culture centers like Milan, Florence, and Naples.

[16] Lynn M. Case: *Franco-Italian Relations 1860-65* (Philadelphia, 1932), 13, footnote, discusses the evidence on the question whether or not this phrase is apocryphal.

Although the chamber overrode Ferrari 190 to 6, the ethnic and geographic facts he stated could not be ignored. "Though no one any longer defends the Italian Confederation," he said, "the Po and the Apennines will never abandon it."

Cavour hoped to meet the resistance of particularistic sentiment with a system of administrative decentralization. A commission of the parliament worked on the plan through the winter of 1860-61. The proposed system would have established great regions more or less corresponding to the historic divisions of Italy. The regions would have had no legislative powers, but would have had their administration largely in their own hands. When the project came before the chamber in March, 1861, it was attacked and defeated by the fusionists, who saw in it the menace of disunion. No definitive action on internal administration was taken for four years thereafter.

In the meantime the Piedmontese heroes of the Risorgimento established what was almost a carpet-bagger régime in the south. Honest and tactless, talking constantly about patriotism and liberty even as they were buying up the lands seized in Sicily from the church foundations, they became exceedingly unpopular. The peasantry that had voted for annexation turned against the new régime, and the white flag of the Bourbons rose from time to time in the villages.[17]

The actors in the political drama of the south now exchanged rôles. The Bourbons from their asylum in Rome sent out leaders of rebellion, even as the liberals had once sent them out from Piedmont. The Piedmontese found themselves ruling the country with the bayonet, unable to adhere to the principles of civil liberty which their theories required. One Piedmontese general in Sicily went so far as to issue an order to shoot "anyone who by word or act insults the coat of arms of Savoy, the portrait of the King, or the national flag of Italy."[18] This overzealous commander was recalled, but the shooting of peasants went on. Over seven thousand were shot in

[17] Bianco di Saint Jorioz, *Il Brigantaggio alla frontiera pontifica dal 1860 al 1863* (Milano, 1864); *Cronaca degli avvenimenti di Sicilia da Aprile 1860 a marzo 1861, Estratto da documenti* (Italia, 1863); G. Racioppi, *Storia dei Moti di Basilicata e delle provincie contermine nel 1860* (Napoli, 1867).

[18] Carlo Tivaroni: *Storia critica del risorgimento italiano* (Turin, 1888-1897), II, 367.

the course of two years. Legitimist leaders appeared to head bands that sometimes numbered up to a thousand. The Catalan Don José Boijas was the Garibaldi of the Bourbon cause; he disembarked at Brancaleone in September, 1861, where he met the bands of the rebel chieftain Donatello. He had a thousand men and two hundred horses. When the Italian parliament was forced by the complaints of the southerners to open an investigation in 1863, a long list of atrocity stories came to light. Thousands of peasants had been deported, whole villages burned. The rebels tortured and killed the soldiers, the soldiers shot the rebels on sight.

The government, faithful to the lexicon of politics as it is read in the New World and the Old, in Ireland, Nicaragua, or Manchuria, regarded these disturbers of the peace as "brigands." Doubtless they conformed more to the type of "brigand" in their aspect and behavior than did the Garibaldini. Since the Rothschilds would make no advances to Francis, they had less money to finance their raids. They were drawn from a lower social class. Theirs was a lost cause, although, unlike the majority of the followers of Garibaldi, *they were native to the soil.*

IX. THE ROMAN QUESTION

Though the chamber overrode Ferrari and the army wiped out the "brigands," the fact remained that Italy would not willingly accept as a permanent system the dictation of a government in Turin. Only one city could be accepted by Italy as the capital of a unified state, and that was not Turin nor Florence, but Rome. Thus the logic of unification as against confederation led inevitably to Rome. Cavour had recognized this need as soon as the annexations in the south were accomplished.

Through two intermediaries, Dr. Pantaleoni and Father Passaglia, he developed a plan for a settlement of the dispute with the Papacy somewhat more favorable to the Pope than the arrangements finally concluded by Mussolini in 1929. Under Cavour's plan a nominal papal sovereignty would have continued over all papal territory, although the "exercise of the government" would have been conferred on Victor Emmanuel. The Pope could have had a little Vatican City on the right bank of the Tiber if necessary. Pope and cardinals would have had their income guaranteed, and the Papacy would have had an endowment of property tax free. The Pope would have been guaranteed free communication with Catholics everywhere. This was the program of "a free church in a free state." It was sweetened even further by a provision that the cardinals were to have rank as princes of Italy, and that some of them were to sit in the Italian senate. Cardinal Antonelli, the influential papal secretary of state, hinted that he would be receptive to further sweetening in the form of a gift of three million scudi "for the expenses of the negotiations."[19] Cavour had no hesitation in proceeding to bribery on this colossal scale, but the political weather changed suddenly in February, 1861, and Antonelli let it be understood that all deals were off.

Cavour thereupon turned to France, where he encountered a plan which Thouvenel, Napoleon's foreign secretary, had worked out—the plan that became famous three years later as the "September Convention." Under Thouvenel's scheme the Kingdom of Italy was to replace France as guarantor of the Pope's independence. The French troops were to be withdrawn, the Pope was to be permitted to enlist two thousand loyal Catholic troops as a foreign legion to keep order at home, and the Italian Kingdom was to guarantee him against attack by regular or irregular forces from abroad. The Italian cabinet accepted these principles after a discussion which revealed Cavour's firm intention to violate the agreement at the first decent opportunity by applying to Rome the formula of revolt and annexation that had worked so well elsewhere. Napoleon probably understood that these were Cavour's secret intentions, and yet he said on June 3 that he expected soon to sign the treaty. Two days later Cavour died.

It had become evident by this time that the rules of the political game had been changed materially since the days when Nicholas feared that a numeral in the title of the French Emperor would undermine the treaty system of Europe. If, at the time of the armistice of Villafranca, Cavour went almost mad with despair, it was because his political experience to that date indicated that when treaties were once duly signed it might be anticipated that they

[19] Cavour's, *La Questione Romana negli Anni 1860-61* (Bologna, 1930), 2 vols.

would be loyally carried out. In the two years since Villafranca the treaty system had been so greatly undermined by the diplomacy of non-intervention and the jurisprudence of insurrection and plebiscite that it seemed the most natural thing in the world to sign a treaty for the purpose of breaking it.

Another strange fact must be noted. When Cavour died, suddenly and in mid-career, like Schwarzenberg, it was seen that his persistent tactics of deceit had won him the confidence of his contemporaries, who seemed to trust him because of the success of his magnificent treacheries. Napoleon hesitated to sign with Ricasoli the treaty he had negotiated with Cavour, thus postponing the French evacuation of Rome for years. The September Convention was signed in 1864, and the French withdrew under its terms in 1867, but they were immediately recalled to the city to defend it against a Garibaldian raid, which they stopped at Mentana. When the Franco-Prussian War finally forced the withdrawal of the French in 1870, the Italian army took the city without any treaty preparation at all.

Chapter Eleven

DUALISM AND FEDERALISM: THE FEDERATIVE CRISIS IN CENTRAL AND EASTERN EUROPE (1860-1864)

I. FEDERALISM, CONFEDERATION AND DUALISM

THE ITALIAN WAR of 1859, like the World War of 1914-18, presented to the whole complex of peoples living east of the Rhine and the Alps the problem of reordering their political life. The problem was threefold: how would the German nationality develop its political organization now that the Italian nationality had marked out a road? How would the non-German nationalities of central Europe, especially the western Slavs, be fitted into the European states-system? How would the middle class establish its political position in the dynastic state?

The three regions in which the impact of the war in Italy was felt most directly were the German Confederation, the Hapsburg Monarchy, and Russian Poland. German patriots were stunned by the failure of the military defensive system of the *Bund*; their feelings were not unlike those of the League of Nations adherents who saw the League machinery fail in Manchuria. The sense of insecurity, the fear of a French movement on the Rhine, affected everyone from the Prince Regent of Prussia down. Yet the attempt to make political and military preparations for the impending war encountered difficulties as complex as those that confronted Europe sixty years later in organizing the reverse process of disarmament.

In the Hapsburg Monarchy, the spirit of unrest had a different character. There the outstanding fact was the discrediting of the bureaucratic Bach system. In 1848 the dynasty had held together peoples that were pulling apart; in the words of Eötvös, it was not the idea of unity that saved the monarchy, but the idea of the monarchy that saved unity. By 1859 the peoples had come to a kind of unity of sentiment, but in opposition to the centralized

Bach bureaucracy. Thus the formula of change was defined for central Europe: tighten up the *Bund*, loosen up the Hapsburg Monarchy.

When the twentieth century reconstructed all central and eastern Europe by setting up centralized national states, it transferred the problem of giving to these peoples a satisfactory political structure, so that it ceased to be an object of statecraft for the Hapsburgs, Hohenzollerns, and Romanovs, but became a European problem instead.[1] Since it has now become a European problem, those chapters of history which could once be enclosed as items in the record of a dynastic state take their place as a part of the general constitutional history of the whole continent.

In the extraordinarily fertile political discussion of the time there were a number of types of solution for the central European problem, all within the prevailing federative polity. Most plans fell into one of two classes, called *Kleindeutsch* and *Grossdeutsch* in Germany; *Dualism* and *Federalism* in the Hapsburg Monarchy.

Dualism in the Hapsburg Monarchy meant that Hungary, as a constitutional state, should gather to itself the subordinate lands of Croatia, the Banat of Temesvar, the Voivodina and Transylvania (Siebenbürgen), and define its relation to a unit composed of all the other Hapsburg lands on the basis of a personal union. The German *Kleindeutsch* plan was simply a Dualism for *Mitteleuropa*: Prussia should gather to itself the lesser German states and define its relations to the whole Hapsburg Monarchy by an alliance treaty on the basis of international law. Some of the dualist plans provided that the Prussian sphere should lie north of the river Main, and the south German states should fall into an Austrian sphere. The dualist plans all involved a division of Germany, whether at the Main or the Inn (the river dividing the Austrian from the Bavarian German lands).

Federalism in the Hapsburg Monarchy meant that the various crown lands should take control of all matters except foreign affairs, defense, customs, communications, coinage, weights and measures. These essential services should be left in the hands of a central government. Federalism in the *Bund* meant that all the German

[1] See Joseph Redlich, *Das Osterreichische Staats- und Reichsproblem* (Leipzig, 1920-26).

states—including those under the Austrian crown—should be drawn closer together under a stronger central authority—in short, that the Confederation should be transformed into a federation.

The crucial test of the dual or federal character of a proposal was the place it gave to the German middle states (that is, middle-sized states), and the great Austrian crown lands. To the extent that Hanover, Saxony, Baden, Württemberg, and Bavaria approached parity with Prussia, or the crown lands of Bohemia, Galicia, Croatia, and Transylvania parity with Hungary, a system was *federal.* A variant plan in Germany called for the union of all the small and middle states in a group which would have been just about large enough to balance Prussia on the one hand, and Austrian Germany on the other. This was called the *Triad* plan.

In theory there might have been yet another program, namely "centralization" or "unification," and the publicists have actually used these words in describing policies and achievements of the time. But true centralization in the Hapsburg Monarchy would have been the perpetuation of the Bach system, and true unification in Germany would have meant the absorption of all the parts of the German Confederation, including the Austrian parts, in a centralized state. Neither of these schemes had any living significance in the period of reform and reconstruction in the 'sixties. No important party, no responsible statesmen, supported either of them. Journalists who disliked Schmerling in 1861 called his program (which will be described below) centralization. Journalists and historians have described Bismarck's achievement as "unification." Both terms are misnomers. In the practical politics of the 'sixties there were only the two alternatives for central Europe: dualism and federalism. In the end it was dualism that won.

What is the meaning of dualism? It is the simplest form of balance of power. To be a member of a group which includes a number of other members on equal terms with the self is always complex and entangling. To reduce the complexity to a dualism simplifies the power relationship. When Danilevsky laid down the Pan-Slav doctrine that Russia is not merely one among five great powers, but a power equal in status to all the other four put together, the ideal of his system was a kind of European dualism. There are points of resemblance between Pan-Slavism and the Monroe Doctrine from this point of view. Each of them was a doctrine of "two worlds" and each of them involved in fact the hegemony of a great state over the lesser units in its own world. Dualism as expressed in the dual monarchy in 1867, the dual alliance of 1879, as well as Pan-Slavism and the Monroe Doctrine, was an alternative or substitute for more completely federative relationships, involving a larger number of equal members. To analyze this concept with the material provided by the Bismarck alliance system, the dualism of the triple alliance and triple entente, the problem of American participation in the League of Nations and the "collective guarantee" problem of post-war Europe would go beyond the compass of this book. It is sufficient to point out that dualism in the experience of modern Europe has been in most cases antithetic to the full realization of federative polity. It was the form given to a house divided that would not stand.

II. FEDERALISM AND DUALISM IN THE HAPSBURG MONARCHY

In 1860 there were three rallying-points for the forces of movement in central Europe: nationalism, liberalism, and great-power status.

The rich symbolism of a national cause was used on behalf of both programs, dualism as well as federalism. It was a lofty ideal to the peoples, a tool in the hands of cabinets. Liberalism was more of a class program. The middle class used it in a war on two fronts, against the bureaucracy and court nobility in Prussia and Hungary, and against the labor movement that Lassalle was calling to life in Germany. The liberals rallied in 1860 to a Prussia that would protect the rights of parliament; the nationalities of Hungary rallied to a free Hungarian state that would protect rights of nationality, and both, in the end, were betrayed.

In the formation of cabinet policy, neither the dogmas of liberalism nor of nationalism were decisive at Berlin or Vienna. The idea of great-power status was dominant at both courts. In the Hapsburg Monarchy, reform was taken up by the ministry in 1859 because financial difficulties threatened to weaken the part that Austria could play as a great power, and brought to a conclusion when

Déak and Francis Joseph, after five years of tension, were able to get together on the common ground that the framework uniting Austria and Hungary must be one that would enable Austria to fulfill its duties as a great power. Prussia's German policy from the time of the Crimean War through the crisis of 1859 and the destruction of the *Bund* in 1866 was defined by the conception of Prussia's great-power status as something that entailed specific privileges and obligations which might be opposed to her privileges and obligations as a member of the *Bund*. After the founding of the Empire it was a corner stone of Bismarck's central European dualism that Austria no less than Germany must be preserved as a great power. The great-power principle and the nationality principle operated in opposite directions both in Germany and on the Danube. In Germany the great-power principle kept Prussia and Austria apart, while the nationality principle drew them together; on the Danube the great-power principle meant union, while the nationality principle meant separation.

At the Austrian court the first repercussion of the Italian crisis was a shake-up in the ministry. Rechberg, friend and pupil of Metternich, replaced Buol at the foreign office, and Goluchowski, an experienced provincial governor, took the post of the hard-working Bach. These appointments foreshadowed more amity toward Prussia and more sympathy with the provinces, but they did not indicate a change of system. The realization that a change of system would be necessary came only gradually, as the government was assailed by financial troubles in the autumn of 1859, and as the high aristocracy, which had access to the Emperor, carried the complaints of the country to his ear. Though the fundamental difficulty of the monarchy was a phenomenon of nationality, the dynamic forces that first imposed themselves on policy were non-national: they were the force of finance with its rapidly developing international institutions of credit, capital accumulation, and exchange, and the force of that political class which had remained nearest to the non-national traditions of feudalism. Though the aristocracy was destined in the later decades of the century to merge its interests more and more with those of other propertied and financial classes, in this historic moment it stood up and played independently the rôle of a political party with a far-reaching program. The leaders of this so-called "High Tory" party were the Hungarians, Count Anton Szécsen von Temerin and Count Georg Apponyi. They drew in as an ally Count Jaroslav von Clam-Martinitz of the high Bohemian nobility, and the great Bishop Strossmayer, leader of the southern Slavs, whose opposition to political centralization in 1860 was no less marked than his opposition to papal centralization in the Vatican Council of 1870.

The first step toward a change in system came in December, 1859, when a commission was appointed to survey the state debt. This step, taken on the advice of the finance minister as a means of bolstering up credit, was followed in January, 1860, by another scheme, that of enlarging the established administrative Reichsrat by adding new members to it. The Reichsrat would thus become an assembly of notables. On March 5, 1860, the Enlarged Reichsrat was summoned. The leaders of the "High Tory" party were appointed to sit in it. They came as enemies of the centralizing bureaucracy and the ministry, but they were equally hostile to the secular dogmas of liberalism. Their hostility to western constitutional ideas put them on a solid footing with the Emperor.

The meetings of the Enlarged Reichsrat continued through the summer and into September of 1860. From being a body of financial counselors, it became almost a constitutional convention, for the consideration of the state of the budget led to the consideration of the state of the country and the need for reconstruction.

Two parties defined themselves in the sessions, the high-tory federalists, led by the Hungarian delegates, and the German bureaucratic centralists, of whom Auersperg, Lichtenfels, and Thun were outstanding spokesmen. The federalist majority wanted to restore all the crown lands to their historic status in the monarchy, leaving the historic ruling class, the aristocrats, as the link between the crown lands and the center. The bureaucratic minority did not dare to advocate the mechanical centralization of the Bach period, which was so evidently bankrupt, but they insisted that the first thought in the reconstruction of the monarchy must be "of what unites us, not of what separates us"; there must be plans for "that great house in which we can all find room."[2] Lichtenfels, speaking for the centralists, declared:

> We must decide whether the Austrian state . . . may develop true greatness, or whether it will fall into the weakness of mere personal union or at best a federated state, and thereby be forced to cease to be a great power, and become a second-rate power in Europe.[3]

Even the bureaucratic party conceded that decentralization was necessary, but saw it as a process of assigning duties to new local organs of government, communal and provincial. They saw the need for a central parliament, but not for the liberal principles of parliamentary control of administration.

Against these ideas the high-tory majority developed the theory that Austria was a collective state created by the free compact of its component parts, which by sacred treaties (such as the Pragmatic Sanction of 1723) were joined together under a common throne. These parts were the "historic-political individualities" whose reciprocal rights were the legal fabric holding the monarchy together. Their thought continually returned to the starting-point: Austria is not a state like other states, but a kind of confederation.

The doctrine of "historic-political individualities" as it was set forth by the majority was peculiarly favorable to Hungary, because the restoration of historic rights would have given Hungary a degree of autonomy and a weight in the monarchy exceeding that of any other crown land. Thus in the Enlarged Reichsrat there predominated not only the class interests of the high aristocracy, but also the state interests of Hungary.

The doctrine of historical-political individualities was not only very favorable to the Hungarians, but very unfavorable to those two leading ideas that were coming in from the west: the mechanical conception of parliamentary liberalism and the geographical conception of a united nationality. Only one member of the Reichsrat spoke in favor of the liberal parliamentary system, and many members turned aside to heap scorn upon it. This was natural, for the high tories had in mind not modern parliaments, but "estates of the

[2] Count Auersperg in *Verhandlungen des österreichischen verstärken Reichsrathes, 1860* (Vienna, 1860), II, 113.
[3] *Ibid,* 173.

realm," and the bureaucrats were the natural enemies of parliamentary control. As to the application of the principle of nationality, it was obvious that most of the historic frontiers were not frontiers of nationality at all. The crown lands, large and small, from Hungary to Tyrol, from Galicia to Carinthia, from Bohemia to Dalmatia, included mixtures of nationalities. Since this multi-national monarchy was composed, historically, of multi-national parts, no return to historic autonomies would have given the nationalities territorial segregation. The high tories realized this; Clam-Martinitz spoke on behalf of the Kingdom of Bohemia, not on behalf of the Slavic race or the Czechish nationality. Though the nationality problem was constantly before the Reichsrat, the solution was conceived of as lying in an application of the catchword "equality of national rights" (*Gleichberechtigung*). This conception was not clearly defined, but seemed to mean that rights of nationality would be guaranteed to individuals, as personal rights; it did not mean that nationalities would be recognized as equal political units.

In the debates between the majority and the minority of the Enlarged Reichsrat, the fundamental problem of structure for the Danubian states-complex was for the first and last time submitted to a deliberative body representing all its regions. The constituent assembly at Kremsier in 1849 had worked without the participation of Hungarian representatives; the Delegations after 1867 included representatives of both halves of the monarchy, but without desire or competence to discuss the structure of the state as a whole. The monarchy ultimately went to its doom without seeing the vital problems of its existence come before any representative organ that could appraise them on the scale of the Reichsrat of 1860.

The majority report of this unique body proposed federalism on an historic and high-tory basis. It was the starting-point of a sequence of events that in the end traversed and nullified the intentions of all the parties to it—of the bureaucrats, the aristocrats, and the Emperor himself. What began as aristocratic federalism ended in 1867 as liberal dualism.

As the first step in this transition, Count Szécsen persuaded the Emperor to accept the principles of the majority report and to promulgate them as an imperial diploma on October 20, 1860. This

"October Diploma" provided that the Emperor should exercise his legislative power only with the coöperation (*Mitwirkung*) of the lawfully assembled diets of the crown lands, and of the central Reichsrat, which was to be made up of delegates from them. The central Reichsrat should have competence in matters of coinage, credit, customs, commerce, communication, new taxes and levies, military duties, and examination of the budget; all other matters should be left to the various crown-land diets. The Hungarian kingdom would act under its old constitution; for the other crown lands new constitutions should be provided. By the accompanying decrees a Croatian-Slavonian assembly was called to determine the relations of that land to Hungary, the local comitat organization was restored in Hungary, and the Magyar language reëstablished as the official language of the kingdom.

The non-Hungarian crown lands were to receive provincial organs of government. The high-tory nobles hoped that these would be designed to break the power of the bureaucracy and leave the provinces in their hands. This was a gross miscalculation, for their class had been displaced since the time of Maria Theresa; the Hungarian nobles were asking for what they had forfeited only ten years before, the Bohemians for what they had not enjoyed for over a century. The ministry did not really expect to allow to the non-Hungarian crown lands the same degree of autonomy that Hungary claimed.

The diploma pleased no one; it showed at once that it had been based on the most complete miscalculations. Sixty thousand copies of it were printed and distributed in Vienna. When the Emperor rode out through the city he received an ovation, but as he rode back sentiment had already cooled. The Viennese realized that the document did not provide for liberal constitutional government, and that Vienna and the middle-class Germans had been sold out to Hungary and the Slavic provincial nobles. In Hungary sentiment turned immediately against the diploma because it surrendered to a Reichsrat in Vienna some powers that had been exercised historically by the diet meeting in Pressburg and Budapest, and because it did not restore in Hungary the system of ministerial responsibility that had been granted by the laws of 1848. As the local comitat meetings were held, it was clear that the Hungarian gentry would not go along with the court nobility in surrendering any legislative powers to a central Reichsrat. The Hungarian high tories had erred completely in appraising the sentiment of their country and their influence in it. The Hungarian gentry, using their restored local government as a weapon, set forth with all the spirit and determination of a gifted political class to sabotage the diploma.

Back of the miscalculation was a genuine difficulty in applying the principle of a restoration of historic rights. To what historic date should the restoration run? This was not a problem peculiar to the Hungarians when they looked to history for a basis of relations with Vienna. It appeared in the debates of the Enlarged Reichsrat when Count Borelli, a delegate from Dalmatia, chose as a starting-point for Dalmatia's historic rights Queen Theuto (228 B.C.), proving thereby the independence of Dalmatia from Croatia. Bishop Strossmayer replied by citing the pragmatic sanction of Charles VI, which proved the union of Dalmatia with Croatia and Slavonia in a triune kingdom. Palácky's Czechish party liked to take the time of King Wenzel as the historical starting-point of a kingdom which should include Moravia and Silesia with Bohemia. Even in German affairs the effort to find an historic basis for policies was by no means simple. One might go back to Metternich, or back to Frederick the Great. But the clearest case of confusion came in the application of this concept of historic right to the Kingdom of Hungary.

It seemed at the outset that there could be but two possible dates to be taken as the basis of historic rights in Hungary: 1847 and 1848. The high tories said 1847, the Hungarian squires replied 1848. Only Kossuth, in exile, stood out for 1849 and the deposition of the dynasty. But in fact neither party was willing to accept in its totality the situation of either date. The high tories dared not return to the electoral system of 1847, which deprived the middle class and peasantry of political rights; the Hungarian patriots, while they desired the system of ministerial responsibility, dared not try to apply the centralizing laws of 1848 to Croatia, for Croatia had resisted Hungarian domination at that time and would resist it again. The issue came up in many forms. Should the Austrian civil code remain in force in Hungary or should the old Hungarian civil law be restored? The ministry at Vienna voted to retain the civil code till a Hungarian diet could alter it, but the restored local judges enforced Hungarian law.

In an effort to make the October Diploma more pleasing to the Hungarians, the high-tory leaders made another miscalculation. They thought that if the diploma were interpreted in a liberal sense in Austria, so that it would attract the Austrian liberals, the Hungarian gentry would be better satisfied. This was a complete about-face. Francis Joseph had adopted the program because he was assured it would protect him from liberal parliamentary institutions in Austria and bring Hungary into a common Reichsrat. Now he was told that he must make liberal concessions. He made them, but was still unable to win over the Hungarians.

The man chosen by the high-tory partisans to sweeten the diploma for the middle-class Germans in the non-Hungarian parts of the monarchy was Anton von Schmerling, a popular Vienna liberal with a background and circle of acquaintances in the higher bureaucracy. The new man took office in December, 1860, and immediately set to work to adapt the October Diploma to the demands of liberalism. The result was the so-called "February Patent," issued February 26, 1861, to provide for the participation of the non-Hungarian lands in the Reichsrat established by the October Diploma. The patent was in form a group of election laws for the crown land diets and the common Reichsrat. The system of voting, by curies representing commerce, towns, large and small landholding, not only preserved some of the marks of the old diet of estates but also assured a German middle-class majority. The Reichsrat was increased in numbers, and its competence extended. The patent was a reinterpretation of the October Diploma in the sense of a retreat from extreme federalism. The bureaucrats, defeated by the high tories in the Enlarged Reichsrat, had turned to make an alliance with the German middle class.

The turn taken in the interpretation of the diploma, far from conciliating the Hungarians, served only to increase their bitterness, because of the increased parliamentary centralization. When the Hungarian diet met in due course in April, 1861, it refused to send

GERMAN CONFEDERATION
Main R.
Rhine R.
BAVARIA
Danube R.
Elbe R.
Prague
BOHEMIA
AUSTRIA
Vienna
AUSTRIAN CROWN LANDS
Inn R.
SALZBURG
TYROL
CARINTHIA
STYRIA
CARNIOLA
ISTRIA
Drave
Agram
CROATIA
CROATIAN MARCHES
Save
DALMATIA (Austrian Crown)
LOMBARDY-VENETIAN KINGDOM
Milan
Po R.
Venice
KINGDOM OF ITALY
ADRIATIC SEA
10
15
50
45
MANHATTAN DRAFTING CO. INC., N.Y.

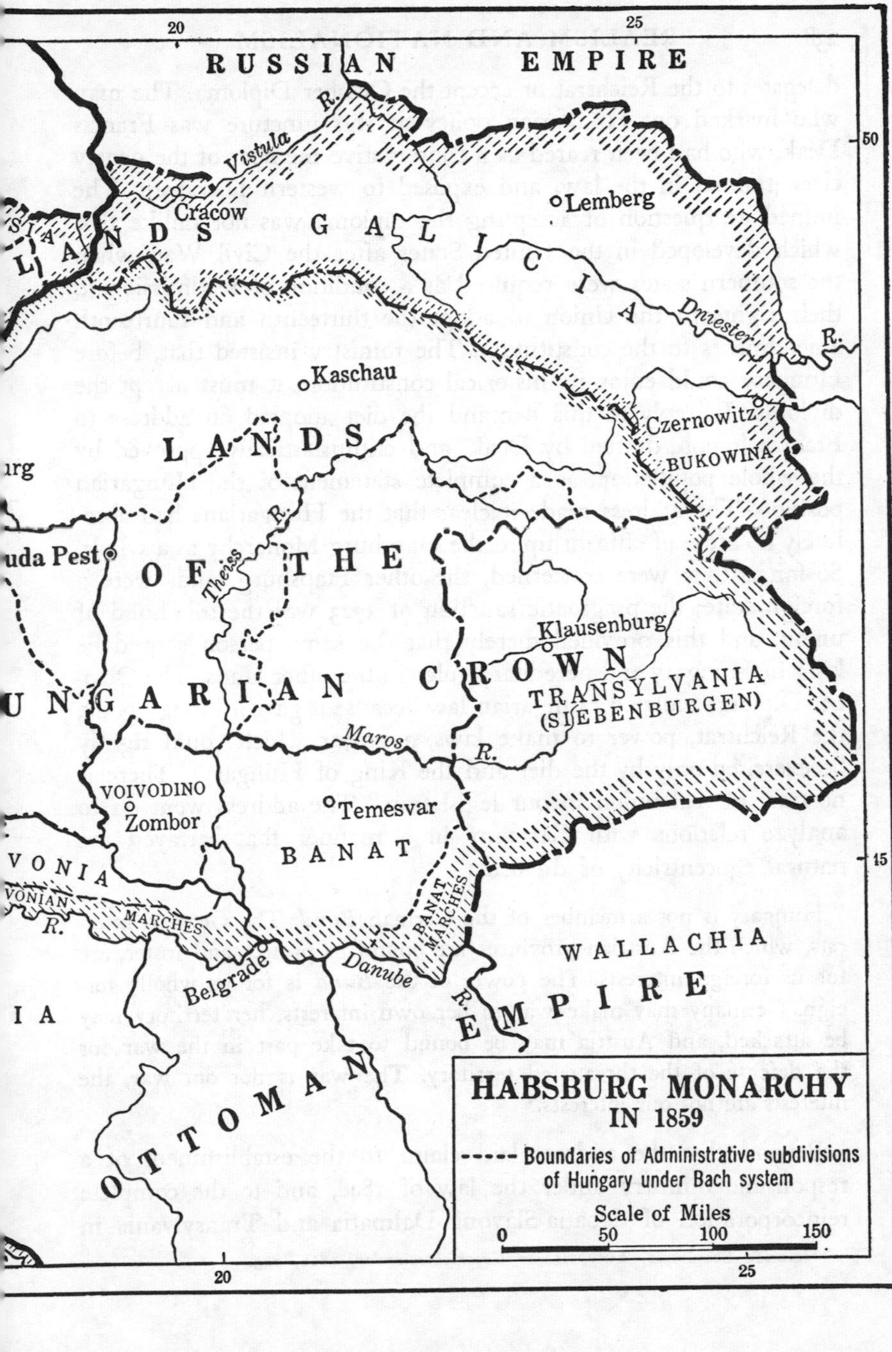

HABSBURG MONARCHY
IN 1859
Boundaries of Administrative subdivisions of Hungary under Bach system
Scale of Miles
0 50 100 150
RUSSIAN EMPIRE
Vistula R.
Cracow
Lemberg
LANDS OF GALICIA
Dniester R.
Kaschau
Czernowitz
BUKOWINA
LANDS OF THE HUNGARIAN CROWN
Buda Pest
Theiss R.
Klausenburg
TRANSYLVANIA
(SIEBENBURGEN)
Maros R.
VOIVODINO
Zombor
Temesvar
BANAT
BANAT MARCHES
SLAVONIA
SLAVONIAN MARCHES
Belgrade
Danube R.
WALLACHIA
OTTOMAN EMPIRE
20
25
50
45

delegates to the Reichsrat or accept the October Diploma. The man who marked out Hungarian policy at this juncture was Francis Déak, who had been reared as a conservative member of the gentry class, trained in the law, and exposed to western liberalism. The immediate question of accepting the diploma was not unlike that which developed in the United States after the Civil War, when the southern states were required as a condition of readmission to their rights in the Union to adopt the thirteenth and fourteenth amendments to the constitution. The ministry insisted that, before Hungary could enjoy its historical constitution, it must accept the diploma. In reply to this demand the diet adopted an address to Francis Joseph, drafted by Déak, and enthusiastically approved by the whole population, as a complete statement of the Hungarian position. The address made it clear that the Hungarians had absolutely no sense of citizenship in the Hapsburg Monarchy as a whole. So far as they were concerned, the other Hapsburg lands were a foreign state; the pragmatic sanction of 1723 was the sole bond of union, and this provided merely that the same person should be king in Hungary and hereditary ruler in the other lands. The October Diploma violated Hungarian law because it gave a foreign body, the Reichsrat, power to make laws, a power which could rightly be exercised only by the diet and the King of Hungary. "There is no trace of real union in our legislation." The address went on to analyze relations with Germany in a manner that betrayed the natural egocentricity of dualism:

> Hungary is not a member of the German *Bund*. The German interests, which the Austrian provinces are bound to protect and foster, are for us foreign interests. The power of the *Bund* is for us wholly foreign. Germany may make war in her own interests, her territory may be attacked, and Austria may be bound to take part in the war for the defense of the threatened territory. The war is not our war, the interests are not our interests.[4]

Beyond that the address laid claim to the establishment of a responsible ministry under the law of 1848, and to the complete reincorporation of Croatia-Slavonia-Dalmatia and Transylvania in

[4] Heinrich Schulthess, *Europaischer Geschichtsalendar*, 1861, 143.

the Hungarian kingdom. It protested against the decree that had called the diets of these lands to send their delegates direct to the Reichsrat in Vienna. One concession only was made to the interests of the monarchy as a whole. Hungary was ready, the address declared,

> to treat in particular cases with the constitutionally organized peoples of the hereditary (Hapsburg) lands, as one free and independent nation with another free and independent nation.[5]

The significance of this address was not alone that it completed the bankruptcy of high-tory federalism, and brought the Vienna government to resort once more to an autocratic administrative system in Hungary, but also that it set forth clearly and completely the full implications of dualism in the Danube area. Personal union under a king who reigned but did not rule would be very little union indeed. Déak evidently contemplated the possibility that the western half of the monarchy might be at war while Hungary remained at peace. The procedure for taking common action with the Austrian lands by making special agreements from occasion to occasion was not much more coöperation than any independent state would offer to any other. In that way England and France had just dealt with each other in preparing their free-trade treaty. The dualism of the address might indeed have destroyed the Hapsburg monarchy as a great power.

As compared with the dualism of the address or the centralism of the Bach system, Schmerling's program became the living program of federalism in the monarchy. When the Hungarian diet was dissolved, the diets of Croatia and Transylvania held the key to Schmerling's success. If they consented to participate in a common Reichsrat in Vienna, the system of the February Patent could be operated without the aid of the diet in Budapest. The Magyars were a minority in their own land, only 4,866,000 of them to 8,525,000 non-Magyars.[6] If the two principal non-Magyar areas of Hungary could be brought to coöperate with Vienna, the resisting power of the remaining area would be greatly reduced. Schmerling made

[5] *Ibid.*, 144.

[6] The figures were compiled by C. Freiherr von Czornig in his *Ethnographie der Österreichischen Monarchie* (Wien, 1857), quoted by Redlich.

due effort to bring the Croatian delegates to Vienna; he set up in the ministry a chancellery for Croatia and gave it equal rank with the chancellery for Hungary. The arrangement foreshadowed something like the scheme that was called "Trialism" in the days of the Archduke Francis Ferdinand just before the World War. But the Croats were not to be tempted. They remained loyal to Budapest. It was otherwise with Transylvania. In July, 1863, Schmerling succeeded in bringing a delegation of Transylvanians to his Reichsrat. That was the high moment of federalism in the Danube monarchy. The opportunity never returned.

While the issue between dualism and federalism was being defined, there arose in both the Hungarian and non-Hungarian parts of the monarchy a number of territorial claims on the part of the nationalities. The Ruthenians, who disliked their Polish overlords, called for the partitioning of Galicia into Polish and Ruthenian sections; the Slovenes demanded a Kingdom of Slovenia; and the Czechs, of course, insisted upon the union of the lands of St. Wenzel's crown. To the Hungarian diet came a petition drawn up at a Serbian congress at Carlowitz, praying for the creation of a separate Serbian region within the Kingdom of Hungary, and from a meeting of Slovaks at Thurocz St. Marton (June, 1861) came a petition for a similar regional organization of the Slovak area in the north. How did Schmerling on the one hand, the Hungarian diet on the other, meet these demands?

Schmerling was willing to make concessions to the Ruthenians in Galicia against the Poles, but not to the Czechs in Bohemia nor to the Slovenes in Carinthia against the Germans. He divided Galicia into three administrative districts, and gave official privilege to the Ruthenian language in the eastern parts. The Hungarian diet offered everything to Croatia, but denied the territorial demands of the Serbs and Slovaks.

As a general policy Schmerling developed his system of communal autonomy, which has been discussed in a previous chapter. His communal laws offered to all peoples a field of action which, though limited, was free. The Hungarian diet also defined a general policy. Under the inspiration of Eötvös, who saw more deeply than most of his contemporaries into the problem of nationality, it adopted a resolution on nationality policy which seven years later became the Nationality Law of 1868. According to the principles of this resolution, nationality was to be respected as a personal right, and given all privileges that did not compromise the unity of the Hungarian state. Eötvös wanted a free nationality in a free state, as Cavour wanted a free church in a free state. He believed that a free Hungarian government could hold the loyalty of the non-Magyar peoples without yielding to the territorial principle of nationality; his epigones took another course, tried to make territory and nationality coincide by Magyarizing the Slovaks, Rumanians, and Serbs, and in the end lost not only the loyalty of these peoples, but the territory as well.

III. FEDERALISM AND DUALISM IN GERMANY

While the Hungarian nation was defining a national policy which an entire population was willing to defend, if necessary, by passive resistance, the Prussian state was developing a cabinet policy to which it was to hold through several changes in the personnel of the ministry and which it was to defend by diplomacy. Hungary's historic claim to political nationhood, Prussia's to great-power status, were the axiomata from which these policies were respectively deduced and by which they were explained and rationalized. Prussian policy during most of the federative crisis was not dictated by Bismarck nor dominated by any strong personality. The purely personal policy such as that which Napoleon had carried on in Italy was not found in Berlin. There is evidence that the Prince Regent was, from time to time, tempted to acts of generosity toward Austria comparable to those of Napoleon toward Italy, but the ministry caused him to waver. Prussia's cabinet policy, without Bismarck, seems always to have been firm enough to resist the development of federal institutions in Germany, but not to substitute for them the clean-cut dualism which Bismarck forced into existence.

The long Prussian filibuster against the development of the *Bund* in the 'fifties had been broken by the New Era only a month before the Italian crisis furnished a new starting-point for Austro-Prussian relations in Germany. Why had Prussia failed to come to Austria's aid? That was the vital question. The answer now stands out clearly in recently published documents. The Prussian cabinet was anxious to play a rôle as a great power in mediating the dispute, and was reluctant to intervene with armed force until Russia and England were lined up. As to military arrangements, Prussian policy in 1859 was quite consistent with Prussian policy in the days of the filibuster. Prussia demanded, (July 4, 1859) that the two northern confederate army corps should be brigaded into the Prussian army; Austria replied by proposing in the confederate assembly (July 7, 1859) that the Prince Regent of Prussia be elected commander-in-chief of all the confederate forces. The Prussian motion did not ask for military leadership of all Germany, but for the "annexation" of the two northern confederate army corps, leaving the two southern army corps momentarily to Bavaria, ultimately to Austria. Austria and the middle states resisted the Prussian motion. The point must be emphasized because so many historians have missed it. It is the very key to subsequent Prussian policy. It implied, not Prussian leadership in uniting Germany, but Prussian desire to divide Germany.[7] Just as Hungary sought to avoid common legislative institutions, so Prussia resisted common military institutions. Prussian policy in 1859 would have partitioned Germany for military purposes at the line of the river Main. It would have left the states of the south as a sphere of Austrian influence, military as well as political.

The Italian War revived German politics. The politics of the reaction period had been Hanoverian, Hessian, Bavarian; now they

[7] Sybel writes that the Austrian motion meant "forbidding Prussia to make war." *Founding of the German Empire* (New York, 1891), II, 380. Actually the exact opposite was the case. Schleinitz resisted the Austrian move on the ground that it would interfere with Prussia's neutrality and hence with Prussian neutral mediation. See also Sir Adolphus Ward, *Germany, 1815-1890* (Cambridge, 1917), II, 35. Friedjung writes that Francis Joseph concluded peace with Napoleon "rather than accept help from Prussia and allow her to take the military lead in Germany" *Cambridge Modern History*, XI, 406. But in *Der Kampf um die Vorherrschaft in Deutschland* (Stuttgart, 1900), I, 29, Friedjung writes that Rechberg offered Prussia the command of the whole army and that Schleinitz refused to accept it. Even Alfred Stern, in *Geschichte Europas* (Stuttgart-Berlin, 1920), 354-356, states that the Prussian motion of July 4 would have given "the command of all German fighting power to Prussia," which leaves out of account the distinction between the Austrian and Prussian motions, both of which gave this supreme command. See also Erich Marcks, *Kaiser Wilhelm I* (Munich and Leipzig, 1918), 145, Erich Brandenburg, *Die Reichsgründung* (Leipzig, 1922). The new documents are published in *Die Auswärtige Politik Preussens, 1858-1871* (Oldenburg, 1933), Bd. I; and in *Quellen zur Deutschen Politik Oesterreichs, 1859-1866* (Oldenburg, 1934), Bd. I.

became German. The standard political alignment appeared in an all-German forum. First to become vocal were the liberals and democrats, who in Germany as in Italy quickly organized a party cutting across state lines. Bennigsen, a Hanoverian, and Schultze-Delitsch, the sponsor of mutual coöperation, were leaders. In a series of meetings through August and September, 1859, they set up a National Society to demand a central authority and liberal parliamentary government for Germany. They were pro-Prussian as an incident to their policy, because Prussia in the New Era stood forth as a liberal state.

The National Society touched hands with the liberal Coburg-Gotha party among the princes. Duke Ernst sheltered the National Society at Gotha, while Duke Fredrick of Baden worked with his friend and counselor, Roggenbach, on a detailed reform plan. Oncken has shown that the demand of the German liberals was not *Kleindeutsch* nor pro-Prussian fundamentally, but was merely a practical way of achieving two old aims, central government and a parliament for Germany.[8]

For the Prussian cabinet liberalism was an incident rather than an aim. The work of the National Society and the Coburgers was useful to Prussia because it provided resources for the defense of great-power status, by contributing to the success of the policy of "moral conquests" in Germany. Already in December, 1859, the possibility that the Prussian state might abandon the highway of liberalism appeared, for a cabinet controversy over army reform resulted in the resignation of minister of war von Bonin, and the appointment of von Roon, whose reform plan was distasteful to the liberal majority in the Prussian diet. For the time being, however, the National Society did not distrust Prussia's liberalism, though it was somewhat sceptical of the Prince Regent's willingness to stand forth with a strong German policy.

The middle state reply to the agitation of the National Society was a conference of ministers at Würzburg in November, 1859, to lay plans for a positive policy of reform and improvement within the framework of the *Bund*. The so-called Würzburg program picked up the threads of German reform, not from 1848, but from

[8] Hermann Oncken, *Rudolf von Bennigsen* (Stuttgart und Leipzig, 1910).

that quiet development of concrete improvements illustrated by the preparation of the common commercial code. The Würzburgers wanted to use the machinery of the *Bund* to frame a common civil law and common law on patents, weights, measures, and right of domicile. They wished to establish a supreme court and to revise the military statutes of the *Bund* to increase defensive efficiency. Led by the Saxon prime minister, Count Beust, they advanced a program of legislation, while the National Society concentrated on a program of reconstruction. The Würzburgers were federalists, the National Society was predominantly dualist. Each party accused the other of lack of patriotism, and each claimed to speak in the name of German nationalism.

While the public debate developed between the Würzburg and Gotha movements, Austrian and Prussian cabinet policy picked up the dispute over military reform where it had been left at Villafranca. Austria supported a Bavarian proposal to elect, in time of peace, a confederate commander-in-chief for a term of five years. It was understood that the office should alternate between Austria and Prussia. The Prussian cabinet countered with a proposal to develop in time of peace a dualistic system by assigning the two northern confederate army corps to Prussia for purposes of inspection and control, and the two southern army corps to Austria. By the spring of 1860 the army reform was deadlocked, and rumors were abroad that Prussia would secede from the *Bund*, and might even bargain with Napoleon to play in Germany the part that Victor Emmanuel had played in Italy.

Count Rechberg, as a good pupil of Metternich, longed to get back to the old system of mutual confidence between Prussia and Austria. Upon what basis could it be restored? William and Francis Joseph met at Töplitz in July, 1860, to make an effort to iron out their differences, and thought they had achieved this object by going back to the basis of 1840. In 1840 there had been a war scare on the Rhine, and specific precautions had been taken to meet it. The two sovereigns agreed that their military experts should be authorized to devise a plan that would apply to the dangers of 1860 the precedents of 1840. Like the high tories of the Austrian Reichsrat (which was meeting at this very time) the monarchs tried to escape from the present into the past, and to restore a vanished world.

In October, three months later, they met the Tsar at Warsaw with a similar purpose—the revival of the Holy Alliance. But the system of Metternich would not return to life—neither in the Hapsburg Monarchy nor in Germany nor in the cabinet policies of the three northern courts. By April, 1861, the failure was complete. The meetings of the military experts in Berlin broke up without reaching an agreement on the basis of 1840; the Hungarian diet rejected the October Diploma; and Tsar Alexander continued to be the friend of Napoleon.

As the two great powers in Germany confessed their failure to agree, the ministers of two lesser states stepped forward with proposals that looked to the future rather than the past. Roggenbach at Baden-Baden persuaded William, who became King of Prussia in 1861, to accept his plan for a liberal United States of Germany, built around Prussia, and yet retaining the tie of the *Bund* with Austria. And Beust collaborated with the Austrian ministry in evolving a complicated plan for a new federal system with a ministerial conference as its principal working organ.

While Roggenbach was working on William, Bismarck was putting down on paper his ideas of reform in Germany. His Baden memorandum of July, 1861, deduced the German reform from the international system. Bismarck argued that since the Holy Alliance group no longer stabilized eastern and central Europe, Prussia had incurred enormous responsibilities for the defense of German territory. This responsibility called for corresponding influence in Germany, which should be obtained by means of a national representative body, based on population, in which Prussia would have a majority. Since Austria could not participate without dividing the monarchy, it would mean the exclusion of Austria and the division of Germany at the Inn. A means of working toward the new system would be to call delegates of the diets of the states which were members of the Customs Union to attend a customs parliament, and to gain control of the military forces of the other states by special agreements outside the framework of the *Bund*. Such a military treaty had been made between Prussia and Saxe-Coburg-Gotha.

The Baden memorandum was the clearest formulation of the system of dualism. But at the time Bismarck was not able to win the King to it, nor could he persuade the conservative party to adopt it.[9]

In this same pregnant summer of 1861, while Bismarck was working out an extreme dualist solution of the German problem, Julius Froebel developed an extreme Federalist solution. Froebel proposed the creation of a central government to consist of three houses: A house of states (corresponding to the existing confederate assembly, and representing the cabinets), a house of delegates from the various diets, and a house of princes. The plan should be launched by a congress of princes. The merit of the scheme lay partly in the probability that it would be easier to get the princes to agree than to get their cabinets to coöperate. A pamphlet written in the autumn of 1861 shows how the idea was gaining currency:

> We ask: if today Emperor Francis Joseph should call a German Diet of Princes, and invite his high federal colleagues to appear in person, in Regensburg or in Frankfurt, to take counsel on the present and future of the common Fatherland, who would remain away?—The King of Prussia?—Perhaps;—but for how long?[10]

The Beust plan and the Roggenbach plan were brought forward officially in the winter of 1861. Beust tried to make his federal solution attractive to Prussia by providing that Prussia should have parity with Austria in the presidency of the *Bund*—(the *Alternat*). Roggenbach tried to make his dualist solution—(a "*Bund* within a *Bund*") palatable to Austria by conceding a guarantee of all Hapsburg territories, German and non-German. No one was satisfied. Austria rejected Beust's plan because it lacked the guarantee of Hapsburg territories; Prussia in December rejected it on the ground that it was insufficient, and that the whole Roggenbach plan of a *Bund* within a *Bund* would be necessary. Then, in February, 1862, Austria and five middle states denounced the Prussian proposal as disruptive of German unity. The two concrete plans of reconstruction, based respectively on principles of federalism and dualism, had defeated each other.

[9] H. Oncken, "Die Baden-Badener Denkschrift Bismarcks über die Deutsche Bundesreform (Juli, 1861)," *Historische Zeitschrift*, CXLV (1931), 106-130.

[10] *Oesterreichs und Preussens Mediatisierung die conditio sine qua non einer monarchisch-parlamentarischem Lösung des deutschen Problems* (Leipzig, 1862), 64.

After another year of tension Bismarck gained a position from which he could press his more extreme Baden plan for the exclusion of Austria from the *Bund*, and Francis Joseph took up the more elaborate federal ideas of Julius Froebel. In the meantime the constitutional conflict in Prussia had reached its climax, and an effort to return to the Würzburg tactics of gradual growth within the *Bund* led to another deadlock.

IV. THE CONFLICT IN PRUSSIA

At the very moment when the Prussian cabinet, by adopting the territorial dualism of the National Society and Coburg-Gotha party, had exasperated Austria and the middle states, it kicked the props out from under its German policy by abandoning the liberalism of the New Era. The essence of the National Society program had been liberalism in Germany, and Prussian hegemony was a means to an end; now the Prussian cabinet was breaking with its liberal allies, while at the same time Schmerling was promoting liberalism in Austria. In 1859 Prussia was liberal and Austria autocratic; in 1862, the situation was reversed.

Neither in Austria nor in Prussia was the change in respect to liberalism brought about in direct response to the German reform situation. The Schmerling ministry was a gift to the Austrian liberals from the Hungarian high tories, who disliked liberalism but thought that a little of it in Austria would do no harm, and might make Hungary more tractable. The retreat from liberalism in Prussia was forced upon the cabinet by a chain of causes that derived directly from the episode of Schwarzenberg's triumph at Olmütz in 1850. For it was from that moment that Prince William dated his interest in a reform of the Prussian army system. The Prussian mobilization of that date had revealed the specific technical deficiencies which the man who later became Prince Regent and then King made it his major interest to correct.

In 1857, two years before the Italian crisis, Prince William and General von Roon had already worked out the basis of the army reform—a longer term of service, sufficient cadres to take up all recruits, and a shelving of the "citizen army" (the *Landwehr*). A coalition of liberals in the diet, despite their widely differing views on other matters, made a common front in using the army reform issue as a means of forcing the King into the system of responsible government. Against the liberals was aligned the conservative squire and army class. The elections of 1862 put the lower chamber of the diet completely into the hands of the liberals, and the conservative deputies were reduced to a handful "who could ride to the parliament building in one omnibus." With an approach to unanimity that almost put the Prussian lower house in a class with the Hungarian diet as the champion of a cause, the liberals refused to pass the budget. The King was ready to abdicate and had the act drawn up. His son Frederick, who was well under the influence of the Coburgers, would have made terms with the liberals. It would have meant the complete defeat of the conservatives and the army. Von Roon, when he saw his army reform and the influence of his whole social class threatened, wired on his own responsibility a hurry call for Bismarck, who was on vacation in the Pyrenees. Bismarck took a fast train to Berlin. Von Roon then suggested to the King that he make one more effort to hold his ground—that Bismarck be called to head the ministry and defy the chamber.

"He is not here and he wouldn't do it," the King answered impatiently. And Roon was able to reply: "He is here and he will do it."[11] On September 22, 1862, as they walked up and down in the park of the castle at Babenburg, Bismarck and the King agreed to stand together against the diet and the country for the army reforms.

Bismarck stood among German leaders as the one who was perhaps least influenced by considerations of German patriotism. His advocacy of a French alliance was a scandal. When he took office, he was none the less ready to embark on a strong German policy because it would either embarrass or win the liberals (who had been praying for two years for that very thing). This was the note he struck in his first meeting with the budget committee when he uttered his memorable warning: "The great questions of the day will not be decided by speeches and resolutions—that was the blunder of 1848 and 1849—but by blood and iron."

[11] Brandenburg: *Die Reichsgründung,* I, 437; see also L. Dehio, "Bismarck und die Heeresvolagen der Konfliktzeit," *Historische Zeitschrift* CXLIV (1931), 31-47.

The liberals took him at his word, but in a different sense. Had not liberal reforms followed in Russia after the defeat of the Crimean War, and in Austria after the defeat in Italy? As Bismarck moved in his German policy from one perilous situation to another he had constantly to deal with the unforgiving opposition of the liberals whose vote he defied. He governed without a legal budget, and the chamber repeatedly warned him that if he carried Prussia into war he could expect no support, moral or legal, from the representatives of the Prussian people.[12]

V. THE FRANKFURT CONGRESS OF PRINCES

The eclipse of Prussia's moral leadership left the field open for the *Grossdeutsch* federalists. In August, 1862, the Würzburgers and Austrians agreed to press forward with a practical reform: they would have the confederate assembly call a meeting of delegates from the diets of different German states to collaborate in drafting a common German code of civil and criminal law. In October, a *Grossdeutsch* Reform Society was founded to campaign for the cause. Bismarck took stern measures to head off the movement. He warned the Austrian minister, Count Karolyi, in December that in the next war Prussia would be either an ally or an enemy of Austria, and that Austria should transfer the center of her interest from Vienna to Budapest. Austria could choose between the middle states and Prussia. And he further warned all the German states that if by majority vote the *Bund* should call this assembly of delegates, Prussia would secede. The threat sufficed to defeat the motion when it came up for a vote on January 14, 1863, and the reform movement headed in a new direction.

Since Bismarck blocked the way to gradual reform by expansion of the functions of the *Bund*, there remained the possibility of thoroughgoing reconstruction. In March, 1863, Francis Joseph gave his attention to Froebel's plan for a congress of princes. The Austrian ministry worked it up with great secrecy through the spring, and adopted it, over Rechberg's protest, on July 5, 1863.[13]

[12] Dehio, "Die Taktik der Opposition während der Konfliktzeit," *Historische Zeitschrift*, CXL (1929), 279-347, an analysis of *Deutscher Liberalismus im Zeitalter Bismarcks. Eine Politische Briefsammlung, 1859-1870* (Leipzig, 1925).

[13] H. Scheller, *Der Frankfurter Fürstentag* (Leipzig, 1929).

It may seem at first sight irrelevant to interrupt the story of Germany for a moment and turn to the story of Japan, and yet there are elements in the Japanese political situation that may help to interpret the history of Germany. In Japan there had existed for centuries two authorities, the Shogun who held military and administrative power at Yedo, and the Emperor who lived, poor in means yet rich in honor, at Kyoto. In the presence of danger from abroad, with the political support of clans that were hostile to the Shogun and with the intellectual support of a school of historical scholarship that developed a doctrine of imperial legitimacy, an imperialist party arose in Japan. The date is a mere coincidence, but it was in 1862 that the Emperor demanded that the Shogun pay homage to him, and through a series of decrees revived powers that had lapsed for centuries. Five years later, in 1867, the Shogun voluntarily resigned his office into the Emperor's hands, the heads of the great feudal clans surrendered their powers at the same time, and as the nation rallied around the throne of the young Emperor, the new Japan was born. Was it impossible that comparable gestures of generous sacrifice for the common good should be made by the princes of Germany? What was asked of them at Frankfurt was not a tithe to what their Japanese counterparts surrendered. And the only strong will that stood firmly in the way was that of Bismarck, who was not only the most unpopular man in Germany, but the most hated man in Prussia.

The German princes met, at the Emperor's invitation, on August 17. They had before them a comprehensive plan for extending the functions of the *Bund* and establishing new organs: a directory, a federal council, an assembly of delegates from the diets, a house of princes and a supreme court. All the princes had come—except the King of Prussia. King John of Saxony was sent as messenger with a collective note from the princes to urge King William to reconsider his decision and join his brothers in the work of national reconstruction. William wavered; it was difficult for him to resist the appeal to his generosity, patriotism, and monarchic sentiment. "Thirty princes and a king as their messenger," he said, "how can one refuse?" Bismarck threatened to resign; the King yielded to his minister; the crisis in Prussian policy passed, and Germany lost her last chance to build on the broad foundations of federalism.

The princes continued their deliberations; they actually agreed upon a federal constitution for a new Germany, but were unwilling to go the full way and confront Prussia with a *fait accompli.*

VI. CONSTITUTIONS AND INTERVENTIONS IN DENMARK

The abrupt transition from federalism to dualism in German politics was made within three months of the failure of the Frankfurt congress of princes, in connection with the Danish question.

The relation of Denmark to the three duchies of Schleswig, Holstein, and Lauenburg had been causing increasing friction in the ten years since the London settlement of 1852. Schleswig and Holstein, "inseparably" united, were both under the Danish crown; Holstein and Lauenburg alone of the Danish crown lands belonged to the German Confederation.

What was there in the London settlement that proved unworkable? Under that settlement the rights of the Danish crown were to remain unimpaired, and also the rights of the two duchies. But how could the Danish kingdom travel along the common road of European political evolution, toward centralization and the substitution of the popular for the monarchic principle, without impairing the rights of the duchies? The question was merely a variant of the general problem confronting all central Europe in the unscrambling of confederate relationships.

In 1854, during the reaction, the Danish ministry set up a common legislative body for the whole monarchy. This new organ, the *Rigsraad,* was to have power over foreign policy, defense, and other common affairs, and to leave only local matters to the four subordinate legislatures of Denmark, Schleswig, Holstein, and Lauenburg. The move was not unlike that made by the Emperor Francis Joseph with his October Diploma, and it had the support of the same social class—a high tory aristocracy represented in Holstein by Scheel-Plessen as in Hungary by Szécsen. The Rigsraad, like the Reichsrat contemplated in the October Diploma, was to be a conservative body; twenty of its fifty members were to be appointed by the King. The Danish liberals in Copenhagen liked the constitution of 1854 as little as the German liberals of Vienna liked the October Diploma. To meet their objections, the constitution was submitted to the parliament of Denmark for amendment and approval, but the diets of the duchies were not permitted to consider it. Just as the February Patent in Austria altered the October Diploma in a sense favorable to the German nationality and middle class, so the Danish constitution of 1855 modified the constitution of 1854 in a way that gave the Danish population more power. The duchies resisted this constitution as Hungary resisted the February Patent, and in this resistance received the support of the German states of the *Bund*, including Prussia and Austria. There were two points of leverage for intervention: Holstein's and Lauenburg's membership in the *Bund*, and the Treaty of London of 1852, under which the Danish Monarchy had agreed to respect the rights of both duchies. The two kinds of intervention tended to take on two different characteristics. The Treaty of London called for action by the great powers, the place of Holstein in the *Bund* permitted action under German confederate law. Thus the Danish question, like the Italian question, offered the option between great power status and *Bund* membership as a basis of policy both in Austria and in Prussia. In 1858 the confederate assembly adopted a motion declaring the constitution of 1855 invalid in Holstein and Lauenburg. The Danish government yielded, and suspended its constitution in those two duchies.

In the face of this action, the Danish nationalists turned to what was called the "Eider Danish" policy. They would let Holstein and Lauenburg remain loosely connected with the monarchy, but incorporate Schleswig in the Danish state. They would accept what Austria in a comparable situation could never concede, namely that the boundary of the German Confederation should stand as a real boundary between two parts of the monarchy. But the Eider Dane policy ran counter to one of the rights of Holstein—namely its right to be forever united to Schleswig. And since the southern part of Schleswig was populated by Germans, it left a nationality grievance unadjusted.

The Danish government tried to get out of the impasse by proclaiming a new constitutional law in March, 1863, the so-called

"March Patent," under which it was admitted that no law enacted by the Danish Rigsraad could go into effect in Holstein and Lauenburg without the consent of the diets of these duchies, but on the other hand neither Holstein nor Lauenburg could veto laws enacted for Schleswig and Denmark. Since this patent had the effect of dissolving the bond between the inseparable duchies, it violated the terms of the London Protocol of 1852. The German confederate assembly demanded its revocation; the Danish ministry refused. The Germans threatened confederate execution in Holstein, and then in November, 1863, while the whole question was still pending, King Frederick died. Prince Christian of Glücksburg became King under the terms of the same London Protocol that was violated by the March Patent. King Christian signed the patent. Scheel-Plessen hurried to Copenhagen to persuade the King to abandon the Eider Dane policy. Had he entered the ministry at that time the London Treaty would not have been broken. But the Danish national sentiment was too strong to be bent from its purpose by the partisans of the high aristocracy.

As Scheel-Plessen stepped out of the picture, there stepped into it Frederick of Augustenburg, who claimed that his rights to the ducal throne were still intact and that King Christian was not the rightful ruler of Schleswig-Holstein. All German patriots sprang to his defense. He became for the time being a national hero.

This was the moment chosen by Austria to change her attitude toward Prussia. There were in the Austrian ministry the heirs of Metternich and the heirs of Schwarzenberg. The former, led by Rechberg, always wanted collaboration with Prussia, and after the collapse of the Frankfurt congress of princes they had their way. The latter, represented by Schmerling and the gifted adviser on German affairs, Rudolf von Biegeleben, had been given their opportunity at Frankfurt and had failed. Rechberg now took command. He and Bismarck coöperated in the Danish question, against the middle states and the *Bund*. The *Bund* voted confederate execution in Holstein to force the Danes to repeal the patent, and tried to call in question the throne right of Christian and to clear the road for Augustenburg. Austria and Prussia held a different line. They agreed (January 17, 1864) to enforce the London protocol and the repeal of the patent by an invasion of Schleswig.

What were Bismarck's aims? Even before he signed the treaty with Austria he had privately expressed his aim of conquering the duchies for Prussia. At the time neither the King nor any political group in Prussia shared the idea. Bismarck during the Frankfurt days had recognized that it would be undesirable to have the duchies become "another middle state on the Elbe to coquette with Austria."[14] The interests of Prussia as Bismarck saw them had nothing in common with Austrian interests in the duchies.

The Austrian and Prussian armies quickly drove the Danes out of Schleswig. Then came the time for a conference. The powers met at London and proposed that the two duchies be retained by King Christian on the basis of personal union with the Danish crown. The Danish nationalist government, mistakenly believing that it would receive armed British aid, rejected this offer. Suggestions were then made for the division of the territory, but it proved impossible to compromise the extreme demands of both parties. Napoleon ultimately put forward the idea of a plebiscite, but this proposal was rejected with horror by the Austrians. The conference ended, leaving Bismarck freed of the obligations of the London protocol of 1852. He then pressed for the continuation of the war, and dragged his reluctant ally into the invasion of Jutland. When Danish military resistance had been completely broken, the Danes made peace by ceding the duchies to Austria and Prussia in common. The war had been both short and inexpensive. It had served to instruct the Prussian staff in the use of railways for troop movement—instruction that was useful in the war against Austria two years later. The London conference was significant in its impotence; its failure to solve the problem of the duchies was an index to the decline of European authority. On the surface, the Austro-Prussian alliance might seem to have been a restoration of the comity of the time of Metternich, but there was something lacking. Everything in Europe had been undermined, nothing was any longer secure, neither the *Bund*, nor the concert, nor the treaties of

[14] A. O. Meyer, "Die Zielsetzung in Bismarcks Schleswig-Holstenische Politik von 1855 bis 1864," *Zeitschrift für Schleswig-Holsteinische Geschichte*, LIII (1923), 124.

1815. What was lacking was the whole context, external and internal, of the Metternich system. Austro-Prussian coöperation was no longer woven into the fabric of the system of the great powers nor of the German Confederation. It was a casual and occasional alliance, such as any state might make with another and as easily discard. And if anything of permanence was to emerge therefrom, it could only take the form of dualism in *Mitteleuropa*.

In Austria, also, the high point of federalism was reached and passed in 1863. In December, 1864, Francis Joseph secretly established contact with Déak, and found the basis of a compromise that would satisfy a Hungarian parliament and still leave to a common government sufficient powers to maintain Austria as a great power. When Déak published his statement of this view at Easter, 1865, the Hapsburg Monarchy turned toward dualism on the Danube.

VII. AUTONOMY AND REVOLUTION IN POLAND

The practical forum of the Polish question in the 1860's was the internal government of Russia. Even as an internal issue in Russia, the Polish question had its territorial aspects. In this respect the relation of the Russian Poles to the Tsar was roughly analogous to the relation of the Hungarians to Francis Joseph, or even of the Germans in Holstein to the King of Denmark. Both in Hungary and in Russian Poland, a socially and economically dominant agrarian nobility maintained the cult of a lost independence and a forfeited constitution. Along with the demand for constitutional government came the demand for territory. As the Hungarians demanded the re-incorporation of Croatia and Transylvania in the Hungarian state, and the Germans of Holstein the maintenance of unity with Schleswig, so the Poles insisted upon the incorporation of Lithuanian and Ukrainian lands in Russian Poland. The Schleswig formula, "Up ewig ungedeelt" (forever inseparable), the Hungarian "lands of the Holy Crown of St. Stephen," and the Polish "frontiers of 1772" were the catchword descriptions of territorial claims made within the Danish monarchy and the Austrian and Russian empires respectively.

The social structure of Poland resembled that of Hungary in several respects. In neither country was there a strong urban middle class; both were agricultural regions which maintained a class of high nobles, a class of impoverished squires, and a peasantry which in eastern Poland and around parts of the outer rim of Hungary belonged to a subject nationality.

In 1815 there had been a class of high nobility in Poland, like the Szécsens of Hungary and the Scheel-Plessens of Holstein, who combined loyalty to their class and land with fealty to their monarch. The revolutions of 1830 had sent them into exile or left them to nurse their grievances at home. The revolutionary party founded on this class was called the party of the "whites." Czartoryski in Paris was the leader until his death in 1861. The Polish "reds" were comparable to the Kossuth party in Hungary.

In the general relaxation of despotism that followed the Crimean War, Count Andrei Zamoyski, one of the whites, was permitted to found an Agricultural Society in Poland. The white nobles used the society, not only to study scientific farming, but also to organize themselves politically throughout the kingdom. The reds found their adherents among the impoverished squires—the szlachta—and the professional classes in the city. They maintained on the ground a Secret Committee in charge of their propaganda and organization.

The effect of the Italian revolution was to stimulate the activity of revolutionists of all colors. A series of manifestations were held; in February, 1861, the soldiers fired on a procession. The Agricultural Society thereupon stepped forward as the representative of the nation, and addressed to the Viceroy Gorchakov a demand for the redress of Poland's wrongs.

The address, coming within a week of the great proclamation emancipating the serfs of Russia, found the Tsar in a reforming frame of mind, disposed to better his relations with his Polish subjects, though reluctant to display weakness in the face of popular demonstrations.

As Alexander's ideas defined themselves, under the influence of a liberal party at court and with the advice of agents from Warsaw, he came to hope that he could make Poland a contented kingdom under his crown, like Norway under the Swedish crown. He was tired of being reproached as a barbarian in a civilized country.

But how could he establish a régime of conciliation? Where was the class with which he could work? Among all the high nobility who elsewhere formed the natural allies of the monarchs in nineteenth-century federative polity, there was only one conspicuous figure who favored a working entente with Russia. That was the Marquis Wielopolski, a strange, powerful, and lonely man.

Wielopolski offered to help with conciliation if the Tsar would grant Poland sufficient autonomy. The Tsar met him halfway, with a decree of March 26, 1861, that set up a state council with power to hear complaints and make investigations, established a ministry of cult and education with Wielopolski in charge, provided for provincial councils with powers of local self-government, and promised the extension of the high school and university system. The grant of power to Poland was very much less than what Francis Joseph offered the Hungarians in the October Diploma, less than the Tsar was at this very time giving to Finland. For it was not easy to find a social and political class in Poland that would make the system of autonomy work.

The Agricultural Society, the Roman Catholic Church, and the secret organization of the reds were three anti-Russian governments spread through the country, all willing to engage in active or passive resistance. Only the serfs might be counted upon to support the Russian rule, and then only to the extent that the Russians helped them against the landlords.

One of Wielopolski's first acts was to dissolve the Agricultural Society. Thenceforth he was regarded by his countrymen as a traitor. He wanted a firm government, but a government of law. He had to contend with Suchosanet, a military governor who had absolutely no idea of legality. "You forget with whom you speak; I am one whom His Majesty has appointed to office," said Suchosanet in anger. Wielopolski replied: "And I am one whom His Majesty begged to accept office." His political problem was to win the whites. If he won them he stood a chance of losing the serfs. The serfs were already refusing to do their compulsory service, and wanted to take their land without payment. Wielopolski issued a decree in the Tsar's name, providing for permanent lease with money payment. The Tsar feared that Wielopolski was sacrificing the one class upon whose loyalty he could count, and called him to St. Petersburg. At St. Petersburg, in November, 1861, the firm Polish statesman won the confidence of the court, and was able to return in the following year with larger powers, and with the Grand Duke Constantine as Viceroy, to hold the military authorities in check. But where could the coöperation of a Polish governing class be found? Russia had no skilled bureaucracy that could be thrown into Poland as Schmerling threw his officials into recalcitrant Hungary; in the presence of disorder, Russia had no resource but martial law and military rule.

Under these conditions, the future of the Tsar's policy depended upon the coöperation of the whites; Grand Duke Constantine had an interview with Count Andrei Zamoyski in September, 1862, to try to reach an understanding. He found that the Count would not coöperate unless the frontiers of 1772 were restored. This was a demand the Tsar could not grant!

Meanwhile the revolutionary tide was rising. The red Secret Committee was provoking manifestations everywhere. Wielopolski's last stroke was an attempt simultaneously to win over the country people and suppress the urban agitation by suspending martial law in the rural districts and arresting the leaders of the patriotic city youth for forced service in the army. When these arrests were attempted in Warsaw in January, 1863, the country sprang to arms.

As the revolution spread through Poland, European opinion was aroused and measures of international intervention proposed. The Poles had long claimed that their cause was international because the treaties of 1815 had defined their status. In 1860 Polish deputies in the Prussian diet introduced a resolution stating that the Polish nation should be regarded as a recognized member of the European community of nations, though for European convenience the task of governing it had been allotted to three princes instead of one. Of course the Prussian cabinet and diet rejected this theory.

A few weeks after the revolution started (February 8, 1863), Prussia signed a convention with Russia under which the two powers agreed to coöperate against the rebels. This convention immediately made the Polish question an international one, and gave the friends of Poland an opportunity to intercede. In a series of diplomatic moves under Napoleon's leadership, from February to September, 1863, France, England, and Austria tried to force the Tsar to grant amnesty and reforms. Gorchakov ended by denying that Europe had any right to intervene in Poland under the treaties of 1815.

VIII. A CONGRESS TO REVISE THE TREATIES OF 1815

The federative crisis of the 1860's was a turning-point in modern political history, for here, at the very moment that the great gear-shift of industry and transport was taking hold, and giving economic life a tremendous acceleration, the peoples throughout the heart of the Continent had an opportunity to readjust their relationships to each other without annexations or cessions of the territory of one monarchy to another, but solely by rearrangements within each monarchy, or by increasing the interdependence of the monarchies.

Why did all this ferment leave so little trace? Why did it fail? Was it because of nationalist sentiment? But the German nationalists in 1863 were pulling with the super-national Austrian state, and the Slavic nationalities on the Danube were working hand in hand with the Magyars. The Polish question showed itself conclusively resistant to solution only when the Polish landlord class insisted on a historical right (not a national-democratic right) to include a Lithuanian and Ukrainian peasantry in the Polish Kingdom.

Among the circumstances that contributed to the failure of these schemes must be reckoned the impotence or paralysis, for different reasons in different places, of the high aristocracy that had in the preceding centuries mediated between thrones and peoples. Another factor was the disintegration of the concert of the five great powers on the basis of the treaties of 1815.

If the dynastic states could not stabilize Europe by internal reforms, was it possible to stabilize a new situation by redistributing territory among them? The question was presented simultaneously in 1863 in Poland, Denmark, Rumania, Italy, and Germany. It led the Imperial couple in Paris to resort again to their map-making. On February 21, at a time when it still seemed that the revolution in Poland might succeed, Empress Eugénie was talking to the

Austrian ambassador about a Franco-Austrian alliance. "We must look at the map," she said, and then unrolled before the eyes of the astonished diplomat a chart on which he saw laid out an independent Poland, with Russia compensated in Asia and Prussia in north Germany. Silesia had been transferred to Austria, Venetia to Italy, and the Austrian Empire had been extended through the Balkans. France had the left bank of the Rhine, the Ottoman Empire had disappeared, and the Greeks had Constantinople. Eugénie explained that the dispossessed princes could set themselves up with thrones in South America. She said she had good news from Mexico, where Maximilian was establishing his imperial throne. The Austrians, of course, were wholly unprepared for any such adventures. On the scale of such projects, the Frankfurt congress of princes was a cautious or even commonplace effort.

To interpret the dreams of Napoleon III as mere bargaining proposals to win for France additional Rhineland territory is to miss the meaning and the tragedy of the man's rôle in history. In 1863 he was perhaps the last genuine European who stood in a place of authority, a successor to Metternich, a precursor of Woodrow Wilson. On the 4th of November he invited all the powers, great and small, to attend a congress in Paris to revise the treaties of 1815, for Gorchakov had encouraged him privately to believe that Russia would be willing to consider the Polish question on an international plane if it were taken up, along with all other troublesome questions, in a European congress. Yet Napoleon's speech to the chambers on the occasion of the invitation to the congress was keyed to a note of pessimism, almost of despair:

> Will the jealous rivalry of the great powers forever obstruct the progress of civilization? Will we always maintain our mutual defiance by exaggerated armaments? . . . Will we forever preserve a state which is neither peace with its security nor war with its chances of fortune?[15]

The only power that dared refuse outright was England. Lord Russell stated his objections on December 26:

> There being no supreme authority in such an assembly to enforce the

[15] A. Pingaud, "Un Projet de Désarmement de Napoléon III (1863)," in *Académie des sciences Morales et Politiques. Compte-Rendu,* XCI, 1931, 475.

decisions of the majority, the Congress would probably separate leaving many of its members on worse terms with each other than they had been when it met.[16]

Lord Russell was probably right, and Napoleon wrong, in the appraisal of the amount of strain that international organization would stand in 1863. Perhaps it is only in the exhaustion or exaltation that follows a general war that governments are willing to readjust their affairs on a comprehensive scale. If that be true, then it must stand as one of the peculiarities of the succeeding era that a readjustment was made without either a general war or a general peace.

[16] *Annual Register*, 1863, 211.

Chapter Twelve

CIVIL WAR AND RECONSTRUCTION

I. BISMARCK'S OBJECTIVES BEFORE THE GERMAN CIVIL WAR

AS THE BONDS of federative polity were relaxed simultaneously among the great powers and within the German *Bund*, the disintegration of the European order became evident. In the words of Count Vitzthum, the anarchy of the mobs of 1848, having been defeated in the streets, had now ascended to the courts.

> Anarchy reigned in the alliances; one united today only with the *arrière pensée* to break apart tomorrow. All efforts to reconstruct a political system in Europe remained sterile, and short-sighted egoism was not able to create the slightest durable combination.[1]

The rapid flux of alliances began in 1864 when Austria and Prussia combined in the Danish question against the middle states and the authority of the *Bund*, cut themselves loose from the concert and the London Protocol, and forced the Danish Kingdom to cede the duchies. Then in the dispute over the disposition of the duchies, Prussia allied herself with Italy against Austria, Austria with the middle states against Prussia. With the object of restraining Prussia from further expansion, an alliance of Austria, France, and Italy was projected between 1867 and 1870, but the negotiations had not been completed when the Franco-Prussian War broke out. After the Franco-Prussian War the Three Emperors' Agreement of 1873, anticipated by a Russo-Prussian understanding in 1867, began to restore some stability to the European system, and finally, in 1879, the Austro-German Dual Alliance reëstablished on a basis of dualism the old military-defensive *Mitteleuropa*. In the meantime Prussia had risen from the least to the highest place among the powers, and Italy was admitted (in 1867, in the Luxemburg question) to

[1] Count Vitzthum to Beust, June 8, 1869, in Hermann Oncken: *Die Rheinpolitik Kaiser Napoleons III von 1863 bis 1870 und der Ursprung des Krieges von 1870-71* (Berlin and Leipzig, 1926), III, 199.

the charmed circle. The German Empire with the annexed territory of Alsace and Lorraine, and the Kingdom of Italy with Venetia and Rome, remained as the permanent products of this era of European disintegration.

In this time of travail Bismarck was so active that the whole period is in a sense a chapter of his biography. This fact would greatly simplify the account if Bismarck's policy had always been directed to the achievement of a single end by a single method. What makes the narrative difficult to interpret is the extraordinary fertility and elasticity of Bismarckian diplomacy. The man was so fully prepared for so great a number of contingencies that the thread of his actual purpose is sometimes lost. Yet there is one thing that stands out very clearly in the copious documentation: that Bismarck before 1866 was not an architect of German unity, but a Prussian statesman striving with demonic energy to build up the power of the Prussian state.

The territorial basis of increased Prussian power he saw in three possible achievements: first, outright annexation of territory in north Germany, especially the duchies conquered from Denmark. Even before the Danish War he resolved to acquire these lands. The second territorial objective was a clear Prussian hegemony north of the Main River. This was the policy foreshadowed in 1859 in the Prussian demand that the two northern confederate army corps should be annexed to the Prussian army. This would have left the hegemony of the remainder of Germany to Austria. Or, as an alternative, if Austria should be driven back upon her own Hapsburg German lands south of the Inn, to Bavarian hegemony. Finally there was the possibility that Germany might be partitioned at the Inn rather than the Main, and the whole non-Austrian area made subject to Prussia.

In the period from the Danish War to the battle of Königgrätz none of these objectives was desired by German national patriots. The liberals from 1859 to 1862 had been willing to accept the partitioning of Germany at the Inn, but the constitutional conflict in Prussia had made them the fixed enemies of Prussian expansion of any kind and hence of the *Kleindeutsch* solution of the German problem. The partitioning at the Main was even less desirable. And so far as the duchies were concerned, German patriotic sentiment was absolutely committed to the Augustenburg cause and hostile to Prussian annexation. German nationalists demanded unanimously that a new German middle state should be established in the territory conquered from Denmark.

Thus Bismarck, in his schemes for increasing the great-power status of Prussia, found himself solidly opposed on all fronts by German nationalism. At the same time he had difficulty in bringing King William to go with him in his policy. William was reluctant to usurp the duchies from Augustenburg, to break way from the federal ties of the *Bund*, or to provoke a civil war in Germany.

Neither a war with Austria nor an alliance with Austria was for Bismarck an end in itself. He was willing to coöperate with Austria against Italy and France, or with Russia, Italy, or France against Austria. For reasons of internal politics he wanted a war if he could get one, but a foreign war would serve his purpose as well as a civil war. Provided Austria met his terms as to territory and hegemony in north Germany, he was willing to continue the alliance with her, and possibly to direct it against France and Italy.

How close did Bismarck come to a peaceful understanding with Austria? There were three occasions upon which this ground was explored. First at Schönbrunn in August, 1864, when Bismarck and Rechberg agreed that Prussia could annex Schleswig and Austria take Holstein, with the thought that Holstein could later be traded for Prussian help in Italy. King William was not at that time sufficiently anxious to annex the territory he had liberated to give Bismarck the bargaining power necessary to reach an agreement with Austria, and the influence of Biegeleben at Vienna was sufficient to check Rechberg's generosity to Prussia.

The second possible basis of understanding with Austria was proposed by Bismarck in February, 1865, as a compromise between giving the duchies to the Duke of Augustenburg and ceding them to Prussia. The duke could have the territory, but subject to conditions that made Prussia virtually a suzerain power. Austria rejected some of these conditions—notably the proposal that the

Schleswig-Holstein army should take an oath of allegiance to the King of Prussia rather than to the duke.

When Austria rejected the February conditions, friction developed in the duchies, and Prussia bargained with the Duke of Oldenburg to make him a stalking-horse for Prussian claims. By a secret contract with Duke Peter Bismarck arranged that as soon as the duchies were awarded to Oldenburg, the latter should sell them to Prussia. Then he championed the Oldenburg claims, and in the summer of 1865 put his demand for the recognition of Oldenburg in the form of an ultimatum to Austria. This was the crisis that ended in the Gastein Agreement (August 14, 1865), under which Prussia took over the administration of Schleswig and Austria of Holstein, leaving the sovereignty undetermined.

The Gastein Convention kept the road open for a return to the principle of division of the duchies as proposed at Schönbrunn the previous year. It mortally offended German national sentiment because the ostensible cause of the Danish War was Denmark's attempt to separate the duchies, and now the two German powers were dividing them.

Then, in the spring and summer of 1866, as the conflict between Austria and Prussia grew more bitter, the two Gablenz brothers, one in Austrian and the other in Prussian service, became mediators in proposing another settlement. The duchies should be given, not to Prussia, but to a younger son of the Hohenzollern house, and Austria should agree to let Prussia organize military hegemony north of the Main, a fulfillment of Prussian desires formulated in 1859. The Gablenz negotiations were kept up till the very last moment; they were not dropped till after the troop trains were moving into Saxony. The principal consideration that kept Francis Joseph from accepting them was his loyalty to the middle states, who would have been sacrificed to Prussia by the Gablenz plan.

As an alternative to an agreement with Austria, Bismarck maintained as an anti-Austrian weapon a plan for German reform. The basic outline of his plan was already laid down in 1861 in the Baden memorandum. It provided for a German parliament exercising such powers over the territories from which it drew delegates that Austria could not join it. At Baden in 1861 he thought of this parliament as a body chosen by the diets of the German states; in 1863 when he brought the plan up again as a counter-project to the program of the Frankfurt congress of princes he would have had the parliament chosen by direct vote of a restricted class of voters. He was then in the midst of his fight with the Prussian diet, and could not hope to have the German diets send to a central parliament delegates friendly to him; he would have made sure of a conservative parliament by means of an electoral law. Then, in 1866, when he was mounting the final attack on Austria, he proposed the same plan with the provision for universal suffrage. On June 10, 1866, he came out openly for the exclusion of Austria and hence the division of Germany at the Inn. This was an effort to win the masses away from Austria. As such it was a complete failure. Liberals and democrats were so hostile to Bismarck that they suspected his sincerity. Not until after the victory at Königgrätz did Bismarck win the nationalists to his side.

Along with the plans for coöperation with Austria against the German middle states, and for coöperation with the democratic masses against Austria, Bismarck recurred to plans for coöperation with foreign states against the German middle states and Austria. Such alliances were forbidden by the constitution of the *Bund*, but Bismarck had no compunctions about violating this particular confederate obligation. In 1863, immediately after the Frankfurt congress of princes, he asked for an immediate Russian alliance against Austria, and hinted to the Russian ambassador that he would be willing to pay France with some of the Rhineland if he could obtain Hanoverian territory on the Weser. In 1865, during the crisis that led to the Gastein Convention, he telegraphed to Italy an alliance suggestion (which was intercepted and decoded by the Austrian secret service). And in 1866, in the decisive meeting of the Prussian crown council on February 28, he obtained permission to contract with Italy an alliance against Austria, and signed the treaty on April 8.

Bismarck's three plans for building up Prussian power: with Austria against the other German states, with German nationalism against Austria, with foreign powers against Austria, were kept constantly ready for use. Against him Austrian policy was inelastic and paralyzed by the conflict within the Austrian ministry between the Metternichean and Schwarzenbergian traditions. Rechberg, the Metternichean, was checkmated because Bismarck would not accept the postulates of Metternichean comity. When he tried to get Bismarck to agree to stop bullying the *Bund* and the middle states, Bismarck said very pleasantly (September 29, 1864):

> We would be surer of progress along our common path if we were both to take our stand on the practical ground of cabinet policy, without befogging the situation with the sentimental doctrines of German politicians.

In other words, as Rechberg sorrowfully admitted to his Emperor, "to hold to the treaty basis is a nebulous and sentimental policy. . . . Such language is worthy of a Cavour."[2]

When Bismarck blocked a genuine return to the policies of Metternich, the alternative for Austria was a clear-cut *Realpolitik* of the Schwarzenberg type. This would have meant making concessions to Prussia in north Germany and using Prussian aid in Italy, or surrendering Venetia to the Italians and striking with full force against Prussia. But Francis Joseph would not go as far as this, and Biegeleben hardly dared to lay his full thought before the Emperor. Moreover, Austrian strength was paralyzed during the critical months by the development of the conflict with Hungary.

II. THE CIVIL WAR IN GERMANY

As the tension between Austria and Prussia increased in the winter of 1865 and 1866, Francis Joseph became convinced that he could not make the system of coöperation with Prussia a workable one. Austria began, thereupon, to return to the old alignment with the middle German states against Prussia. At the same time both Prussian and Austrian diplomacy worked hard at Paris for an understanding with Napoleon. In March Napoleon offered Richard Metternich, the son of the great chancellor, an assurance of diplomatic coöperation with Austria if Austria would surrender Venetia to Italy. It was Austria's last chance to make this a profitable bargain, for the Prusso-Italian treaty was already under negotiation.

[2] C. W. Clark: *Franz Joseph and Bismarck, The Diplomacy of Austria before the war of 1866* (Cambridge, 1934), 115.

Austria lost this chance, and then, on the very eve of the war, when it was evident at Vienna that there would be an attack on both the Italian and German fronts, Napoleon forced the Viennese cabinet to agree to surrender Venetia to Italy regardless of the outcome of the fighting, as a price of French neutrality.

Bismarck, in an effort to counter the Austrian move to line up the middle states, set out in April with his move toward German reform. On the day after the alliance treaty with Italy was signed the Prussian representative in the confederate assembly moved to call a constituent convention elected by universal suffrage to reorganize Germany. Bismarck later declared that the greatest mistake of his career was the introduction of universal suffrage. It was intended, of course, to break down liberal power without offending national sentiment. This was the gesture that was regarded by the German nationalists as a trap. It also brought Napoleon into an anti-Prussian attitude. Napoleon had assured Bismarck that he did not have any objection to the creation of a strong Prussian state in the north, but he made it clear that a union of forty million Germans in a reorganized state would meet French armed opposition. Bismarck calmed him with assurances that Prussia would divide Germany at the Main, and tempted him with the prospect of some territory in the Rhineland, though he made it clear that he dared not, at the moment, propose such a solution to King William, who would prefer making terms with Austria to a surrender of German land to France.

The Prussian treaty with Italy was a short-term alliance that ran only for three months from April 8. In order to make use of it, Bismarck had to start a war. The time limits within which he had to work were more restricted than those within which Cavour worked in bringing about the war of 1859.

In May the approach to civil war was marked by military preparations in Bohemia and in Prussia. The sequence by which military preparations lead to war had been somewhat standardized in the Crimean and Italian Wars, and ran in this case its regular course. Austria almost forced Prussia into a bad position by offering to begin demobilization a day before Prussia, but then by an unfortunate decision the Vienna government spoiled the effect of this diplomatic victory by proceeding with mobilization against Italy. When Napoleon issued the usual call for a European conference, Austria nullified the move by making a condition that the Pope must be invited to attend, and that the participants must agree in advance not to take any territory. The bitterness of German sentiment against Prussia made it easier than it would otherwise have been to bring the middle states into line against a disturber of the German peace. Then a Prussian military demonstration in Holstein forced the Austrian troops to withdraw from that duchy, and Austria brought before the *Bund* a motion to mobilize the confederate army against Prussia. On June 14, 1866, the motion was adopted by a vote of nine to six. The Prussian delegate announced Prussia's secession, and declared the *Bund* dissolved. The war began at once on all fronts.

On June 24 the Austrian army in Italy inflicted a decisive defeat on the Italians at Custozza. The Prussians overran the German middle states which had sided with Austria, forced the blind King George of Hanover to capitulate on June 28, and moved south against the Bavarians. The Saxon army had withdrawn into Bohemia to join the Austrians, who were coming up into the decisive theater of the war. Benedek, the Austrian commander, who had unwillingly taken command in Bohemia, wanted to retreat and wait for reinforcements from the victorious army in Italy, but a telegram from Vienna caused him to make a stand against the Prussians at Königgrätz, where his troops were decisively defeated on July 3.

This German Gettysburg was won by the secessionists. The military history of the campaign proves that several factors contributed to the victory. Benedek might have saved his army but for the telegram from Vienna. The Prussian army had superior equipment for the infantry in the breech-loading needle gun, but more than any other single factor in turning the tide of victory was the successful use of railways by the Prussian army. The use of railways for the mass transport of troops had been carefully studied by the Prussian staff. The Danish War had taught the lesson that the military commanders in the field must not be permitted to give orders directly to the railway administration, but that every order

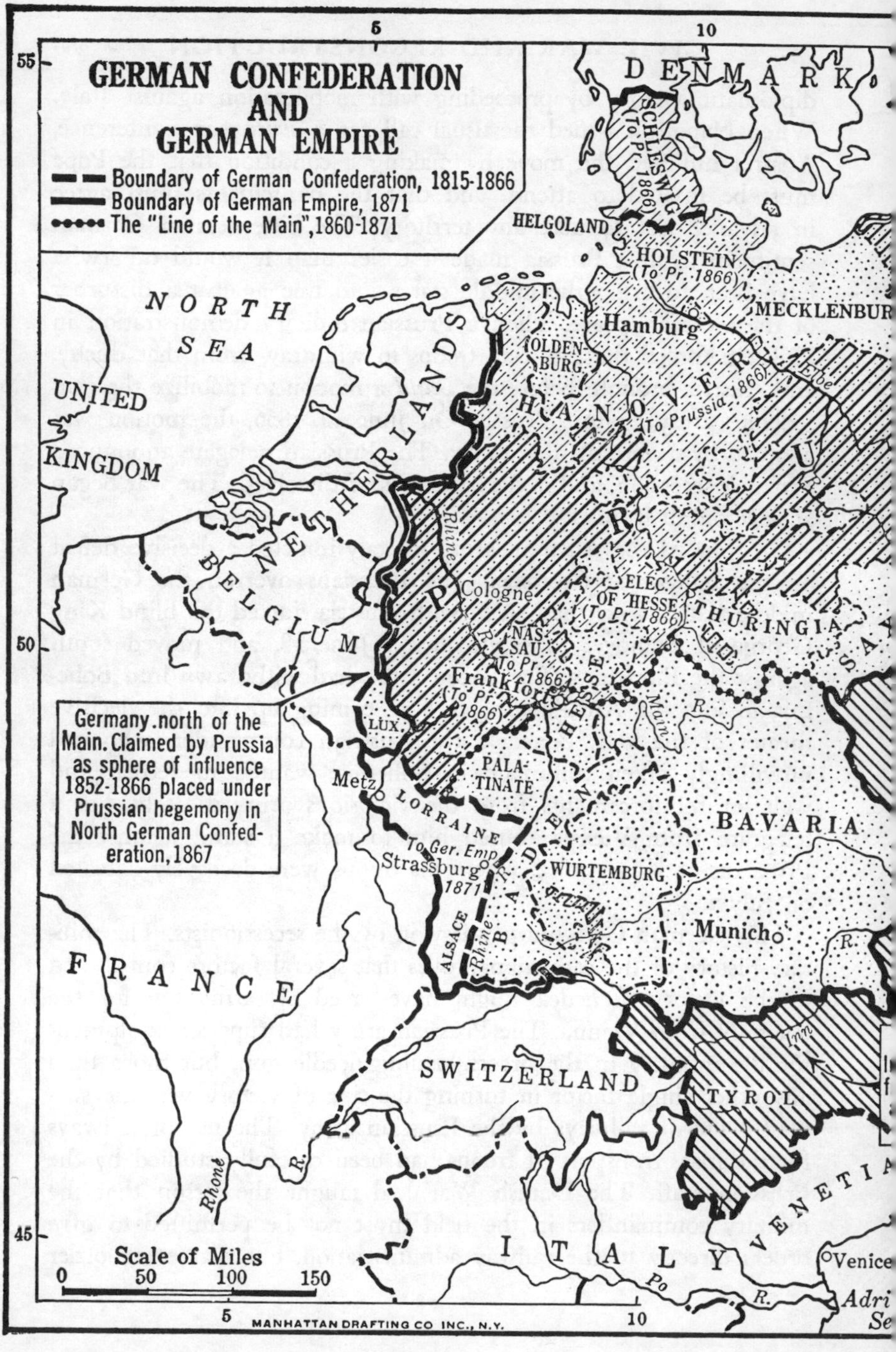
GERMAN CONFEDERATION AND GERMAN EMPIRE
Boundary of German Confederation, 1815-1866
Boundary of German Empire, 1871
The "Line of the Main", 1860-1871
Germany north of the Main. Claimed by Prussia as sphere of influence 1852-1866 placed under Prussian hegemony in North German Confederation, 1867
NORTH SEA
UNITED KINGDOM
DENMARK
SCHLESWIG (To Pr. 1866)
HELGOLAND
HOLSTEIN (To Pr. 1866)
MECKLENBURG
Hamburg
OLDENBURG
HANOVER (To Prussia 1866)
NETHERLANDS
BELGIUM
PRUSSIA
Elbe
Rhine
Cologne
ELEC. OF HESSE (To Pr. 1866)
THURINGIA
NASSAU To Pr. 1866
Frankfort (To Pr. 1866)
HESSE
Main R.
LUX.
PALATINATE
Metz
LORRAINE To Ger. Emp.
Strassburg 1871
ALSACE
BADEN
WURTEMBURG
BAVARIA
Munich
FRANCE
SWITZERLAND
TYROL
Inn
Rhone R.
ITALY
VENETIA
Venice
Po R.
Scale of Miles
0 50 100 150
5 10
55 50 45
MANHATTAN DRAFTING CO INC., N.Y.

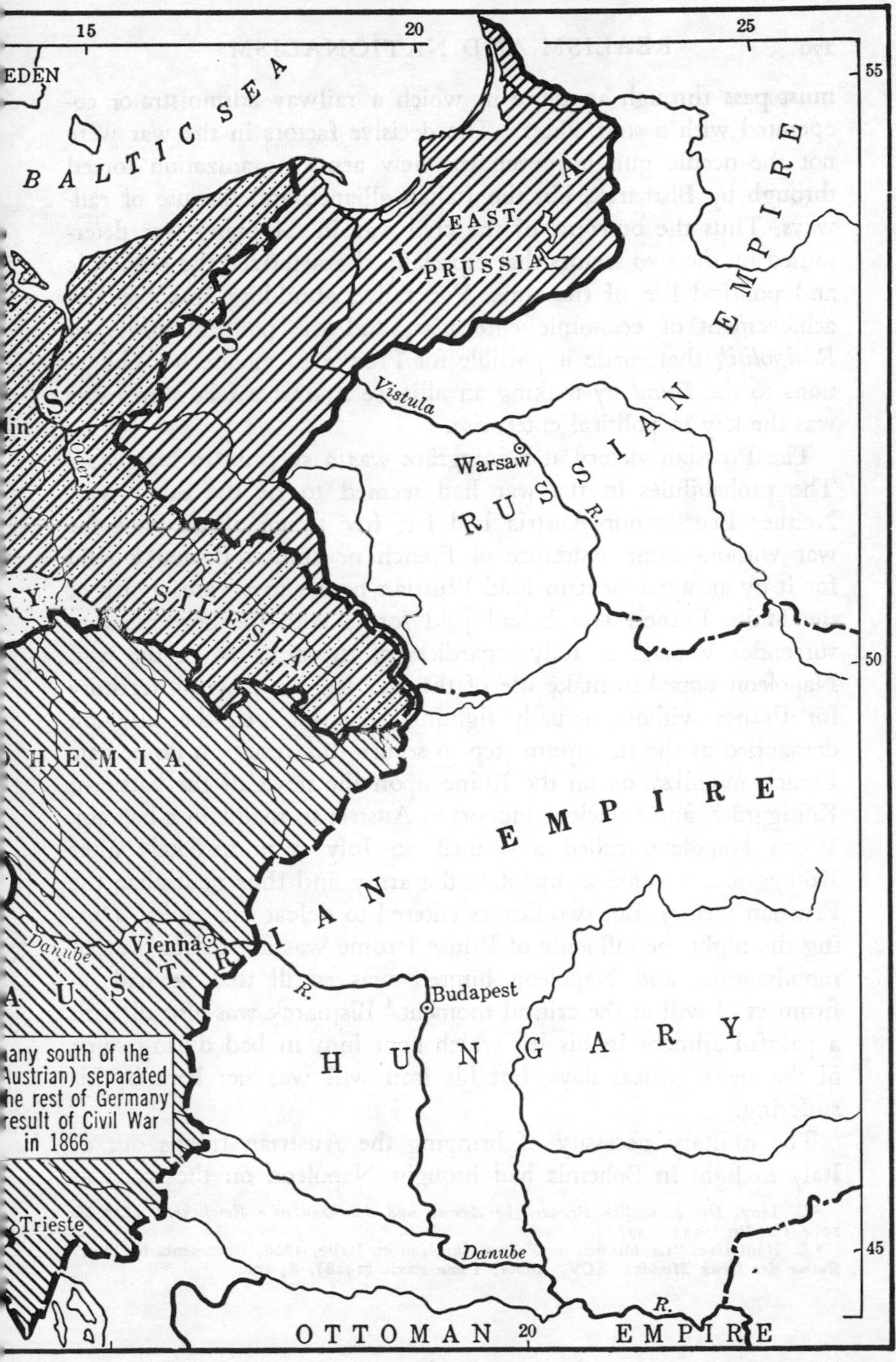

EDEN
BALTIC SEA
EAST PRUSSIA
PRUSSIA
RUSSIAN EMPIRE
Vistula
Warsaw
Oder
SILESIA
HEMIA
AUSTRIAN EMPIRE
Vienna
Danube
R.
Budapest
HUNGARY
Trieste
Danube
R.
OTTOMAN EMPIRE
any south of the
Austrian) separated
he rest of Germany
result of Civil War
in 1866
15
20
25
55
50
45
20

must pass through an office in which a railway administrator co-operated with a staff officer.[3] The decisive factors in the war were not the needle gun nor even the new army organization forced through by Bismarck, but the Italian alliance and the use of railways. Thus the outcome of the civil war in Germany was determined by the two factors that especially characterized the economic and political life of the time. For railway-building was the key achievement of economic enterprise, and the political ethics of *Realpolitik* that made it possible for Prussia to violate her obligations to the *Bund* by making an alliance against a fellow member was the key to political enterprise.

The Prussian victory at Königgrätz was a surprise to Napoleon. The probabilities in the war had seemed to lie the other way. Neither Prussia nor Austria had felt free to go ahead with the war without some assurance of French neutrality. Bismarck paid for it by an agreement to hold Prussian power to an area north of the Main, Francis Joseph had paid for it with the agreement to surrender Venetia to Italy regardless of the outcome of the war. Napoleon hoped to make use of the war to gain Rhenish territory for France without actually fighting. The logic of the situation demanded as the minimum step to secure this result an immediate French mobilization on the Rhine upon the news of the battle of Königgrätz, and sufficient support to Austria to maintain a balance. When Napoleon called a council on July 5, immediately after Königgrätz, it voted to mobilize the army and thus neutralize the Prussian victory. But two factors entered to defeat this policy. During the night the influence of Prince Jerome was exerted to prevent mobilization, and Napoleon himself was so ill that he had no firmness of will at the critical moment.[4] Bismarck was also ill with a painful ailment in his leg which kept him in bed during some of the most critical days, but his iron will was not bent by his suffering.

The military necessity of bringing the Austrian troops out of Italy to fight in Bohemia had brought Napoleon on the scene as

[3] C. Jany, *Die Königlich Preussische Armee und das Deutsche Reichsheer, 1807 bis 1914* (Berlin, 1933), 237.

[4] E. Hauterive, "La Mission du Prince Napoléon en Italie, 1866. Documents inédites," *Revue des Deux Mondes*, XCV, Année, Tome xxvii (1928), 83-120.

a mediator under the terms of his agreement with Austria, for it was necessary to clear up the cession of Venetia to Italy before the Austrian troops could be withdrawn to the north. But before these diplomatic arrangements were completed the Prussian victory changed the focus of French diplomacy. The question confronting Napoleon, as well as the Prussian and Austrian governments, was how to determine the extent to which Prussia should be permitted to reap the fruits of victory.

Bismarck formulated three fundamental war aims: the rounding out of the Prussian state in the north by annexations of middle-state territory, the exclusion of Austria from the *Bund*, and the right to organize all territory north of the Main in a North German Confederation. Napoleon gave his consent provided the south German states were left free to form other alliances and to organize themselves as a third unit (July 13). Francis Joseph made sure that the French terms would not involve cession of Austrian or Saxon territory to Prussia, and Bismarck, after an argument with the King, prevailed upon William to accept them on July 18. On July 23 the Austrian plenipotentiaries appeared at the Prussian headquarters at Nikolsburg to conclude the political terms of the armistice. They reluctantly accepted the separation of Austria from the rest of Germany. Thus there was drawn that frontier at the Inn which is one of the most troublesome nationality grievances of the twentieth century.

While the Austrian armistice plenipotentiaries were still at Nikolsburg the French ambassador, Benedetti, made his appearance, bearing a demand that France be given compensations on the Rhine. Bismarck put him off until the peace with Austria was made, and then refused. This refusal was the first decisive act in which Bismarck utilized successfully the German sentiment of nationalism. Benedetti returned to the attack after the peace preliminaries had been signed, as will be related below.

With marvelous rapidity Bismarck concluded peace with the south German states, and brought them to sign secret alliance treaties with Prussia at the same time. He hurried Bavaria into the alliance by telling of Napoleon's compensation claims at Bavaria's expense. These alliance treaties were a violation of the agreement with Napoleon not to extend the Prussian zone south of the Main, but how could Napoleon expect a letter-perfect fidelity to engagements from one who had just torn up the German federal pact by the Italian alliance? Then Bismarck turned to the annexations. King William did not wish to wipe out whole princely houses in Germany; he would have preferred to take some territory from each of his enemies, coming down upon them like a Nemesis to punish them according to their deserts.[5] For this reason he was especially reluctant to let Austria go without loss of any territory except Venetia. But Bismarck had his way. The outright annexation of Hanover, Schleswig-Holstein, Electoral Hesse, Nassau, and the Free City of Frankfurt gave Prussia a compact territory and an overwhelming physical preponderance, especially in the north.

III. RECONSTRUCTION IN GERMANY

The victory made Bismarck a popular hero. He immediately offered peace to the Prussian liberals by proposing an indemnity bill to legalize the unconstitutional financing of the past four years. The liberals accepted the olive branch. The conservatives were offended not only at universal suffrage, but because Bismarck would not make the liberals eat dirt. The King made it clear that he would act in the same way if the safety of the state should again demand it, "But, gentlemen, it will not happen again"—and it did not happen again so long as there were kings in Prussia. The relationship of monarch to parliament thereby established was transferred from Prussian to German practice when the German Empire was founded, and remained unshaken until the panic of defeat in the autumn of 1918, when the Reichstag established the system of responsible government at the behest of Woodrow Wilson. The liberals as a class and liberalism as an idea sold out to Bismarck. Though the Prussian diet and the later Reichstag filled a large place in the political machine, the political life of Germany never became what the hopes of the liberals of the New Era would have made it.

As the breach with the liberals was healed, Bismarck was ready

[5] G. Roloff, "Brünn und Nikolsburg. Nicht Bismarck sondern der König isoliert," *Historische Zeitschrift*, CXXXVI (1927), 457-501.

to press forward the organization of the North German Confederation. The draft of a constitution that emerged from his collaboration with his experts retained as many features as possible of the constitution of the old *Bund*. The old confederate assembly hung on with the states south of the Main excluded, with its name changed to *Bundesrat*, and with voting power still distributed as in the old plenum of the *Bund*. Since Prussia assumed the votes allotted in the old *Bund* to the states she had annexed, this gave her seventeen out of forty-three votes—though in population she had twenty-four out of twenty-nine million. With the army in the hands of the King of Prussia, Prussian dominion over the *Bund* was assured. The chancellor of the *Bund*, in Bismarck's draft, was to be simply the president of the *Bundesrat*, with duties resembling those once discharged by the Austrian delegate at Frankfurt. Bismarck would have left the separate states free to maintain consulates and legations abroad. The Prussian draft was laid before the plenipotentiaries of the other north German states in December, 1866. The spirit of the draft itself was fairly close to the Baden memorandum of 1861; the procedure of cabinet preparation and submission to a popularly elected constituent assembly was in line with the procedure Bismarck had suggested in 1863 and 1866. The political tradition of Germany had already established the general character of reconstruction. The question was: how far would it go? At what point between confederation and federal state would the political institutions crystallize and set themselves?

The plenipotentiaries of the lesser states limited the power Bismarck would have given the *Bund* in deciding internal constitutional questions in the individual states, and extended the power of the chancellor. Then the draft went before the constituent assembly elected by universal suffrage in February, 1867. The old liberal desire for a German ministry responsible to a German parliament encountered Bismarck's resistance, for he was hardly willing to concede to the new *Bund* what he had just wrested from the Prussian diet. The effect of liberal pressure in the constituent was to increase the powers of the North German Confederation as a means of increasing the powers of its parliament. The conservatives would have liked to see an upper house representing the high nobility, rather than a *Bundesrat* representing the governments of the states. Thus the pressure exerted by the representatives of the people was all in the direction of strengthening the powers of the new *Bund* at the expense of the separate states. The German nation ran ahead and pulled Bismarck with it. The powers of the chancellor were further increased under the pressure of the delegates. Bismarck had at first planned to let Savigny be chancellor, but when the assembly voted that the chancellor must countersign all acts of the new *Bund* and be politically responsible for them, Bismarck realized that he himself must fill that office. The rights of the separate states to maintain separate consular and diplomatic services abroad were eliminated by the force of the movement for concentration of power.

The effect of Königgrätz and the peace preliminaries at Nikolsburg was like the effect of Solferino and the peace preliminaries of Villafranca in that they called forth and directed national energies. The effect of nationalism as a unifying force was felt after the military decision, not before it. In Italy the men implicated in the central Italian revolutions began defending themselves against the very real danger that their bitter enemies might be restored to power; in Germany the movement had the character of a rush for the band wagon.

In making peace with the south German states Bismarck had not only brought them into an alliance with Prussia, but had also persuaded them to yield their rights in tariff-making in the Customs Union to a customs parliament that would act by majority vote. Thus the new Germany took form with the old Prussian state at the center, and the rest of Germany north of the Inn ranged around the center in three tiers. The first tier was annexed outright, the second tier united in the North German Confederation, and the third by the alliance treaties and the customs parliament. The line of the Main was already subsiding as a frontier; only the line of the Inn would stand.

IV. RECONSTRUCTION IN THE HAPSBURG EMPIRE

While German politics was moving through civil war and reconstruction the politics of the Hapsburg Monarchy passed through another cycle of conservatism—a hopeless attempt to go back to the aristocratic federalism of the October Diploma, which in its actual effects led directly to dualism. It was in December, 1864, that secret negotiations between Déak and the court were opened. Déak receded from the position that Hungarian law would permit no common organs to treat of common affairs, for he was willing to deduce from the reference to "common defense" in the Pragmatic Sanction of 1723 an implication that a common authority for defense and diplomacy might be established. When Francis Joseph was convinced that this common authority might have sufficient competence to preserve the great-power status of his empire, the road was opened to compromise. Déak's letter, published in the newspapers at Easter, 1865, was the signal for the change in policy. Schmerling was dismissed in July, and the Czech nobleman, Count Belcredi, called to head a new ministry.

Belcredi began by undoing all of Schmerling's work. He suspended the Reichsrat that had been functioning under the February Patent on the theory that the whole question of the application of the October Diploma was now to be reopened with Hungary and Croatia, and that the February Patent could not be constitutional law in one part of the monarchy while that part was negotiating with the other part. Then he undid Schmerling's work in Transylvania by turning the Transylvanian diet over to the Magyars, sacrificing the Rumanians and Saxons who had coöperated with Vienna. The next step was to call the Hungarian diet and confront it, not with the October Diploma as a *fait accompli*, but with the open problem of reaching an understanding on the management of the affairs that must in the nature of things be of common interest to all Hapsburg subjects.

In February, 1866, the Hungarian diet met. Francis Joseph in his speech from the throne declared that the relations of the Hungarian Kingdom to the other Hapsburg lands could be adjusted on the basis of the Pragmatic Sanction of 1723 (not the October Diploma). And Déak in his reply to the address conceded that some common organs of government were necessary to the monarchy.

Belcredi and his friends of the high Hungarian aristocracy had allowed themselves to hope that it would not be necessary to concede the whole system of liberal parliamentary mechanism that was provided for in the laws of 1848. He repeated the same gross and fundamental miscalculation that had nullified the proposals of the Enlarged Reichsrat of 1860 and ruined the October Diploma. Déak quickly cleared the air with a speech in which he declared that there could be no return to 1847. The principle of continuity of law required that not one single step in lawmaking could be taken by a Hungarian diet until a Hungarian King had appointed a responsible Hungarian ministry to countersign its legal acts. Nevertheless, a committee of the diet elaborated the points upon which an agreement with Francis Joseph and the Vienna ministry could be negotiated. This punctation allowed the transfer of only three subjects from the competence of the Hungarian diet to the competence of a joint legislative body. The three subjects were defense, foreign affairs, and finance for defense and foreign affairs. Neither recruiting nor the floating of war loans was to be surrendered to a common authority. And the common authority itself was to be established on a basis of absolute parity. A delegation from the Hungarian diet should meet a delegation from the parliament of the remaining Hapsburg lands, and sitting as a legislature of two coördinate houses, deal with the restricted list of common affairs. The report of this committee was adopted and the diet adjourned just before the decisive battle of Königgrätz.

Meanwhile the Vienna ministry had drawn up its list of common affairs. These included not only military and foreign affairs (counting recruiting and war loans as military matters), but also a long list of fiscal and economic matters; indirect taxes, communications, customs, and monopolies.

The effect of Königgrätz upon the internal situation of the monarchy was greatly to weaken the prestige of the dynasty and also to bring in, as the most important adviser to the crown, Count Beust, who had retired from Saxon service because he was *persona non grata* at Berlin. With a clarity, and perhaps a superficiality, that only an outsider could bring to these intricate problems, Beust pressed forward the understanding with Hungary in order to hasten the day when the monarchy could again assert itself in European affairs.

In December and January, 1866-67 the negotiation of the compromise was continued with a few leading Hungarians who were understood to be the prospective Hungarian ministers—among them Count Julius Andrássy. It is said that Déak was about to concede the extension of common authority over recruiting and war loans in his dealing with Belcredi, but that Beust came in and let Déak have his way. The long list of common economic and fiscal matters were left to be agreed upon between the two halves of the monarchy in much the same way as the south German states were to agree with the North German Confederation on matters of railway communication—that is, by a separate act of the legislatures on each point. The compromise was accepted by the Vienna ministry about as Déak had outlined it. Then the Hungarian ministry was appointed, and the question was closed so far as Hungary was concerned.

But what of Austria and the Slavs? The German middle class was just as determined as it had been in the time of the October Diploma that it would not allow its interest to be sacrificed to the provincial Slavic nobility. Belcredi's policy in the western half of the monarchy, as in Hungary, repeated the error of 1860. And in the meantime the Czechs had been taught by their experience with Schmerling to fear German political domination. In August, 1866, as the war clouds were clearing after Königgrätz, a Slavic congress met in Vienna. Palaćky and Rieger represented the Czechs, Goluchowski the Poles, Strossmayer the Croats. They made plans for federalism in the interest of the Slavs. Their scheme called for a fivefold division or "pentarchy." There were to be five provincial units, the Upper Austrian, Lower Austrian, Bohemian, South Slavic and Polish. A supreme central Reichstag was to control foreign affairs, war, commerce, customs, and finance. Five chancellors were to enter the ministry, each to guard the autonomy and interests of each of the groups of crown lands. This was the practical, nationalist federalism that was opposed by the Austrian Slavs to dualism.

Belcredi wanted to give bargaining power to the Slavs in the negotiation of the compromise with Hungary. He would have submitted the compromise to the different diets and would have called an extraordinary constituent Reichsrat to deliberate upon it. But Beust saw that such a procedure could not satisfy Hungary, for the Hungarians were opposed to federalism, even if it were limited to the western parts of the monarchy. Count Julius Andrássy expounded his objections in a memorandum in 1866.

> To substitute the federal idea for the Pragmatic Sanction would estrange Hungary and remove the strongest basis of the Monarchy. The German provinces would lose their cultural-historical mission, and the result would be that soon in Berlin or Munich the "cry of anguish" of the German provinces would be heard, just as in Florence the cry of the Italian provinces was heard.[6]

Moreover, there was the danger that federalism in the Austrian half would threaten the integrity of Hungary.

The final crisis in the reconstruction of the Hapsburg Monarchy was the conflict between Beust and Belcredi in January, 1867. When Belcredi was defeated, the Czechs were defeated with him. The German liberals came into the Reichsrat prepared to accept the compromise with Hungary, but determined to make sure of their own influence in their half of the common realm. They presented constitutional amendments making their ministers responsible to the Reichsrat, and introducing the guarantees of liberal parliamentary government; they made their own amendments part of the same law as the Hungarian compromise, and adopted the whole program at once.

The Czechs were furious. Some of them made a pilgrimage to Moscow in May, 1867, to attend a Pan-Slav congress. Their leaders undertook to give to Czechish claims the character of an international problem. Palaćky gave warning that the effect of dualism in the monarchy would be to stimulate Pan-Slavism in its most aggravated form. He said that he regretted the turn events were taking, but did not fear it: "The Slavs existed before Austria, and they will exist after her." And in 1872 he formally repudiated the much-quoted phrase he had coined in 1849—that if Austria did not exist it would be necessary to invent her.

The new order divided the Hapsburg monarchy at the Leitha almost as clearly as Germany was divided at the Inn when, after

[6] Eduard von Wertheimer: *Graf Julius Andrássy, sein Leben und seine Zeit* (Stuttgart, 1910-13), I, 224.

1879, the Dual Alliance had provided for Austro-German coöperation in defense. It left the peoples of the Danube monarchy gerrymandered into political relations which allowed some of them to domineer over others. The Germans sold out the Ruthenians to the Poles in order to make sure of Polish coöperation against the Czechs; the Croats sold out the South Slavs in order to gain for themselves a strong position in the Hungarian kingdom. The advent of dualism made impossible in the Danube basin the development of that free collaboration of peoples of different language and race that took place in Switzerland. And when Francis Joseph in a solemn ceremony at Budapest received the Holy Crown of St. Stephan, and swore to defend forever the integrity of the lands of that crown, he burned the bridges that might in the stress of later times have made possible the conciliation of the dynasty with the Slavs.

Thus the unsolved nationality problems that were destined to disturb the peace of the twentieth century—the division of Germany at the Inn, and the quarrels of German, Slav, and Magyar on the Danube, were institutionalized in the reconstruction of central Europe after the German civil war. And the list was not yet complete; within four years there was to be added the most bitter grievance of all—the annexation to Germany of Alsace and Lorraine.

V. THE SPREAD OF PARLIAMENTARY GOVERNMENT AND DEMOCRACY

Despite the limitations upon the powers of the Reichstag of the North German Confederation, and the actual friction within the new Austrian Reichsrat, the reconstruction in *Mitteleuropa* that followed the German civil war brought the legislative institutions of the whole region close to a common norm. At the same time the Paris government took a comparable course in the successive steps, beginning in 1860 and concluded in the spring of 1870, by which Napoleon changed France from the authoritarian empire into the liberal empire.

The disturbance of opinion in France that followed the Italian War led Napoleon in November, 1860, to empower the *corps législatif* to discuss freely an address to the throne, and hence to criticize the government. The same kind of financial pressure that had forced a reform policy upon Francis Joseph carried Napoleon in 1861 a step further toward liberal government. He renounced the right to borrow money without a vote of the legislature, and gave the deputies the right to vote separately on the separate items of the budget. The public disapproval of Napoleon's intervention in Mexico and of his failure in European foreign policy increased the power of the opposition in the succeeding years, and led in 1867 to the introduction of a limited right of interpellation. In 1868 Napoleon faced the same kind of a difficulty that William had faced in Prussia in 1862: he needed an army reform bill, and found a liberal opposition intrenched in a strong position in the *corps législatif*. To conciliate the opposition he granted a qualified freedom of the press and of public assembly in January, 1868. The elections of 1869 showed that the spirit of opposition had grown still stronger in the country. In September, 1869, Napoleon yielded to the liberals by issuing a decree that made the legislative body a parliament after the English fashion, with the right to choose its own officers and initiate laws. This was followed in December, 1869, by the appointment of Émile Ollivier as prime minister to organize a cabinet that would have the confidence of a majority of the legislature. In April, 1870, the constitutional change was completed and France became a constitutional monarchy of the English type, with a ministry responsible to parliament. The change was ratified by seven million votes in a plebiscite. The internal adjustment was completed just in time for the Franco-Prussian War.

While in France a system of parliamentary government was introduced to supplement a system of universal suffrage, in England a system of almost universal suffrage came into existence to supplement the long established parliamentary government. Franchise extension had come up in British politics in 1852, in 1858, and again in 1860. It was a chronic political problem, upon which various compromises were offered. The effect of the victory of the North in the American Civil War was to further the cause of electoral reform in England. Gladstone spoke in favor of universal suffrage in 1864 in a speech that "set the Thames on fire," and in 1866, as a member of the Russell ministry, proposed to lower the property qualifications for voting. John Bright, who had been Cobden's colleague in the anti-corn law agitation, was the great crusader for electoral reform, and the rising trades-union organization lent its weight to the movement. The Russell ministry, having failed with Gladstone's suffrage bill, fell from power on the very day the civil war in Germany began, and the months that saw the reconstruction in central Europe witnessed the extension of the franchise in England to include all urban householders. The reform bill was carried through in August, 1867, by a conservative ministry led by the venerable Lord Derby. In 1868 Disraeli succeeded Derby as prime minister. Then, when the conservatives were turned out of office by the voters they had just enfranchised, English politics entered the late-Victorian phase as these two seasoned parliamentarians, who had crossed swords in 1852, came at last to the leadership of their respective parties.

Britain's politics in the decade following the Crimean War had been played in three arenas—internal, colonial, and continental European. The various issues of internal politics were of the same class as those arising in other states. English liberalism was escaping from the dogma of *laissez-faire*; education was nationalized, local government rationalized, and judicial system systematized, and just as Catholic countries broke away from clerical dominance, so England turned away from it, not only in such minor matters as the opening of museums on Sunday, but in the disestablishment of the Anglican church in Ireland, and of course the control of education. The bankruptcy law of 1861 made it possible for debtors to escape imprisonment; an act of 1867 abolished flogging in the army in time of peace; in general, English internal politics responded to what the nineteenth century learned to expect as "progress."

In imperial relations the responsibilities of the English home government were greatly increased by the great Indian mutiny of 1857. Lord Stratford de Redcliffe had been a firm believer in the possibility of converting a social and political system based on religious ties, as he found it in the Ottoman Empire, into a system based on the western conception of citizenship. But the English administrators in India had found this road a difficult one to follow. The English army in India before the mutiny was made up of a small force of English and a large force of native troops officered by English. Hindu religious practices did not sit well with the western idea of military organization; one might see a low-caste sergeant on his knees before a high-caste recruit. There were social discontents in the valley of the Ganges resulting from the English conversion of the fiduciary tenure of the *zemindars*, the collectors of the land tax, into ownership tenures of the type known to English law. This was the conversion that the English had effected in Ireland and wished to effect in the Ottoman Empire. Moreover, there were political discontents resulting from the displacement of certain Indian dynasts. The incident that set off the mutiny was the well-known affair of the greased cartridges. The munitions distributed to the infantry were greased and the infantryman had to bite the cartridges before loading his rifle. A lascar at Dum-Dum, near Calcutta, asked a Brahman sepoy for water from his drinking-cup; the Brahman refused on the ground that the use of the cup by a low-caste man would contaminate him. The lascar replied that the Brahman would be contaminated anyway by biting his cartridge; the story spread; it was marvelous propaganda material; a commander tried to force the use of the greased cartridges; the sepoys attacked their officers and soon the whole Ganges valley was in turmoil. The dispossessed rajahs called up their old retainers, a successor to the moghul set himself up at Delhi, there was a jacquerie in the villages. The mutiny had become a political and social war.

The English army, with the aid of some of the Indian princes, succeeded in recovering control, but a new policy for India was necessary. The government of the territory passed from the company to the British realm; large-scale railroad building and a stronger and more expensive English army gave new strength to British rule, new outlets for English capital, new opportunities of employment to the sons of English families.

The mutiny was hardly quelled before trouble with China came to a head. One Fong Ah-Ming, a pirate whose vessel, the *Arrow*, had at a previous date been registered in Hongkong as a British vessel, was arrested by Chinese officials at Canton. Harry Parkes, the British representative on the ground, made an issue of the incident, and called upon the admiral of the British squadron to bombard Canton. When the news reached England, Palmerston defended the bombardment, but in parliament the conservatives under Lord Derby and the free-traders under Cobden combined with John Russell and Gladstone in a great assault on the ministry. Palmerston was defeated in parliament, but went to the country and won the election on the plea of having defended the security of the lives and property of Englishmen in China. The ensuing war, fought with the active help of the French and to the equal advantage of the Russians, caught the Chinese government in the throes of its own difficulties with the Taiping rebels, and ended with the humiliating defeat of the Chinese Empire, and an expansion of British trading opportunities.

In Ethiopia a brilliant chieftain, Lij Kassa, who had made himself Emperor in 1855, came into conflict with Britain. A clerical error in the British Foreign Office was the cause of a small colonial war. A letter from the Emperor to Queen Victoria in 1862 was not answered; the Emperor took umbrage, and put the British consul in chains. An expeditionary force of 32,000 British, with the cooperation of rebel chiefs, succeeded in penetrating 400 miles into Ethiopian territory, and capturing the Imperial citadel at Magdala in 1868. The Emperor committed suicide, and the British withdrew.

On the European continent, British policy was active until Palmerston's death in 1865, but not particularly effective. British influence was felt more in what Britain refused to do than in what she actually did. In the Italian question Britain gave moral support to Cavour's expansion to the south and protested against the annexation of Nice and Savoy by France; in the Polish and Danish crises, the German civil war, and again in the Franco-Prussian War the net result of Britain's participation was an extension into the political realm of the principle of *laissez-faire*. When Bright joined the Gladstone ministry in 1869, the policy that even Palmerston had been held to by the reluctance of the British to engage in continental adventure received formal recognition in the preamble to the mutiny bill. The bill, passed annually in parliament, had always stated in the preamble that the army was maintained, not only for the protection of the dominions of the Crown, but for the defense of "the balance of power in Europe." When the phrase "balance of power in Europe" was dropped from the preamble, Britain was formally embarked upon a policy of splendid isolation.

As the inventor and leading example of responsible government, England made some steps in perfecting and extending it. The complete control of the Commons over the budget was perfected in an event that took place in 1860 in connection with Gladstone's move to abolish the duties on paper. The Lords threw out the bill abolishing the duties; then Gladstone included the same item in his budget in 1861 and the Lords let it pass. This constitutional question was not again raised till 1909.

The most interesting and creative experiments in the development of parliamentary institutions took place, however, in the extension of responsible government to British colonies in North America, Australia, and Africa.

In the North American British colonies the system of responsible government developed gradually in the 'forties, first in Nova Scotia and Canada, then in New Brunswick (1848), Prince Edward Island (1851), and Newfoundland (1855). It came to all the Australian colonies between 1855 and 1870, to New Zealand in 1855, and to Cape Colony in 1872. The Colonial Laws Validity Act of 1865 gave the colonial parliaments the right to alter their own constitutions. The British government did not even withhold from these colonies the right to establish protective tariffs against British goods. When in 1867 the colonies of British North America united in a federal union as the Dominion of Canada it was evident that the Anglo-Saxon world was to take up the rôle that central Europe had dropped as the leader in constructive experiments in federative polity.

For the tradition of federative polity in Europe was a monarchic tradition except in Switzerland, and the leadership of the federative movements of 1858-63 had been in the class that was nearest to the monarchic system. To weld into one system responsible government and federation required great political tact. The granting of responsible government in the dominions, without the creation of an imperial parliament, meant that Britain was pioneering on a new road. The pioneering would have been impossible had it not been for a widespread sentiment in Britain that the colonies were as much a liability as an asset, and that the loss of them could be envisaged with equanimity.

Another new development in political structure was the initiative and referendum—so-called "direct democracy." Here Switzerland was the pioneer.

The tradition of direct democracy in Switzerland had continued in the small forest cantons from the most remote times, but the adaptation to modern political society took place in other cantons. A Zürich democratic movement turned out Adolf Escher and his wealthy partisans in 1867, and in the ensuing years a flood of democracy swept through the cantons. New constitutions in Zürich, Thurgau, Berne, Lucerne and Aargau, all in 1869, established initiative or referendum or both. The reform movement in cantonal politics was accompanied by a movement to reform the federal constitution, especially to provide for a better military system. The reform was proposed in 1869, defeated at that time, and finally accomplished in 1874.

Northern Europe brought itself into line with the general political development. Belgium had been governed under the parliamentary system since its foundation, and the Netherlands and Denmark since 1849. After the loss of the duchies in 1866 the Danish constitution of 1849 was revamped, but without establishing clearly whether the lower or upper house would control the ministry. In Sweden a reform movement forced the abolition of the old diet of four estates and the introduction of a modern parliament in 1866.

In the Balkans the western political forms were imitated. In Greece (1862) and Rumania (1866) the rulers were deposed, and the new monarchs, George of the Danish house in Greece, and Carol of the younger branch of the Hohenzollern in Rumania, granted the standard type of constitution. In Serbia the old patriarchal prince, Miloš Obrenovič, with his informal ways of doing business, died in 1860, and his son Michael took steps not only to modernize the government, but also to make Serbia the Piedmont of the Balkans. The presence of a Turkish garrison in Belgrad gave him an occasion for agitation, which he used with effect until the garrison was withdrawn in 1867. He bought 200,000 modern rifles in Belgium, sold them at a nominal price to the people, and organized a national army with annual training-camps. An insurrection in Crete in 1866 seemed to give the signal for a Balkan war. The beginnings of a Balkan alliance against the Turks were made in 1867 in a Serbian treaty with Greece. A supplementary military convention providing for the use of guerilla bands against the Turks was signed in February, 1868. The plans for a Balkan rising were quashed by the assassination of Michael, June 10, 1868.

It had been the dream of Stratford Canning to see the Turkish Empire itself adopt western constitutional institutions, but the first steps in this direction—which meant giving citizenship to Christians—aroused the fury of the Moslems to such a degree that the resulting atrocities led to French intervention in Syria in 1860. A national and liberal opposition appeared in Turkey in the late 'sixties—a "Young Turk" movement, led by exiles in Paris, and hostile to European influence even while it took over some of the standard liberal European dogmas.

When in 1868 a revolutionary movement in Spain deposed Queen Isabella, the event did not signify in any sense a triumph of liberal principles in the Iberian peninsula, although the mere fact of deposition contributed, like the deposition of Otto in Greece and of Cuza in Rumania, to the evidence of the weakness of the throne as a European institution.

Another shock to European monarchic sentiment was given by the fate of Francis Joseph's brother, Maximilian, who had married the Coburg princess Charlotte. The conservative and Catholic faction in Mexico, defeated in civil war by the republican Juarez, a full-blooded Indian, made an alliance with a profiteering banker by the name of Jecker, who reached Napoleon's court by offering to share his profits with the Duc de Morny, won the enthusiasms of the Empress Eugénie and aroused the expectations of the Hapsburg and his wife with the prospect of an imperial throne in Mexico. While the influence of the United States in Central America was paralyzed by the Civil War, Napoleon joined with England and Spain in a military intervention to collect claims against Mexico, and then went forward to set Maximilian upon his throne. But Maximilian had no military resources except those loaned by France, and when the French army withdrew in 1867 he was left to the mercy of the Juaristas, who shot him at Querataro in 1867.[7] Maximilian was in a sense an imitator of Napoleon III; he thought in terms of plebiscites, and dreamed of an expansion of the empire of Mexico throughout Central America.

Another unfortunate follower of the Napoleonic tradition was the dictator Lopez of Paraguay, who had spent some of his youth in Paris. In 1864 he began a war of aggression and conquest against Brazil and Argentine that did not end until 1870, when his country was completely drained of its manhood. Prince Cuza of Rumania was yet another of the imitators of Napoleon.

In the political reconstruction that was taking place in the late 'sixties, the secular dogma of liberalism triumphed everywhere. No longer could it be said that the crux of the political problem lay in the relations of peoples to thrones; rather it was evident that the crux of the problem lay in the relations of peoples to peoples. What would those relations be? Prussian hegemony in northern Germany, dualism on the Danube, responsible government in France, democracy in England were established facts. And more than that there was established so far as the relations of peoples in Europe were concerned the principles of *Realpolitik*, the pattern of violence. What remained for Europe was the carrying out to their ultimate conclusion of the principles already established, and therefore the last part of the story took on the character of a dénouement in a drama wherein the characters were already presented, the situations made clear.

[7] E. Corti, *Maximilian and Charlotte of Mexico* (New York and London, 1929).

Chapter Thirteen

DÉNOUEMENT

I. FRENCH COMPENSATIONS

WHILE RECONSTRUCTION took place throughout central Europe, and while all governments in consequence of parliamentary or electoral reform were becoming mechanically more responsive to public opinion than they had been before, the changing structure of international organization reflected the new conditions.

In the negotiation of the Treaty of Prague, which converted into a definitive peace treaty the armistice of Nikolsburg, Napoleon made his influence felt in two respects. As a mediator he secured recognition for his principle of nationalities in a provision that the Danish population of North Schleswig should be allowed to vote their union to Denmark. This union was not effected till after the World War. He also wrote into the treaty a statement that the south German states were to have an independent international personality—a provision intended to halt Prussia permanently at the Main.

But Napoleon was not unwilling, provided he could make sure of compensations, to permit the advance of Prussian power to the Inn. Instructions approved by Napoleon were sent to Benedetti, the French ambassador to Prussia, on August 16, authorizing him to ask for the Rhineland up to Mainz, The Grand Duchy of Luxemburg, and Belgium, as the price of a Franco-Prussian alliance and a French permit for further Prussian expansion. Bismarck made it clear that no cessions of Rhineland territory could be allowed, but hinted that he might be brought to agree to some French compensation in Belgium and Luxemburg. Benedetti drafted a treaty providing for French expansion in these regions, and for a Franco-Prussian alliance. Bismarck took the draft and filed it away, but delayed completion of the negotiation. Napoleon himself changed his mind about Belgium in the course of the autumn, but he had to take account of rising public resentment in France against what seemed to be a complete failure of his foreign policy. Therefore he made a diplomatic campaign in the spring of 1867 to secure Luxemburg for France.

Luxemburg was another of those areas in which European federative polity had preserved an intricate arrangement of political authority. The grand duchy was united by personal union with the Netherlands; it had been a member of the dissolved German *Bund* and of the Customs Union, and its fortress was garrisoned by Prussian troops. The situation resulted not alone from the treaties of 1815, but also from the treaties of 1839, which had separated Luxemburg and Limburg from that part of the Netherlands which achieved its independence as the new state of Belgium. The unscrambling of these relationships gave France a chance to acquire the territory, provided the King-and-Grand-Duke could be brought to consent, and the people of Luxemburg induced to vote in a plebiscite for union with France. On March 30, 1867, the King of the Netherlands was ready to sign a treaty selling the grand duchy to France. Bismarck told Benedetti that he did not want to be brought into the deal in any capacity, for he did not wish to be put in the position of defending before his new parliament of the North German Confederation the cession of territory to France. He made it clear that the thing for France to do was to confront Germany with a *fait accompli*. But he allowed Bennigsen to interpellate him in parliament on the rumor that "German soil" in Luxemburg was to be surrendered. Public opinion in Germany and passive diplomatic resistance at The Hague ruined the chances of the treaty. There was war talk everywhere, but Napoleon backed down. Then Bismarck asked the powers signatory to the treaties of 1839 to determine the future of the grand duchy. Beust proposed that it be given to Belgium, and that France be compensated with the two Belgian fortresses of Marienburg and Philippeville, but the powers decided to establish Luxemburg as an independent neutral state under their collective guarantee.

The settlement of the Luxemburg question by a conference of the powers did not by any means indicate that the old days of the

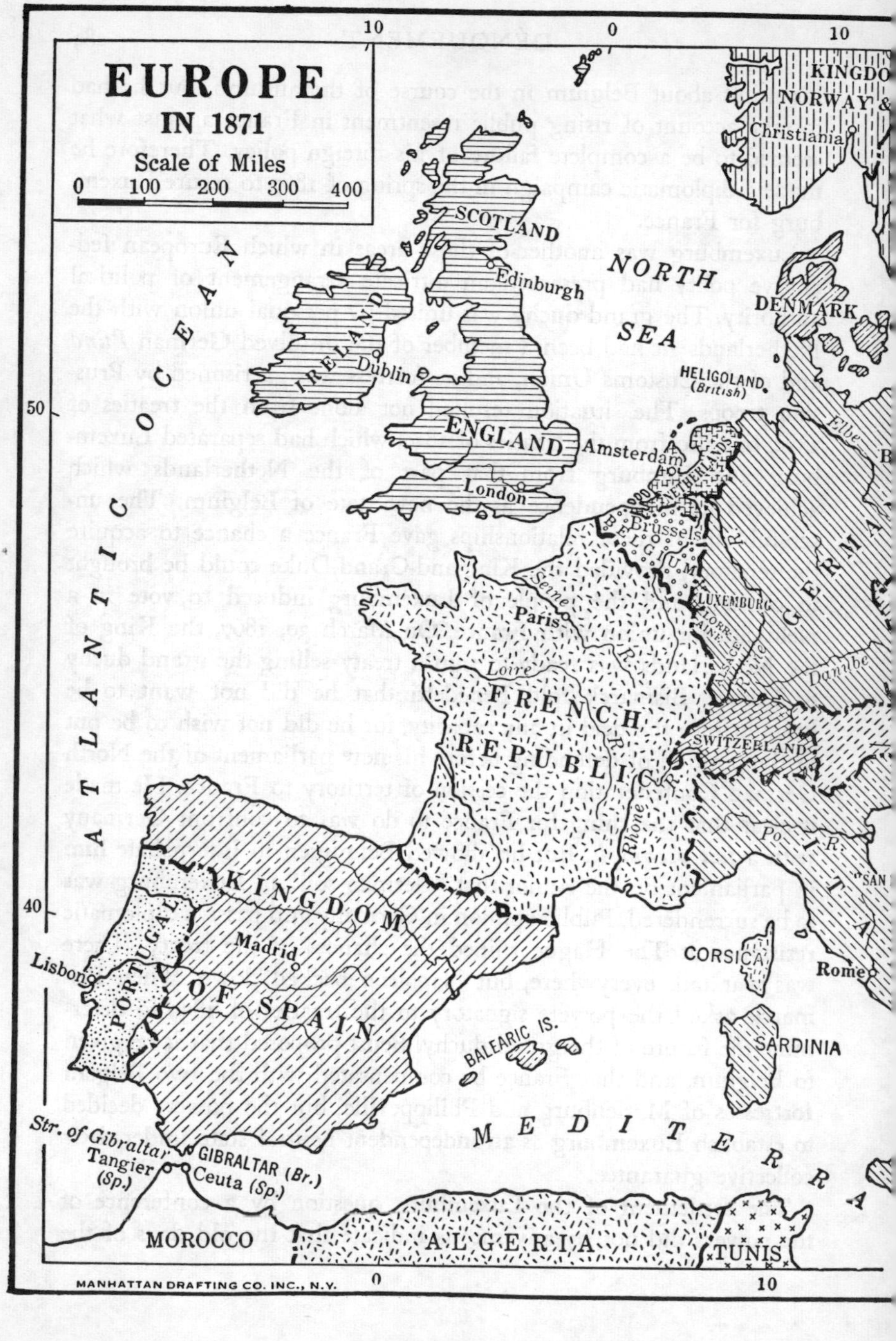
EUROPE
IN 1871
Scale of Miles
0 100 200 300 400
10
0
10
50
40
0
10
KINGDO
NORWAY &
Christiania
ATLANTIC OCEAN
SCOTLAND
Edinburgh
NORTH SEA
DENMARK
IRELAND
Dublin
HELIGOLAND (British)
ENGLAND
Amsterdam
NETHERLANDS
London
Elbe
Brussels
BELGIUM
Seine
Paris
LUXEMBURG
LORRAINE
ALSACE
GERMAN
Rhine R.
Loire
Danube
FRENCH REPUBLIC
SWITZERLAND
Rhone R.
Po R.
ITAL
SAN
PORTUGAL
KINGDOM OF SPAIN
Madrid
Lisbon
CORSICA
Rome
BALEARIC IS.
SARDINIA
Str. of Gibraltar
GIBRALTAR (Br.)
Tangier (Sp.)
Ceuta (Sp.)
MEDITERRA
MOROCCO
ALGERIA
TUNIS
MANHATTAN DRAFTING CO. INC., N.Y.

FINLAND
St. Petersburg
Stockholm
BALTIC SEA
Volga R.
Moscow
Dvina R.
RUSSIAN EMPIRE
Danzig
EMPIRE
Vistula
Warsaw
POLAND
Dnieper R.
GALICIA
DUAL MONARCHY OF AUSTRIA-HUNGARY
Vienna
Budapest
RUMANIA
Bucharest
Belgrade
BOSNIA
SERBIA
Danube R.
BULGARIA
BLACK SEA
Constantinople
OTTOMAN EMPIRE
MONTE NEGRO
ADRIATIC SEA
Athens
GREECE
CRETE
CYPRUS
MALTA (Br.)
SEA
20
30
40
50

authority of the concert had returned. It meant rather that the prospect of a Franco-Prussian friendly alliance was dead. Though Bismarck since his days at Frankfurt had been the partisan of a Prussian alliance with France, he was now allied with the German national patriots. Antagonism to France became, therefore, the line of least resistance for him.

II. GROPING TOWARDS AN ALLIANCE SYSTEM

During the three years that followed the Luxemburg crisis there was a groping in Europe toward some more stable arrangement. For anarchy and insecurity create a yearning for permanent alliances, and a state that has achieved the liberty of a free hand begins to fear the perils of isolation. In the spring of 1868 King William and the Tsar made a secret agreement that they would coöperate against Austria.[1] And through the whole three-year period from 1868 to 1870 a Franco-Italo-Austrian alliance was the subject of secret negotiations.

The still-born triple alliance of Austria, France, and Italy went through a long development, from an interview of Napoleon with Francis Joseph in August, 1867, to the military conversations that closed just five days before the outbreak of the Franco-Prussian War. It began as a French suggestion that the two countries ally themselves and then pick a quarrel with Prussia. The alliance would then have been the exact counterpart of the Prussian-Italian treaty of 1866. In May, 1868, Francis Joseph gave Count Vitzthum a secret commission to negotiate some kind of an alliance treaty with France. Napoleon put the question clearly to the Austrians: should the alliance be active or passive? Beust declared that Austria could promise nothing more than neutrality. Napoleon then sought to use an entente with Austria to prepare a European congress that would impose checks on Prussia's expansion south of the Main.

Beust preferred to make a diplomatic issue of disarmament, for the lesson of Prussia's success in 1866 was already resulting in a round of army reforms all over Europe. The psyche of the armed peace was developing. Count Quadt wrote to King Ludwig of

[1] W. Platzhoff, "Die Anfänge des Dreikaserbundes, 1867-1871," *Preussische Jahrbücher*, CLXXXVIII (1922), 283-306.

Bavaria in 1868, "everyone is cognizant of the unstable state of affairs and above all of the impossibility of maintaining indefinitely the ruinous system of the armed peace." And Count Vitzthum referred to the feeling of the commercial classes who said "war is better than this peace which is nothing but a ruinous armed truce."[2] Beust realized that Bismarck was in the midst of the task of bringing the newly annexed Prussian territories and the North German Confederation up to the Prussian military standard, and that he would certainly reject a proposal for limitation of armaments. To propose disarmament would make possible a diplomatic victory; it would put Prussia in the wrong.

When Napoleon, who was working against the resistance of his own Corps Législatif to expand the French army, cooled to Beust's scheme, the facile Austrian chancellor worked out a new basis for coöperation. He proposed that an alliance with France be pointed to the east, which was the region "most favorable for diplomatic action that might develop into a war that would yield large results."[3] It was Beust's idea, moreover, to draw Italy into the alliance. This suggestion placed the whole enterprise on a new footing. More and more clearly there came into the foreground those diplomatic postulates of the armed peace that were to be so completely realized ten years later in the Bismarckian system of alliances.

Beust's diplomacy was restrained by the fact that the Austro-Germans (who were in control of the Reichsrat in Vienna) would not support an anti-German war, and the Hungarians, who were now enjoying their system of parliamentary control, would not indorse a return of Austrian influence in Germany. Napoleon did not feel drawn by any direct interest in the question of the disposition of Rumania or other Ottoman territories; he wanted a treaty that would be good on the Rhine. Out of this situation there emerged in March 1869 a series of treaty projects of which the principal stipulations resembled in form those that were later found in Bismarck's Dual and Triple Alliances and Three Emperors' League. The French project of March 1, 1869 provided that if Austria should be at war with Prussia, France would come to Austria's aid. The re-

[2] Hermann Oncken: *Die Rheinpolitik Kaiser Napoleon III von 1863 bis 1870 und der Ursprung des Krieges von 1870-71* (Berlin and Leipzig, 1926), III, 17.
[3] Beust to Richard Metternich, November 6, 1868, in Oncken, III, 59.

ciprocal engagement would be that Austria, in case of a war between France and Prussia, should mobilize, and in case Russia intervened to help Prussia, come actively to the aid of France. Andrássy on behalf of Hungary interposed his veto upon such a treaty (March 12, 1869), but Beust continued the search for a workable alliance formula. He was willing to promise Italy some territory in the Trentino provided the war should result in conquests for Austria.

As the treaty bargaining continued through 1869 another difficulty became apparent. Italy demanded as the price of her coöperation that the French troops be withdrawn from Rome. Napoleon was just in the midst of the final political shift that converted the Second Empire into a liberal parliamentary state. He was not, therefore, in a position to ignore the actual state of Catholic opinion in France, at least until he had prepared the ground by developing the political power of the anti-clericals. Just as Beust and Francis Joseph found themselves restrained by their public and their parliaments, so Napoleon discovered that he no longer had a free hand in foreign policy. At the same time he had to reckon with a vociferous party that was demanding some kind of action against the rising power of Prussia.

As the treaty formulæ and the relation of foreign policy to the public were assuming the character that was to continue through all the years of the armed peace, the rôle of the "military conversations" appeared, and the influence of the mobilization time-table was felt, in a way that foreshadowed the alliance system of later decades. Archduke Albrecht as military representative of Austria met General Lebrun as military representative of France and agreed (May 19, 1870) that in case of a war in Germany the allied powers should attack with an army of 1,300,000 men. But Albrecht said it would take forty-two days to get the Austrian army to the frontier, and this operation should be covered diplomatically by "armed neutrality."

Moreover, German national sentiment operated to restrain Austria as it had governed Bismarck in bargaining with France over Luxemburg. Francis Joseph explained to Lebrun (June 14, 1870) that he could only join France in a war in Germany if Napoleon appeared as a liberator; he could not (like Bismarck in 1866) take action that would outrage German national sentiment.

If the triple alliance of 1868-70 had been perfected before the breaking of the next European crisis, it would probably have functioned to make the war continental in scope: Prussia and Russia against the triple alliance. A victory of the triple alliance would then have meant not only the reunion and reconstruction of Germany as a confederation of middle-sized states, but the restoration of Poland. A defeat might have meant the liquidation of the Danubian problem in favor of the Slavs. In any event a general war would have taken place instead of a localized war, and would doubtless have resulted in some kind of a general European peace.

III. THE FRANCO-PRUSSIAN WAR

Up to 1870 the full possibilities of war as an instrument of political destruction had hardly been realized, for in none of these mid-century wars had both state and people of one political society been locked in a death battle with state and people of another. The Crimean War, though it aroused a rabid public enthusiasm in some places, notably England—was still essentially a cabinet war. In 1859 the Italian people, rallying around the symbols of nationality, had participated, especially in liberating Italy after the war was over, but the conflict was not at any time a war between peoples, for the Austrian peoples did not regard it as such, and the French were fighting for a foreign state.

In Poland in 1863, the Polish people fought against the Russian state. The German civil war was a struggle between two states, not between hostile peoples, and the people quickly accepted the military decision. But in 1870 there came a war that was fought on a different plane. For the two most highly organized states in Europe, each with parliamentary institutions that were for the time being holding the administrative machine in line with the popular will, each with a population highly indoctrinated with the secular dogma of nationalism, tore at each other's throats.

A generation that has learned to associate the study of diplomatic history with efforts to apportion responsibility for precipitating a war is likely to inquire concerning the origins of the war of 1870-71, whether it was brought on by the French or by the Prussians. Certainly it is evident that in both countries ministers who enjoyed the confidence of popularly elected parliaments welcomed the appeal to arms. The sequence of events out of which the war arose was such as to suggest that they were a pretext rather than a cause. The deposition of Queen Isabella in Spain led to a search for a new monarch for that country; the search led to Prince Leopold of Hohenzollern. Bismarck encouraged the candidature, hoping to confront France with a threat of war on two fronts as he had confronted Austria in 1866.[4] Though Napoleon had at one time favored Leopold as a candidate as a means of blocking an Orléans prince, the news of the Hohenzollern candidacy resulted in a French protest on the ground that it would upset the balance of power to have the same royal family ruling on both the northern and southern frontiers of France.[5] Prince Leopold withdrew his candidacy. But the withdrawal took place in such a fashion as not to constitute a great diplomatic victory for France. Gramont, the French minister for foreign affairs, instructed Benedetti to secure from King William, whose authority over the Prince was complete under the Hohenzollern house law, an assurance that the candidacy would not be renewed. On July 13 Benedetti met the King under the trees on the public promenade of the quiet vacation resort at Ems, and pressed for the guarantee. The King was offended, not only by the nature of the demand, but also by the effort to bring him to commit himself on a matter of this kind in a public place. A crowd of people from a distance watched the interview. The King broke it off without giving any assurance as to the future. Twice again on the same day Benedetti sought an audience with the King. Finally, at 6 P.M., the King's adjutant told him categorically that the King refused further discussion.

The King meanwhile had telegraphed to Bismarck at Berlin an account of the episode, together with his decision not to receive Benedetti again. Bismarck edited the telegram to sharpen the point that the King refused to receive the ambassador, and gave it to the

[4] F. Frahm, "Bismarcks Briefwechsel mit General Prim," *Historische Vierteljahrschrift*, XXIII (1926), 64-86.

[5] F. Frahm, "Frankreich und die Hohenzollernkandidature bis zum Fruhjahr, 1869," *Historische Vierteljahrschrift*, XXIX (1934), 342-70.

press. The news rallied patriotic sentiment in Germany and aroused the political leaders of France. Napoleon, in a last attempt at personal politics behind the backs of his newly "responsible" ministers, sent word to Vienna and Florence suggesting that Austria and Italy propose a congress. But the ministry carried the chamber, and the chamber carried the country, directly into war.

War was declared by France on July 19. The French army, contrary to many later judgments, was in some respects not ill-prepared. The French rifle had almost double the range of the Prussian, and the French infantrymen carried more rounds of ammunition. The Prussians had not been trained to seek cover and advance in thin and open formation; they were at a tactical disadvantage which could only be made to disappear if they could stand behind intrenchments to stave off attacks. The incredible incompetence of the French leadership actually made it possible for the Prussian army to win the war in this way. Marshal Bazaine allowed the army of the Rhine to be bottled up in the fortress of Metz, which the Prussians surrounded with trenches. The French at Sedan were surrounded and pounded with artillery. The last phase of the war was the siege of Paris.

When Bazaine was besieged in Metz, the remaining field army, commanded by Marshal McMahon and accompanied by the Emperor, violated all military rules in a maneuver intended to have some political effect, and possibly to help in relieving the siege of Metz. Instead of falling back on Paris, the army advanced to the northeast. At Sedan, where the river Meuse turns west, the main Prussian army caught the French in the angle of the river. Marshal McMahon was wounded; he turned over the command to General Ducrot, who was about to withdraw the army to the west to escape from the jaws of the Prussian nut-cracker. But an order from the minister of war replaced Ducrot by Wimpffen, and Wimpffen postponed retreat till it was too late. Though Napoleon was with the army, he was there almost as a tourist or observer; the command changed twice without his intervention, and changed for the last time on order of the responsible ministry that had voted the war. When the Prussian troops had the French completely surrounded and the artillery was pounding the town, Napoleon took control. When the generals refused to sign a request for an armistice, the Emperor signed it himself. On September 1, he sent across the lines to the King of Prussia the letter that ended the Second Empire, "Nothing remains for me but to give my sword into your hands." On the following day he crossed the lines in his carriage. Bismarck, unwashed and unbreakfasted, hurried to meet him, and encountered the Imperial carriage on the road to the village of Donchéry. In the deserted house of a weaver in Donchéry the two men held their interview. Bismarck was ready to discuss peace terms, but Napoleon refused. Only the government in Paris could speak for France, he said. Despite the unprecedented military disaster, the war went on.

When the news of Sedan reached Paris, the left-wing faction of the *corps législatif* combined with the republicans of the city to proclaim the fall of the Empire and to organize a Government of National Defense. Jules Favre, the new minister for foreign affairs, met Bismarck in the middle of September to arrange an armistice, but found that he could not purchase peace without ceding Alsace and Lorraine. He pleaded in vain that the day of conquests and military glory was over, and that the seizure of these provinces would permanently embitter European life. When the Government of National Defense learned of the Prussian demands, it set itself with the energy of desperation to organize the country for resistance. It sent a delegation to Tours to raise forces in the provinces, while it remained in Paris to organize defense. The German lines closed around the city. Gambetta, minister of the interior, escaped by balloon to join the "delegation" at Tours. He installed republican patriots in the prefectures throughout the unoccupied departments, and called upon the country for sacrifices. In a feverish effort to extemporize an army, half a million men were placed under arms in one formation or another, some in Paris, some in the eastern departments, some on the Loire and some in the north. The resistance was desperate but vain.

The food shortage in Paris made ultimate capitulation inevitable. The people ate up the horses, hunted rats in the sewers, and butchered the elephants at the Jardin des Plantes, while they waited vainly for rescue, cursed the incompetence of their leaders, and dreamed of 1793. Bismarck thought, erroneously, that the capitulation could be hastened by a bombardment; the King's entourage and the Prussian staff had objections to this experiment in barbarism, but Bismarck overrode them. Two days of bombardment killed a number of civilians, aroused the ire of the neutral states, but failed to break the nerve of the defenders. Then the imminent prospect of the exhaustion of the food supplies forced the Government of National Defense to yield. On January 28, Jules Favre signed an armistice which included no peace terms, but made possible an election to constitute an authority that could sign a peace.

IV. THE GERMAN EMPIRE AND THE THIRD REPUBLIC

Elections to a national assembly took place hurriedly and without much preparation. The republicans appeared before the electors as the partisans of war to the bitter end; the monarchists as partisans of peace. The royalists entered the national assembly, which met at Bordeaux, with a clear two-thirds majority. Everyone recognized that it was not the time for a party conflict. The assembly elected Adolph Thiers as chief of executive power. Thiers brought into his cabinet men of all shades of political opinion, and gave his pledge of neutrality between the royalist and republican factions. This was the "pact of Bordeaux," the party truce in the face of national disaster.

While the German armies moved from one triumph to another, Bismarck worked on the south German princes to bring them into the North German Confederation, rechristened the German Empire. War enthusiasm made the task easier than it would have been in time of peace. The south German princes had proved in the Frankfurt congress of 1863 that they were not unwilling to coöperate in national reconstruction, yet it required careful management to bring the head of the House of Wittelsbach, King Ludwig II of Bavaria, to offer the title of German Emperor to a Hohenzollern. Bavaria received a special position in the new constitution of the Empire, with the right to maintain a foreign service and a special control of her army. Bismarck, with German national sentiment supporting him, overcame all obstacles. Finally, in a stirring ceremony at Versailles on January 18, 1871, King William of Prussia was proclaimed German Emperor. Thus the great political achievement of dividing Germany at the Inn and subjecting the northern part to Prussian hegemony was completed.

In February, Adoph Thiers and Jules Favre appeared as the agents of the national assembly to negotiate the peace preliminaries at Versailles. Bismarck's first conditions called for an indemnity of six billion francs, and the cession of three-fourths of Lorraine and Alsace, including Belfort. Thiers persuaded him to reduce the indemnity to five billions, and to concede Belfort. When the national assembly ratified the peace preliminaries, the deputies from Alsace and Lorraine solemnly protested "we declare null and void the pact that disposes of us without our consent."

This statement of the principle of nationality under these circumstances served only to call attention to the limitations of nationalism as a program for Europe, for what the French nation called a brutal violation of national right was hailed by the German nation as the just satisfaction of a national claim. The founding of the German Empire meant not only that Germany must be partitioned at the Inn, but also that France should be partitioned at the Vosges.

While the annexation of Alsace and Lorraine was making nationalism inconsistent with the conciliation of peoples, the Commune, an expression of Parisian patriotism and republicanism, was interposing its annals of terror to obstruct the future conciliation of classes.

It was quite in line with the character of the times that the monarchist deputies in the national assembly should establish a republic. When the legitimist heir, the aging Count of Chambord, published a proclamation (July 6, 1871) declaring that he would not sacrifice his principles or his flag, that he would not take the French throne unless the white flag and three lilies of the Bourbons were restored as the national emblem, the national assembly resorted to a provisional constitution for a provisional republic. The tricolor had become a necessary symbol of French nationalism. In a contest between the monarchic principle and a national symbol only one issue was possible.

The year of violence "settled" other matters. Tsar Alexander took advantage of the general upheaval to announce (October 31, 1870) that he would no longer be bound by the Black Sea naval clauses of the Treaty of Paris. The unilateral denunciation of a multilateral treaty shocked such legalistic sensitivities as remained in Europe at the time. The Italian government took advantage of the opportunity to seize the city of Rome (September 20, 1870). All these events were parts of the same great action on the same great stage. It resulted from them that for the whole life-span of the next generation nationalism, socialism, and catholicism were tuned to the echoes of the guns of Sedan, the guns of Paris, the breaching of the walls at Porta Pia and the massacres of the Commune.

V. THE FATE OF FEDERATIVE POLITY

There are moments in history the whole record of which is not contained in the story of what happened, and the meaning of which is not disclosed except in an estimate of what never came to be. It was in such a moment that federative polity ceased to be a living principle in the European states-system. It yielded to centralization in Italy, to dualism in the Hapsburg Monarchy, to Prussian hegemony in that part of Germany that lay north of the Inn, to anarchy in the relations of the great powers. There was in Europe a great interregnum. There remained only a few vestigial remnants of the federative spirit: the non-militant political attitudes that had once been standard for all Europe's *Kleinstaaterei* remained in the Scandinavian kingdoms, in the Netherlands and Switzerland. Elsewhere standards of political conduct and ambition came to be patterned upon the exploits of Piedmont and Prussia.

There was one other area in which federative polity survived. In 1818, the year in which the European rulers at Aix-la-Chapelle were cementing a general peace by admitting a defeated enemy to equality with themselves, there was signed an agreement that the frontier between the United States and the British territory in North America should not be fortified nor patrolled by ships of war. At the time this treaty was signed, it did not symbolize any greater degree of comity and peaceful coöperation in the new world than the politics of Metternich, Castlereagh, and Alexander exemplified in the old world. But by 1867 Europe had gone so far from the Metternichean spirit that the situation on the three-thousand mile frontier in North America was something exceptional. The agreement was denounced by the United States, but the denunciation was then withdrawn. In that year the attempt of some Irish-Americans to start a war between the United States and Great Britain by invading Canada was foiled. Then in 1871 the long and bitter controversy between Britain and the United States over damage done to American shipping by the confederate cruiser *Alabama* was settled by the procedure of arbitration. It was the year that Paris fell, the year of the Treaty of Frankfurt, and the moment when it seemed on the European continent that all that remained of law and comity in international relations was being swept away. Here at least were two great states that kept their relations on the footing of federative polity.

The political complex of North America had in it possibilities of the same type of development that took place in Europe. The southern states might have been subjected, like Poland, to a permanent military régime in which the negro would have been used against the upper classes, as the Polish peasant was used against the Polish political class. The disturbance in the United States might have been followed by a war and annexation of Canada to complete the union of British North America as the German civil war was followed by an international war and the annexation of Alsace-Lorraine. But fate decreed otherwise. The federal system was gradually restored to the United States; the tension of Anglo-American relations furthered the development of the federation of the provinces of Canada, and the evolution of that political arrangement which later became "dominion status."[6] The relations of Britain to the United States, instead of coming to a climax in a war, took the road that made them resemble the relations of Prussia, Austria, and Russia in the old Metternichean days when war between those European great powers was, in the language of later Anglo-American relations, "unthinkable."

Thus, while federative polity was preserved on a new basis in the United States, and given a fresh start in the British Empire, especially in Canada, the foreign relations of a few small European

[6] R. G. Trotter, "Canada as a Factor in Anglo-American Relations of the 1860's," *Canadian Historical Review*, XVI (1935), 19-26.

states and of the two great Anglo-Saxon nations remained to illustrate what all European international relations might have been, but did not come to be.

Was it because of community of blood and speech that the Anglo-Saxon world preserved federative polity? Why then did Latin America, which also possessed a community of blood and speech, take the other road? The adventure of Lopez, the Paraguayan dictator, in his aggressive war on the eastern side of the continent, and the politics of Chile, Peru and Bolivia on the Pacific coast followed the European rather than the Anglo-Saxon model. In 1866 Chile and Bolivia made a treaty for the joint conquest of Peruvian territory, quite in the style of the Italo-Prussian "robber treaty" of the same year. Emperor Maximilian in Mexico seems to have considered trying to make a deal with the United States, offering some Mexican territory in exchange for permission to expand in Central America. When the Bolivian envoy to London advocated the purchase of warships in 1872 he argued

> I am convinced of the urgency of this necessity by the reflection that, to the end of the world, right will never be anything without the aid of might. In all international disputes it is always the case.[7]

The War of the Pacific confirmed his prophecy within a few years.

Yet other policies had in fact prevailed under other circumstances. Even as late as 1865 the Prussian forts on the Austrian frontier were equipped only with antiquated guns, as if to testify that there had been a period when war between Austria and Prussia was outside the realm of practical politics. And yet, when the spirit of *Realpolitik* had once become a dogma of a foreign office, diplomats became incapable of understanding that any other spirit could exist. When William Martin, the Swiss journalist, visited Berlin in 1915 he discussed with Zimmermann in the Wilhelmstrasse the probability that the United States might enter the war. Zimmermann explained that the possibility of the conquest of Canada would make it more probable that the United States would fight against England than for her. This was the Zimmermann of the famous note on Mexican reconquest of Texas. His mind worked according to rules

[7] J. J. Dennis, *Tacna and Arica* (New Haven, 1931), 56.

that he thought to be universally true of political relations, and under these rules the desire for territorial expansion at the expense of neighbors was normal political motivation. How different was the situation of 1864, when Bismarck had stood alone in planning for the Prussian conquest of the duchies! The Zimmermann of 1915 and 1917 illustrates the magnitude of the change that brought into power a generation of European leaders who were unable, not alone to share, but even to understand, the ideas that had been part of the great political system that fell to pieces in the 'sixties.

VI. CONCLUSION

Professor Whitehead writes that steam in modern times, like the inrush of barbarians into the Roman Empire, was an accidental and senseless agency, driving civilization from its inherited modes of order. It brought new concentrations of wealth and poverty, of power and insecurity. Its freight trains gave a new tempo to business, its troop trains to politics. From it came the laws of thermodynamics that crowned the synthesis of the natural sciences, the investment opportunities that brought economic society into its phase of "high capitalism." If in the decline of the great mediæval intuitions of the nature of the universe the seventeenth century saw an alternative pattern in the movement of the planets and the eighteenth century in the clock at Strassburg, the nineteenth century could draw the imagery for its intuitions from the steam-engine; this possibility came to be fully realized only in the second half of the century. Matter and energy, commodity and enterprise, the nation as territory and the state as power, do they not in a sense say over again what is said in iron and steam? The mechanics of bureaucratic administration, of responsible parliamentary government, of the monetary and credit system—do they not appeal with especial force to minds that believe in machines? Inductive science, literary and artistic realism, commodity economics and *Realpolitik* betray a certain harmony of design. It was in the presence of these cultural facts that federative polity yielded to centralization and violence in the basic group relations of Europe—political, clerical, social.

The relationships between the facts here brought together are not relationships of cause and effect, but of pattern and design. They suggest a syntax in history, not a dynamic. And yet the historian (himself entangled in the thought-modes of the nineteenth century), is impelled to seek out and establish relationships of cause and effect. The cause-effect sequence has two possible manifestations, corresponding to the metaphysics of natural law on the one hand, and of will on the other. In natural law causal relationships are sequences so established that whenever A takes place, B follows. In the experience of will they are sequences in which A, a free agent, desires to bring into existence B, a new fact, and then creates the events that realize B. The first of these kinds of cause is alleged to be present in so far as nationalism resulted in the making of national states, the second in so far as the national states were the products of the political leadership of certain individuals, notably Cavour and Bismarck.

Neither of these concepts of historical causation yields satisfactory results in the interpretation of the data in hand. In general it might be expected that the conditions for the application of the natural-law idea of cause are lacking in history, for A and B, moments in the great and unique time-series, do not recur; there is, therefore, no historic evidence that whenever A takes place, B will follow.

Historians sometimes try to avoid this pitfall by distinguishing between immediate and underlying causes, though they will discover that the immediate causes are never sufficient causes, and the underlying causes are not linked to the effects in a nexus of necessity. History gives short change when it "explains" the causes of the Franco-Prussian War by relating the incident of the Ems telegram; it dodges the issue when it explains it by alluding to nationalism, for the question is still left open; why did nationalism of necessity issue in the particular political structure that Europe assumed in 1871?

Molièré's medical student received high honor when he answered the question "why does opium produce sleep?" by saying that it contained a dormative principle, the quality of which was to produce sleep. The priests of primitive cults explained the growth of corn by the potency of the corn spirit. In the same way it can be explained that the rise of national states was the result of nationalism. Of course tne thinkers of the nineteenth century could not give nationalism an anthropomorphic quality; they made it resemble rather those great synthetic generalizations of natural science—gravitation, conservation of energy, evolution—which prevailed with majestic omnipotence in the world of nature. Still, the explanation that the national states arose because of nationalism is just as good—or just as bad—as the explanation that corn grows because of the corn spirit.

Turning, then, to the analysis of the historic sequence in terms of will and leadership, how often were the intentions of the leaders realized by their acts of leadership in accord with their predictions? What was the coefficient of correlation between intention and result? National hagiography reads a high correlation, but detailed analysis of the political sequence shows that the correlation was low. The events attributed to the leaders were in some cases the direct products of miscalculation, and in other cases came about as a fortuitous by-product of their designs.

The Crimean War undermined European stability and the supremacy of the concert because Palmerston and Stratford de Redcliffe intended to preserve the balance of power by restraining Russia in the east. They defeated their intentions by imposing upon Russia treaty terms that upset European equilibrium because they made Russia a revisionist power.

The only great leader who acted to realize for Europe a reorganization on lines of nationality was Napoleon. His intentions in Italy, in Poland, in the duchies, and in Germany itself were travestied by events. For he would have realized national aims within the framework of federative polity, yet he could only act by undermining federative polity as he went along. He visioned a Europe that would accept confederation in the various national areas, and defer to the authority of the concert as expressed in a congress. When he died at Chiselhurst, a sad and broken man, he was a tragic hero of miscalculation, his career great in its pathos, like that of Woodrow Wilson.

Cavour's intentions were of the hand-to-mouth variety. Not he, but Napoleon, set on foot the great events in Italian history. The armistice of Villafranca, which destroyed the autonomists in central Italy and thus played into the hands of the unification program, he met by resigning his post. He sought to stop Garibaldi at the Straits; success would probably have been fatal to unification, for he had completely miscalculated the possibility of arousing an indigenous revolution against the Bourbon dynasty. The only truly indigenous risings in the Neopolitan kingdom came after the unification, and were directed against Piedmont, not against the Bourbons.

The reorganization of the Hapsburg Monarchy was a sequence in which miscalculation was the prevailing nexus between intention and result. The October Diploma was promulgated because the Hungarian high tories thought they could deliver Hungary to the dynasty on its terms, and Francis Joseph thought the high tories could save him from liberalism. The appointment of Schmerling was the result of a second miscalculation by the high tories, and the Czechs miscalculated when they worked with Hungary against Vienna in the time of Belcredi and Beust.

And what of Bismarck? He came to power on a local Prussian issue, despite his foreign policy, not because of it. His ideal was to build up the great-power status of Prussia, and such satisfaction as he gave to national sentiment was a by-product of his intentions. Each of his three wars increased the disequilibrium of Europe in terms of nationality: the Danish settlement put Danes under German rule, the civil war in Germany divided Germany at the line of the Inn, the war with France created the most chronic nationality grievance in western Europe. The line of the Inn and the ridges of the Böhmerwald still separate politically peoples of Germanic speech and culture whose opportunity for union lay not in the rise of Prussia's great-power status, but in the growth of the federative institutions of the old German *Bund*. And when in those conversations with Jules Favre in September, 1870, he disregarded the warning that the annexation of Alsace and Lorraine would compromise Europe's whole future, Bismarck did not foresee that his triumph of the moment would end forty-seven years later in the ruin of his whole edifice.

These were the personal agents of change, these their intentions, these the results. National hagiography can indeed recreate them as giants who ruled the very tides, but can they not with equal accuracy be portrayed as midgets playing around the fingers of the great hand of destiny before it closed upon them?

It is easier to summarize events than to explain them. It seems clear that the outstanding fact of European history from 1852 to 1871 was the turning away from federative polity. The traditions of monarchy, aristocracy, and church had been favorable to federative polity. The interests of business were ambivalent in that business had much to gain from the service of international organization, and yet could obtain some satisfaction from an alliance with the national state. The bureaucracies that had built up state centralization were the interested opponents of federative polity. The insecurities bred of rapidly changing economic organization contributed to the fervor with which people welcomed the power-formation of the national state. The extension of the franchise and of parliamentary government increased their sense of participation, even while it threatened the political monopoly of the propertied classes. The voters became sharers in the newly created wealth; within seven years of the Reform Bill of 1867 the export of British capital ended. And the next political-economic formation was already in sight in 1871; it was a formation called "imperialism." Just as the rivalries of agrarian and business classes were being ended in common alliance of property against the unpropertied, so the propertied and unpropertied in Europe were to become allies against the fellaheen, the cooly, and the savage. In 1871 Cecil Rhodes landed in South Africa, and Stanley met Livingstone at Lake Nyanza in an encounter that was a triumph of newsmongering to the public. The postulates of *Realpolitik* that had been proved in Europe were to receive a more extended application by men who had learned them in twenty years of schooling. On all fronts, intellectual, economic, and political, the way was cleared for a generation of materialism.

BIBLIOGRAPHICAL ESSAY

(Revised as of December, 1958)

In 1935, when Robert C. Binkley published his study of European history from 1852 to 1871, he could justly complain that ". . . the principal lacuna in European history of this period is a deficiency of histories of Europe." Since then most historians have continued to concentrate their attention on individual nation states, and most authors of general histories of nineteenth-century Europe have continued to break up their accounts into separate national chapters. A distinguished exception is David Thomson, *Europe since Napoleon* (New York, 1957). Meanwhile a second world war and renewed efforts at world organization, as well as a widespread concern to formulate a philosophy of history, have quickened interest in world history and the comparative study of civilizations. This interest is reflected in a new review, *The Journal of World History,* founded in 1953, and in the work of polyhistors such as Jacques Pirenne whose *Les grands courants d'histoire universelle,* 7 vols. (Neuchâtel, 1945-1956), devotes its fifth volume to the nineteenth century. It is reflected further in the many historical series whose volumes, while centered on Europe, include chapters on other areas. Such volumes, treating the 1850's and 1860's, are: in the *Clio* series, J. Droz, *et al., L'époque contemporaine,* I, *Restaurations et révolutions, 1815-1871* (Paris, 1953); and in the *Histoire générale des civilisations,* Robert Schnerb, *Le XIXe siècle: l'apogée de l'expansion européenne, 1815-1914* (Paris, 1955). Another French series, *Peuples et civilisations.* divides this period between C. H. Pouthas, *Démocraties et capitalisme, 1848-1860,* 2nd ed. (Paris, 1948), and Henri Hauser, *et al., Du libéralisme à l'impérialisme, 1860-1878,* 2nd ed. (Paris, 1952). Neither the Swiss series, *Historia Mundi: ein Handbuch der Weltgeschichte,* nor *The New Cambridge Modern History* has reached the nineteenth century, although the latter has announced as its tenth volume *The Zenith of European Power, 1830-1870.* The student may still profit from volumes in older series: E. Lavisse and

A. Rambaud, eds., *Histoire générale,* XI, *Révolution et guerres nationales, 1848-1870* (Paris, 1899); *The Cambridge Modern History,* X, *The Growth of Nationalities* (New York, 1909); and *Propyläen Weltgeschichte,* VIII, *Realismus und Nationalismus* (Berlin, 1930).

Bibliographical aids may be found in most of the volumes listed above, but special mention should be made of the Droz volume in the *Clio* series which has extensive, critical bibliographical notes. L. J. Ragatz has provided a useful compilation in his *Bibliography for the Study of European History, 1815-1939* (Ann Arbor, Mich., 1942), with supplements published in 1943, 1945, and 1956. On one of Binkley's central themes there are: K. S. Pinson, *A Bibliographical Introduction to Nationalism* (New York, 1935); and Karl W. Deutsch, *Interdisciplinary Bibliography on Nationalism, 1935-1953* (Cambridge, Mass., 1956). More specialized bibliographies will be mentioned below under appropriate headings.

I. POLITICAL HISTORY

International Affairs: The publication of documents on the diplomacy of the period continues. Just as the French Foreign Ministry completed its collection, *Les origines de la guerre de 1870-1871,* 29 vols. (Paris, 1910-1932), the Historische Reichskommission in Germany began to publish *Die auswärtige Politik Preussens, 1858-1871,* 10 vols. (Oldenburg, 1932-   ), two volumes of which have yet to appear. In Rome a special commission has launched *I documenti diplomatici Italiani,* which is designed to span the years 1861 to 1943. More specialized collections of documents include: H. von Srbik and Oskar Schmid, eds., *Quellen zur deutschen Politik Oesterreichs, 1859-1866,* 5 vols. (Oldenburg, 1934-1938); A. Friis, ed., *Det Nordslesvigske Spørgsmaal, 1864-1879,* 6 vols. (Copenhagen, 1921-1946) which published Danish sources; A. Friis and P. Bagge, eds., *Europa, Danmark og Nordslesvig, 1864-1879,* 4 vols. (Copenhagen, 1939-1949), which published documents of the European powers; H. Oncken, *Die Rheinpolitik Napoleons III,* 3 vols. (Berlin, 1926), drew heavily on Austrian archives; G. Bonnin, ed., *Bismarck and the Hohenzollern Candidature for the Spanish Throne* (London, 1957), brought to light new German sources. No great collections of Russian or British documents for this period have yet appeared, although much of the correspondence of British statesmen has been published as is noted below.

As a detailed and comprehensive diplomatic history of these decades, Alfred Stern, *Geschichte Europas seit den Verträgen von 1815 bis zum Frankfurter Frieden von 1871,* volumes VIII-X (Berlin, 1894-1924), is still useful. Recent surveys are H. Kramer, *Die grossmächte und die Weltpolitik, 1789 bis 1945* (Vienna, 1952); P. Renouvin, *Histoire des relations internationales,* V, *Le XIXe siècle,* I, *De 1815 à 1871* (Paris, 1954); A. J. P. Taylor, *The Struggle for Mastery in Europe, 1848-1918* (New York, 1954); R. Albrecht-Carié, *A Diplomatic History of Europe since the Congress of Vienna* (New York, 1958).

On the origins of the Crimean War see: B. D. Gooch, "A Century of Historiography on the Origins of the Crimean War," *American Historical Review,* LXII (1956), 33-58; H. W. V. Temperley, *England and the Near East: the Crimea* (New York, 1936); F. E. Bailey, *British Policy and the Turkish Reform Movement* (Cambridge, Mass., 1942); V. J. Puryear, *International Economics and Diplomacy in the Near East: a Study of British Commercial Policy in the Levant, 1834-1853* (Stanford, 1935). On the war itself and its aftermath see: E. de Guichen, *La guerre de Crimée (1854-1856) et l'attitude des puissances européennes* (Paris, 1936); F. Vulliamy, *Crimea, the Campaign of 1854-56* (London, 1939); C. Woodham-Smith, *The Reason Why* (New York, 1953); E. V. Tarlé, *Krymskaya Voina,* 2nd ed., 2 vols. (Moscow, 1950); G. B. Henderson, *Crimean War Diplomacy* (Glasgow, 1947); F. Valsecchi, *Il Risorgimento e l'Europa: l'Alleanza di Crimea* (Milan, 1949); R. L. Cummings, *The Italian Question at the Congress of Paris,* 2 vols. (Washington, 1952): E. Schüle, *Russland und Frankreich von Ausgang des Krimkrieges bi szum italienischen Krieg, 1856-1859* (Berlin, 1935); C. Friese, *Russland und Preussen vom Krimkrieg bis zum polnischen Aufstand* (Berlin, 1931).

International complications arising out of Italian unification are discussed in: F. Valsecchi, *L'unificazione italiana e la politica europea dalla guerra di Crimea alla guerra di Lombardia, 1854-1859* (Milan, 1939); L. M. Case, *Franco-Italian Relations, 1860-1865* (Philadelphia, 1932); S. Bortolotti, *La guerra del 1866* (Milan, 1941) and Wilhelm

Deutsch, *Habsburgs Rückzug aus Italien* (Leipzig, 1940). The role of Napoleon III in such nationalist movements is debated by G. I. Bratianu, *Napoléon III et les nationalités* (Paris, 1934), and P. Henry, *Napoléon III et les peuples* (Clermont-Ferrand, 1943). C. W. Hallberg in *Franz Joseph and Napoleon III, 1852-1864* (New York, 1955) argues that for Napoleon nationalism was a convenient tool for prying apart the Hapsburg Empire.

The unification of Germany has been the subject of countless histories. Those dealing with relations between Prussia and Austria will be listed below with other works on Germany. The impact of the unification on European diplomacy may be studied in: W. E. Mosse, *The European Powers and the German Question, 1848-1871* (Cambridge, 1958); E. M. Carroll, *Germany and the Great Powers, 1866-1914* (New York, 1938); R. Sontag, *Germany and England: Background of Conflict, 1848-1894* (New York, 1938); V. Valentin, *Bismarcks Reichsgründung im Urteil englischer Diplomaten* (Amsterdam, 1937). The three best studies on the outbreak of the wars of 1864, 1866, and 1870 are: L. D. Steefel, *The Schleswig-Holstein Question* (Cambridge, Mass., 1932); C. W. Clark, *Franz Joseph and Bismarck* (Cambridge, Mass., 1934); and R. H. Lord, *The Origins of the War of 1870* (Cambridge, Mass., 1924). Repercussions of the American war on Europe may be noted in E. D. Adams, *Great Britain and the American Civil War,* 2 vols. (New York, 1925).

Great Britain: Detailed narratives of English politics which have some of the value of contemporary reporting are: Herbert Paul, *History of Modern England,* 5 vols. (London, 1904-1906); and J. McCarthy, *History of Our Own Times,* 7 vols. (London, 1879-1905). Unfortunately Élie Halévy did not deal with the middle years of the century; his *Victorian Years, 1841-1895* (London, 1951), is a posthumous fragment. E. L. Woodward, *The Age of Reform, 1815-1870* (New York, 1938), is brief on this period but ranges over economic and cultural as well as political history. An extended essay which did much to counteract twentieth-century belittling of eminent Victorians is G. M. Young, *Victorian England: Portrait of an Age* (New York, 1936). The development of the empire may be followed in J. H. Rose, et al., *The Cambridge History of the British Empire,* II, *The Growth of the New Empire* (Cambridge, 1940).

On the actual working of the government, the student should consult Walter Bagehot's classic, *The English Constitution,* first published in 1867. On the effects of various reform bills, see: J. A. Thomas, *The House of Commons, 1832-1901* (Cardiff, 1939); and K. B. Smellie, *A History of Local Government,* 2nd ed. (London, 1950). Particular political groups and pressures are the subjects of: F. E. Gillespie, *Labour and Politics in England, 1850-1867* (Durham, N. C., 1927); S. Maccoby, *English Radicalism, 1853-1886* (Chicago, 1938); J. H. Whyte, *The Independent Irish Party, 1850-1859* (Oxford, 1958). On Ireland itself, see N. Mansergh, *Ireland in the Age of Reform and Revolution, 1840-1921* (London, 1940).

Some of the most important political history of this period has appeared in the form of "life and letters," which combines biographical narrative with the publication of private papers. An excellent example is H. C. F. Bell, *Lord Palmerston,* 2 vols. (New York, 1936). Other standard works of this kind are: S. Walpole, *The Life of Lord Russell,* 2 vols. (London, 1889); W. F. Monypenny and G. E. Buckle, *The Life of Benjamin Disraeli,* 5 vols. (New York, 1910-1920); J. Morley, *Life of William Ewart Gladstone,* 3 vols. (New York, 1903); and his *Life of Cobden,* 10th ed. (London, 1903); G. M. Trevelyan, *The Life of John Bright* (New York, 1913); S. Lane Poole, *The Life of Stratford de Redcliffe,* 2 vols. (New York, 1890).

Correspondence published without a connecting narrative includes: A. C. Benson and G. E. Buckle, eds., *Letters of Queen Victoria,* 9 vols. (New York, 1907-1932); P. Guedalla, ed., *The Queen and Mr. Gladstone* (Garden City, 1934); H. Bolitho, ed., *Letters of Queen Victoria from the Archives of the House of Brandenburg-Prussia* (New Haven, 1938); K. Jagow, ed., *Letters of the Prince Consort, 1831-1861* (New York, 1938); A. Ramm, ed., *The Political Correspondence of Mr. Gladstone and Lord Granville,* 2 vols. (London, 1952).

Shorter, more interpretive biographies and monographs, which economize on both time and publication costs, are successors to the older "life and letters" genre. Victoria has been the subject of such distinguished biographers as Sidney Lee (1903), Lytton Strachey (1921), and Edith Sitwell (1936). Particular aspects of her reign are treated in F. Hardie, *The Political Influence of Queen Victoria,*

1861-1901, 2nd ed. (London, 1938), and Algernon Cecil, *Queen Victoria and Her Prime Ministers* (New York, 1953). Among Victoria's statesmen, Gladstone has attracted the most attention recently. P. M. Magnus, *Gladstone* (London, 1954), is a thorough recapitulation written with a perspective impossible to Morley. E. Eyck, *Gladstone* (Erlenbach-Zürich, 1938; trans., London, 1938), is a tribute paid by a continental liberal. Specialized studies of Gladstone include: F. W. Hirst, *Gladstone as a Financier and an Economist* (London, 1931); P. Knaplund, *Gladstone and Britain's Imperial Policy* (London, 1927), and his *Gladstone's Foreign Policy* (New York, 1935); W. E. Williams, *The Rise of Gladstone to the Leadership of the Liberal Party, 1859-1868* (Cambridge, 1934); J. L. Hammond, *Gladstone and the Irish Nation* (New York, 1938). No one has yet done for Disraeli what Magnus did for Gladstone, although there has been no shortage of popular biographies. The most recent of these is H. Pearson, *Dizzy* (New York, 1951). Cecil Roth, *Benjamin Disraeli* (New York, 1952), is notable for its emphasis on Jewish influences in Disraeli's life and thought. Scholarly resurrections of two neglected figures are: A. B. Erickson, *The Public Career of Sir James Graham* (Cleveland, 1952); Wilbur D. Jones, *Lord Derby and Victorian Conservatism* (Athens, Ga., 1957). W. B. Pemberton, *Lord Palmerston* (London, 1954), is a thoughtful interpretation of Palmerston's use of British power in world affairs. Asa Briggs, *Victorian People: a Reassessment of Persons and Themes, 1851-1867* (Chicago, 1955), has brilliant essays on Bright, Disraeli, and Robert Lowe.

France: Early histories of the Second Empire, whether the work of a journalist like T. Delord, *Histoire du second empire,* 6 vols. (Paris, 1869-1876), or that of an ex-minister like É. Ollivier, *L'empire libéral: études, récits, souvenirs,* 17 vols. (Paris, 1895-1915), for all their bias, are rich sources of information. The first effort at objectivity was P. de La Gorce, *Histoire du second empire,* 7 vols. (Paris, 1894-1905), which still treated Napoleon with some conservative disdain. F. Simpson, *Louis Napoleon and the Recovery of France, 1848-1856* (New York, 1923), did much to refurbish Napoleon's reputation, and Albert Guérard with his *Napoleon III, an Interpretation* (Cambridge, Mass., 1943) and his *Napoleon III*

(New York, 1955) argued that in his ideas on international relations and social welfare Napoleon anticipated the visions of Woodrow Wilson and Franklin Roosevelt. J. S. Schapiro, *Liberalism and the Challenge of Fascism: Social Forces in England and France, 1815-1870* (New York, 1949), treated the Emperor rather as the forerunner of fascist dictators. These extreme views are avoided in two compact and judicious syntheses: M. Blanchard, *Le second empire* (Paris, 1950) and J. M. Thompson, *Louis Napoleon and the Second Empire* (New York, 1955).

On particular aspects of the Empire see: F. C. Palm, *England and Napoleon III: a Study of the Rise of a Utopian Dictator* (Durham, N. C., 1948); L. M. Case, *French Opinion on War and Diplomacy during the Second Empire* (Philadelphia, 1954); T. Zeldin, *The Political System of Napoleon III* (New York, 1958); H. N. Boon, *Rêve et réalité dans l'oeuvre économique et sociale de Napoléon III* (The Hague, 1936); Louis Girard, *La politique des travaux publics du second empire* (Paris, 1951); D. H. Pinkney, *Napoleon III and the Rebuilding of Paris* (Princeton, N. J., 1958); J. Maurain, *La politique ecclésiastique du second empire de 1852 à 1869* (Paris, 1930). Napoleon's associates have been the subjects of some excellent biographies: J. Maurain, *Un bourgeois français au XIXe siècle: Baroche, ministre de Napoléon III* (Paris, 1936); P. Poirson, *Walewski, fils de Napoléon* (Paris, 1943); H. Farat, *Persigny: un ministre de Napoléon III, 1808-1872* (Paris, 1957); R. Schnerb, *Rouher et le second empire* (Paris, 1949); P. Saint Marc, *Émile Ollivier, 1825-1913* (Paris, 1950); J. M. and Brian Chapman, *Life and Times of Baron Haussmann* (New York, 1957). Some interesting essays on prominent men and women appear in Roger L. Williams, *Gaslight and Shadow: the World of Napoleon III* (New York, 1957).

On the collapse of the Empire and the agony of 1871, see: P. Lehaucourt, *Histoire de la guerre de 1870-71*, 7 vols. (Paris, 1901-1907); J. P. T. Bury, *Gambetta and the National Defense* (New York, 1936); J. Demarest, *La défense nationale, 1870-1871* (Paris, 1949); M. Kranzberg, *The Siege of Paris, 1870-1871* (Ithaca, N. Y., 1950). The myth of the Commune as a working-class uprising has been re-examined in G. Laronze, *Histoire de la commune de 1871*

(Paris, 1928), and E. Mason, *The Paris Commune* (New York, 1930), a point which seems to have been lost in the lively narrative of F. Jellinek, *The Paris Commune of 1871* (New York, 1937). An analysis of the ideas of the communards is provided by C. Rihs, *La commune de Paris, sa structure et ses doctrines* (Geneva, 1955).

Italy: The main stream of *risorgimento* history has led not toward critical reappraisal, but toward deeper understanding of the spirit of the movement and the problems which it entailed. Political narratives such as F. Bertolini, *Italia dal 1814 al 1878* (Milan, 1881), or A. de Gori, *Il Risorgimento italiano* (Milan, 1897), or even the valuable critique, C. Tivaroni, *L'Italia degli Italiani,* 3 vols. (Milan, 1895-1897), have given way to histories penetrated by "Crocean" idealism, with heavy emphasis on the role of ideas. On this point see: K. R. Greenfield, "The Historiography of the Risorgimento since 1920," *Journal of Modern History,* VII (1935), 49-67; A. M. Ghisalberti, *Introduzione alla Storia del Risorgimento* (Rome, 1942); and F. Valsecchi, *La Storiografia del Risorgimento e i suoi problemi* (Milan, 1953). A Marxist-materialist interpretation is available in A. Gramsci, *Il Risorgimento* (Turin, 1949); much more typical of recent Italian writing are A. Monti, *Il Risorgimento,* 2 vols. (3rd ed., Milan, 1948), and A. Omodèo, *L'Età del Risorgimento Italiano* (2nd ed., Messina, 1939).

Official and semi-official agencies in Italy have published the speeches, writings, and private papers of figures like Mazzini, Garibaldi, Bettino Ricasoli, and Nino Bixio. M. de Rubris has edited *Massimo d'Azeglio: Scritti e discorsi politici,* 3 vols. (Florence, 1931-1938). To earlier collections such as *Il Carteggio Cavour-Nigra dal 1858 al 1861, 4 vols.* (Bologna, 1926-1929), and *Cavour e Inghilterra: Carteggio con V. E. d'Azeglio* (Bologna, 1933), the Commission per la pubblicazione dei Carteggi di Camillo Cavour has added *La liberazione del Mezzogiorno e la formazione del Regno d'Italia,* 5 vols. (Bologna, 1949-1954). A. Omodèo and others have edited Cavour's *Discorsi parlamentari,* 11 vols. (Florence, 1932-1957).

On Cavour's life there is the popular A. Panzini, *Il conte di Cavour,* 4th ed. (Milan, 1939); on his early career, A. Omodèo, *L'opera politica del conte di Cavour, Part I: 1848-1857,* 3rd ed., 2 vols. (Florence, 1945); on the development of his thought, two works by F. Ruffini, *La giovinezza di Cavour,* 2nd ed., 2 vols. (Turin, 1937-1938), and *Ultimi studi sul conte di Cavour* (Bari, 1936). Cavour's contemporaries meanwhile have begun to emerge from his shadow. Recent studies of them include: L. Lipparini, *Minghetti,* 2 vols. (Bologna, 1942-1947); D. Guccerelli and E. Sestini, *Bettino Ricasoli* (Florence, 1950); A. M. Ghisalberti, *Massimo d'Azeglio, un moderato realizzatore* (Rome, 1953).

Shortly after the settlement of the Roman question in 1929, several monographs appeared which threw new light on that problem during the period of unification. Documents on the negotiations between the papal and secular governments were published in F. Salata, *Per la storia diplomatica della questione Romana* (Milan, 1929); A. Piola presented a documented summary in *La questione Romana* (Padua, 1931). On relations between the pope and the king of Italy see P. Pirri, *pio IX c Vittorio Emanuele dal loro carteggio* 2 vols. (Rome, 1944-1951). R. de Cesare, *Roma e lo stato del Papa dal ritorno di Pio IX al 20 settembre, 1850-1870* (Rome, 1907; trans., New York, 1909) is a spirited narrative; A. Ventrone, *L'amministrazione dello stato pontificio dal 1814 al 1870* (Rome, 1942) is a useful analysis. On the problem of southern Italy, see: R. Rosario, *Il Risorgimento in Sicilia* (Bari, 1950): R. de Cesare, *Le fine de un regno dal 1855 al 5 settembre, 1860,* 3 vols. (Citta di Castello, 1909).

Some important writing on the *risorgimento* has been done in English. Bolton King, *History of Italian Unity, being a Political History of Italy from 1814 to 1871,* 2 vols. (London, 1899); W. R. Thayer, *Life and Times of Cavour,* 2 vols. (Boston, 1911); G. M. Trevelyan, *Garibaldi and the Thousand* (New York, 1909), and his *Garibaldi and the Making of Italy* (New York, 1911); all these breathe the spirit of Italian patriotism. A. Whyte, *Political Life and Letters of Cavour* (London, 1925), used new materials from the papers of the British minister at Turin; W. K. Hancock, *Ricasoli and the Risorgimento in Tuscany* (London, 1926) made extensive use of family archives. D. Mack Smith, *Cavour and Garibaldi, 1860* (New York, 1954), depicted the great puppet master at work.

Germany: Because the history of the *Reichsgründung* is so interwoven with the biography of Bismarck, his *Gedanken und Erinnerungen,* 2 vols. (Stuttgart, 1898), translated as *Bismarck, the Man and the Statesman* (New York, 1899), is an indispensable source. His speeches and writings are collected in F. Thimme, ed., *Bismarck: Die gesammelten Werke,* 15 vols. (Berlin, 1924-1935). Collections of diplomatic correspondence from the Austrian and Prussian archives are noted above. H. Rosenberg, *Die nazionalpolitische Publizistik Deutschlands vom Eintritt der neuen Ära in Preussen bis zum Ausbruch des deutschen Krieges,* 2 vols. (Munich, 1935), is a critical bibliography and a collection of abstracts from some thirteen hundred pamphlets and articles.

The first general history of German unification was H. von Sybel, *Die Begründung des deutschen Reichs durch Wilhelm I,* 6th ed., 7 vols. (Munich, 1904), in translation, *The Founding of the German Empire by William I,* 7 vols. (New York, 1890-1898). Sybel's classical ode to Bismarck and William I was followed by more balanced studies: M. Lenz, *Geschichte Bismarcks* (Leipzig, 1902); E. Zechlin, *Bismarck und die Grundlegung der deuschen Grossmacht* (Stuttgart, 1930), and, above all, E. Brandenburg, *Die Reichsgründung,* 2nd ed., 2 vols. (Leipzig, 1922). H. von Srbik, *Deutsche Einheit,* 4 vols. (Munich, 1935-1942), is the best criticism of Bismarck from a "gesammtdeutsch" viewpoint. A brilliant "kleindeutsch" rebuttal is E. Marcks, *Der Aufstieg des Reichs,* 2 vols. (Stuttgart, 1936). More recently a Dutch scholar, Z. R. Dittrich, has emphasized the role of circumstances in the shaping of Bismarck's policies in *De Opkomst van het moderne Duitsland,* II, *De Oplosing van Bismarck, 1862-1871* (Groningen, 1956). The best account in English is F. Darmstaedter, *Bismarck and the Creation of the Second Reich* (London, 1948).

Since the reduction of Bismarck's Germany in 1919 and its partition in 1945 there has been a flood of reinterpretatations of the man and his work. For a review of this material see O. Pflanze, "Bismarck and German Nationalism," *American Historical Review,* LX (1955), 548-566. Interpretive essays in this vein by F. Schnabel and A. von Martin are available in Hans Kohn, ed., *German History: Some New German Views* (Boston, 1954). Much of the writing on Bismarck since World War II has had as its point of departure E. Eyck, *Bismarck: Leban und Werk,* 3 vols. (Erlenbach-Zürich, 1941-1944), a hostile treatment which has aroused some strong reactions. A. O. Meyer, *Bismarck: der Mensch und der Staatsmann* (Stuttgart, 1949), is a eulogy; W. Mommsen in *Stein, Ranke, Bismarck* (Munich, 1954), and L. von Muralt in *Bismarcks Verantwortlichkeit* (Göttingen, 1955), stress the principles on which Bismarck's policies were founded; G. A. Rein, in *Die Revolution in der Politik Bismarcks* (Göttingen, 1957), stresses rather Bismarck's intuitive grasp of conditions in the determination of his policies. No first-rate biography of Bismarck has appeared in English. E. Eyck, *Bismarck and the German Empire* (London, 1950), is an unsatisfactory abridgment and redaction of his original work; A. J. P. Taylor's *Bismarck: The Man and the Statesman* (New York, 1955), tends toward caricature; although faulty, the best life is still C. G. Robertson, *Bismarck* (New York, 1919).

In their search for alternatives to Bismarck's solution of the German problem, his critics have revived the "grossdeutsch" and federalist ideals. During World War I and just after it these ideals merged with Friedrich Naumann's vision of a *Mitteleuropa* and produced such works as: R. Charmatz, *Minister Freiherr von Bruck: ein Vorkämpfer Mitteleuropas* (Leipzig, 1916); F. W. Förster, *Bismarcks Werk im Lichte der föderalistischen Kritik* (Ludwigsburg, 1921); R. F. Kaindl, *Österreich, Preussen, und Deutschland* (Vienna, 1926). Hitler's drive toward *Anschluss* inspired W. von Klöber, *Die deutsche Frage, 1859-71, in grossdeutscher und antiliberaler Beleuchtung* (Munich, 1936). Srbik's great work noted above made the best case for a central European rather than a German interpretation of German history. For a searching inquiry into the whole concept see H. C. Meyer, *Mitteleuropa in German Thought and Action, 1815-1945* (The Hague, 1955). World War II and the constitution making which followed it revived interest in the early advocates of federalism: E. Schaper, *Konstantin Frantz: Versuch einer Darstellung seines Systems des Föderalismus* (Berlin, 1940); W. von Klopp, *Onno Klopp: Leben und Wirken* (Munich, 1950); E. von Puttkamer, *Föderative Elemente im deutschen Staatsrecht seit 1648* (Göttingen, 1955); W. Mommsen, "Julius Froebel," *Historische Zeitschrift*, CLXXXI (1956), 497-532.

On the breakdown of the German Confederation and the Austro-

German war see: K. Fischer, *Die Nation und der Bundestag* (Leipzig, 1880); A. O. Meyer, *Bismarcks Kampf mit Österreich am Bundestag zu Frankfurt* (Berlin, 1927); H. Friedjung, *Der Kampf um die Vorherrschaft in Deutschland 1859 bis 1866* (Stuttgart, 1900; trans., New York, 1935). Fischer and Meyer reflect Prussian hostility toward the Confederation; Friedjung's viewpoint is that of an Austrian liberal. Two more objective studies are: C. W. Clark, *Franz Joseph and Bismarck: The Diplomacy of Austria before the War of 1866* (Cambridge, Mass., 1934); and R. Stadelmann, *Das Jahr 1865 und das Problem von Bismarcks deutscher Politik* (Munich, 1933).

The best guide to German constitutional history is F. Hartung, *Deutsche Verfassungsgeschichte,* 5th ed. (Stuttgart, 1950). The constitutional conflict in Prussia in the early 1860's has been dealt with in K. Kaminski, *Verfassung und Verfassungsstreit, 1862-1866* (Königsberg, 1938), and E. N. Anderson, *The Social and Political Conflict in Prussia, 1858-1864* (Lincoln, Neb., 1954). Bismarck's biographers are eloquent on this subject, but should be supplemented by E. Marcks, *Kaiser Wilhelm I,* 8th ed. (Leipzig, 1918), and H. M. Elster, *Graf Albrecht von Roon* (Berlin, 1938). The role of the military in shaping Prussian policy is clarified by G. Ritter, *Staatskunst und Kriegshandwerk,* I, *Die altpreussische Tradition, 1740-1890* (Munich, 1954); G. A. Craig, *The Politics of the Prussian Army, 1640-1945* (Oxford, 1955); and R. Stadelmann, *Moltke und der Staat* (Krefeld, 1950).

On the smaller German states see: W. P. Fuchs, *Die deutschen Mittelstaaten und die Bundesreform, 1853-1860* (Berlin, 1934); W. Schübelin, *Das Zollparlament und die Politik von Baden, Bayern, und Württemberg, 1866-1870* (Berlin, 1935); T. Schieder, *Die kleindeutsche Partei in Bayern, 1863-1871* (Munich, 1936); M. Doeberl, *Bayern und die Bismarcksche Reichsgründung* (Munich, 1925). Two biographies by Hermann Oncken describe the roles of non-Prussian statesmen in the unification movement: *Rudolf von Bennigsen* (Stuttgart, 1910); and *Grossherzog Friedrich von Baden* (Stuttgart, 1927). W. Richter, *Ludwig II, König von Bayern,* 4th ed. (Munich, 1956), is a better book than its English translation, *The Mad Monarch* (Chicago, 1954), which omits the important historical sections. A good introduction to the reaction of a religious minority to Bismarck's work is G. C. Windell, *The Catholics and German Unity, 1866-1871* (Minneapolis, 1954). Finally, it should be noted that German history in the nineteenth century has been interpreted not in terms of Bismarck's achievement but in terms of the liberals' failure. See: L. Krieger, *The German Idea of Freedom* (Boston, 1957); T. S. Hamerow, *Restoration, Revolution, Reaction: Economics and Politics in Germany, 1815-1871* (Princeton, N. J., 1958); H. Heffter, *Die deutsche Selbstverwaltung im 19. Jahrhundert* (Stuttgart, 1950).

Austria-Hungary: After such *ex parte* accounts as W. Rogge, *Österreich von Vilagos bis zur Gegenwart,* 3 vols. (Leipzig, 1872-1873), and H. Friedjung, *Österreich von 1848 bis 1860,* 2 vols. (Stuttgart, 1908-1912), Joseph Redlich's *Das österreichische Staats- und Reichsproblem,* 2 vols. (Leipzig, 1920-1926), made clear that neither the dynastic policies of the Hapsburgs nor the national policies of the Prussians and Hungarians had succeeded in solving the problem of central Europe. Redlich's account broke off in 1867; for later constitutional experiments, see B. Weisz, *Die Verfassungen Österreichs seit 1848 und ihre unitarischen und föderalistischen Elemente* (Innsbrück, 1937). English works which help to unravel the complexities of the nationalities problem are: R. A. Kann, *The Multinational Empire: National Reform in the Habsburg Monarchy, 1848-1918,* 2 vols. (New York, 1950); A. J. P. Taylor, *The Habsburg Monarchy, 1809-1918* (London, 1948); A. J. May, *The Habsburg Monarchy, 1867-1914* (Cambridge, Mass., 1951).

Material by, or about, Austrian statesmen is not abundant. Count Friedrich Beust published his apologia, *Aus drei Vierteljahrhunderten,* 2 vols. (Stuttgart, 1887; trans., 2 vols., London, 1887), and E. von Wertheimer published important papers in his *Graf Julius Andrássy, sein Leben und seine Zeit,* 3 vols. Stuttgart, 1910-1913). The best biography of the Emperor is J. Redlich, *Kaiser Franz Joseph von Österreich* (Berlin, 1928; trans., New York, 1928). See also: F. Engel-Janosi, *Graf Rechberg* (Munich, 1927); P. Molisch, *Schmerling* (Vienna, 1947). Brief essays on Kuhn and John are to be found in H. Von Srbik, *Aus Österreichs Vergangenheit* (Salzburg, 1949), and on Alexander Bach, in R. Charmatz, *Lebensbilder aus der Geschichte Österreichs* (Vienna, 1947). Georg Franz, *Liberalismus: die deutschliberale Bewegung in der Habsburgischen Monarchie* (Munich, 1956), is an account of the quarrels and lost opportunities of the liberals in the 1860's.

The *Ausgleich* of 1867 has been the subject of a masterful analysis, L. Eisenmann, *Le compromis austro-hungrois de 1867* (Paris, 1904). A. Apponyi, *Die rechtliche Natur der Beziehungen zwischen Österreich und Ungarn* (Vienna, 1910), explored the constitutional effects of the settlement. On Hungary between 1848 and 1866, see A. Berzeviczy, *Az absolutismus kora Magyarországon,* 3 vols. (Budapest, 1922); for the period, 1867 to 1914, see: Gustav Gratz, *A dualismus kora,* 2 vols. (Budapest, 1934). On the Croatians, see J. Horvat, *Političha Povijest Hrvatske* (Zagreb, 1936); on the east Slavs, see: Josef Macurek, *Dejiny Východnick Slovanu,* 3 vols. (Prague, 1947).

Russia: The great surge of interest in Russian history which followed World War II has produced some excellent works on Russia in western languages. Two good introductions are: L. I. Strakhovsky, *A Handbook of Slavic Studies* (Cambridge, Mass., 1949); and Charles Morley, *Guide to Research in Russian History* (Syracuse, N. Y., 1951). Among the many general histories of Russia which have appeared, these are especially good on the 1850's and 1860's: H. Seton-Watson, *The Decline of Imperial Russia, 1855-1914* (New York, 1952); M. T. Florinsky, *Russia: a History and an Interpretation,* 2 vols. (New York, 1953). See also: K. *Stählin, Geschichte Russlands,* 4 vols. (Berlin, 1923-1939); and V. Giterman, *Geschichte Russlands,* 3 vols. (Zürich, 1944-1949). An interesting study of federalist ideas and forces in Russia history is G. von Rauch, *Russland: staatliche Einheit und nationale Vielfalt* (Munich, 1953). On the Polish revolt, see: H. Scheidt, *Konvention Alvensleben und Interventionspolitik der Mächte in der polnischen Frage, 1863* (Munich, 1937); W. F. Reddaway, *et al., Cambridge History of Poland,* 2 vols. (Cambridge, 1950-1951). On Finland, see L. Krusius-Ahrenberg, *Der Durchbruch des Nationalismus und Liberalismus im politischen Leben Finlands, 1856-1863* (Helsinki, 1934). The eastward movement is sketched in: D. J. Dallin, *The Rise of Russia in Asia* (New Haven, 1949); and V. Sincokov, *La colonisation russe en Asie*

(Paris, 1929). C. de Grunwald, *Tsar Nicholas I* (New York, 1955), and Stephen Graham, *The Tsar of Freedom: the Life and Reign of Alexander II* (New Haven, 1935) are superficial, but not without merit.

While Soviet historians have looked into their past to discover precursors of the Bolsheviks, western scholars have traced the genealogy of both revolutionary and reactionary ideas. As a result some of the liveliest writing on Russia in the mid-nineteenth century has been done in the field where intellectual history joins political and social history. Outstanding among such works are: A. Yarmolinsky, *The Road to Revolution: a Century of Russian Radicalism* (London, 1957); S. R. Tompkins, *The Russian Intelligentsia: Makers of the Revolutionary State* (Norman, Okla., 1957); George Fischer, *Russian Liberalism: from Gentry to Intelligentsia* (Cambridge, Mass., 1958); Richard Hare, *Pioneers of Russian Social Thought* (New York, 1951); N. Riasanovsky, *Russia and the West in the Teaching of the Slavophiles* (Cambridge, Mass., 1952); A. Coquart, *Dmitri Pisarev (1840-1868) et l'idéologie du nihilisme russe* (Paris, 1946); F. Venturi, *Il populismo russo,* 2 vols. (Turin, 1952); J. H. Billington, *Mikhailovsky and Russian Populism* (New York, 1958). Hans Kohn has provided excerpts from Russian publicists in *The Mind of Modern Russia* (New Brunswick, N. J., 1955). Kohn's *Pan-Slavism: Its History and Ideology* (Notre Dame, Ind., 1953), has been largely superseded for this period by M. Petrovich, *The Emergence of Russian Panslavism, 1856-1870* (New York, 1956). See also the pioneer work of A. Fischel, *Der Panslawismus bis zum Weltkrieg* (Stuttgart, 1919), and B. Hepner, *Bakounine et le panslavisme révolutionnaire* (Paris, 1950). No student should neglect the classic work of T. G. Masaryk translated into English as *The Spirit of Russia,* 2nd ed., 2 vols. (New York, 1955).

Lesser States: For a general introduction to Scandinavian history, see B. J. Hovde, *The Scandinavian Countries, 1720-1865,* 2 vols. (Boston, 1943); a socio-economic interpretation which should be balanced by more conventional histories such as: Ingvar Andersson, *Sveriges Historia* (Stockholm, 1943; trans., London, 1956); D. V. Verney, *Parliamentary Reform in Sweden, 1866-1921* (Oxford,

1957); T. Jorgenson, *Norway's Relation to Scandinavian Unionism, 1815-1871* (Northfield, Minn., 1935); N. Neergard, *Under Junigrundloven: en Fremstilling af det danske Folks politiske Historie fra 1848 tel 1866,* 2 vols. (Copenhagen, 1896-1907).

The history of Switzerland as the evolution of a Swiss nationality is the theme of W. Oechsli, *History of Switzerland, 1499-1914* (Cambridge, 1922). For a federalist reply, see W. Martin, *Histoire de la Suisse* (Paris, 1927; trans., London, 1931). See also W. Rappard, *La constitution fédérale de la suisse, 1848-1948* (Neuchâtel, 1948). Both E. Fueter, *Die Schweiz seit 1848* (Leipzig, 1928), and E. Gagliardi, *Geschichte der Schweiz,* 3 vols. (3rd ed., Zürich, 1938), stress economic and social forces. On the Low Countries, see J. A. van Houtte, *et al., Algemene Geschiednis der Nederlanden,* X, *Liberaal Getij, 1840-1885* (Utrecht, 1955). A more nationalist treatment is H. Pirenne, *Histoire de Belgique,* VII, *De la révolution de 1830 à la guerre de 1914,* 2nd ed. (Brussels, 1948). King Leopold I has been the subject of biographies by E. Corti (Vienna, 1922; trans., London, 1923); by L. Lichtervelde (New York, 1929); and by C. Bronne (Brussels, 1947). A great Belgian liberal is the subject of J. Garsou, *Frère-Orban,* 2 vols. (Brussels, 1946); the plight of Luxemburg is described in Garsou's *Le grand-duché de Luxembourg entre la Belgique, la France et la Prusse, 1867-1871* (Luxemburg, 1937).

Of the Iberian countries, Portugal has been badly served by historians. For detailed coverage of this period, see Oliveira Martins, *Portugal contemporaneo,* 2 vols. (Lisbon, 1881). An introduction to Spanish history is provided by R. Altamira, *Manual de Historio de España,* 2nd ed. (Buenos Aires, 1946); specifically on the nineteenth century, there is A. Ballestros y Beretta, *Historia de España,* vols. VIII-IX (Barcelona, 1936-1941). The first volume of M. Fernandez Almagro, *Historia politica de la España contemporanea* (Madrid, 1956), covers the period 1867-1885. On the revolution, see Roman Oyarzún, *Historia del Carlismo,* 2nd ed. (Madrid, 1944). In English there are: E. H. Strobel, *The Spanish Revolution, 1868-1875* (Boston, 1898); J. A. Brandt, *Toward the New Spain* (Chicago, 1933); and J. B. Trend, *The Origins of Modern Spain* (Cambridge, 1934).

On the Balkan states, L. S. Stavrianos, *The Balkans since 1453*

(New York, 1958), has an excellent bibliography. The history of Serbia after the return of the Obrenoviches is dealt with in: Slobodan Jovanović, *Druga vlada Miloša i Mihaila, 1858-1868* (Belgrade, 1923); and V. Cubrilović and V. Corović, *Srbija od 1858 do 1903 godine* (Belgrade, 1938). The history of Greece is inseparable from its position vis-à-vis the great powers. See: E. Driault and M. L'Héritier, *Histoire diplomatique de la Grèce,* 5 vols. (Paris, 1925-1926); J. A. Levandis, *The Greek Foreign Debt and the Great Powers, 1821-1898* (New York, 1944); E. Prevalakis, *British Policy toward the Change of Dynasty in Greece, 1862-1863* (Athens, 1953). For the development of the royal government, see N. Kaltchas, *Introduction to the Constitutional History of Modern Greece* (New York, 1940); and L. Bower and G. Bolitho, *Otho I: King of Greece* (London, 1939). Three important works on Rumania are: P. Henry, *L'abdication du Prince Cuza et l'avènement de la dynastie de Hohenzollern au trône de Roumanie: documents diplomatiques* (Paris, 1930); W. G. East, *The Union of Moldavia and Wallachia* (New York, 1929); T. W. Riker, *The Making of Rumania: a Study of an International Problem, 1856-1866* (Oxford, 1931). On Bulgaria, see: A. Hajek, *Bulgarien unter der Türkenherrschaft* (Stuttgart, 1925); D. Mishew, *The Bulgarians in the Past* (Lausanne, 1919). J. K. Birge, *A Guide to Turkish Area Study* (Washington, 1949); Kerim Kami Key, *An Outline of Modern Turkish Historiography* (Istanbul, 1954); C. Ritter von Lax, *Geschichte des Machtverfalls der Türkei,* 2nd ed., (Vienna, 1913); W. Miller, *The Ottoman Empire and Its Successors* (Cambridge, 1936); L. Lamouche, *Histoire de la Turquie* (Paris, 1934); and Morgan P. Price, *A History of Turkey* (London, 1956), provide an introduction to Turkish history. On efforts at reform, see: E. Engelhardt, *La Turquie et le tanzimat,* 2 vols. (Paris, 1882-1884); and, in Turkish, Maarif Vekeleti, ed., *Tanzimat* (Istanbul, 1940); Resat Kaynar, *Mustafa Resit Pasa ve Tanzimat* (Ankara, 1954).

II. SOCIAL AND ECONOMIC HISTORY

The complex economic development of Europe in the nineteenth century is best approached through some general survey such as W. Bowden, M. Karpovich, and A. P. Usher. *An Economic History of*

Europe Since 1750 (New York, 1937), or through an interpretive synthesis such as W. Sombart, *Wirtschaftsleben im Zeitalter des Hochkapitalismus,* 2 vols. (Munich, 1928). Histories of national economies include: J. H. Clapham, *Economic History of Modern Britain,* 3 vols. (Cambridge, 1930-1938); and his *Economic History of France and Germany, 1815-1914,* 4th ed. (Cambridge, 1945); H. Sée, *Histoire économique de la France: les temps modernes, 1789-1914,* rev. ed. (Paris, 1951); H. Bechtel, *Wirtschaftsgeschichte Deutschlands,* 3 vols. (Munich, 1951-1956); P. I. Lyashchenko, *History of the National Economy of Russia to the 1917 Revolution* (New York, 1949).

Estimates of population are available in the *Almanach de Gotha* after 1823 and in the *Statesman's Year Book* since 1863. A corrective to overconfidence in such figures is J. Koren, *The History of Statistics* (New York, 1918). Statistical studies by professional demographers include: R. Kuczynski, *Balance of Births and Deaths,* 2 vols. (London, 1928-1931); E. Levasseur, *La population française,* 3 vols. (Paris, 1889-1892); P. Mombert, *Bevölkerungslehre* (Jena, 1929); H. Haufe, *Die Bevölkerung Europas* (Berlin, 1936); D. S. Thomas, *Social and Economic Aspects of Swedish Population Movements, 1750-1933* (New York, 1941). The best general account of population changes is M. R. Reinhard, *Histoire de la population mondiale de 1700 à 1948* (Paris, 1949). Economists and biologists have advanced various explanations for the growth and decline of population; see, for example: M. B. Hexter, *Social Consequences of the Business Cycle* (Boston, 1925); A. M. Carr-Saunders, *World Population* (Oxford, 1936); R. Pearl, *The Biology of Death* (Philadelphia, 1920), and his *The Biology of Population Growth* (New York, 1925). H. Boner, *Hungry Generations: The Nineteenth Century Case against Malthusianism* (New York, 1955), is especially good on the 1850's and 1860's.

On migration, see: M. L. Hansen, *The Atlantic Migration* (Cambridge, Mass., 1940); W. A. Corrothers, *Emigration from the British Isles* (London, 1929); T. Blegen, *Norwegian Migration to America* (Minneapolis, 1931); F. Foerster, *The Italian Emigration of Our Times* (Cambridge, 1919). For statistical data, see the United States Bureau of Economic Research, *International Migrations* (New

York, 1931). On urbanization, there is an old but comprehensive study, A. F. Weber, *The Growth of Cities in the Nineteenth Century* (New York, 1899). A new synthesis must await the publication of more monographs such as L. Chevalier, *La formation de la population parisienne au XIXe siècle* (Paris, 1950), and W. Brepohl, *Der Aufbau des Ruhrvolkes* (Recklinghausen, 1948).

Contemporary British reports on agrarian conditions are a mine of information on this subject. See, for example, J. Probyn, *Systems of Land Tenure in Various Countries* (London, 1881). A good general history is M. Augé-Laribé, *La revolution agricole* (Paris, 1955). On the Russian agrarian reforms, the best book in English is G. T. Robinson, *Rural Russia under the Old Regime,* 2nd ed. (New York, 1949). See also: G. Pasvolsky, *Agricultural Russia on the Eve of Revolution,* 2nd ed. (London, 1949); and R. Stupperich, *Die Anfänge der Bauernbefreiung in Russland* (Berlin, 1939). The first volume of the *Bolshaia Sovietskaia Entsiklopediia* carries an article on the agrarian question which classifies writers according to their political bias. The foremost Soviet authorities on the subject are E. A. Morokovets, N. M. Druzhinin, and IA. Linkov. Linkov has investigated the background of reform in his *Ocherki Istorii Krest'ianskogo Dvizheniia v Rossii v 1825-1861* (Moscow, 1952).

No comprehensive history of industrialization in Europe has yet appeared. For Britain, see: C. R. Fay, *Round about Industrial Britain, 1830-1860* (London, 1952); W. O. Henderson, *Britain and Industrial Europe, 1750-1870* (Liverpool, 1954). The best brief account of French industry in this period is in G. Duveau, *La vie ouvrière en France sous le second empire* (Paris, 1946). P. Benaerts, *Les origines de la grande industrie allemande* (Paris, 1933), is indispensable for Germany. See also: R. Morandi, *Storia della grande industria in Italia* (Bari, 1931); Arthur Montgomery, *The Rise of Modern Industry in Sweden* (London, 1939).

A good general history of commerce is B. Nogaro and W. Oualid, *L'évolution du commerce* (Paris, 1914). On tariffs and free trade, see: R. L. Schuyler, *The Fall of the Old Colonial System: a Study in British Free Trade, 1770-1870* (New York, 1945); S. B. Clough, *France: a History of National Economics, 1789-1939* (New York, 1939); F. A. Haight, *A History of French Commercial Policies*

(New York, 1941); A. L. Dunham, *The Anglo-French Treaty of 1860* (Ann Arbor, 1930); W. O. Henderson, *The Zollverein* (New York, 1939); E. Frantz, *Der Entscheidungskampf um die Wirtschaftspolitische Führung Deutschlands* (Munich, 1933). The rise of modern financial institutions and the mobilization of European capital have been the subject of numerous studies. See: R. R. Formoy, *Historical Foundations of Modern Company Law* (London, 1924); J. Plenge, *Gründung und Geschichte des Crédit Mobiliers* (Tübingen, 1903); E. Corti, *The Reign of the House of Rothschild, 1848-1870* (New York, 1928); Adolph Weber, *Depositenbanken und Spekulationsbanken,* 4th ed. (Munich, 1938); R. Bigo, *Les banques françaises au cours du XIXe siècle* (Paris, 1947); H. Feis, *Europe, the World's Banker* (New Haven, 1930); D. Landes, *Bankers and Pashas: International Finance and Economic Imperialism in the Egypt of the 1860's* (Cambridge, Mass., 1958). The last is an important contribution to the history of the Suez Canal. See also: C. W. Hallberg, *The Suez Canal* (New York, 1931); G. Edgar-Bonnet, *Ferdinand de Lesseps* (Paris, 1951). On the business crisis of 1857, see H. Rosenberg, *Die Weltwirtschaftskrisis von 1857-1859* (Berlin, 1934).

Social histories dealing chiefly with the upper and middle classes are: G. M. Young, ed., *Early Victorian England, 1830-1865,* 2 vols. (New York, 1934); M. Allem, *La vie quotidienne sous le second empire* (Paris, 1948); E. Kohn-Bramstedt, *Aristocracy and the Middle Classes in Germany* (London, 1937). J. Kuczynski, *A Short History of Labour Conditions under Capitalism,* 4 vols. (London, 1942-1945), has a heavy Marxist bias. On working-class movements, see: E. Dolléans and M. Crozier, *Mouvements ouvrier et socialiste: chronologie et bibliographie: Angleterre, France, Allemagne, États-Unis, 1750-1918* (Paris, 1950); G. D. H. Cole and R. Postgate, *The British People, 1746-1946* (New York, 1946); H. Herkner, *Die Arbeiterfrage,* 8th ed., 2 vols. (Berlin, 1922); É. Halévy, *Histoire du socialisme européen,* 4th ed. (Paris, 1948); A. Sargent and C. Harmel, *Histoire de l'anarchie* (Paris, 1949). Studies of socialism as an intellectual movement will be listed below. On the efforts of the churches to come to grips with the social problem, see: R. F. Wearmouth, *Methodism and the Struggle of the Working Class, 1850-*

1900 (Leicester, 1954); W. O. Shanahan, *German Protestants Face the Social Question,* I, *The Conservative Phase, 1815-1871* (Notre Dame, Ind., 1954); J. Duroselle, *Les débuts du catholicisme social en France, 1822-1870* (Paris, 1951).

Other titles of interest in the field of social and economic history include: A. Berglund, *Ocean Transportation* (New York, 1931); D. B. Tyler, *Steam Conquers the Atlantic* (New York, 1939); O. S. Nock, *The Railway Engineers* (London, 1955); André Lefèvre, *Sous le second empire: chemins de fer et politique* (Paris, 1951); A. von Mayer, *Geschichte und Geographie der deutschen Eisenbahnen,* 2 vols. (Berlin, 1890-1891); P. Trajani, *Storia delle ferrovie italiana* (Milan, 1944); R. Isay, *Panorama des expositions universelles* (Paris, 1937); H. L. Jenks, *The Migration of British Capital to 1875* (New York, 1927); D. C. Blaisdell, *European Financial Control in the Ottoman Empire* (New York, 1929); E. Dolléans, *Histoire du movement ouvrier,* 3rd ed. (Paris, 1947); B. S. Chlepner, *Cent ans d'histoire sociale en Belgique* (Brussels, 1956); E. Comin Colomer, *Historia del anarquismo español,* 2nd ed. (Barcelona, 1956); M. Gumpert, *Dunant: the Story of the Red Cross* (New York, 1938); C. Woodham-Smith, *Florence Nightingale* (New York, 1951).

III. INTELLECTUAL HISTORY

For a large-scale treatment of intellectual currents during this period, see Theodore Merz, *History of European Thought in the Nineteenth Century,* 4 vols. (Edinburgh, 1896-1914). Good synoptic chapters will be found in: E. Friedell, *Cultural History of the Modern Age,* vol. III (New York, 1933); J. H. Randall, *The Making of the Modern Mind,* rev. ed. (Boston, 1940); Hans Meyer, *Geschichte der abendländischen Weltanschauung,* vol. V. (Würzburg, 1949). K. Löwith, *Von Hegel bis Nietzsche* (Zürich, 1941) argues that European thought took a decisive turn during this period; J. Barzun, *Darwin, Marx, Wagner* (Boston, 1941) argues that it took a turn for the worse. Two influential thinkers of these decades are the subjects of P. Lamy, *Claude Bernard et le matérialisme* (Paris, 1939), and F. Copleston, *Arthur Schopenhauer* (London, 1946).

The history of science is set in perspective by A. N. Whitehead, *Science and the Modern World* (New York, 1926). The progress of science since this period can be followed in H. Dingle, ed., *A Century of Science, 1851-1951* (New York, 1951). On individual fields, see: Carl T. Chase, *The Evolution of Modern Physics* (New York, 1947); A. Findlay, *A Hundred Years of Chemistry,* 2nd ed. (London, 1948); Charles Singer, *A History of Biology,* 2nd ed. (New York, 1951); E. Boring, *History of Experimental Psychology,* 2nd ed. (New York, 1950). On individual scientists, see: Thomas Martin, *Faraday* (London, 1934); J. M. D. Olmstead, *Claude Bernard, Physiologist* (New York, 1938); H. de Terra, *The Life and Times of Alexander von Humboldt, 1769-1859* (New York, 1955); Geoffrey West, *Charles Darwin* (New Haven, 1938). On the impact of Darwin's theory, see: Arthur M. Davies, *Evolution and Its Modern Critics* (London, 1937); W. Irvine, *Apes, Angels and Victorians* (New York, 1955). On the history of medicine, see: C. D. Haagensen and W. E. B. Lloyd, *A Hundred Years of Medicine* (New York, 1943); C. E. A. Winslow, *The Conquest of Epidemic Diseases* (Princeton, N. J., 1943).

On the relations between social sciences and class interests, see J. A. Hobson, *Free Thought in the Social Sciences* (London, 1926). Particular schools of thought are discussed in: G. de Ruggiero, *History of European Liberalism* (London, 1927); H. Marcuse, *Reason and Revolution* (New York, 1941). National traditions are dealt with in: C. Brinton, *English Political Thought in the Nineteenth Century* (New York, 1931); L. Salvatorelli, *Il pensiero politico italiano dal 1800 al 1870,* 5th ed. (Turin, 1949); R. Soltau, *French Political Thought in the Nineteenth Century* (New York, 1931). Individual political theorists are discussed in: W. Irvine, *Walter Bagehot* (New York, 1939); M. S. Packe, *The Life of John Stuart Mill* (New York, 1954); A. B. Spitzer, *The Revolutionary Theories of Louis Auguste Blanqui* (New York, 1957). On the history of economic theory, J. A. Schumpeter, *History of Economic Analysis* (New York, 1954), is more stimulating than the text of Gide and Rist. On the development of historical writing and scholarship, see J. W. Thompson and B. W. Holm, *A History of Historical Writing,* Vol. II (New York, 1942).

On socialist thought, see: G. D. H. Cole, *A History of Socialist Thought,* II, *Marxism and Anarchism, 1850-1890* (New York, 1954); D. Footman, *Ferdinand Lassalle* (New Haven, 1947); Gustav Mayer, *Friedrich Engels,* 2nd ed., 2 vols. (The Hague, 1934; trans., London, 1936); E. H. Carr, *Bakunin* (New York, 1937). Good biographies of Marx are numerous; see those by E. H. Carr (London, 1938), L. Schwarzschild (New York, 1947), and I Berlin (London, 1952). Helpful introductions to Marx's thought are: S. Hook, *From Hegel to Marx* (New York, 1936); A. Cornu, *Karl Marx et la pensée moderne* (Paris, 1948); P. Bigo, *Marxisme et humanisme* (Paris, 1953). Among the many studies of Proudhon, that by E. Dolléans (Paris, 1948) is the most solid, that by G. Woodcock (New York, 1956) is the best in English.

Invaluable guides to the study of English literature of this period are: F. W. Bates, ed., *The Cambridge Bibliography of English Literature,* III, *1800-1900* (New York, 1941), with a supplement published in 1957; F. E. Faverty, *The Victorian Poets, A Guide to Research* (Cambridge, Mass., 1956). The influence of science is the subject of M. Cazamian, *Le roman et les idées en Angleterre* (Strasbourg, 1923). See also: Walter E. Houghton, *The Victorian Frame of Mind* (New Haven, 1957); J. Drinkwater, ed., *The Eighteen Sixties* (Cambridge, 1932); J. Holloway, *The Victorian Sage* (London, 1953); B. Willey, *Nineteenth Century Studies* (London, 1950); T. E. Welby, *The Victorian Romantics, 1850-1870* (London, 1929); D. Welland, *The Pre-Raphaelites in Literature and Art* (London, 1953); Harold Nicolson, *Tennyson,* 2nd ed. (London, 1925); Edgar Johnson, *Charles Dickens,* 2 vols. (New York, 1952); G. Tillotson, *Thackeray, the Novelist* (Cambridge, 1954); L. Trilling, *Matthew Arnold,* 2nd ed. (New York, 1949); D. A. Wilson, *Carlyle to Threescore and Ten* (New York, 1929); Joan Evans, *John Ruskin,* (London, 1954); Betty Miller, *Robert Browning* (London, 1952); Kenneth Robinson, *Wilkie Collins* (London, 1951); L. P. and R. P. Stebbins, *The Trollopes* (New York, 1945).

On French literature, see R. Dumesnil, *Le réalisme* (Paris, 1936); on the great realist, Philip Spencer, *Flaubert* (London, 1952). The track of romanticism in an age of science is followed by K. Allott's *Jules Verne* (London, 1941). See also E. M. Grant, *French Poetry and Modern Industry* (Cambridge, Mass., 1931). On Hugo, see: A. Maurois, *Olympio* (New York, 1956); E. M. Grant, *The Career of Victor Hugo* (Cambridge, Mass., 1946). On Baudelaire, see: M. P. Ruff, *Baudelaire, l'homme et l'oeuvre* (Paris, 1955); E. Starkie, *Baudelaire,* rev. ed. (New York, 1957). On schools of criticism, see: S. J. Kahn, *Science and Aesthetic Judgment: a Study in Taine's Critical Method* (London, 1953); H. Nicolson, *Sainte-Beuve* (Garden City, 1957); L. W. Wylie, *Saint-Marc Girardin, Bourgeois* (Syracuse, N. Y., 1947). German literature of this period is less rich and varied than English or French. See: H. Bieber, *Der Kampf um die Tradition: die deutsche Dichtung im europäischen Geistesleben, 1830-1880* (Stuttgart, 1928); or F. Koch, *Idee und Wirklichkeit: deutsche Dichtung zwischen Romantik und Naturalismus,* 2 vols. (Düsseldorf, 1956). On realism in the theater, see: B. W. Downs, *Ibsen: the Intellectual Background* (Cambridge, 1946); J. Müller, *Das Weltbild Friedrich Hebbels* (Halle, 1955). The great Russian novelists are discussed in: G. Lukacs, *Der russische Realismus in der Weltliteratur* (Berlin, 1951); D. Magarshack, *Turgenev* (New York, 1954); E. J. Simmons, *Dostoevski* (London, 1940).

On the history of art, see: E. Waldman, *Die Kunst des Realismus und des Impressionismus im 19. Jahrhundert* (Berlin, 1927); R. Moser, *L'impressionisme français* (Geneva, 1952). A. Hauser, *The Social History of Art,* 2 vols. (London, 1952), tries to relate art to social environment in the style of Marxist criticism. On particular artists, see: J. Adhémar, *Honoré Daumier* (Paris, 1954); G. Mack, *Gustave Courbet* (New York, 1951); G. H. Hamilton, *Manet and His Critics* (New Haven, 1954); and P. Lemoisne, *Dégas et son oeuvre,* 4 vols. (Paris, 1947-1949). On the history of music, consult E. Dannreuther, *Oxford History of Music,* Vol. VI (London, 1931); the flowering of grand opera is discussed in J. Gregor, *Kulturgeschichte der Oper,* 2nd ed. (Vienna, 1950). See also: E. Newman, *The Life of Richard Wagner,* 4 vols. (New York, 1933-1946); S. Krakauer, *Orpheus in Paris: Offenbach and the Paris of his Time* (New York, 1938); C. Gatti, *Verdi: the Man and His Music* (New York, 1955).

On the conflict over religion, see: J. M. Robertson, *A History of Free Thought in the Nineteenth Century* (New York, 1930); P.

van Tieghem, *Renan* (Paris, 1948); B. Willey, *More Nineteenth Century Studies: a Group of Honest Doubters* (New York, 1956). On the battles between the church and liberalism, see: G. Weill, *Histoire de l'idée laïque en France au XIXe siècle* (Paris, 1929); S. Jacini, *La crisi religiosa del Risorgimento* (Bari, 1938); Georg Franz, *Kulturkampf: Staat und katholische Kirsche in Mitteleuropa* (Munich, 1954), which treats the period 1859 to 1879. On the Catholic Church generally, see: R. Aubert, *Le pontificat de Pie IX, 1846-1878* (Paris, 1952); E. E. Y. Hales, *Pio Nono* (London, 1954); K. S. Latourette, *Christianity in a Revolutionary Age,* I, *The Nineteenth Century in Europe* (New York, 1958); E. Perrier, *The Revival of Scholastic Philosophy in the Nineteenth Century* (New York, 1909); E. C. Butler, *The Vatican Council,* 2 vols. (New York, 1930). On the Protestant churches, consult: F. W. Cornish, *The English Church in the Nineteenth Century* (London, 1910); J. R. Fleming, *A History of the Church in Scotland, 1843-1874* (Edinburgh, 1927); J. Tulloch, *Movements of Religious Thought in Britain during the Nineteenth Century* (New York, 1886); L. E. Elliott-Binns, *The Development of English Theology in the Later Nineteenth Century* (London, 1952); L. Perriraz, *Histoire de la théologie protestante au XIXe siècle,* I, *Les doctrines* (Neuchâtel, 1949); R. Seeberg, *Die Kirche Deutschlands im neunzehnten Jahrhundert* 2nd ed. (Leipzig, 1904); K. Barth, *Die protestantische Theologie im 19. Jahrhundert* (Zürich, 1947). Judaism and its position in European intellectual history are discussed in A. Lewkowitz, *Das Judentum und die geistigen Strömungen des 19. Jahrhunderts* (Breslau, 1935).

See also, for the general field of intellectual history: W. Kaegi, *Jacob Burckhardt,* 3 vols. (Basel, 1947-1956), one volume still to be published; W. Bussmann, *Treitschke, sein Welt-und Geschichtsbild* (Göttingen, 1952); A. Dorpalen, *Heinrich von Treitschke* (New Haven, 1957); B. Weinberg, *French Realism: the Critical Reaction, 1830-1870* (Chicago, 1937); A. Billy, *Sainte-Beuve,* 2 vols. (Paris, 1952); J. Dresch, *Le roman social en Allemagne, 1850-1900* (Paris, 1913).

INDEX

CLEMENT EATON: The Freedom-of-Thought Struggle in the Old South. *Revised and Enlarged. Illus.* TB/1150
CLEMENT EATON: The Growth of Southern Civilization: 1790-1860. † *Illus.* TB/3040
LOUIS FILLER: The Crusade Against Slavery: 1830-1860. † *Illus.* TB/3029
DIXON RYAN FOX: The Decline of Aristocracy in the Politics of New York: 1801-1840. ‡ *Edited by Robert V. Remini* TB/3064
WILLIAM W. FREEHLING, Ed.: The Nullification Era: *A Documentary Record* ‡ TB/3079
FELIX GILBERT: The Beginnings of American Foreign Policy: *To the Farewell Address* TB/1200
FRANCIS GRIERSON: The Valley of Shadows: *The Coming of the Civil War in Lincoln's Midwest: A Contemporary Account* TB/1246
FRANCIS J. GRUND: Aristocracy in America: *Social Class in the Formative Years of the New Nation* TB/1001
ALEXANDER HAMILTON: The Reports of Alexander Hamilton. ‡ *Edited by Jacob E. Cooke* TB/3060
THOMAS JEFFERSON: Notes on the State of Virginia. ‡ *Edited by Thomas P. Abernethy* TB/3052
JAMES MADISON: The Forging of American Federalism: *Selected Writings of James Madison. Edited by Saul K. Padover* TB/1226
BERNARD MAYO: Myths and Men: *Patrick Henry, George Washington, Thomas Jefferson* TB/1108
JOHN C. MILLER: Alexander Hamilton and the Growth of the New Nation TB/3057
RICHARD B. MORRIS, Ed.: The Era of the American Revolution TB/1180
R. B. NYE: The Cultural Life of the New Nation: 1776-1801. † *Illus.* TB/3026
JAMES PARTON: The Presidency of Andrew Jackson. *From Vol. III of the Life of Andrew Jackson.* ‡ *Ed. with an Intro. by Robert V. Remini* TB/3080
FRANCIS S. PHILBRICK: The Rise of the West, 1754-1830. † *Illus.* TB/3067
TIMOTHY L. SMITH: Revivalism and Social Reform: *American Protestantism on the Eve of the Civil War* TB/1229
ALBION W. TOURGÉE: A Fool's Errand. ‡ *Ed. by George Fredrickson* TB/3074
A. F. TYLER: Freedom's Ferment: *Phases of American Social History from the Revolution to the Outbreak of the Civil War. 31 illus.* TB/1074
GLYNDON G. VAN DEUSEN: The Jacksonian Era: 1828-1848. † *Illus.* TB/3028
LOUIS B. WRIGHT: Culture on the Moving Frontier TB/1053

American Studies: The Civil War to 1900

W. R. BROCK: An American Crisis: Congress and Reconstruction, 1865-67 ° △ TB/1283
THOMAS C. COCHRAN & WILLIAM MILLER: The Age of Enterprise: *A Social History of Industrial America* TB/1054
W. A. DUNNING: Essays on the Civil War and Reconstruction. *Introduction by David Donald* TB/1181
W. A. DUNNING: Reconstruction, Political and Economic: 1865-1877 TB/1073
HAROLD U. FAULKNER: Politics, Reform and Expansion: 1890-1900. † *Illus.* TB/3020
HELEN HUNT JACKSON: A Century of Dishonor: *The Early Crusade for Indian Reform.* ‡ *Edited by Andrew F. Rolle* TB/3063
ALBERT D. KIRWAN: Revolt of the Rednecks: *Mississippi Politics, 1876-1925* TB/1199
ROBERT GREEN MC CLOSKEY: American Conservatism in the Age of Enterprise: 1865-1910 TB/1137
ARTHUR MANN: Yankee Reformers in the Urban Age: *Social Reform in Boston, 1880-1900* TB/1247
WHITELAW REID: After the War: *A Tour of the Southern States, 1865-1866.* ‡ *Edited by C. Vann Woodward* TB/3066
CHARLES H. SHINN: Mining Camps: *A Study in American Frontier Government.* ‡ *Edited by Rodman W. Paul* TB/3062
VERNON LANE WHARTON: The Negro in Mississippi: 1865-1890 TB/1178

American Studies: 1900 to the Present

RAY STANNARD BAKER: Following the Color Line: *American Negro Citizenship in Progressive Era.* ‡ *Illus. Edited by Dewey W. Grantham, Jr.* TB/3053
RANDOLPH S. BOURNE: War and the Intellectuals: *Collected Essays, 1915-1919.* ‡ *Edited by Carl Resek* TB/3043
A. RUSSELL BUCHANAN: The United States and World War II. † *Illus.* Vol. I TB/3044; Vol. II TB/3045
ABRAHAM CAHAN: The Rise of David Levinsky: *a documentary novel of social mobility in early twentieth century America. Intro. by John Higham* TB/1028
THOMAS C. COCHRAN: The American Business System: *A Historical Perspective, 1900-1955* TB/1080
FOSTER RHEA DULLES: America's Rise to World Power: 1898-1954. † *Illus.* TB/3021
JOHN D. HICKS: Republican Ascendancy: 1921-1933. † *Illus.* TB/3041
SIDNEY HOOK: Reason, Social Myths, and Democracy TB/1237
ROBERT HUNTER: Poverty: *Social Conscience in the Progressive Era.* ‡ *Edited by Peter d'A. Jones* TB/3065
WILLIAM L. LANGER & S. EVERETT GLEASON: The Challenge to Isolation: *The World Crisis of 1937-1940 and American Foreign Policy* Vol. I TB/3054; Vol. II TB/3055
WILLIAM E. LEUCHTENBURG: Franklin D. Roosevelt and the New Deal: 1932-1940. † *Illus.* TB/3025
ARTHUR S. LINK: Woodrow Wilson and the Progressive Era: 1910-1917. † *Illus.* TB/3023
GEORGE E. MOWRY: The Era of Theodore Roosevelt and the Birth of Modern America: 1900-1912. † *Illus.* TB/3022
RUSSEL B. NYE: Midwestern Progressive Politics: *A Historical Study of Its Origins and Development, 1870-1958* TB/1202
WILLIAM PRESTON, JR.: Aliens and Dissenters: *Federal Suppression of Radicals, 1903-1933* TB/1287
WALTER RAUSCHENBUSCH: Christianity and the Social Crisis. ‡ *Edited by Robert D. Cross* TB/3059
JACOB RIIS: The Making of an American. ‡ *Edited by Roy Lubove* TB/3070
PHILIP SELZNICK: TVA and the Grass Roots: *A Study in the Sociology of Formal Organization* TB/1230
IDA M. TARBELL: The History of the Standard Oil Company: *Briefer Version.* ‡ *Edited by David M. Chalmers* TB/3071
GEORGE B. TINDALL, Ed.: A Populist Reader ‡ TB/3069
TWELVE SOUTHERNERS: I'll Take My Stand: *The South and the Agrarian Tradition. Intro. by Louis D. Rubin, Jr., Biographical Essays by Virginia Rock* TB/1072

Anthropology

JACQUES BARZUN: Race: *A Study in Superstition. Revised Edition* TB/1172
JOSEPH B. CASAGRANDE, Ed.: In the Company of Man: *Twenty Portraits of Anthropological Informants. Illus.* TB/3047
W. E. LE GROS CLARK: The Antecedents of Man: *Intro. to Evolution of the Primates.* ° △ *Illus.* TB/559
CORA DU BOIS: The People of Alor. *New Preface by the author. Illus.* Vol. I TB/1042; Vol. II TB/1043
RAYMOND FIRTH, Ed.: Man and Culture: *An Evaluation of the Work of Bronislaw Malinowski* ¶ ° △ TB/1133
DAVID LANDY: Tropical Childhood: *Cultural Transmission and Learning in a Puerto Rican Village* ¶ TB/1235

L. S. B. LEAKEY: Adam's Ancestors: *The Evolution of Man and His Culture.* △ *Illus.* TB/1019

EDWARD BURNETT TYLOR: Religion in Primitive Culture. *Part II of "Primitive Culture."* § *Intro. by Paul Radin* TB/34

W. LLOYD WARNER: A Black Civilization: *A Study of an Australian Tribe.* ¶ *Illus.* TB/3056

Art and Art History

WALTER LOWRIE: Art in the Early Church. *Revised Edition. 452 illus.* TB/124

EMILE MÂLE: The Gothic Image: *Religious Art in France of the Thirteenth Century.* § △ *190 illus.* TB/44

MILLARD MEISS: Painting in Florence and Siena after the Black Death: *The Arts, Religion and Society in the Mid-Fourteenth Century. 169 illus.* TB/1148

ERICH NEUMANN: The Archetypal World of Henry Moore. △ *107 illus.* TB/2020

DORA & ERWIN PANOFSKY : Pandora's Box: *The Changing Aspects of a Mythical Symbol. Revised Edition. Illus.* TB/2021

ERWIN PANOFSKY: Studies in Iconology: *Humanistic Themes in the Art of the Renaissance.* △ *180 illustrations* TB/1077

ALEXANDRE PIANKOFF: The Shrines of Tut-Ankh-Amon. *Edited by N. Rambova. 117 illus.* TB/2011

JEAN SEZNEC: The Survival of the Pagan Gods: *The Mythological Tradition and Its Place in Renaissance Humanism and Art. 108 illustrations* TB/2004

OTTO VON SIMSON: The Gothic Cathedral: *Origins of Gothic Architecture and the Medieval Concept of Order.* △ *58 illus.* TB/2018

HEINRICH ZIMMER: Myth and Symbols in Indian Art and Civilization. *70 illustrations* TB/2005

Business, Economics & Economic History

REINHARD BENDIX: Work and Authority in Industry: *Ideologies of Management in the Course of Industrialization* TB/3035

GILBERT BURCK & EDITORS OF FORTUNE: The Computer Age: *And Its Potential for Management* TB/1179

THOMAS C. COCHRAN: The American Business System: *A Historical Perspective, 1900-1955* TB/1080

THOMAS C. COCHRAN: The Inner Revolution: *Essays on the Social Sciences in History* △ TB/1140

THOMAS C. COCHRAN & WILLIAM MILLER: The Age of Enterprise: *A Social History of Industrial America* TB/1054

ROBERT DAHL & CHARLES E. LINDBLOM: Politics, Economics, and Welfare: *Planning and Politico-Economic Systems Resolved into Basic Social Processes* TB/3037

PETER F. DRUCKER: The New Society: *The Anatomy of Industrial Order* △ TB/1082

EDITORS OF FORTUNE: America in the Sixties: *The Economy and the Society* TB/1015

ROBERT L. HEILBRONER: The Great Ascent: *The Struggle for Economic Development in Our Time* TB/3030

ROBERT L. HEILBRONER: The Limits of American Capitalism TB/1305

FRANK H. KNIGHT: The Economic Organization TB/1214

FRANK H. KNIGHT: Risk, Uncertainty and Profit TB/1215

ABBA P. LERNER: Everybody's Business: *Current Assumptions in Economics and Public Policy* TB/3051

ROBERT GREEN MC CLOSKEY: American Conservatism in the Age of Enterprise, 1865-1910 △ TB/1137

PAUL MANTOUX: The Industrial Revolution in the Eighteenth Century: *The Beginnings of the Modern Factory System in England* ° △ TB/1079

WILLIAM MILLER, Ed.: Men in Business: *Essays on the Historical Role of the Entrepreneur* TB/1081

RICHARD B. MORRIS: Government and Labor in Early America △ TB/1244

HERBERT SIMON: The Shape of Automation: *For Men and Management* TB/1245

PERRIN STRYKER: The Character of the Executive: *Eleven Studies in Managerial Qualities* TB/1041

Education

JACQUES BARZUN: The House of Intellect △ TB/1051

RICHARD M. JONES, Ed.: Contemporary Educational Psychology: *Selected Readings* TB/1292

CLARK KERR: The Uses of the University TB/1264

JOHN U. NEF: Cultural Foundations of Industrial Civilization △ TB/1024

Historiography & Philosophy of History

JACOB BURCKHARDT: On History and Historians. △ *Introduction by H. R. Trevor-Roper* TB/1216

WILHELM DILTHEY: Pattern and Meaning in History: *Thoughts on History and Society.* ° △ *Edited with an Introduction by H. P. Rickman* TB/1075

J. H. HEXTER: Reappraisals in History: *New Views on History & Society in Early Modern Europe* △ TB/1100

H. STUART HUGHES: History as Art and as Science: *Twin Vistas on the Past* TB/1207

RAYMOND KLIBANSKY & H. J. PATON, Eds.: Philosophy and History: *The Ernst Cassirer Festschrift. Illus.* TB/1115

ARNALDO MOMIGLIANO: Studies in Historiography ° △ TB/1283

GEORGE H. NADEL, Ed.: Studies in the Philosophy of History: *Selected Essays from* History and Theory TB/1208

JOSE ORTEGA Y GASSET: The Modern Theme. *Introduction by Jose Ferrater Mora* TB/1038

KARL R. POPPER: The Open Society and Its Enemies △
Vol. I: The Spell of Plato TB/1101
Vol. II: The High Tide of Prophecy: Hegel, Marx and the Aftermath TB/1102

KARL R. POPPER: The Poverty of Historicism ° △ TB/1126

G. J. RENIER: History: Its Purpose and Method △ TB/1209

W. H. WALSH: Philosophy of History: *An Introduction* △ TB/1020

History: General

WOLFGANG FRANKE: China and the West. *Trans by R. A. Wilson* TB/1326

L. CARRINGTON GOODRICH: A Short History of the Chinese People. △ *Illus.* TB/3015

DAN N. JACOBS & HANS H. BAERWALD: Chinese Communism: *Selected Documents* TB/3031

BERNARD LEWIS: The Arabs in History △ TB/1029

BERNARD LEWIS: The Middle East and the West ° △ TB/1274

History: Ancient

A. ANDREWES: The Greek Tyrants △ TB/1103

ADOLF ERMAN, Ed. The Ancient Egyptians: *A Sourcebook of Their Writings. New material and Introduction by William Kelly Simpson* TB/1233

MICHAEL GRANT: Ancient History ° △ TB/1190

SAMUEL NOAH KRAMER: Sumerian Mythology TB/1055

NAPHTALI LEWIS & MEYER REINHOLD, Eds.: Roman Civilization. *Sourcebook I: The Republic* TB/1231

NAPHTALI LEWIS & MEYER REINHOLD, Eds.: Roman Civilization. *Sourcebook II: The Empire* TB/1232

History: Medieval

P. BOISSONNADE: Life and Work in Medieval Europe: *The Evolution of the Medieval Economy, the 5th to the 15th Century.* ° △ *Preface by Lynn White, Jr.* TB/1141

HELEN CAM: England before Elizabeth △ TB/1026

NORMAN COHN: The Pursuit of the Millennium: *Revolutionary Messianism in Medieval and Reformation Europe* △ TB/1037

G. G. COULTON: Medieval Village, Manor, and Monastery TB/1022

CHRISTOPHER DAWSON, Ed.: Mission to Asia: *Narratives and Letters of the Franciscan Missionaries in Mongolia and China in the 13th and 14th Centuries* △ TB/315

HEINRICH FICHTENAU: The Carolingian Empire: *The Age of Charlemagne* △ TB/1142

GALBERT OF BRUGES: The Murder of Charles the Good. *Trans. with Intro. by James Bruce Ross* TB/1311

F. L. GANSHOF: Feudalism △ TB/1058

DENO GEANAKOPLOS: Byzantine East and Latin West: *Two Worlds of Christendom in the Middle Ages and Renaissance* TB/1265

EDWARD GIBBON: The Triumph of Christendom in the Roman Empire *(Chaps. XV-XX of "Decline and Fall," J. B. Bury edition).* § △ *Illus.* TB/46

W. O. HASSALL, Ed.: Medieval England: *As Viewed by Contemporaries* △ TB/1205

DENYS HAY: Europe: The Emergence of an Idea TB/1275

DENYS HAY: The Medieval Centuries ° △ TB/1192

J. M. HUSSEY: The Byzantine World △ TB/1057

ROBERT LATOUCHE: The Birth of Western Economy: *Economic Aspects of the Dark Ages.* ° △ *Intro. by Philip Grierson* TB/1290

FERDINAND LOT: The End of the Ancient World and the Beginnings of the Middle Ages. *Introduction by Glanville Downey* TB/1044

ACHILLE LUCHAIRE: Social France at the Time of Philip Augustus. *New Intro. by John W. Baldwin* TB/1314

MARSILIUS OF PADUA: The Defender of the Peace. *Trans. with Intro. by Alan Gewirth* TB/1310

G. MOLLAT: The Popes at Avignon: 1305-1378 △ TB/308

CHARLES PETIT-DUTAILLIS: The Feudal Monarchy in France and England: *From the Tenth to the Thirteenth Century* ° △ TB/1165

HENRI PIRENNE: Early Democracies in the Low Countries: *Urban Society and Political Conflict in the Middle Ages and the Renaissance. Introduction by John H. Mundy* TB/1110

STEVEN RUNCIMAN: A History of the Crusades. △
Volume I: *The First Crusade and the Foundation of the Kingdom of Jerusalem. Illus.* TB/1143
Volume II: *The Kingdom of Jerusalem and the Frankish East, 1100-1187. Illus.* TB/1243
Volume III: *The Kingdom of Acre and the Later Crusades* TB/1298

SULPICIUS SEVERUS et al.: The Western Fathers: *Being the Lives of Martin of Tours, Ambrose, Augustine of Hippo, Honoratus of Arles and Germanus of Auxerre.* △ *Edited and trans. by F. O. Hoare* TB/309

J. M. WALLACE-HADRILL: The Barbarian West: *The Early Middle Ages, A.D. 400-1000* △ TB/1061

History: Renaissance & Reformation

JACOB BURCKHARDT: The Civilization of the Renaissance in Italy. △ *Intro. by Benjamin Nelson & Charles Trinkaus. Illus.* Vol. I TB/40; Vol. II TB/41

JOHN CALVIN & JACOPO SADOLETO: A Reformation Debate. *Edited by John C. Olin* TB/1239

ERNST CASSIRER: The Individual and the Cosmos in Renaissance Philosophy. △ *Translated with an Introduction by Mario Domandi* TB/1097

FEDERICO CHABOD: Machiavelli and the Renaissance △ TB/1193

EDWARD P. CHEYNEY: The Dawn of a New Era, 1250-1453. * *Illus.* TB/3002

G. CONSTANT: The Reformation in England: *The English Schism, Henry VIII, 1509-1547* △ TB/314

R. TREVOR DAVIES: The Golden Century of Spain, 1501-1621 ° △ TB/1194

G. R. ELTON: Reformation Europe, 1517-1559 ** ° △ TB/1270

DESIDERIUS ERASMUS: Christian Humanism and the Reformation: *Selected Writings. Edited and translated by John C. Olin* TB/1166

WALLACE K. FERGUSON et al.: Facets of the Renaissance TB/1098

WALLACE K. FERGUSON et al.: The Renaissance: *Six Essays. Illus.* TB/1084

JOHN NEVILLE FIGGIS: The Divine Right of Kings. *Introduction by G. R. Elton* TB/1191

JOHN NEVILLE FIGGIS: Political Thought from Gerson to Grotius: 1414-1625: *Seven Studies. Introduction by Garrett Mattingly* TB/1032

MYRON P. GILMORE: The World of Humanism, 1453-1517. * *Illus.* TB/3003

FRANCESCO GUICCIARDINI: Maxims and Reflections of a Renaissance Statesman *(Ricordi). Trans. by Mario Domandi. Intro. by Nicolai Rubinstein* TB/1160

J. H. HEXTER: More's Utopia: *The Biography of an Idea. New Epilogue by the Author* TB/1195

HAJO HOLBORN: Ulrich von Hutten and the German Reformation TB/1238

JOHAN HUIZINGA: Erasmus and the Age of Reformation. △ *Illus.* TB/19

JOEL HURSTFIELD: The Elizabethan Nation △ TB/1312

JOEL HURSTFIELD, Ed.: The Reformation Crisis △ TB/1267

ULRICH VON HUTTEN et al.: On the Eve of the Reformation: *"Letters of Obscure Men." Introduction by Hajo Holborn* TB/1124

PAUL O. KRISTELLER: Renaissance Thought: *The Classic, Scholastic, and Humanist Strains* TB/1048

PAUL O. KRISTELLER: Renaissance Thought II: *Papers on Humanism and the Arts* TB/1163

NICCOLÒ MACHIAVELLI: History of Florence and of the Affairs of Italy: *from the earliest times to the death of Lorenzo the Magnificent.* △ *Introduction by Felix Gilbert* TB/1027

ALFRED VON MARTIN: Sociology of the Renaissance. *Introduction by Wallace K. Ferguson* TB/1099

GARRETT MATTINGLY et al.: Renaissance Profiles. △ *Edited by J. H. Plumb* TB/1162

MILLARD MEISS: Painting in Florence and Siena after the Black Death: *The Arts, Religion and Society in the Mid-Fourteenth Century.* △ *169 illus.* TB/1148

J. E. NEALE: The Age of Catherine de Medici ° △ TB/1085

ERWIN PANOFSKY: Studies in Iconology: *Humanistic Themes in the Art of the Renaissance.* △ *180 illustrations* TB/1077

J. H. PARRY: The Establishment of the European Hegemony: 1415-1715: *Trade and Exploration in the Age of the Renaissance* △ TB/1045

BUONACCORSO PITTI & GREGORIO DATI: Two Memoirs of Renaissance Florence: *The Diaries of Buonaccorso Pitti and Gregorio Dati. Ed. with an Intro. by Gene Brucker. Trans. by Julia Martines* TB/1333

J. H. PLUMB: The Italian Renaissance: *A Concise Survey of Its History and Culture* △ TB/1161

A. F. POLLARD: Henry VIII. ° △ *Introduction by A. G. Dickens* TB/1249

A. F. POLLARD: Wolsey. ° △ *Introduction by A. G. Dickens* TB/1248

CECIL ROTH: The Jews in the Renaissance. *Illus.* TB/834

A. L. ROWSE: The Expansion of Elizabethan England. ° △ *Illus.* TB/1220

GORDON RUPP: Luther's Progress to the Diet of Worms ° △ TB/120

FERDINAND SCHEVILL: The Medici. *Illus.* TB/1010

FERDINAND SCHEVILL: Medieval and Renaissance Florence. *Illus.* Volume I: *Medieval Florence* TB/1090
Volume II: *The Coming of Humanism and the Age of the Medici* TB/1091

R. H. TAWNEY: The Agrarian Problem in the Sixteenth Century. *New Intro. by Lawrence Stone* TB/1315

G. M. TREVELYAN: England in the Age of Wycliffe, 1368-1520 ° △ TB/1112

VESPASIANO: Renaissance Princes, Popes, and Prelates: *The Vespasiano Memoirs: Lives of Illustrious Men of the XVth Century. Intro. by Myron P. Gilmore* TB/1111

History: Modern European

FREDERICK B. ARTZ: Reaction and Revolution, 1815-1832. * *Illus.* TB/3034

MAX BELOFF: The Age of Absolutism, 1660-1815 △ TB/1062

ROBERT C. BINKLEY: Realism and Nationalism, 1852-1871. * *Illus.* TB/3038

EUGENE C. BLACK, Ed.: European Political History, 1815-1870: *Aspects of Liberalism* TB/1331

ASA BRIGGS: The Making of Modern England, 1784-1867: *The Age of Improvement* ° △ TB/1203

CRANE BRINTON: A Decade of Revolution, 1789-1799. * *Illus.* TB/3018

D. W. BROGAN: The Development of Modern France. ° △ Volume I: *From the Fall of the Empire to the Dreyfus Affair* TB/1184
Volume II: *The Shadow of War, World War I, Between the Two Wars. New Introduction by the Author* TB/1185

J. BRONOWSKI & BRUCE MAZLISH: The Western Intellectual Tradition: *From Leonardo to Hegel* △ TB/3001

GEOFFREY BRUUN: Europe and the French Imperium, 1799-1814. * Illus. TB/3033

ALAN BULLOCK: Hitler, A Study in Tyranny. ° △ *Illus.* TB/1123

E. H. CARR: German-Soviet Relations Between the Two World Wars, 1919-1939 TB/1278

E. H. CARR: International Relations Between the Two World Wars, 1919-1939 ° △ TB/1279

E. H. CARR: The Twenty Years' Crisis, 1919-1939: *An Introduction to the Study of International Relations* ° △ TB/1122

GORDON A. CRAIG: From Bismarck to Adenauer: *Aspects of German Statecraft. Revised Edition* TB/1171

DENIS DIDEROT: The Encyclopedia: *Selections. Ed. and trans. by Stephen Gendzier* TB/1299

WALTER L. DORN: Competition for Empire, 1740-1763. * *Illus.* TB/3032

FRANKLIN L. FORD: Robe and Sword: *The Regrouping of the French Aristocracy after Louis XIV* TB/1217

CARL J. FRIEDRICH: The Age of the Baroque, 1610-1660. * *Illus.* TB/3004

RENÉ FUELOEP-MILLER: The Mind and Face of Bolshevism: *An Examination of Cultural Life in Soviet Russia. New Epilogue by the Author* TB/1188

M. DOROTHY GEORGE: London Life in the Eighteenth Century △ TB/1182

LEO GERSHOY: From Despotism to Revolution, 1763-1789. * *Illus.* TB/3017

C. C. GILLISPIE: Genesis and Geology: *The Decades before Darwin* § TB/51

ALBERT GOODWIN, Ed.: The European Nobility in the Eighteenth Century △ TB/1313

ALBERT GOODWIN: The French Revolution △ TB/1064

ALBERT GUÉRARD: France in the Classical Age: *The Life and Death of an Ideal* △ TB/1183

CARLTON J. H. HAYES: A Generation of Materialism, 1871-1900. * *Illus.* TB/3039

J. H. HEXTER: Reappraisals in History: *New Views on History and Society in Early Modern Europe* △ TB/1100

STANLEY HOFFMANN et al.: In Search of France: *The Economy, Society and Political System in the Twentieth Century* TB/1219

A. R. HUMPHREYS: The Augustan World: *Society, Thought, & Letters in 18th Century England* ° △ TB/1105

DAN N. JACOBS, Ed.: The New Communist Manifesto *and Related Documents. Third edition, revised* TB/1078

LIONEL KOCHAN: The Struggle for Germany: *1914-45* TB/1304

HANS KOHN: The Mind of Germany: *The Education of a Nation* △ TB/1204

HANS KOHN, Ed.: The Mind of Modern Russia: *Historical and Political Thought of Russia's Great Age* TB/1065

WALTER LAQUEUR & GEORGE L. MOSSE, Eds.: Education and Social Structure in the 20th Century. ° △ *Vol. 6 of the* Journal of Contemporary History TB/1339

WALTER LAQUEUR & GEORGE L. MOSSE, Eds.: International Fascism, 1920-1945. ° △ *Volume 1 of* Journal of Contemporary History TB/1276

WALTER LAQUEUR & GEORGE L. MOSSE, Eds.: The Left-Wing Intellectuals between the Wars 1919-1939. ° △ *Volume 2 of* Journal of Contemporary History TB/1286

WALTER LAQUEUR & GEORGE L. MOSSE, Eds.: Literature and Politics in the 20th Century. ° △ *Vol. 5 of the* Journal of Contemporary History TB/1328

WALTER LAQUEUR & GEORGE L. MOSSE, Eds.: The New History: *Trends in Historical Research and Writing since World War II.* ° △ *Vol. 4 of the* Journal of Conporary History TB/1327

WALTER LAQUEUR & GEORGE L. MOSSE, Eds.: 1914: *The Coming of the First World War.* ° △ *Volume 3 of* Journal of Contemporary History TB/1306

FRANK E. MANUEL: The Prophets of Paris: *Turgot, Condorcet, Saint-Simon, Fourier, and Comte* TB/1218

KINGSLEY MARTIN: French Liberal Thought in the Eighteenth Century: *A Study of Political Ideas from Bayle to Condorcet* TB/1114

ROBERT K. MERTON: Science, Technology and Society in Seventeenth Century England ¶ *New Intro. by the Author* TB/1324

L. B. NAMIER: Facing East: *Essays on Germany, the Balkans, and Russia in the 20th Century* △ TB/1280

L. B. NAMIER: Personalities and Powers: *Selected Essays* △ TB/1186

L. B. NAMIER: Vanished Supremacies: *Essays on European History, 1812-1918* ° TB/1088

NAPOLEON III: Napoleonic Ideas: *Des Idées Napoléoniennes, par le Prince Napoléon-Louis Bonaparte. Ed. by Brison D. Gooch* TB/1336

FRANZ NEUMANN: Behemoth: *The Structure and Practice of National Socialism, 1933-1944* TB/1289

FREDERICK L. NUSSBAUM: The Triumph of Science and Reason, 1660-1685. * *Illus.* TB/3009

DAVID OGG: Europe of the Ancien Régime, 1715-1783 ** ° △ TB/1271

JOHN PLAMENATZ: German Marxism and Russian Communism. ° △ *New Preface by the Author* TB/1189

RAYMOND W. POSTGATE, Ed.: Revolution from 1789 to 1906: *Selected Documents* TB/1063

PENFIELD ROBERTS: The Quest for Security, 1715-1740. * *Illus.* TB/3016

PRISCILLA ROBERTSON: Revolutions of 1848: *A Social History* TB/1025

GEORGE RUDÉ: Revolutionary Europe, 1783-1815 ** ° △ TB/1272

LOUIS, DUC DE SAINT-SIMON: Versailles, The Court, and Louis XIV. ° △ *Introductory Note by Peter Gay* TB/1250

HUGH SETON-WATSON: Eastern Europe Between the Wars, 1918-1941 TB/1330

ALBERT SOREL: Europe Under the Old Regime. *Translated by Francis H. Herrick* TB/1121

N. N. SUKHANOV: The Russian Revolution, 1917: *Eyewitness Account.* △ *Edited by Joel Carmichael*
Vol. I TB/1066; Vol. II TB/1067

A. J. P. TAYLOR: From Napoleon to Lenin: *Historical Essays* ° △ TB/1268

A. J. P. TAYLOR: The Habsburg Monarchy, 1809-1918: *A History of the Austrian Empire and Austria-Hungary* ° △ TB/1187

G. M. TREVELYAN: British History in the Nineteenth Century and After: *1782-1919.* ° △ *Second Edition* TB/1251

H. R. TREVOR-ROPER: Historical Essays ° △ TB/1269

ELIZABETH WISKEMANN: Europe of the Dictators, 1919-1945 ** ° △ TB/1273

JOHN B. WOLF: The Emergence of the Great Powers, 1685-1715. * *Illus.* TB/3010

JOHN B. WOLF: France: 1814-1919: *The Rise of a Liberal-Democratic Society* TB/3019

Intellectual History & History of Ideas

HERSCHEL BAKER: The Image of Man: *A Study of the Idea of Human Dignity in Classical Antiquity, the Middle Ages, and the Renaissance* TB/1047

R. R. BOLGAR: The Classical Heritage and Its Beneficiaries: *From the Carolingian Age to the End of the Renaissance* △ TB/1125

RANDOLPH S. BOURNE: War and the Intellectuals: *Collected Essays, 1915-1919.* △ ‡ *Edited by Carl Resek* TB/3043

J. BRONOWSKI & BRUCE MAZLISH: The Western Intellectual Tradition: *From Leonardo to Hegel* △ TB/3001

ERNST CASSIRER: The Individual and the Cosmos in Renaissance Philosophy. △ *Translated with an Introduction by Mario Domandi* TB/1097

NORMAN COHN: The Pursuit of the Millennium: *Revolutionary Messianism in Medieval and Reformation Europe* △ TB/1037

C. C. GILLISPIE: Genesis and Geology: *The Decades before Darwin* § TB/51

G. RACHEL LEVY: Religious Conceptions of the Stone Age *and Their Influence upon European Thought.* △ *Illus. Introduction by Henri Frankfort* TB/106

ARTHUR O. LOVEJOY: The Great Chain of Being: *A Study of the History of an Idea* TB/1009

FRANK E. MANUEL: The Prophets of Paris: *Turgot, Condorcet, Saint-Simon, Fourier, and Comte* △ TB/1218

PERRY MILLER & T. H. JOHNSON, Editors: The Puritans: *A Sourcebook of Their Writings* Vol. I TB/1093; Vol. II TB/1094

RALPH BARTON PERRY: The Thought and Character of William James: *Briefer Version* TB/1156

GEORG SIMMEL et al.: Essays on Sociology, Philosophy, and Aesthetics. ¶ *Edited by Kurt H. Wolff* TB/1234

BRUNO SNELL: The Discovery of the Mind: *The Greek Origins of European Thought* △ TB/1018

PAGET TOYNBEE: Dante Alighieri: *His Life and Works. Edited with Intro. by Charles S. Singleton* △ TB/1206

W. WARREN WAGAR, Ed.: European Intellectual History since Darwin and Marx TB/1297

PHILIP P. WIENER: Evolution and the Founders of Pragmatism. △ *Foreword by John Dewey* TB/1212

BASIL WILLEY: Nineteenth Century Studies: *Coleridge to Matthew Arnold* ° △ TB/1261

BASIL WILLEY: More Nineteenth Century Studies: *A Group of Honest Doubters* ° △ TB/1262

Law

EDWARD S. CORWIN: American Constitutional History: *Essays edited by Alpheus T. Mason & Gerald Garvey* TB/1136

ROBERT H. JACKSON: The Supreme Court in the American System of Government TB/1106

LEONARD W. LEVY, Ed.: American Constitutional Law: *Historical Essays* TB/1285

LEONARD W. LEVY: Freedom of Speech and Press in Early American History: *Legacy of Suppression* TB/1109

LEONARD W. LEVY, Ed.: Judicial Review and the Supreme Court TB/1296

LEONARD W. LEVY: The Law of the Commonwealth and Chief Justice Shaw TB/1309

RICHARD B. MORRIS: Fair Trial: *Fourteen Who Stood Accused, from Anne Hutchinson to Alger Hiss. New Preface by the Author.* TB/1335

Literature, Poetry, The Novel & Criticism

JAMES BAIRD: Ishmael: *The Art of Melville in the Contexts of International Primitivism* TB/1023

JACQUES BARZUN: The House of Intellect △ TB/1051

W. J. BATE: From Classic to Romantic: *Premises of Taste in Eighteenth Century England* TB/1036

RACHEL BESPALOFF: On the Iliad TB/2006

JAMES BOSWELL: The Life of Dr. Johnson & The Journal of a Tour to the Hebrides with Samuel Johnson LL.D.: *Selections.* ° △ *Edited by F. V. Morley. Illus. by Ernest Shepard* TB/1254

ERNST R. CURTIUS: European Literature and the Latin Middle Ages △ TB/2015

ADOLF ERMAN, Ed.: The Ancient Egyptians: *A Sourcebook of Their Writings. New Material and Introduction by William Kelly Simpson* TB/1233

ALFRED HARBAGE: As They Liked It: *A Study of Shakespeare's Moral Artistry* TB/1035

STANLEY R. HOPPER, Ed: Spiritual Problems in Contemporary Literature § TB/21

A. R. HUMPHREYS: The Augustan World: *Society, Thought and Letters in 18th Century England* ° △ TB/1105

ARNOLD KETTLE: An Introduction to the English Novel. △
Volume I: *Defoe to George Eliot* TB/1011
Volume II: *Henry James to the Present* TB/1012

RICHMOND LATTIMORE: The Poetry of Greek Tragedy △ TB/1257

J. B. LEISHMAN: The Monarch of Wit: *An Analytical and Comparative Study of the Poetry of John Donne* ° △ TB/1258

J. B. LEISHMAN: Themes and Variations in Shakespeare's Sonnets ° △ TB/1259

ROGER SHERMAN LOOMIS: The Development of Arthurian Romance △ TB/1167

JOHN STUART MILL: On Bentham and Coleridge. △ *Introduction by F. R. Leavis* TB/1070

KENNETH B. MURDOCK: Literature and Theology in Colonial New England TB/99

SAMUEL PEPYS: The Diary of Samuel Pepys. ° *Edited by O. F. Morshead. Illus. by Ernest Shepard* TB/1007

ST.-JOHN PERSE: Seamarks TB/2002

V. DE S. PINTO: Crisis in English Poetry, 1880-1940 ° TB/1260

ROBERT PREYER, Ed.: Victorian Literature TB/1302

GEORGE SANTAYANA: Interpretations of Poetry and Religion § TB/9

C. K. STEAD: The New Poetic: *Yeats to Eliot* △ TB/1263

HEINRICH STRAUMANN: American Literature in the Twentieth Century. △ *Third Edition, Revised* TB/1168

PAGET TOYNBEE: Dante Alighieri: *His Life and Works. Edited with Intro. by Charles S. Singleton* TB/1206

DOROTHY VAN GHENT: The English Novel: *Form and Function* TB/1050

BASIL WILLEY: Nineteenth Century Studies: *Coleridge to Matthew Arnold* △ TB/1261

BASIL WILLEY: More Nineteenth Century Studies: *A Group of Honest Doubters* ° △ TB/1262

RAYMOND WILLIAMS: Culture and Society, 1780-1950 ° △ TB/1252

RAYMOND WILLIAMS: The Long Revolution. ° △ *Revised Edition* TB/1253

MORTON DAUWEN ZABEL, Editor: Literary Opinion in America Vol. I TB/3013; Vol. II TB/3014

Myth, Symbol & Folklore

MIRCEA ELIADE: Cosmos and History: *The Myth of the Eternal Return* § △ TB/2050

MIRCEA ELIADE: Rites and Symbols of Initiation: *The Mysteries of Birth and Rebirth* § △ TB/1236

THEODOR H. GASTER: Thespis: *Ritual, Myth and Drama in the Ancient Near East* △ TB/1281

C. G. JUNG & C. KERÉNYI: Essays on a Science of Mythology: *The Myths of the Divine Child and the Divine Maiden* TB/2014
DORA & ERWIN PANOFSKY: Pandora's Box: *The Changing Aspects of a Mythical Symbol.* △ *Revised edition. Illus.* TB/2021
ERWIN PANOFSKY: Studies in Iconology: *Humanistic Themes in the Art of the Renaissance.* △ *180 illustrations* TB/1077
JEAN SEZNEC: The Survival of the Pagan Gods: *The Mythological Tradition and its Place in Renaissance Humanism and Art.* △ *108 illustrations* TB/2004
HELLMUT WILHELM: Change: *Eight Lectures on the I Ching* △ TB/2019
HEINRICH ZIMMER: Myths and Symbols in Indian Art and Civilization. △ *70 illustrations* TB/2005

Philosophy

G. E. M. ANSCOMBE: An Introduction to Wittgenstein's Tractatus. ° △ *Second Edition, Revised* TB/1210
HENRI BERGSON: Time and Free Will: *An Essay on the Immediate Data of Consciousness* ° △ TB/1021
H. J. BLACKHAM: Six Existentialist Thinkers: *Kierkegaard, Nietzsche, Jaspers, Marcel, Heidegger, Sartre* ° △ TB/1002
CRANE BRINTON: Nietzsche. *New Preface, Bibliography and Epilogue by the Author* TB/1197
MARTIN BUBER: The Knowledge of Man. △ *Ed. with an Intro. by Maurice Friedman. Trans. by Maurice Friedman and Ronald Gregor Smith* TB/135
ERNST CASSIRER: The Individual and the Cosmos in Renaissance Philosophy. △ *Translated with an Introduction by Mario Domandi* TB/1097
ERNST CASSIRER: Rousseau, Kant and Goethe. *Introduction by Peter Gay* TB/1092
FREDERICK COPLESTON: Medieval Philosophy ° △ TB/376
F. M. CORNFORD: Principium Sapientiae: *A Study of the Origins of Greek Philosophical Thought. Edited by W. K. C. Guthrie* TB/1213
F. M. CORNFORD: From Religion to Philosophy: *A Study in the Origins of Western Speculation* § TB/20
WILFRID DESAN: The Tragic Finale: *An Essay on the Philosophy of Jean-Paul Sartre* TB/1030
A. P. D'ENTRÈVES: Natural Law: *An Historical Survey* △ TB/1223
MARVIN FARBER: The Aims of Phenomenology: *The Motives, Methods, and Impact of Husserl's Thought* TB/1291
MARVIN FARBER: Phenomenology and Existence: *Towards a Philosophy within Nature* TB/1295
HERBERT FINGARETTE: The Self in Transformation: *Psychoanalysis, Philosophy and the Life of the Spirit* ¶ TB/1177
PAUL FRIEDLÄNDER: Plato: *An Introduction* △ TB/2017
J. GLENN GRAY: The Warriors: *Reflections on Men in Battle. Intro. by Hannah Arendt* TB/1294
WILLIAM CHASE GREENE: Moira: *Fate, Good, and Evil in Greek Thought* TB/1104
W. K. C. GUTHRIE: The Greek Philosophers: *From Thales to Aristotle* ° △ TB/1008
G. W. F. HEGEL: The Phenomenology of Mind ° △ TB/1303
F. H. HEINEMANN: Existentialism and the Modern Predicament △ TB/28
ISAAC HUSIK: A History of Medieval Jewish Philosophy JP/3
EDMUND HUSSERL: Phenomenology and the Crisis of Philosophy. *Translated with an Introduction by Quentin Lauer* TB/1170
IMMANUEL KANT: The Doctrine of Virtue, *being Part II of the Metaphysic of Morals. Trans. with Notes & Intro. by Mary J. Gregor. Foreword by H. J. Paton* TB/110
IMMANUEL KANT: Groundwork of the Metaphysic of Morals. *Trans. & analyzed by H. J. Paton* TB/1159
IMMANUEL KANT: Lectures on Ethics. § △ *Introduction by Lewis W. Beck* TB/105
IMMANUEL KANT: Religion Within the Limits of Reason Alone. § *Intro. by T. M. Greene & J. Silber* TB/67
QUENTIN LAUER: Phenomenology: *Its Genesis and Prospect* TB/1169
MAURICE MANDELBAUM: The Problem of Historical Knowledge: *An Answer to Relativism. New Preface by the Author* TB/1338
GABRIEL MARCEL: Being and Having: *An Existential Diary.* △ *Intro. by James Collins* TB/310
GEORGE A. MORGAN: What Nietzsche Means TB/1198
H. J. PATON: The Categorical Imperative: *A Study in Kant's Moral Philosophy* △ TB/1325
PHILO, SAADYA GAON, & JEHUDA HALEVI: Three Jewish Philosophers. *Ed. by Hans Lewy, Alexander Altmann, & Isaak Heinemann* TB/813
MICHAEL POLANYI: Personal Knowledge: *Towards a Post-Critical Philosophy* △ TB/1158
WILLARD VAN ORMAN QUINE: Elementary Logic: *Revised Edition* TB/577
WILLARD VAN ORMAN QUINE: From a Logical Point of View: *Logico-Philosophical Essays* TB/566
BERTRAND RUSSELL et al.: The Philosophy of Bertrand Russell. *Edited by Paul Arthur Schilpp* Vol. I TB/1095; Vol. II TB/1096
L. S. STEBBING: A Modern Introduction to Logic △ TB/538
ALFRED NORTH WHITEHEAD: Process and Reality: *An Essay in Cosmology* △ TB/1033
PHILIP P. WIENER: Evolution and the Founders of Pragmatism. *Foreword by John Dewey* TB/1212
WILHELM WINDELBAND: A History of Philosophy
Vol. I: *Greek, Roman, Medieval* TB/38
Vol. II: *Renaissance, Enlightenment, Modern* TB/39
LUDWIG WITTGENSTEIN: The Blue and Brown Books ° TB/1211

Political Science & Government

JEREMY BENTHAM: The Handbook of Political Fallacies: *Introduction by Crane Brinton* TB/1069
C. E. BLACK: The Dynamics of Modernization: *A Study in Comparative History* TB/1321
KENNETH E. BOULDING: Conflict and Defense: *A General Theory* TB/3024
CRANE BRINTON: English Political Thought in the Nineteenth Century TB/1071
ROBERT CONQUEST: Power and Policy in the USSR: *The Study of Soviet Dynastics* △ TB/1307
EDWARD S. CORWIN: American Constitutional History: *Essays edited by Alpheus T. Mason and Gerald Garvey* TB/1136
ROBERT DAHL & CHARLES E. LINDBLOM: Politics, Economics, and Welfare: *Planning and Politico-Economic Systems Resolved into Basic Social Processes* TB/3037
JOHN NEVILLE FIGGIS: The Divine Right of Kings. *Introduction by G. R. Elton* TB/1191
JOHN NEVILLE FIGGIS: Political Thought from Gerson to Grotius: 1414-1625: *Seven Studies. Introduction by Garrett Mattingly* TB/1032
F. L. GANSHOF: Feudalism △ TB/1058
G. P. GOOCH: English Democratic Ideas in the Seventeenth Century TB/1006
J. H. HEXTER: More's Utopia: *The Biography of an Idea. New Epilogue by the Author* TB/1195
SIDNEY HOOK: Reason, Social Myths and Democracy △ TB/1237
ROBERT H. JACKSON: The Supreme Court in the American System of Government △ TB/1106
DAN N. JACOBS, Ed.: The New Communist Manifesto *and Related Documents. Third Edition, Revised* TB/1078
DAN N. JACOBS & HANS BAERWALD, Eds.: Chinese Communism: *Selected Documents* TB/3031

HANS KOHN: Political Ideologies of the 20th Century TB/1277

ROY C. MACRIDIS, Ed.: Political Parties: *Contemporary Trends and Ideas* TB/1322

ROBERT GREEN MC CLOSKEY: American Conservatism in the Age of Enterprise, 1865-1910 TB/1137

KINGSLEY MARTIN: French Liberal Thought in the Eighteenth Century: *Political Ideas from Bayle to Condorcet* △ TB/1114

ROBERTO MICHELS: First Lectures in Political Sociology. *Edited by Alfred de Grazia* ¶ ° TB/1224

JOHN STUART MILL: On Bentham and Coleridge. △ *Introduction by F. R. Leavis* TB/1070

BARRINGTON MOORE, JR.: Political Power and Social Theory: *Seven Studies* ¶ TB/1221

BARRINGTON MOORE, JR.: Soviet Politics—The Dilemma of Power: *The Role of Ideas in Social Change* ¶ TB/1222

BARRINGTON MOORE, JR.: Terror and Progress—USSR: *Some Sources of Change and Stability in the Soviet Dictatorship* ¶ TB/1266

JOHN B. MORRALL: Political Thought in Medieval Times △ TB/1076

JOHN PLAMENATZ: German Marxism and Russian Communism. ° △ *New Preface by the Author* TB/1189

KARL R. POPPER: The Open Society and Its Enemies △
Vol. I: *The Spell of Plato* TB/1101
Vol. II: *The High Tide of Prophecy: Hegel, Marx and the Aftermath* TB/1102

JOHN P. ROCHE, Ed.: American Political Thought: *From Jefferson to Progressivism* TB/1332

HENRI DE SAINT-SIMON: Social Organization, The Science of Man, and Other Writings. *Edited and Translated by Felix Markham* TB/1152

CHARLES I. SCHOTTLAND, Ed.: The Welfare State TB/1323

JOSEPH A. SCHUMPETER: Capitalism, Socialism and Democracy △ TB/3008

BENJAMIN I. SCHWARTZ: Chinese Communism and the Rise of Mao TB/1308

CHARLES H. SHINN: Mining Camps: *A Study in American Frontier Government.* ‡ *Edited by Rodman W. Paul* TB/3062

PETER WOLL, Ed.: Public Administration and Policy: *Selected Essays* TB/1284

Psychology

ALFRED ADLER: The Individual Psychology of Alfred Adler. △ *Edited by Heinz L. and Rowena R. Ansbacher* TB/1154

ALFRED ADLER: Problems of Neurosis. *Introduction by Heinz L. Ansbacher* TB/1145

ARTHUR BURTON & ROBERT E. HARRIS, Eds.: Clinical Studies of Personality
Vol. I TB/3075; Vol. II TB/3076

HADLEY CANTRIL: The Invasion from Mars: *A Study in the Psychology of Panic* ¶ TB/1282

HERBERT FINGARETTE: The Self in Transformation: *Psychoanalysis, Philosophy and the Life of the Spirit* ¶ TB/1177

SIGMUND FREUD: On Creativity and the Unconscious: *Papers on the Psychology of Art, Literature, Love, Religion.* § △ *Intro. by Benjamin Nelson* TB/45

C. JUDSON HERRICK: The Evolution of Human Nature TB/545

WILLIAM JAMES: Psychology: *The Briefer Course. Edited with an Intro. by Gordon Allport* TB/1034

C. G. JUNG: Psychological Reflections △ TB/2001

C. G. JUNG: Symbols of Transformation: *An Analysis of the Prelude to a Case of Schizophrenia.* △ *Illus.*
Vol. I TB/2009; Vol. II TB/2010

C. G. JUNG & C. KERÉNYI: Essays on a Science of Mythology: *The Myths of the Divine Child and the Divine Maiden* TB/2014

KARL MENNINGER: Theory of Psychoanalytic Technique TB/1144

ERICH NEUMANN: Amor and Psyche: *The Psychic Development of the Feminine* △ TB/2012

ERICH NEUMANN: The Archetypal World of Henry Moore. △ *107 illus.* TB/2020

ERICH NEUMANN : The Origins and History of Consciousness △ Vol. I *Illus.* TB/2007; Vol. II TB/2008

RALPH BARTON PERRY: The Thought and Character of William James: *Briefer Version* TB/1156

JOHN H. SCHAAR: Escape from Authority: *The Perspectives of Erich Fromm* TB/1155

MUZAFER SHERIF: The Psychology of Social Norms TB/3072

Sociology

JACQUES BARZUN: Race: *A Study in Superstition. Revised Edition* TB/1172

BERNARD BERELSON, Ed.: The Behavioral Sciences Today TB/1127

ABRAHAM CAHAN: The Rise of David Levinsky: *A documentary novel of social mobility in early twentieth century America. Intro. by John Higham* TB/1028

KENNETH B. CLARK: Dark Ghetto: *Dilemmas of Social Power. Foreword by Gunnar Myrdal* TB/1317

LEWIS A. COSER, Ed.: Political Sociology TB/1293

ALLISON DAVIS & JOHN DOLLARD: Children of Bondage: *The Personality Development of Negro Youth in the Urban South* ¶ TB/3049

ST. CLAIR DRAKE & HORACE R. CAYTON: Black Metropolis: *A Study of Negro Life in a Northern City.* △ *Revised and Enlarged. Intro. by Everett C. Hughes*
Vol. I TB/1086; Vol. II TB/1087

EMILE DURKHEIM et al.: Essays on Sociology and Philosophy: *With Analyses of Durkheim's Life and Work.* ¶ *Edited by Kurt H. Wolff* TB/1151

LEON FESTINGER, HENRY W. RIECKEN & STANLEY SCHACHTER: When Prophecy Fails: *A Social and Psychological Account of a Modern Group that Predicted the Destruction of the World* ¶ TB/1132

ALVIN W. GOULDNER: Wildcat Strike: *A Study in Worker-Management Relationships* ¶ TB/1176

CÉSAR GRAÑA: Modernity and Its Discontents: *French Society and the French Man of Letters in the Nineteenth Century* ¶ TB/1318

FRANCIS J. GRUND: Aristocracy in America: *Social Class in the Formative Years of the New Nation* △ TB/1001

KURT LEWIN: Field Theory in Social Science: *Selected Theoretical Papers.* ¶ △ *Edited with a Foreword by Dorwin Cartwright* TB/1135

R. M. MAC IVER: Social Causation TB/1153

ROBERT K. MERTON, LEONARD BROOM, LEONARD S. COTTRELL, JR., Editors: Sociology Today: *Problems and Prospects* ¶ Vol. I TB/1173; Vol. II TB/1174

ROBERTO MICHELS: First Lectures in Political Sociology. *Edited by Alfred de Grazia* ¶ ° TB/1224

BARRINGTON MOORE, JR.: Political Power and Social Theory: *Seven Studies* ¶ TB/1221

BARRINGTON MOORE, JR.: Soviet Politics—The Dilemma of Power: *The Role of Ideas in Social Change* ¶ TB/1222

TALCOTT PARSONS & EDWARD A. SHILS, Editors: Toward a General Theory of Action: *Theoretical Foundations for the Social Sciences* TB/1083

ARNOLD ROSE: The Negro in America: *The Condensed Version of Gunnar Myrdal's* An American Dilemma TB/3048

GEORGE ROSEN: Madness in Society: *Chapters in the Historical Sociology of Mental Illness.* ¶ *Preface by Benjamin Nelson* TB/1337

KURT SAMUELSSON: Religion and Economic Action: *A Critique of Max Weber's* The Protestant Ethic and the Spirit of Capitalism. ¶ ° *Trans. by E. G. French. Ed. with Intro. by D. C. Coleman* TB/1131

PHILIP SELZNICK: TVA and the Grass Roots: A Study in the Sociology of Formal Organization TB/1230
GEORG SIMMEL et al.: Essays on Sociology, Philosophy, and Aesthetics. ¶ Edited by Kurt H. Wolff TB/1234
HERBERT SIMON: The Shape of Automation: For Men and Management △ TB/1245
PITIRIM A. SOROKIN: Contemporary Sociological Theories. Through the First Quarter of the 20th Century TB/3046
MAURICE R. STEIN: The Eclipse of Community: An Interpretation of American Studies TB/1128
WILLIAM I. THOMAS: The Unadjusted Girl: With Cases and Standpoint for Behavior Analysis. ¶ New Intro. by Michael Parenti TB/1319
EDWARD A. TIRYAKIAN, Ed.: Sociological Theory, Values and Sociocultural Change: Essays in Honor of Pitirim A. Sorokin ¶ △ ° TB/1316
FERDINAND TÖNNIES: Community and Society: Gemeinschaft und Gesellschaft. Translated and edited by Charles P. Loomis TB/1116
W. LLOYD WARNER & Associates: Democracy in Jonesville: A Study in Quality and Inequality TB/1129
W. LLOYD WARNER: Social Class in America: The Evaluation of Status TB/1013

RELIGION

Ancient & Classical

J. H. BREASTED: Development of Religion and Thought in Ancient Egypt. Intro. by John A. Wilson TB/57
HENRI FRANKFORT: Ancient Egyptian Religion: An Interpretation TB/77
G. RACHEL LEVY: Religious Conceptions of the Stone Age and their Influence upon European Thought. △ Illus. Introduction by Henri Frankfort TB/106
MARTIN P. NILSSON: Greek Folk Religion. Foreword by Arthur Darby Nock TB/78
ALEXANDRE PIANKOFF: The Shrines of Tut-Ankh-Amon. △ Edited by N. Rambova. 117 illus. TB/2011
ERWIN ROHDE: Psyche: The Cult of Souls and Belief in Immortality Among the Greeks. △ Intro. by W. K. C. Guthrie Vol. I TB/140; Vol. II TB/141
H. J. ROSE: Religion in Greece and Rome △ TB/55

Biblical Thought & Literature

W. F. ALBRIGHT: The Biblical Period from Abraham to Ezra TB/102
C. K. BARRETT, Ed.: The New Testament Background: Selected Documents △ TB/86
C. H. DODD: The Authority of the Bible △ TB/43
M. S. ENSLIN: Christian Beginnings △ TB/5
M. S. ENSLIN: The Literature of the Christian Movement △ TB/6
JOHN GRAY: Archaeology and the Old Testament World. △ Illus. TB/127
JAMES MUILENBURG: The Way of Israel: Biblical Faith and Ethics △ TB/133
H. H. ROWLEY: The Growth of the Old Testament △ TB/107
GEORGE ADAM SMITH: The Historical Geography of the Holy Land. ° △ Revised and reset TB/138
D. WINTON THOMAS, Ed.: Documents from Old Testament Times TB/85
WALTHER ZIMMERLI: The Law and the Prophets: A Study of the Meaning of the Old Testament △ TB/144

The Judaic Tradition

LEO BAECK: Judaism and Christianity. Trans. with Intro. by Walter Kaufmann TB/823
SALO W. BARON: Modern Nationalism and Religion TB/818
MARTIN BUBER: Eclipse of God: Studies in the Relation Between Religion and Philosophy △ TB/12
MARTIN BUBER: For the Sake of Heaven TB/801
MARTIN BUBER: Hasidism and Modern Man. △ Ed. and Trans. by Maurice Friedman TB/839
MARTIN BUBER: The Knowledge of Man. △ Edited with an Introduction by Maurice Friedman. Translated by Maurice Friedman and Ronald Gregor Smith TB/135
MARTIN BUBER: Moses: The Revelation and the Covenant △ TB/837
MARTIN BUBER: The Origin and Meaning of Hasidism △ TB/835
MARTIN BUBER: Pointing the Way. △ Introduction by Maurice S. Friedman TB/103
MARTIN BUBER: The Prophetic Faith TB/73
MARTIN BUBER: Two Types of Faith: the interpenetration of Judaism and Christianity ° △ TB/75
ERNST LUDWIG EHRLICH: A Concise History of Israel: From the Earliest Times to the Destruction of the Temple in A.D. 70 ° △ TB/128
MAURICE S. FRIEDMAN: Martin Buber: The Life of Dialogue △ TB/64
GENESIS: The NJV Translation TB/836
SOLOMON GRAYZEL: A History of the Contemporary Jews TB/816
WILL HERBERG: Judaism and Modern Man TB/810
ARTHUR HERTZBERG: The Zionist Idea TB/817
ABRAHAM J. HESCHEL: God in Search of Man: A Philosophy of Judaism TB/807
ISAAC HUSIK: A History of Medieval Jewish Philosophy TB/803
JACOB R. MARCUS: The Jew in the Medieval World TB/814
MAX L. MARGOLIS & ALEXANDER MARX: A History of the Jewish People TB/806
T. J. MEEK: Hebrew Origins TB/69
JAMES PARKES: The Conflict of the Church and the Synagogue: The Jews and Early Christianity TB/821
PHILO, SAADYA GAON, & JEHUDA HALEVI: Three Jewish Philosophers. Ed. by Hans Lewey, Alexander Altmann, & Isaak Heinemann TB/813
CECIL ROTH: A History of the Marranos TB/812
CECIL ROTH: The Jews in the Renaissance. Illus. TB/834
HERMAN L. STRACK: Introduction to the Talmud and Midrash TB/808
JOSHUA TRACHTENBERG: The Devil and the Jews: The Medieval Conception of the Jew and its Relation to Modern Anti-Semitism TB/822

Christianity: General

ROLAND H. BAINTON: Christendom: A Short History of Christianity and its Impact on Western Civilization. △ Illus. Vol. I TB/131; Vol. II TB/132

Christianity: Origins & Early Development

AUGUSTINE: An Augustine Synthesis. △ Edited by Erich Przywara TB/335
W. D. DAVIES: Paul and Rabbinic Judaism: Some Rabbinic Elements in Pauline Theology. New Intro. by the Author △ ° TB/146
ADOLF DEISSMANN: Paul: A Study in Social and Religious History TB/15
EDWARD GIBBON: The Triumph of Christendom in the Roman Empire (Chaps. XV-XX of "Decline and Fall," J. B. Bury edition). § △ Illus. TB/46
EDGAR J. GOODSPEED: A Life of Jesus TB/1
ROBERT M. GRANT: Gnosticism and Early Christianity. △ Revised Edition TB/136
ADOLF HARNACK: The Mission and Expansion of Christianity in the First Three Centuries. Introduction by Jaroslav Pelikan TB/92
R. K. HARRISON: The Dead Sea Scrolls: An Introduction ° △ TB/84
EDWIN HATCH: The Influence of Greek Ideas on Christianity. § △ Introduction and Bibliography by Frederick C. Grant TB/18

GERHART B. LADNER: The Idea of Reform: *Its Impact on Christian Thought and Action in the Age of the Fathers* TB/149

ARTHUR DARBY NOCK: Early Gentile Christianity and Its Hellenistic Background TB/111

ARTHUR DARBY NOCK: St. Paul ° △ TB/104

ORIGEN: On First Principles. △ *Edited by G. W. Butterworth. Introduction by Henri de Lubac* TB/311

JAMES PARKES: The Conflict of the Church and the Synagogue: *The Jews and Early Christianity* TB/821

SULPICIUS SEVERUS et al.: The Western Fathers: *Being the Lives of Martin of Tours, Ambrose, Augustine of Hippo, Honoratus of Arles and Germanus of Auxerre.* △ *Edited and translated by F. R. Hoare* TB/309

JOHANNES WEISS: Earliest Christianity: *A History of the Period A.D. 30-150. Introduction and Bibliography by Frederick C. Grant* Volume I TB/53; Volume II TB/54

Christianity: The Middle Ages and The Reformation

ANSELM OF CANTERBURY: Truth, Freedom and Evil: *Three Philosophical Dialogues. Ed., trans., and Intro. by Jasper Hopkins & Herbert Richardson* TB/317

JOHN CALVIN & JACOPO SADOLETO: A Reformation Debate. *Edited by John C. Olin* TB/1239

G. CONSTANT: The Reformation in England: *The English Schism, Henry VIII, 1509-1547* △ TB/314

CHRISTOPHER DAWSON, Ed.: Mission to Asia: *Narratives and Letters of the Franciscan Missionaries in Mongolia and China in the 13th and 14th Centuries* △ TB/315

JOHANNES ECKHART: Meister Eckhart: *A Modern Translation by R. B. Blakney* TB/8

DESIDERIUS ERASMUS: Christian Humanism and the Reformation: *Selected Writings. Edited and translated by John C. Olin* TB/1166

ÉTIENNE GILSON: Dante and Philosophy △ TB/1089

WILLIAM HALLER: The Rise of Puritanism △ TB/22

HAJO HOLBORN: Ulrich von Hutten and the German Reformation TB/1238

JOHAN HUIZINGA: Erasmus and the Age of Reformation. △ *Illus.* TB/19

A. C. MC GIFFERT: Protestant Thought Before Kant △ *Preface by Jaroslav Pelikan* TB/93

JOHN T. MC NEILL: Makers of the Christian Tradition: *From Alfred the Great to Schleiermacher* △ TB/121

G. MOLLAT: The Popes at Avignon, 1305-1378 △ TB/308

GORDON RUPP: Luther's Progress to the Diet of Worms ° △ TB/120

Christianity: The Protestant Tradition

KARL BARTH: Church Dogmatics: *A Selection* △ TB/95

KARL BARTH: Dogmatics in Outline △ TB/56

KARL BARTH: The Word of God and the Word of Man TB/13

RUDOLF BULTMANN et al: Translating Theology into the Modern Age: *Historical, Systematic and Pastoral Reflections on Theology and the Church in the Contemporary Situation. Volume 2 of* Journal for Theology and the Church, *edited by Robert W. Funk in association with Gerhard Ebeling* TB/252

WHITNEY R. CROSS: The Burned-Over District: *The Social and Intellectual History of Enthusiastic Religion in Western New York, 1800-1850* △ TB/1242

NELS F. S. FERRÉ: Swedish Contributions to Modern Theology. *New Preface by the Author. Additional chapter by William A. Johnson* TB/147

ERNST KÄSEMANN, et al.: Distinctive Protestant and Catholic Themes Reconsidered. *Volume 3 of* Journal for Theology and the Church, *edited by Robert W. Funk in association with Gerhard Ebeling* TB/253

SOREN KIERKEGAARD: On Authority and Revelation: *The Book on Adler. Translated by Walter Lowrie. Intro. by Frederick Sontag* TB/139

SOREN KIERKEGAARD: Crisis in the Life of an Actress *and Other Essays on Drama.* △ *Trans. with Intro. by Stephen D. Crites* TB/145

SOREN KIERKEGAARD: Edifying Discourses. *Edited with an Introduction by Paul Holmer* TB/32

SOREN KIERKEGAARD: The Journals of Kierkegaard. ° △ *Ed. with Intro. by Alexander Dru* TB/52

SOREN KIERKEGAARD: The Point of View for My Work as an Author: *A Report to History.* § *Preface by Benjamin Nelson* TB/88

SOREN KIERKEGAARD: The Present Age. § △ *Translated and edited by Alexander Dru. Introduction by Walter Kaufmann* TB/94

SOREN KIERKEGAARD: Purity of Heart △ TB/4

SOREN KIERKEGAARD: Repetition: *An Essay in Experimental Psychology.* △ *Translated with Introduction & Notes by Walter Lowrie* TB/117

SOREN KIERKEGAARD: Works of Love: *Some Christian Reflections in the Form of Discourses* △ TB/122

WALTER LOWRIE: Kierkegaard: *A Life* Vol. I TB/89; Vol. II TB/90

JOHN MACQUARRIE: The Scope of Demythologizing: *Bultmann and His Critics* △ TB/134

PERRY MILLER & T. H. JOHNSON, Editors: The Puritans: *A Sourcebook of Their Writings* Vol. I TB/1093; Vol. II TB/1094

WOLFHART PANNENBERG, et al.: History and Hermeneutic. *Volume 4 of* Journal for Theology and the Church, *edited by Robert W. Funk in association with Gerhard Ebeling* TB/254

JAMES M. ROBINSON et al.: The Bultmann School of Biblical Interpretation: New Directions? *Volume 1 of* Journal for Theology and the Church, *edited by Robert W. Funk in association with Gerhard Ebeling* TB/251

F. SCHLEIERMACHER: The Christian Faith. △ *Introduction by Richard R. Niebuhr* Vol. I TB/108; Vol. II TB/109

F. SCHLEIERMACHER: On Religion: *Speeches to Its Cultured Despisers. Intro. by Rudolf Otto* TB/36

TIMOTHY L. SMITH: Revivalism and Social Reform: *American Protestantism on the Eve of the Civil War* TB/1229

PAUL TILLICH: Dynamics of Faith △ TB/42

PAUL TILLICH: Morality and Beyond TB/142

EVELYN UNDERHILL: Worship △ TB/10

Christianity: The Roman and Eastern Traditions

DOM CUTHBERT BUTLER: Western Mysticism: *The Teaching of Augustine, Gregory and Bernard on Contemplation and the Contemplative Life* § ° △ TB/312

A. ROBERT CAPONIGRI, Ed.: Modern Catholic Thinkers I: *God and Man* △ TB/306

A. ROBERT CAPONIGRI, Ed.: Modern Catholic Thinkers II: *The Church and the Political Order* △ TB/307

THOMAS CORBISHLEY, S.J.: Roman Catholicism △ TB/112

CHRISTOPHER DAWSON: The Historic Reality of Christian Culture TB/305

G. P. FEDOTOV: The Russian Religious Mind: *Kievan Christianity, the 10th to the 13th centuries* TB/370

ÉTIENNE GILSON: The Spirit of Thomism TB/313

GABRIEL MARCEL: Being and Having: *An Existential Diary.* △ *Introduction by James Collins* TB/310

GABRIEL MARCEL: Homo Viator: *Introduction to a Metaphysic of Hope* TB/397

FRANCIS DE SALES: Introduction to the Devout Life. *Trans. by John K. Ryan* TB/316

GUSTAVE WEIGEL, S. J.: Catholic Theology in Dialogue TB/301

Oriental Religions: Far Eastern, Near Eastern

TOR ANDRAE: Mohammed: *The Man and His Faith* △ TB/62

EDWARD CONZE: Buddhism: *Its Essence and Development.* ° △ *Foreword by Arthur Waley* TB/58

EDWARD CONZE et al., Editors: Buddhist Texts Through the Ages △ TB/113

ANANDA COOMARASWAMY: Buddha and the Gospel of Buddhism. △ *Illus.* TB/119

H. G. CREEL: Confucius and the Chinese Way TB/63

FRANKLIN EDGERTON, Trans. & Ed.: The Bhagavad Gita TB/115

SWAMI NIKHILANANDA, Trans. & Ed.: The Upanishads: *A One-Volume Abridgment* △ TB/114

HELLMUT WILHELM: Change: *Eight Lectures on the* I Ching △ TB/2019

Philosophy of Religion

NICOLAS BERDYAEV: The Beginning and the End § △ TB/14

NICOLAS BERDYAEV: Christian Existentialism: *A Berdyaev Synthesis.* △ *Ed. by Donald A. Lowrie* TB/130

NICOLAS BERDYAEV: The Destiny of Man △ TB/61

RUDOLF BULTMANN: History and Eschatology: *The Presence of Eternity* ° TB/91

RUDOLF BULTMANN AND FIVE CRITICS: Kerygma and Myth: *A Theological Debate* △ TB/80

RUDOLF BULTMANN and KARL KUNDSIN: Form Criticism: *Two Essays on New Testament Research.* △ *Translated by Frederick C. Grant* TB/96

MIRCEA ELIADE: Myths, Dreams, and Mysteries: *The Encounter between Contemporary Faiths and Archaic Realities* § △ ° TB/1320

MIRCEA ELIADE: The Sacred and the Profane TB/81

LUDWIG FEUERBACH: The Essence of Christianity. § *Introduction by Karl Barth. Foreword by H. Richard Niebuhr* TB/11

ÉTIENNE GILSON: The Spirit of Thomism TB/313

ADOLF HARNACK: What is Christianity? § △ *Introduction by Rudolf Bultmann* TB/17

FRIEDRICH HEGEL: On Christianity: *Early Theological Writings. Ed. by R. Kroner and T. M. Knox* TB/79

KARL HEIM: Christian Faith and Natural Science △ TB/16

IMMANUEL KANT: Religion Within the Limits of Reason Alone. § *Intro. by T. M. Greene & J. Silber* TB/67

K. E. KIRK: The Vision of God: *The Christian Doctrine of the Summum Bonum* § △ TB/137

JOHN MACQUARRIE: An Existentialist Theology: *A Comparison of Heidegger and Bultmann.* ° △ *Preface by Rudolf Bultmann* TB/125

PAUL RAMSEY, Ed.: Faith and Ethics: *The Theology of H. Richard Niebuhr* TB/129

EUGEN ROSENSTOCK-HUESSY: The Christian Future *or the Modern Mind Outrun. Intro. by Harold Stahmer* TB/143

PIERRE TEILHARD DE CHARDIN: The Divine Milieu ° △ TB/384

PIERRE TEILHARD DE CHARDIN: The Phenomenon of Man ° △ TB/383

Religion, Culture & Society

JOSEPH L. BLAU, Ed.: Cornerstones of Religious Freedom in America: *Selected Basic Documents, Court Decisions and Public Statements. Revised and Enlarged Edition* TB/118

WILLIAM A. CLEBSCH & CHARLES R. JAEKLE: Pastoral Care in Historical Perspective: *An Essay with Exhibits. New Preface by the Authors* TB/148

C. C. GILLISPIE: Genesis and Geology: *The Decades before Darwin* § TB/51

KYLE HASELDEN: The Racial Problem in Christian Perspective TB/116

WALTER KAUFMANN, Ed.: Religion from Tolstoy to Camus: *Basic Writings on Religious Truth and Morals. Enlarged Edition* TB/123

KENNETH B. MURDOCK: Literature and Theology in Colonial New England TB/99

H. RICHARD NIEBUHR: Christ and Culture △ TB/3

H. RICHARD NIEBUHR: The Kingdom of God in America TB/49

R. B. PERRY: Puritanism and Democracy TB/1138

PAUL PFUETZE: Self, Society, Existence: *Human Nature and Dialogue in the Thought of George Herbert Mead and Martin Buber* TB/1059

WALTER RAUSCHENBUSCH: Christianity and the Social Crisis. ‡ *Edited by Robert D. Cross* TB/3059

KURT SAMUELSSON: Religion and Economic Action: *A Critique of Max Weber's* The Protestant Ethic and the Spirit of Capitalism ¶ ° △ *Trans. by E. G. French. Ed. with Intro. by D. C. Coleman* TB/1131

TIMOTHY L. SMITH: Revivalism and Social Reform: *American Protestantism on the Eve of the Civil War* △ TB/1229

NATURAL SCIENCES AND MATHEMATICS

Biological Sciences

CHARLOTTE AUERBACH: The Science of Genetics Σ △ TB/568

JOHN TYLER BONNER: The Ideas of Biology. Σ △ *Illus.* TB/570

A. J. CAIN: Animal Species and their Evolution. △ *Illus.* TB/519

W. E. LE GROS CLARK: The Antecedents of Man: *An Introduction to Evolution of the Primates.* ° △ *Illus.* TB/559

W. H. DOWDESWELL: Animal Ecology. △ *Illus.* TB/543

W. H. DOWDESWELL: The Mechanism of Evolution. △ *Illus.* TB/527

R. W. GERARD: Unresting Cells. *Illus.* TB/541

J. E. MORTON: Molluscs: *An Introduction to Their Form and Functions. Illus.* TB/529

P. M. SHEPPARD: Natural Selection and Heredity. △ *Illus.* TB/528

EDMUND W. SINNOTT: Cell and Psyche: *The Biology of Purpose* TB/546

C. H. WADDINGTON: The Nature of Life: *The Main Problems and Trends in Modern Biology* △ TB/580

Chemistry

J. R. PARTINGTON: A Short History of Chemistry. △ *Illus.* TB/522

Communication Theory

J. R. PIERCE: Symbols, Signals and Noise: *The Nature and Process of Communication* △ TB/574

Geography

R. E. COKER: This Great and Wide Sea: *An Introduction to Oceanography and Marine Biology. Illus.* TB/551

F. K. HARE: The Restless Atmosphere △ TB/560

History of Science

MARIE BOAS: The Scientific Renaissance, 1450-1630 ° △ TB/583

W. DAMPIER, Ed.: Readings in the Literature of Science. *Illus.* TB/512

A. HUNTER DUPREE: Science in the Federal Government: *A History of Policies and Activities to 1940* △ TB/573

ALEXANDRE KOYRÉ: From the Closed World to the Infinite Universe: *Copernicus, Kepler, Galileo, Newton, etc.* △ TB/31

A. G. VAN MELSEN: From Atomos to Atom: *A History of the Concept* Atom TB/517

STEPHEN TOULMIN & JUNE GOODFIELD: The Architecture of Matter: *Physics, Chemistry & Physiology of Matter, Both Animate & Inanimate, As it Evolved Since the Beginning of Science* ° △ TB/584

STEPHEN TOULMIN & JUNE GOODFIELD: The Discovery of Time ° △ TB/585

Mathematics

E. W. BETH: The Foundations of Mathematics: *A Study in the Philosophy of Science* △ TB/581

S. KÖRNER: The Philosophy of Mathematics: *An Introduction* △ TB/547

GEORGE E. OWEN: Fundamentals of Scientific Mathematics TB/569

WILLARD VAN ORMAN QUINE: Mathematical Logic TB/558

FREDERICK WAISMANN: Introduction to Mathematical Thinking. *Foreword by Karl Menger* TB/511

Philosophy of Science

R. B. BRAITHWAITE: Scientific Explanation TB/515

J. BRONOWSKI: Science and Human Values. △ *Revised and Enlarged Edition* TB/505

ALBERT EINSTEIN et al.: Albert Einstein: Philosopher-Scientist. *Edited by Paul A. Schilpp* Vol. I TB/502
Vol. II TB/503

WERNER HEISENBERG: Physics and Philosophy: *The Revolution in Modern Science* △ TB/549

KARL R. POPPER: Logic of Scientific Discovery △ TB/576

STEPHEN TOULMIN: Foresight and Understanding: *An Enquiry into the Aims of Science.* △ *Foreword by Jacques Barzun* TB/564

STEPHEN TOULMIN: The Philosophy of Science: *An Introduction* △ TB/513

Physics and Cosmology

JOHN E. ALLEN: Aerodynamics: *A Space Age Survey* △ TB/582

P. W. BRIDGMAN: Nature of Thermodynamics TB/537

C. V. DURELL: Readable Relativity. △ *Foreword by Freeman J. Dyson* TB/530

ARTHUR EDDINGTON: Space, Time and Gravitation: *An Outline of the General Relativity Theory* TB/510

GEORGE GAMOW: Biography of Physics Σ △ TB/567

STEPHEN TOULMIN & JUNE GOODFIELD: The Fabric of the Heavens: *The Development of Astronomy and Dynamics.* △ *Illus.* TB/579